THE JEWISH PEOPLE
IN AMERICA

THE JEWISH PEOPLE IN AMERICA

A Series Sponsored by the American Jewish Historical Society

Henry L. Feingold, General Editor

A Time for Building
The Third Migration

THE JEWISH PEOPLE IN AMERICA

A TIME FOR
BUILDING
The Third Migration
1880–1920

Gerald Sorin

The Johns Hopkins University Press

Baltimore and London

Second printing, 1992

The Johns Hopkins University Press
701 West 40th Street
Baltimore, Maryland 21211-2190
The Johns Hopkins Press Ltd., London

Library of Congress Cataloging-in-Publication Data

Sorin, Gerald, 1940–
A time for building : the third migration, 1880–1920 /
Gerald Sorin.
     p.   cm. — (The Jewish People in America ; v. 3)
Includes bibliographical references and index.
ISBN 0–8018–4345–6 (alk. paper)
   1. Jews—United States—History. 2. Jews, East
European—United States—History. 3. United States—
Emigration and immigration. 4. Immigrants—United
States—History. 5. United States—Ethnic relations.
I. Title. II. Series.
E184.J5S664   1992
973'.04924—dc20   91–40700

In Memory of My Parents
John Lewis Sorin
1905–1973
Ruth Gass Sorin
1909–1979

✡

CONTENTS

Contents

✡

SERIES EDITOR'S FOREWORD

OVER the generations, there has been much change in the content of Jewish culture. Some writers argue that in the benevolent and absorbent atmosphere of America, Jewish culture has been thinned beyond recognition. But one ingredient of that culture—a deep appreciation of history—continues to receive the highest priority. The motto on the seal of the American Jewish Historical Society enjoins us, "Remember the Days of Old." It is taken from the Pentateuch, itself a historical chronicle.

Indeed, the Jewish community boasts almost one hundred local historical societies and two professional archives for preserving source material. The cherishing of its history goes beyond any biblical or cultural injunction. History is especially important for Diaspora communities because corporate memory rather than territorial space ultimately ensures their survival. That is what Bal Shem Tov, founder of the Hasidic movement, may have meant when centuries ago he counseled his followers that "memory is the key to redemption."

The American Jewish Historical Society offers this history of the Jews in America to both the Jewish community and the general reading public as a repository of memory. For Jewish readers this series provides an opportunity to enrich their self-understanding, quickening Jewry's energies and enhancing its potential for survival. We hope to remind the general reading public that, at a time when the American dream may be found wanting, the American Jewish experience is evidence that the promise of America can still be realized. Without the opportunities, freedom, and openness found in this land, American Jewry would not have been able to realize its energies and talents and become what it is today.

How that has happened over the generations is a story the American Jewish Historical Society is committed to tell. In fact, the society could think of no better way to honor its historical task and its rich hundred-year history than by recounting that story through this series. No single volume by a single historian can do justice to the multilevel historical experience of American Jewry. Drawing on the talents of five historians with a common vision and purpose, this series offers a historical synthesis at once comprehensible to the intelligent lay reader and useful to the professional historian. Each of these volumes integrates common themes: the origins of Jewish immigrants, their experience of settling in America, their economic and social life, their religious and educational efforts, their political involvement, and the change the American Jewish community experienced over time.

Predictably, the project encountered many conceptual problems. One of the most vexing stemmed from the difficulty of classifying American Jewry. To treat American Jews solely as members of a religious denomination, as was once the practice of the Reform branch, was a distortion, because most American Jews are not religious in the sectarian sense. And though some sociologists have classified Jews as a race, clearly that category does not adequately describe how they differ from other Americans. More than other ethnic communities, American Jewry is influenced by two separate historical streams: the American and the Jewish. To be sure, American Jewry is but one of the many ethnic groups woven into the American national fabric. Yet it is something beyond that as well. It is part of an evolving religious civilization that has persisted for millennia. This persistent tension between assimilation and group survival—the will to remain part of the universal community of Israel—is well evinced in the volumes of this series.

In this third volume, Gerald Sorin focuses on how the eastern European Jewish migration, which set the tone for American Jewry in the final decades of the nineteenth century, confronted the issue of accommodation and group survival. A distinctive political and general culture, which amalgamated traditional Jewish and new American values, was established by the immigrant generation. That Yiddish-speaking transitional culture, which prevailed in the ethnic enclaves of the cities, was considerably modified once Jews left these core communities and after World War I, the cultural energy of the immigrant generation waned.

On behalf of the society, I thank the many participants of this venture, which had its beginnings over fifteen years ago as a way of commemorating the society's 1992 centennial. Dr. Abraham Kanof, Rosemary Krensky, and the late David Lubart provided initial support for the project. Dr. Kanof has been repeatedly generous in his financial contributions over the years, while the Max and Dora L. Starr Foundation has provided additional welcome assistance. The authors, Eli Faber, Hasia R. Diner, Gerald Sorin, and Edward S. Shapiro, deserve special thanks. In addition, we are grateful to Ruth B. Fein and the late Phil Fine for their efforts on behalf of the project. For their technical and legal expertise in making publishing arrangements for the series, Robert L. Weinberg and Franklin Feldman need to be singled out. Words of thanks also go to Henry Y. K. Tom, executive editor of the Johns Hopkins University Press, and to his colleagues for their dedication and professionalism in bringing the society's dream to realization. Last, a special appreciation is in order for the society's untiring staff, particularly Bernard Wax and the late Nathan M. Kaganoff, for their administrative support.

Henry L. Feingold
General Editor

✡

PREFACE AND ACKNOWLEDGMENTS

THE JEWISH MIGRATION to America, beginning in earnest in the 1880s, constituted a momentous decision of a whole people. A stunning one-third of eastern European Jews had left the persecution, pogroms, and poverty of the Old World by 1920. But these Jews were not merely fleeing the old countries. From their attempts in eastern Europe to combine their religious ideals with the demands of modern secularism, they had experienced a cultural renewal, and from that renewal Jewish aspirations for freedom and achievement grew stronger.

The United States—long known as a land of opportunity and, in the 1880s and 1890s, being in a period of vast industrial expansion—provided the context for the fulfillment of these hopes. Their struggle to synthesize the modern and the traditional intensified in America and led these Jewish immigrants to forge a unique transitional culture fashioned from Old World values and New World experiences. This Yiddish-speaking immigrant culture, which lasted almost four decades, served to ease the bewilderment and pain of adjustment.

Jewish immigrants acculturated rapidly but often on their own terms. They became Americans and made important contributions to American life, but they retained and reshaped their distinctive Jewish characteristics. In short, they changed, but they did not "melt." All over the United States, and particularly in cities, immigrant Jews transplanted and nourished recognizably Jewish communities. As a people, they retained their identification with Jewish civilization; as a religious community, they attempted to fashion a group identity that would enhance their integration into American life.

Integration was made easier by the presence of a small, but well-established, German Jewish elite and by important confluences of Jewish and

American values and institutions. The liberal values of the modern democratic republic, themselves partly founded on biblical precepts, meshed well with the covenantal Hebraic tradition and its emphasis on the pursuit of justice; the American idea of progress was compatible with the Jewish injunction to repair and perfect the world in an ongoing partnership with God; and the rational, secular American pursuit of individual happiness within an orderly community complemented modern Jewish this-worldliness and aspiration for personal achievement and communal fulfillment. Integration was also made easier by the absence of a virulent anti-Semitism; America's heterogeneity and liberal constitutionalism protected Jews. Although America has "not been utter heaven for Jews" in regard to anti-Semitism, it has been very far from the hell of Europe's persistently violent and state-sponsored persecutions of Jews.[1]

In addition, American pluralism, which was partly shaped by Jewish thinkers, came to imply a positive obligation on the part of groups to participate fully in society so that society might benefit from their diverse contributions. And indeed Jews and America did enrich each other. Increasingly, Jews found in the United States not only a refuge but a home. The culture that immigrant Jews nurtured in the period from 1880 to 1920 was temporary but powerful; its accomplishments reverberated not only in the second generation but even into the late twentieth century, continuing to inform American, as well as American Jewish, social and political values.

I owe thanks first and foremost to the American Jewish Historical Society for its generous support of this project. I am also grateful to the State University of New York, the College at New Paltz, and to United University Professionals. A debt is owed also to the many historians of the American Jewish experience whose names and works are cited in the notes and bibliography. Librarians and archivists in the following institutions were cooperative and indispensable: SUNY, New Paltz, particularly the division of interlibrary loans; YIVO; Hebrew Union College Jewish Institute of Religion, in New York and Cincinnati; William Weiner Oral History Collection at the American Jewish Committee; Columbia University Oral History Collection; Tamiment Library at New York University; New York Public Library Jewish Division; and most especially, the American Jewish Historical Society, on the campus of Brandeis University, where Bernard Wax was eminently professional, amiable, and indefatigable in his efforts to help me, and where Nathan Kaganoff was all of these and, in addition, a walking treasure of information.

Several colleagues in the various disciplines of English, women's studies, economics, religious studies, history, and Jewish studies read and commented upon one or more chapters and often moved me to make changes. Special thanks are due Jay Bloom, Carole Levin, Robert Miraldi, Deborah Dash Moore, and William Strongin. General editor Henry Feingold carefully read the entire manuscript and made very valuable suggestions in every section. Copy editor Diane Hammond was extraordinarily thorough and helped clean up the occasional infelicities. She sometimes even persuaded me to shorten an overloaded sentence. I am especially grateful once again to my wife, Myra Sorin, for her fine editorial talent, her perceptive reading, her ability to ask probing questions, and most, for her patience and loving support.

A Time for Building
The Third Migration

✡

PROLOGUE: ON THE EVE OF
THE GREAT TRANSFORMATION

BETWEEN 1880 and 1920, more than two million Jews from the countries of eastern Europe chose to come to the United States. This choice, though made over a forty-year period, can be seen as a collective decision, as fully one-third of the Jews of eastern Europe migrated during these years, and more than 80 percent of them came to America. The decision to emigrate was molded in part by the economic decline and physical oppression of Jews in the Old World. But it was also the result of a renewed and transformed Jewish vitality.[1]

Many of the immigrants had already begun to confront social change in the old countries; even before emigration they were struggling to synthesize the ideals and values of their familiar Jewish religious culture with the demands and enticements of the modern secular world. This struggle, a remarkably creative force for cultural resurgence, was carried to the New World, where it intensified and accelerated.

Beginning in the 1880s, Jews from eastern Europe transplanted themselves to dozens of America's cities and hundreds of its small towns. In America they developed over time a unique transitional culture, which borrowed supports from the Old World and the New. By 1920 the dynamic of acculturation—fed by American pressures and opportunities and by immigrant aspiration—had eaten deeply into that transitional culture and was promoting a new synthesis.[2] But between 1880 and 1920, these Jewish immigrants created in America the most populous, concentrated, and vibrant Jewish community in the world.

It is well to remind ourselves that in 1880, before the arrival of masses of Jews from Poland, Russia, Romania, Galicia, Silesia, Bohemia, and Slovakia, the number of Jews in the United States was only about a quarter of a million, and only one-sixth of them were from eastern Europe. More than two hundred thousand were German Jews—or more precisely, Jews who had come mainly in the 1830s and 1840s from central European communities that resonated German culture.[3] The minority of Jewish immigrants from eastern Europe took their cues from the dominant German Jewish majority.

However, their numbers were growing. As early as 1852, the membership of New York's Beth Hamidrash synagogue was largely Russian and Polish Jews, and by 1872 there were nearly thirty additional eastern European congregations in New York City.[4] On the other end of the continent—in San Francisco, Los Angeles, Sacramento, and San Jose, eastern European Jews, though relatively few, outnumbered German Jews as early as the 1860s. But these Jews—whether in California, New York, or a point of settlement in between—desired to become "respectable" American Jews; this required not only Americanization but "acculturation to German Jewish standards" as well.[5]

Ever since the colonial era, when the Sephardim—descendants of Jews who had lived on the Iberian peninsula before the expulsions of 1492 and 1497—had established their preeminence in the American Jewish community, there was a social hierarchy among Jews in America. Time of arrival was important, but so was geography. The farther west in Europe one's origins, the higher one's status. Even though German Jews resented the snobbishness of Iberian Jews who preceded them to these shores, they accepted the geographic origins rule and, when they quickly achieved hegemony over the Sephardim, applied it to Jewish immigrants unlucky enough to have been born even farther east.[6]

Up to the early 1880s, eastern Europeans accepted, indeed anxiously desired, Germanization, as part of the larger process of Americanization. German Jews had, after all, managed to carve out of their immigrant experience a distinctly attractive, and at least temporarily successful, cultural synthesis: Jewish, German, and American. German Jews had also managed to fulfill the immigrant ambition for a better life and more material comfort. Some even had made fortunes. Their stories fit the American rags-to-riches mythology and provided lessons in economic and social mobility for other nineteenth-century Jewish immigrants to the United States.[7]

German Jews, who had been for the most part petty traders and dealers in the Old World, had left such places as Bavaria, Baden, and Württemberg

because of repressive legislation and the disintegration of the peasant economies they had served.[8] They were ambitious and courageous enterprisers,
searching for better opportunity; they moved across the American continent, forming a configuration of Jewish communities that has remained
essentially intact to the present.[9]

Few groups chose a more fortuitous moment to come to America than
these Jews of central Europe. The frontier was still open and moving, and
the economy was expanding.[10] At the same time, however, the transportation system of the country was relatively undeveloped. Despite railroad
speculation, turnpike construction, and canal building in the 1840s and
1850s, huge areas in the interior of the United States had few stores and few
links to factories that produced goods or to port cities that received goods.[11]
German Jews helped fill this merchandising vacuum; in less than a generation they came to dominate the men's and women's clothing trades, both
manufacturing and retailing. Jewish entrepreneurs were attracted to the
soft-goods industry because it was a low-capitalization, labor-intensive enterprise. It also entailed significant risk, which the more established inves-
tors in mining and hard-goods manufacturing avoided. In any case, names
such as Hart, Schaffner, and Marx and Florsheim still serve as reminders of
early Jewish initiative in wearing apparel.

Many German Jewish immigrants started as peddlers. We do not know
precisely how many, but memoir literature and historical studies suggest
significant percentages. One analysis, for example, demonstrates that more
than half of the adult Jewish males in Easton, Pennsylvania, between 1845
and 1855 were peddlers.[12] These pack carriers needed little initial inventory
and paid no rent for storage. Often they began their businesses with borrowed funds—risk capital acquired from family or from fraternal orders or
other social institutions, including religious congregations. The early development of an intragroup credit system was a major ingredient in the
extraordinary business success of German Jews. In response to the growing
system of distribution, a mutually beneficial network developed, strongly
marked by family ties. It connected peddler, creditor, supplier, retailer,
wholesaler, clerk, bookkeeper, skilled worker, clothing manufacturer, and
importer.[13]

The expansion of this distribution system, particularly from east to
west, shaped the grid of Jewish settlement, and points on the primary routes
to the interior became the sites of new Jewish communities. Inland cities
like Albany, Rochester, Cleveland, Milwaukee, and St. Louis witnessed the

3

clustering of Jewish peddlers in the 1830s and 1840s. Some of these men, dreaming of one day becoming "businessmen," failed, their backs giving out under the weight of their 150-pound packs. But an important number graduated from carriers to wagon barons and, finally, to owners of retail stores or peddler supply depots. This sequence happened often enough that the legend of peddler to department store owner—reinforced by names like Adam Gimbel (New York, Philadelphia, and Milwaukee), Benjamin Bloomingdale (New York), Edward Filene (Boston), A. L. Neiman and Herbert and Carrie Marcus (Dallas), Benjamin Altman (New York), Gerson Fox (Boston), the Strauses (Macy's and Abraham and Straus), Julius Rosenwald (Sears, Roebuck), and many others—became a part of American Jewish history.[14]

Between 1850 and 1880 the inland cities filled with enough Jews and Jewish institutions to stimulate the development of satellite communities. Cincinnati is a good example: an inland port serving the Ohio River system and having a sizable German population, Cincinnati attracted thousands of German Jewish immigrants. By the 1850s Jewish peddlers in the city had moved up to the retail clothing trade and had turned Cincinnati into a center for the manufacture of garments. Growing factories, stores, depots, supply routes, and credit operations required additional family members and countrymen, many of whom settled in towns surrounding the Greater Cincinnati area.

By 1855 there were five synagogues in Cincinnati and two prominent rabbis. Isaac Mayer Wise (1819–1900), founder of the Reform movement in America, and Max Lilienthal (1815–1882), the first person with both a rabbinic and a university degree to settle in the United States, held pulpits in the city. Cincinnati soon became the religious center for smaller Jewish communities in Ohio, Indiana, Illinois, Tennessee, Kentucky, and Missouri.[15]

Jewish settlers, connected in one way or another to the ever-expanding merchandising network, also penetrated the South and the Far West. By 1880, Mobile and Montgomery, Alabama, had Jewish populations of 530 and 600, respectively; Jews in New Orleans numbered 5,000. San Francisco, which experienced rapid growth following the California gold rush, had more than 16,000 Jews by 1880.[16] Jewish peddlers trailed prospectors into mining towns, supplied clothes and tools, and eventually established stores. Small communities developed around these stores in Sacramento and Stockton, as well as in mining areas in Arizona, Colorado, and Nevada. The story of Alexander Ritmaster is typical. From a pack strapped to his back, he peddled notions and essential merchandise to miners' wives in

Central City, Colorado. Eventually, Ritmaster's trips up and down the mountainsides of Black Hawk and Nevadaville brought him enough prosperity to open his own store and employ other young immigrants.[17]

Throughout the country, Jewish immigrants found economic opportunities in retailing, ranching, real estate, agriculture, and other enterprises simply by responding to local or regional needs. They provided specialized clothing in the West (the famous riveted Levi's denim trousers, for example), encouraged black customership in the South, and introduced smaller profits, lower prices, direct selling, "bargain basements," and time purchasing everywhere.[18] In isolated areas, some even became local "bankers." I. E. Solomon, for example, a retailer in the Arizona Territory, began keeping his customers' valuables in his safe. Soon he was making "handshake" loans to his friends and then dealing in drafts and checks. In 1899 he and a group of Arizona businessmen opened the Gila Valley Bank in a corner of the Solomon Commercial Company store. From this sprang the Valley National Bank of Arizona—and Solomonville was on the map.[19] Similar stories could be told about dozens of other towns, including Sutro, Nevada; Goldtree (named for Morris Goldbaum), California; Ehrenberg, Arizona; and Jewtown, Georgia. By 1880 across America there were nearly a thousand significant Jewish settlements in at least thirty-two of the thirty-eight states, four territories, and Washington, D.C.[20]

Successful Jewish businessmen accumulated wealth, and some were ready as early as the 1850s to enter the capital market. Mobility and capital accumulation, however, were not necessarily marks of successful integration into the general American business system. Despite the open economy, there was discrimination against Jews in a number of areas, particularly banking. This barrier helped stimulate the establishment of separate Jewish banking houses in America.[21] To some degree this was a product of an established Jewish banking group in Europe, which sent its agents to the United States. But ultimately, in addition to their ambition and willingness to take risks, it was the bond of trust supplied by religious, family, and social networks of the German Jewish settlers in America that lay behind their success as bankers.

The Seligmans, beginning as peddlers in Pennsylvania, Alabama, and Missouri, went on to become wholesale clothiers in New York and gold merchants in California. With capital accumulated in these states, they established the banking firm of J. and W. Seligman and Company, opening offices in leading cities in the United States and Europe. The company helped finance innumerable industrial enterprises, including railroads, public utilities, and the Panama Canal.[22] The Goldmans, Kuhns, Loebs, and Lehmans also had little help from old country financiers, but once established in banking they soon developed European connections to facilitate overseas business.[23]

The combination of American economic needs and Jewish industriousness, commercial experience, and cultural attributes underlay many business success stories. Not all of these prosperous Jewish families—the department store owners, the manufacturers, the financiers—were desperately poor when they began; nor did their collective fortunes ultimately match the wealth and economic power of the American oligarchy that controlled heavy industry and directed the flow of investment capital in the late nineteenth and early twentieth centuries. "Rags to riches," then, is perhaps too extreme a description of their histories. But there was impressive mobility. In numerous quantitative accounts by urban historians of Jews in nineteenth-century cities like Atlanta, Boston, Columbus, Omaha, Poughkeepsie, Los Angeles, and San Francisco similar conclusions were reached: Jews outpaced non-Jews in occupational and social mobility.[24] In fact, German Jews did well enough to allow the careful historian John Higham to conclude that, "proportionately speaking, in no other immigrant group have so many men ever risen so rapidly."[25]

The commercial elite was part of a growing Jewish population (see table 1), the vast majority of whom, by 1880, lived in urban centers of five thousand or more. At a time when urban centers were home to only 25 percent of all Americans, 83 percent of the Jews in the United States lived in them.[26] Although innumerable individual Jews lived in relative isolation from their coreligionists, as itinerant peddlers or as merchants in villages and towns with fewer than twenty Jewish inhabitants, American Jewry in general was concentrated in relatively few communities, both large and small.[27]

The German culture was an important unifying force for Jews in these communities. Many Jews subscribed to the German language press and were patrons of the German language theater and members of German clubs.[28] Toward 1880, however, growing numbers of German Jews were identified as American *and* Jewish or, as they were wont to say, Americans of "Hebrew persuasion." This is partly reflected in the fact that, by 1880, Jewish organizations of one kind or another existed in 90 percent of the 160 U.S. communities with 100 or more Jews. And nearly 70 towns with fewer

Table 1. Jewish Population in the United States, 1790–1920

Year	U.S. Population	U.S. Jews	U.S. Jews as % of U.S. Population	U.S. Jews as % of World Jewry
1790	3,930,000	1,350	0.03	
1800	5,310,000	1,600	0.03	0.06
1810	7,340,000	2,000	0.03	
1820	9,640,000	2,700	0.03	
1830	12,866,000	4,500	0.03	
1840	17,070,000	15,000	0.09	
1850	23,192,000	50,000	0.22	1.05
1860	31,443,000	150,000	0.48	
1870	38,558,000	200,000	0.52	
1880	50,156,000	250,000	0.50	3.27
1890	62,947,715	450,000	0.71	
1900	75,994,575	1,050,000	1.38	9.91
1910	91,972,265	2,043,000	2.22	15.91
1920	105,710,630	3,600,000	3.41	22.86

Source: Abraham Karp, *Haven and Home* (New York: Schocken, 1985), 374–75.

than 100 Jewish residents had at least a small number of Jewish institutions—more often than not, organized religious congregations.[29]

By 1868 Jewish hospitals could be found in Cincinnati, New York, Philadelphia, and Chicago. By 1880 New York City was home to some fifty Jewish charitable and educational institutions. Philadelphia boasted twenty, and Cincinnati a dozen or more. B'nai B'rith chapters dedicated to "uniting Israelites in the work of promoting their highest interests and those of humanity" and Young Men's Hebrew associations appeared in larger cities. Jewish societies for poor relief, free loans, mutual aid, and literary pursuits were founded in at least eleven major cities of the South, as well as in San Francisco, Los Angeles, San Diego, and Sacramento. The German Jews' reputation for philanthropy in the nineteenth century was impressive—and well earned.[30]

The expanding philanthropic network provided some Jews with a substitute for religion and a secular framework for the preservation of ethnic identity, but the growing number of religious congregations was also impressive. Well over 200, many with their own synagogue buildings, were constituted in more than 100 cities and towns by 1880. Most congregations, aside from a small number established by newly arriving eastern Europeans, were Reform—in practice, if not in name. From as early as the 1820s, and accelerating in the 1840s, demands were made for innovations, or "reforms," in the conduct of religious services. Many things combined to spur the movement toward Reform Judaism: the liberal spirit of the United States, the desire to reformulate Jewish ritual in the idiom of the times, and a desire to Americanize the synagogue with a more decorous English language service. In addition, there was no vigorous, traditional Jewry to oppose such changes. Finally, the arrival of authoritative, ordained Reform rabbis steeped in philosophical rationalism and the idea of progressive revelation provided leadership for the movement.[31]

I. M. Wise of Cincinnati was a moderate Reform Jew; through diligent compromise and improvisation, he shaped an American Judaism that enabled nineteenth-century German Jews to maintain their religious allegiance while taking their place in American society. Wise did not seek to be a sectarian, but his activities, along with those of the more radical Reformer David Einhorn (1809–79) of Baltimore, resulted in the evolution and crystallization of a Reform denomination. Wise's hope for unity was reflected in his establishment of both the Union of American Hebrew Congregations, in 1873, and Hebrew Union College, a rabbinical seminary, in 1875. That hope foundered on a variety of obstacles, not the least of which was the arrival of masses of poorer, less modernized eastern European Jews wedded to a greater traditionalism, if not to theological Orthodoxy or rigorous ritual observance.[32]

In 1880, however, the flow of immigrants from eastern Europe, though growing (only seventy-five hundred between 1820 and 1870, but more than thirty thousand between 1870 and 1880), was still small, and German Jewry in America remained preeminent. By this time, the German Jewish community had built a network of viable institutions and organizations crossing the entire continent, established a multilingual press, attracted a body of able, European-ordained rabbis, and was supporting a seminary to train an American rabbinate.

The Jewish community became affluent and influential. But some members who aspired to social acceptance were rejected by leading social clubs in large cities in the 1870s. In the status-hungry years following the Civil War, Jews' upward mobility contributed to the erection of social barriers like restricted hotels and exclusive clubs. In the scramble for prestige, Gentiles could use these noneconomic status markers in their competition with Jews, and social discrimination was intensified. In the late 1870s, German Jewish arrivistes found themselves increasingly excluded from upper-crust private schools, college fraternities, and "desirable" neighborhoods.[33]

In the decade's most prominent exclusionary incident, the Grand Union Hotel in Saratoga Springs, owned by Judge Hilton, refused accommodations to Joseph Seligman, a long-time patron, whose name meant wealth and status in the Jewish community. Leading Jewish merchants, incensed by this public humiliation, boycotted Hilton's wholesale firm, the A. T. Stewart Company. The company was forced into bankruptcy, but general social exclusion against Jews continued and increased. San Francisco's *Elite Directory* for 1879 included Jews but on a separate list from Christians. The New York *Social Register* closed its lists to Jews entirely; and in 1893 the city's prestigious Union League Club, which Jews had helped establish, barred Jews.[34]

Such snubs paled into insignificance compared to the violence Jews experienced in the Deep South during the 1890s. Farmers, burdened by debt, sacked the stores of Jewish merchants in several states, including Louisiana and Georgia. And in 1893, in their attempts to drive Jewish merchants out of southern Mississippi, marauding horsemen burned dozens of farmhouses belonging to Jews.[35]

In the late nineteenth century, America was being transformed from a relatively rural, relatively homogeneous, Protestant society into an industrial nation marked by urbanization, heterogeneity, and mobility. The radical changes of the 1880s and 1890s produced economic grievance, fear of displacement, and social insecurities. These in turn significantly strengthened anti-Semitism. It is important to remember, however, that such hatred of Jews, although in evidence even earlier than the 1890s—indeed, visible as early as the birth of the nation itself—never became part of the national political agenda and that prejudice and discrimination against Jews in America have been mild compared to the violent and increasingly political anti-Semitism of the Old World.[36] This does not make it unimportant; Jews in America whose property was attacked, who were physically assaulted, or who were closed off from social acceptability and enterprises at the upper reaches of the American economy suffered.

When anti-Semitism intensified in the United States in the last quarter of the nineteenth century, German Jews were more ready to blame the new immigrants from eastern Europe than to recognize that their own conspicuous success also played a role in the unfortunate turn of events. Fearing an even greater anti-Semitism as the numbers of immigrants increased exponentially in the 1880s, and anxious over the potential burden of masses of poor dependents, German Jews, in their cultural and class arrogance, initially took an anti-immigration position. But ultimately—indeed relatively quickly, as we will see in later chapters—their stance changed, and they played an important role in the fight against immigration restriction.

They also provided—despite a strained, ofttimes bitter, relationship with eastern European Jews—significant aid, including jobs, social welfare philanthropy, and political support.[37] The more positive attitude, a combination of condescension and empathy, was reflected in the columns of the *American Hebrew*. From May to December 1881, the editors insisted that every effort be made "to rescue our own and give them a space wherein they may breath the air of peace." There is "plenty of room for them all in this 'haven of the oppressed,'" the paper argued, and went on to remind readers that "all of us should be sensible of what we owe not only to these . . . coreligionists but to ourselves, who will be looked upon by our Gentile neighbors as the natural sponsors for these our brethren."[38]

By the 1880s, German Jews had become significantly acculturated. This was reflected in their rapid economic and social mobility, their institutionalization of Reform Judaism, and the intensification of their collective identity as Americans and Jews. German Jews had some trouble with the second of these identifications as they faced the flood of eastern European Jews. They feared, with some reason, that the distinction between "the better class of Jews" and the "vulgar Jews" would collapse and that everything they had worked for would be destroyed.[39]

Though they never relinquished their significant influence—which they maintained particularly through their philanthropy—German Jews did witness, between 1890 and 1920, the end of their total dominance of the American Jewish community. But "everything they had worked for" would not be destroyed. German Jews had created the institutional framework and even many of the modes of behavior and values that, with some important qualifications, continue to mark the American Jewish world.[40] Eastern European Jews, after all, established no new communities; they followed the Germans to their settlements, the largest of which remained the important centers of Jewish population, organizational activity, and cultural continuity throughout the era of massive eastern European immigration.[41]

Like German Jews before them, eastern European immigrants and their children became Americanized, even if not at the same remarkable pace. Many also achieved economic and occupational mobility—sometimes, as in the garment business, by displacing Germans. And like their German predecessors, eastern Europeans retained and reshaped a distinctive, if attenuated, ethnoreligious Jewish culture. Indeed, if German Jews set the stage for the new immigrants, eastern Europeans supplied the biological and cultural reinforcement needed to save American Jewry from assimilation. German Jewish population increases in the nineteenth century were notable, but they did not keep pace with even greater increases in the general American population. It is at least arguable that, without the eastern European Jews, a viable Jewish culture in America would have ultimately disappeared.

CHAPTER ONE

✡

SOURCES OF THE EASTERN
EUROPEAN MIGRATION

IN 1880 close to 6 million of the world's 7.7 million Jews, or about 75 percent, lived in eastern Europe, and only 3 percent lived in the United States. By 1920, however, after a series of large-scale migrations, nearly 23 percent of world Jewry called America home. In order to understand what produced this massive uprooting and transplantation of Jews, and to understand the social and cultural baggage the immigrants carried with them to the United States, we need to briefly examine the traditional world of eastern European Jews—their physical wretchedness and the forces for cultural renewal and spiritual hope that emerged.

The great bulk, more than 73 percent, of Jewish immigrants to the United States between 1880 and 1920 came from the Russian Empire, particularly from the Pale of Settlement, the fifteen western provinces of European Russia, and the ten provinces of Russian-held Poland. Nearly four million Jews, considered by the Russians a pariah people, were confined to the Pale and, for more than two centuries, to the ethnically homogeneous shtetlekh (small towns) therein. Although Jews rarely constituted more than 5 percent of the population of the Russian Empire, they were often close to 15 percent of the population of the Pale; even more often, they constituted the majority, if not all, of the inhabitants of their shtetlekh.

It is true that by 1897 almost half the Jewish population of the Russian Empire, though still confined to the Pale, no longer lived in shtetlekh but in larger towns or cities. And another 30 percent lived in *miesteckos*, settlements that served as commercial and industrial centers for the surrounding countryside. Shtetl life, however, had flourished in eastern Europe for several hundred years. That life, through powerful spiritual ties, through the common language of Yiddish and the sacred language of Hebrew, and through a sense of shared history, had firmly molded Jewish values and behavior. Even when they left their small towns, therefore, Jews carried with them much of their shtetl culture, which they reformulated and transplanted to new locales.[1]

Populations of some shtetlekh, like Bzin, south of Warsaw and not far from Lodz, or Sislevitch, which lay east of Bialystok, engaged in manufacturing. But most Jewish towns provided surrounding agricultural villages with commercial services, especially marketing and milling. Since Jews, the least favored minority in eastern Europe, were mostly forbidden to own land and were limited to a small base of occupational and economic operations, they earned their livelihoods by trade and artisanship, thereby filling an important need in the underdeveloped agrarian economies of the Russian Empire, Galicia (Austria-Hungary), and Romania.[2]

At the center of the shtetl was the marketplace, to which peasants from many miles around brought livestock, fish, hides, grain, fruits, and vegetables. They bought in exchange city products that the Jews imported—dry goods, clothing, lamps, and tools.[3] In Kolibishov (east of Cracow) on market day a great "human stream, together with containers and merchandise, pour[ed] fourth from all of the back streets." Jewish men and women bearing crates, poles, and barrels, got ready for business. And endless trains of peasant wagons arrived, bearing every sort of produce, including "the things Jews need[ed] for their Sabbath table. Onions for fish, parsley for soup, little cucumbers with dill for pickling, and carrots for tsimes." After selling their produce, the peasant men and women did their shopping in the Jewish stalls and shops, the air "filled with a grating mixture of shouting voices. All the voices flowed together into a chorus expressing one word and one word only: Par-no-se (livelihood!)."[4]

The hurly-burly of the shtetl marketplace has been described as "one of the great wonders of the world." Despite the seeming frenzy of economic activity, however, and even though Jews possessed a virtual monopoly of the business life of the Pale, poverty was the general condition in the shtetl from at least as far back as the 1650s, and became worse in the late eighteenth century and through the nineteenth century. Outside of the shtetl, some Jews were relatively well off. One-third of the Pale's factories were owned by Jews, and there were also Jewish dealers in grain, fur, cattle, and lumber, as well as innkeepers, stewards, estate administrators, storekeepers, and peddlers. A number of Jews were in professions, particularly nearer Galicia. But the economic position of these Jews became increasingly precarious. And in any case, the great mass of Jews in the shtetlekh and in eastern Europe generally were the *proste yidn*—the simple and poor.5

Poverty was one of the absolutes in Jewish life, a fact reflected in the language and literature of eastern European Jews. Yiddish, based on a mixture of Middle High German dialects and borrowing freely from almost every other European language, developed innumerable words for *poverty*. A Yiddish thesaurus needs nineteen columns of fine print for all the synonyms for *misfortune*; *good fortune* needs only five. And the theme of poverty with its attendant ills and ironies appears again and again in the stories of such eastern European Yiddish writers as Sholom Aleichem, I. L. Peretz, and Mendele Mokher Sforim.6

Hand in hand with poverty went fear. A Jew in eastern Europe, often marked by distinctive dress and speech, was free game for all, from schoolchildren to government officials. Jews who ventured outside the shtetl to peddle considered themselves lucky if they were not set upon and beaten. Even within the town, Jews were vulnerable to the invasions and excesses of the occasional drunken mob or discontented peasants intent on violence.

The shtetl was not only an economic entity; at its heart, it was a community of faith built upon a deeply rooted religious culture. The community acknowledged an awesome God, whose revelation was filled with power and the possibility of human salvation.7 The shtetl was not, however, a monastic or ascetic community, withdrawn from the world. Indeed, life was seen as a gift to be nourished and enjoyed and, most important, to be fulfilled. Even when Jews used the Hebrew term *olam haba* (the hereafter), they were often referring to the world to come *on this earth* and not necessarily to *yene velt*, the other world.8

Much of Jewish theology looked forward to the future, which was envisaged as a return to the good, older times. But this theology also included the more daring and messianic vision of the prophets, like Isaiah, who expected the future not merely to be like the past but significantly better. Supernatural, other-worldly elements were added to the messianic concept over time, but worldy, historical messianism was a permanent feature of Jewish history. And "thirst for the future" was already significant in Jewish life by the time Jews began their long exile—dispersed, despised, and often physically persecuted.9

Beginning in the seventeenth century and up to the nineteenth century, when Jewish communities in eastern Europe underwent a transformation of values and expectations, this future was assumed to be far off. Meanwhile, the community derived its religion, its values, and its very meaning from the past. In some ways, then, Jewish society had no present. It hoped for an improved future, and its tradition did envisage redemption in that long term. In the interim, however, Jews believed that life, public and private, could be made tolerable, even meaningful, by adherence to tradition and by following the law of God as revealed in the Torah, the Hebrew Scriptures.[10]

Scholarship was one of the important pathways to God and to the future, and every shtetl maintained at least one *kheyder* (elementary school) and a *khevre* (society or committee) for the purpose of providing poor boys with religious education through their thirteenth year. Sometimes there was a yeshiva, a school for advanced Jewish learning, which was chiefly, but not exclusively, for students preparing for the rabbinate.

Many young men, even those not interested in becoming rabbis, immersed themselves in the sacred texts, because study had clear ethical value. Since the Torah was God's law and as such was the only appropriate guide to the good life, the more a student studied the Torah and the Talmud—sixty-three volumes with 5,800 folio pages of elucidation and elaboration of the written law—the more he gained in ethical understanding and reach. On an individual level, study fulfilled the critically important religous value of *takhles,* an orientation to ultimate outcomes rather than to immediate benefits. And study was a *mitzvah,* an ordained obligation whose fulfillment not only brought honor and status in the community but was pleasing to God. Furthermore, it was believed that "he who busies himself with the law for its own sake brings harmony into the universe. . . . He protects the whole world. He brings near redemption." Study, then, was not only the way to a socially useful profession; it was the route to ethical awareness and to immortality, a power-laden enterprise full of cosmic significance.[11]

Study in eastern Europe was also a form of cultural differentiation: scholarship set Jews apart from surrounding peoples and enabled them to maintain a high opinion of themselves, despite their tribulations. As part of the celebration marking the completed study of a talmudic tractate (*siyyum massekhet*), Jewish students chanted: "We arise early and they arise early; we for Torah matters and they for matters of nonsense. . . . We run and they run; we to a life in the world to come and they to the pit." This *hadran,* or benediction, dates from as early as 900 C.E., but in the nineteenth century it reflected the value system that had emerged in the shtetlekh of eastern Europe to help Jews maintain morale in the face of circumscription and persecution. No matter who appeared to be winning in the present, Jews, because of their commitment to religious study, were convinced they would win in the end.[12]

Jewish boys as young as three years old were traditionally wrapped in *talesim* (prayer shawls) and carried to kheyder by their fathers and mothers. Here the other children waited expectantly for the candy or cookies that parents of new students distributed to mark the auspicious occasion. The *melamed* (teacher) brought the new student to a large chart of the Hebrew alphabet and, before starting the lesson, gave the boy a taste of honey. After a short recitation, the teacher would drop a coin on the table from high above, telling the student that "an angel had dropped it from heaven . . . because [he] was a good little boy and wanted to learn."[13]

That traditional world is lovingly recalled by many in the memoir literature. But for some boys, *kheyder* was more like torture. Yoysef Fridman, whose poor parents sent him to the Talmud Torah (the free *kheyder* supported by charity) because they did not "want their child to grow up to be a non-Jew," remembered all too well that his teacher

> had a vicious temper. . . . Woe to the child that made the teacher angry. [He would] let out all of his bitterness on the child's backside. And he knew how to beat children better than he knew how to teach them. . . . I was very frightened of being struck. . . . Therefore I studied hard [and by] the second or third day of the week, I would have already memorized the week's Torah portion. Thus I became the best student in the class. When Reb Yosef came to examine us I would always get a few kopeks and a pinch on the cheek. The other children envied me bitterly. Precisely those children who were incapable of learning were the ones who were physically strong, and they made my life miserable.
>
> I don't remember whether I or someone else thought of having me creep under the table, whisper the Torah portion to the other children, and thereby save them the beatings. [But the melamed] was satisfied . . . and the children were even happier. [Eventually the teacher caught on.] He went over to the stove, picked up a poker and fell on me so viciously I thought I was about to die. . . . I went outside, gathered all the boys together, and made a "speech". . . . I called on them to refuse to be beaten anymore and to strike in protest.[14]

Although education at the *kheyder* often degenerated into rote memorization and at the yeshiva, into obscurantism, for many it meant saturation in

Jewish ethics and in the prophetic tradition, with its emphasis on *tzedakah* (charity as justice and righteousness), and *tikkun olam* (repair or improvement of the world), messianism, and communal responsibility.

Religious education was formally the domain of boys and men, who often spent ten hours a day at it. Girls were generally discouraged from studies, their energies and ambition directed instead toward homemaking and marriage. Girls did often receive a year or two of instruction in reading and writing Yiddish, the so-called *mamaloshen* (mother's tongue). Girls also learned to recite, but not translate, Hebrew prayers. They had access to the content of the holy books only through the *tsene urene,* the traditional Yiddish version of the Pentateuch (the first five books of Hebrew Scriptures).[15]

Although through their own piety women provided models and an informal religious education for their daughters, with whom they spent at least part of the day, we should not overstate this. The lessons were neither direct nor necessarily conscious, and mothers were often preoccupied with work. One daughter's memories reflect the memories of many: "Trouble is the parents did not have much time. There was a lot of work. Already they had three children [who] . . . were always crying. And it was such a pity— my mother was . . . angry, and . . . frustrated—working very hard. And my father was free [to study]."[16]

This picture of the scholarly husband spending all his time in the *bet hamidrash* (house of study) and the *shul* while his wife slaved away at home or market, although true in some instances, has been overdrawn in Jewish historical literature and memory. Few families in impoverished Jewish eastern Europe could afford so unproductive an economic arrangement. Jewish women, however, did indeed play an extraordinarily time-consuming and essential role in providing for their families. Some, like Pearl Halpern's mother, worked in a cigarette factory, but most employed women were involved in a nonindustrial commercial enterprise of one kind or another. The most successful owned shops, where they sold food and dry goods. Clara Lemlich's mother kept a store; Sidney Hillman's mother had a small grocery shop in the front room of their house; she also kept a cow, sold milk, and managed a small bakery. More often, like Clara Weissman's mother, women were peddlers with stalls in the marketplace, where they sold the things they had made or had bought in the city. Or they went from house to house, selling bagels or tea and beans and potato pancakes.[17]

When Sarah Reznikoff was a girl, she kneaded the dough for the rolls her mother peddled, and by crushing a mixture of chalk and oil with her feet, made putty for her father to sell to a shopkeeper. Girls and women often worked together, baking items to peddle, sewing clothing to sell (independently or through small contractors), caring for smaller children, or simply doing the innumerable, seemingly unending domestic chores. All the tasks were performed within the overarching context of religious duty, ritual, regulation, and spirit. Mothers "set important examples of service and self-sacrifice" and taught their daughters to achieve satisfaction by living their lives for and through others. Although learning these traditional values did not bring to girls the status that scholarly achievement brought to boys, daughters were part of an important educational dynamic, and "in many cases a mother's lessons were more vivid than those of the . . . melamed."[18]

In addition to education, formal and informal, many other communal institutions helped transmit values. Every shtetl had a *mikvah* (ritual bath), a *shokhet* (ritual slaughterer), and at least one shul, where the daily prayers were recited and, on *shabbos* (the Sabbath), the Torah was read and studied.

Even though most shtetl Jews were poor, in shul there was not only a rigid separation of men and women but also a separation of the *shayna yidn* (refined or gentlepeople) and the *proste yidn* (common people). Scholarship was the most important determination of *yikhes* (status), but wealth and family background also clearly counted. Sometimes workers' *khevrot* (committees or guilds) had their own shuln, in which artisans and craftsmen could sit unsegregated and stand equal before God. In these humble houses of prayer, artisans were not relegated to the rear and could even occupy the coveted benches near the eastern wall, closest to Jerusalem. Moreover, honors, in liturgical readings or ceremonials were distributed democratically and were never sold. This prohibition avoided the problem of richer members outbidding, and thus outclassing, poorer ones. Congregants were called up in alphabetical order to recite the blessing on the Torah, and money for maintenance of the shul was collected from all on an equal basis.[19]

Although in the shtetl the somewhat better off merchant was generally set off from the worker, and the tutored from the untutored, neither scholarship nor wealth conferred caste privileges. Scholarship was theoretically open to all, and many poor boys did pursue religious studies. Some were even chosen as husbands for daughters of wealthy families that wanted to add to the status of riches the even more important yikhes of scholarship. Nor did being poor and untutored engender a sense of inferiority. As radical a writer as Moishe Olgin could say about his upbringing in traditional Jewish society that even the poorest always remained a "free man, poverty did not corrode his soul, did not break his spirit."[20]

Whenever possible, artisans asserted their spirit and their independence. Their *khevrot* and shuln were manifestations of this. So was the custom of *Ikkuv ha-Kereah,* interrupting or delaying the reading of the Torah on the Sabbath to voice a grievance. A complainant had the right to prevent the religious service from continuing until a promise of arbitration was exacted. Women apparently took advantage of this practice more often than men. Sometimes the rabbi would seize this opportunity to remind prosperous householders that Jewish religious literature, particularly the Prophets and the Psalms, repeatedly exalts the poor and exhorts the affluent to provide for the needy.[21]

Affluence, though not undervalued in worldly terms, had after all a social and religious purpose: tzedakah. Individuals often performed philanthropic acts, but tzedakah was in the main dispensed by the kehillah (Jewish community council) and by the many volunteer organizations this central authority helped administer. Run by a coaliton of rabbis and prosperous merchants, the kehillah did not always satisfy its constituents. At least from as early as the 1750s, the poor chronically voiced complaints and even sporadically rioted against the wealthier Jews and the clergy.[22] But the kehillah did maintain orphanages and schools for the poor, and its khevrot provided free loans, dowries, Passover supplies, fuel, and clothes for the needy. Well-off Jews were obligated to give, as well as to participate in, the *khevrot.* Ideally, "recipients of aid were in no way beholden to donors: it was their due. The word for benefice—tzedakah—derives from the word for justice. In fact the donor owed thanks to the recipient for the opportunity to do a mitzva."[23] If reality deviated at times from the ideals, if the not-so-poor lorded it over the very poor, if scholars behaved arrogantly toward the untutored, or if wealthy merchants were too openly proud and condescending in their charitable giving, still the ideals established the moral tone. And even the simplest, least learned Jew was judged, and judged himself, by the ideals of the Torah.

Whatever the tensions between the poor and the well-to-do, all Jews in the towns of eastern Europe up to the nineteenth century can be classified in relative terms as *kleine menshn* (little people) rather than as rival classes.

And all shared in the embrace of personal and communal ties as well as powerful family loyalties. The Jews were responsible for one another; their concept of human relations, reinforced by religious philosophy, generally promoted mutuality and interdependence. The life of eastern European Jews, with its isolation, provincialism, poverty, and sporadic violence, was anything but ideal. But Jews were at least spared the brutality and indifference that consistently attended the world of lord and peasant. In the face of oppression, they were sustained by their belief in a common destiny, buoyed by their feeling of moral superiority, and strengthened by their sense of community.

The classic eastern European shtetl was never as stable as it has sometimes been portrayed. In the 1800s, moreover, the instability of the shtetl community increased in the face of significant economic changes and under the pressure and appeal of the new social and political thought impinging on Jewish culture generally. The world of the shtetl had already begun to experience the decline of the authority of the rabbis and the kehillot by the middle of the eighteenth century. Hasidism, an enthusiastic, pietistic movement of religious renewal, emerging in the 1750s, temporarily challenged rabbinic traditionalism. In demanding spontaneity and rejecting rote and overly formal ritual, the Hasidim appealed to and brightened the spiritual life of many Jews, particularly the numerous *proste yidn*. But the Mitnagdim (literally, opponents) were extremely critical of the movement and resented what they saw as the uninhibited behavior of the Hasidim as well as the claim that the Hasidic *tzaddik* (wise man) could act as an intermediary between the simple believer and God. It was only in the latter part of the nineteenth century that the bitter hostility between the Hasidim and the Mitnagdim began to fade, partly because the more secular Haskalah (enlightenment) movement provided a common enemy.

A more enduring challenge and split became manifest, however, when Jewish community councils were forced to significantly increase the taxes on their own people. The Polish government demanded inordinately heavy payments from the Jews to help finance its wars with Russia and Sweden and to put down rebellions of cossacks within its own borders. These taxes were collected by the community councils, and the legitimacy of the leaders of the kehillah thus eroded in the eyes of many Jews.[24]

Legitimacy eroded further when Russia, piece by piece, annexed most of Poland in the late eighteenth century. Czarist regimes forced Jewish community leaders not only to tax more heavily but to supply men for the Russian army. Until 1827 only peasants had to face the draft and twenty-five years of military service. Under Czar Nicholas I, Jewish men aged eighteen to twenty-five were called up, and younger recruits, aged twelve to seventeen, were given "preparatory" military training as cantonists.

The high draft quotas, as many as thirty boys for every thousand Jews, moved community leaders to conscript Jews as punishment for failure to pay taxes and to hire *khapers*—professional kidnappers—to ferret young boys out of hiding. At the same time, members of the kehillah and Jews of means bought exemption for their own sons. Under pressure from the government to deliver more and more recruits, and in order to protect their own sons, kehillah leaders delivered up seven- and eight-year-olds, took boys from poor families that had already given a son, and even drafted only sons.[25] Rose Schneiderman, who immigrated to the United States in 1904, remembered with some bitterness that "as an only son [my father] was supposed to be exempt from military service, but it happened that a wealthy Jewish family had bought their son's way out, and my father was drafted to fill the village quota."[26]

By the middle of the nineteenth century, it was clear that czarist Jewish policy was designed to promote conversion and assimilation. Young Jews were to be recruited either for the Crown schools, which were dedicated to the "eradication of the superstitions and harmful prejudices instilled by the study of the Talmud," or for extremely long service in the military, where if explicit conversion pressures did not work, time and distance would.[27] The experiences of the cantonist period, which lasted until the middle of the 1850s, was a source of enduring and divisive resentment in the Jewish community. The corruption of the kehillah, the feared *khaper,* and the pain of separated families found expression in folk songs, snatches of which were sung and remembered until the twentieth century:

> They drag me off to the draft board
> Everyone lowers their head in shame
> They put me through the physical test—
> And announce: A Soldier, one of the best!

and the ironic:

> It's a mitzva to hand over the simple people
> Shoemakers, tailors are good-for-nothings[28]

By the 1850s the split between the poor and the prosperous—or more accurately, between the poor and the less poor—had grown deep and painful. It was the rare shtetl now of which one could say that "Jewish households were tightly knit one with the other, as if all were . . . one family."[29] The leaders of the community never regained their esteem or influence.

Communal solidarity was even further undermined by new and complex economic forces surrounding and penetrating Jewish collectivities. In many areas in the late nineteenth century, the peasant-based economies of eastern Europe were slowly eroding. For Jews this meant increased poverty, intensified competition among themselves, and the further disintegration of communal cohesiveness. The modernization of agriculture and the very beginnings of industrialization—particularly in the Pale, where Jews in the 1890s constituted approximately 70 percent of those engaged in commerce and 30 percent of those engaged in crafts—led to the displacement of petty merchants, peddlers, artisans, teamsters, factors, and innkeepers.

Other effects of modernization were felt as well. Railroads and peasant cooperatives changed the role played by large numbers of Jews in the small market towns, virtually eliminating local fairs. By 1880 some sections of eastern Europe had one Jewish peddler for every ten peasant customers.[30] In addition, the emancipation of the serfs (1861–62) left the peasants with heavy, long-term mortgages and unable to afford the services of Jewish middlemen. And nobles, relieved of their obligations by the freeing of the serfs, needed fewer stewards and administrators for their diminished estates.

The Russian economy was experiencing long periods of instability, and as the need for scapegoats intensified in the face of Russian restlessness in the 1860s and 1870s, the government did not hesitate to promote anti-Semitism by focusing on the Jews' preeminence as middlemen. Native middlemen organized boycotts of Jewish merchants, and the government offered loans to a nascent class of Russian commercial men waiting for businesses to be abandoned by Jews.

The pressures on Jews throughout eastern Europe to seek livelihoods elsewhere mounted year by year. They were intensified by an unsuccessful Polish nationalist uprising in 1863, a famine in Lithuania in 1867–69, and a cholera epidemic in Poland in 1869.[31] In Galicia (Austria-Hungary) in the 1880s, 60 percent of the Jews had to be supported by the community; five thousand a year were dying of starvation or of diseases brought on by malnutrition. Galician Jews migrated toward eastern Hungary and Vienna; Polish Jews flocked to cities like Lodz, Warsaw, and Vilna.

Table 2. Jewish Population in Russia and Poland, as Percentage of
Total Population, 1897–1898

Area	Total	Urban Areas
Northwest Russia	14.1	57.9
Southwest Russia	9.7	38.1
Southern Russia	9.0	26.3
Poland	14.1	40.9
Pale of Settlement	11.6	40.9

Source: Adapted from Simon Kuznets, "Immigration of Russian Jews to the United States:
Background and Structure," *Perspectives in American History* 9 (1975): 71.

All of this was exacerbated after terrorists assassinated Alexander II in
1881. Confusion reigned, and scapegoating was intensified. Murderous
violence took place against Jews in pogroms that erupted in 225 cities and
towns between 1881 and 1882. In addition, the draconian May Laws (1882)
were promulgated, prohibiting Jewish settlement in villages. This meant
the expulsion of a half-million Jews from rural areas. An additional seven
hundred thousand, including twenty thousand expelled from Moscow in
chains, were driven into the Pale by 1891.[32]

Between 1894 and 1898 the number of Jewish paupers increased by 30
percent, and in many communities the number of families of *luftmenshn,*
people without marketable skills or capital (literally, people who live on
air), approached 40 percent of the entire Jewish population. Sam Davis,
born in a Lithuanian shtetl, remembered that his father had three trades,
"and with the three trades we were starving." His family somehow got
permission to move to the city of Riga, outside the Pale of Settlement.[33] The
vast majority of Jews, of course, remained inside the Pale, but the numbers
moving from shtetl to urban concentrations increased significantly between
1885 and 1915.[34] Table 2 shows percentages of Jews in urban areas by 1898.

Economic dislocation and government policy changed the geography of
Jewish life in eastern Europe. Lodz, which counted eleven Jews in 1797, had
almost 100,000 a century later, 32 percent of the population of the city; and
by 1910 the Jewish population was more than 166,000. Warsaw's Jewish
population soared from 3,500 in the late eighteenth century to nearly
220,000, 33 percent of the population, in 1897. Bialystok drew uprooted
shtetl dwellers, artisans, and laborers and, by the turn of the century, was 63
percent Jewish. But even cities offered only a precarious existence. Jews,
victims of Russian paranoia and xenophobia, were excluded from many

branches of the economy. They were forbidden to purchase real estate or even to negotiate mortgages. No business at all could be conducted by Jews in the larger towns, nor could Jews conduct business on Sunday anywhere.

All of this was aggravated by the fact that the Jewish population of eastern Europe continued to grow at a steady rate between 1800 (1,250,000) and 1900 (6,500,000), despite considerable emigration. Now, in addition to luftmenshn, there would be schnorrers (professional beggars) and *gass-menshn,* unskilled workers available for any job regardless of hazard or legality.[35]

In the newer centers of population, the material condition of Jews continued to decline. And it was primarily here that a Jewish proletariat developed, as did further hardening of class feeling. In the major urban centers of the northwest, including Vilna, Minsk, Bialystok, Grodno, Vitebsk, and Kovno, Jewish workers were significantly disproportionate to the general population. This Jewish proletariat, however, was a proletariat of craftsmen and artisans, with very few factory workers.

According to Ezra Mendelsohn, the foremost student of class struggle in the Pale, of the nearly 200,000 workers in the northwest at the turn of the century, some 90 percent were artisans and craftsmen, specializing mainly in small-shop tailoring and carpentry. The very low percentage of Jews employed in factories reflects the backward character of the northwest. Only Bialystok, a major textile center in Grodno province, was highly industrial. In that city, however, the owners of large modern factories preferred Christian to Jewish workers, so that even the "sizeable Jewish weaver proletariat of Bialystok remained a proletariat of shops."[36]

Although factory owners preferred Christian workers partly because of prejudice against Jews, there were undoubtedly other reasons as well, especially since Jewish factory owners also tended to prefer Christian workers. Jewish workers were less experienced, did not want to work on the Sabbath, and were considered troublemakers. Thus the Jewish proletariat, with the exception of workers in cigarette and match factories, remained a "proletariat of small shops and declining fortunes."[37]

In the new urban areas there were few well-organized associations for philanthropic or mutual support in the face of these declining fortunes, and Jewish artisans and the small-shop proletariat tended to look to co-workers rather than to the larger Jewish community for solidarity. They set up *kases,* or unions, for self-help and mutual aid. These were not only expressions of immediate need "but [were] in full accord with the traditions of the Jewish community." Indeed, as the *kases* began to become *kampf-kases* (unions of class struggle), they sometimes used the synagogue as an arena for the presentation of grievances against employers. Workers brought their complaints to a traditional *din* Torah—a lawsuit conducted before a rabbi who played the role of arbitrator.[38]

Although Jewish communal life in the cities of eastern Europe continued to suffer the disintegration that had begun earlier in the shtetl, many Jews, including workers, remained in touch with shtetl culture and ideals. In the cities, "the majority of the Jews (Jews comprised 41 percent of the urban populations of Russia and Poland by 1897) . . . resided in the same locality and led their own social life." City Jews, like shtetl Jews, had economic ties with Gentiles, but the focus of their cultural life was almost exclusively Jewish. Indeed, it is at least arguable that by the late 1890s the larger towns and cities were the "real centers of Jewish culture in Eastern Europe" and that the so-called "shtetl community" was no longer confined to shtetlekh. In the midst of oppression and dislocation, shtetl culture experienced a reawakening and a reweaving into creative and vibrant forms in urban contexts.[39]

The reweaving was not accomplished, however, without significant struggle, missed stitches, wrong turns, and bitter disappointments. As early as the 1850s, the Haskalah, or "enlightenment," originally a product of western European Jewry, had gained a foothold among some secularly educated Jews living in the more urbanized areas of eastern Europe. By 1870 the Haskalah began to penetrate shtetl society. Most of the Maskilim (enlightened ones) did seek a path that would preserve the national-religious identity of the Jews, but they strove toward a complete emancipation, increased secularization, full Jewish citizenship, and the virtual elimination of the kehillah as an intermediary between Jews and the state.

Among the most distinguished Maskilim were novelist Abraham Mapu (1808–67), through whose primitive romances modern Hebrew fiction emerged, and poet Judah Lieb Gordon, a leading but somewhat intemperate advocate of the liberalization of Judaism and a promoter of secular education. At first, the writers and journalists involved in the movement, particularly those in St. Petersburg who in 1863 founded the Society for the Promotion of Culture among the Jews of Russia, strongly favored Russian over Yiddish, but it was not long before some of the Maskilim created a secular Yiddish literature. The books and newspapers of these enlightened ones, in a variety of languages, soon found their way into the heretofore prohibited environment of the yeshivas and houses of prayer.

As long as the Haskalah opposed traditional Jewish leadership and expressed no disloyalty to the czar, the Russian government assisted its spread. Indeed, Judah Lieb Gordon received the title Honorary Citizen for his support of the Russian government's educational policy toward Jews. The proselytizing activities of the Maskilim and the liberalization of Jewish educational policy by Alexander II (1855–81), in combination with the general draft law of 1874, which granted exemption to students in Russian secondary schools, resulted in a massive increase of Jewish youth in Russian-Jewish and general Russian educational institutions. Even young girls pressured their parents, often successfully, into sending them to the gymnasia.[40]

Russian secular education reinforced the growing alienation of the Jewish intellectual youth from the Jewish people in general. This was a serious blow to the nationalist wing of the Maskilim, but it was they who had helped loosen forces over which they now had little control. Secularization and acculturation, if not assimilation and conversion, made inroads into the Jewish world, particularly in the cities. "As soon as we settled in Petersburg," wrote Pauline Wengeroff, "I had to discard the peruke [wig] which pious Jewish women wore" [and after a struggle with my husband] I ceased to keep a kosher kitchen. . . [Then] what a time of heartbreak when my son attended the gymnasium! . . . But ought I to expect that my children, growing up under alien influences, would follow the ways of their mother? . . . I felt alone and abandoned."[41]

Jewish students continued to enroll in Russian schools. They apparently believed with George Price that "the Russian school was an educational shrine and a source of educational nourishment to those who crave it. . . . It seemed to me that a person would be judged not by his wealth, fame or race, but by his knowledge and character." But Price, along with many others, was bitterly disappointed: "The Russian Realschule had nothing in store for the Jew. The education he receives is incomplete; . . . he is left without means of earning a livelihood. . . . Yes, a Jew has no future in Russia."[42]

The rabbis had warned the Maskilim about the dangers of pursuing the gods of secular progress. Throwing off the yoke of the past, they said, would mean suffering great communal and spiritual loss, with no compensatory gain in integration or equality. Whatever their motives, the traditionalists had certainly seen some things about Russia more clearly than had the enlightened ones. Even under Alexander II, Jews were generally kept out of the economic centers. Kiev, with few exceptions, was closed; the same was true of Kharkov and Moscow. And St. Petersburg was open only to the upper bourgeoisie and a handful of students. Despite increases in the "right of residence" outside of the Pale for "useful Jews" and the increasing enrollment of Jews in Russian secondary schools and universities, legal humiliation and economic harassment continued.

In western Europe, Jews had achieved, at least temporarily, some individual liberty in return for the communal autonomy and corporate rights that the several European states had abolished. In Russia, however, where neither individual nor corporate rights had ever been guaranteed, the integration of Jews became repressive. Instead of genuine emancipation, there was a "revolutionary dismemberment of the legal integrity of Jewish society" and a further breakdown of communal interdependence and wholeness.[43] This led in the last quarter of the nineteenth century to great turmoil but, also, to effervescence. There emerged a number of new cultural forms, including devotion to secular yiddishkayt, as well as important political movements—socialism, Zionism, and various combinations thereof. Traditional Jewry, although still seriously split, came together in Orthodoxy in order to mount a defense against secularism. All the movements competed for converts.

In that competition, socialism quite often won. In the late nineteenth century, a context and constituency was being created for a fledgling socialist movement among Jews. The small-shop Jewish proletariat found it increasingly difficult to compete with the factories or with the handcraft enterprises of the masses of emancipated peasants. And Jewish employers, themselves squeezed, intensified their exploitation of Jewish workers. An increasingly self-conscious Jewish proletariat emerged and participated in a series of strikes in the 1870s and 1880s. The action was spontaneous, sporadic, and at first generally uninfluenced by Jewish socialists. An organized movement developed only after the Jewish socialist intelligentsia established significant contact with the Jewish working masses.[44]

Russian schools and universities, which were centers of revolutionary ferment, particularly in the last third of the nineteenth century, helped mold that intelligentsia. Morris Winchevsky, the grand old man of Jewish socialism, was enrolled in the tuition-free training college for state rabbis in Vilna in 1874. The school was seething with student radicalism. Winchevsky said that for his socialist orientation he had "to thank [Isaiah] that poet-preacher who entered [his] heart and mind with love for . . . oppressed people," but he undoubtedly experienced a reinforcement of his radical inclinations at the Vilna school.[45]

Abe Cahan, later to become a foremost American Jewish journalist, in

1878 also attended the Vilna institute. By 1880 the young Cahan, who had been anxious to train for the rabbinate, had had significant contact with the revolutionary students and was converted to socialism. In remembering the experience later, Cahan implicitly connected his newfound political identity and his religious background. Cahan had read the radical student political literature, which he described as a forbidden object. "Its publishers are those people . . . who live together like brothers and are ready to go to the gallows for freedom and justice. . . . I took the pamphlet in hand as one touches a holy thing. . . . All of this became part of my new religion, and had a great effect on my feelings. After my conversion to socialism, I was definitely a better, more serious and philosophical man."[46]

Aaron Lieberman, the virtual founder of Jewish socialism, had graduated from the Vilna school several years before; he articulated the connection between Jewishness and socialism even more explicitly than Cahan. By 1875 Lieberman had developed the belief that Jewish history and religious teachings had prepared the Jews for progressive secular movements: "Socialism is not alien to us. The community is our existence; the revolution—[is in] our tradition . . . [and in] our legislation . . . on equal rights [and] fraternity. . . . In the spirit of our people, the great prophets of our time such as Marx and Lassalle were educated and developed."[47]

Between 1884 and 1890, Jews—approximately 4.5 percent of the general population of the Russian Empire and only a little more than that of the university population—provided more than 13 percent of those who stood trial for subversive activities. By 1901–3 that figure rose to 29 percent and included increasing and disproportionate numbers of young, unmarried Jewish women. The outside influences on, and internal changes within, shtetl culture were raising aspirations for all but perhaps most for previously hemmed-in girls.[48]

Numerous Jewish student radicals and intellectuals, men and women, were, at least until the pogroms of 1881–82, convinced assimilationists. Gregory Weinstein was aware that, "like zealots of a new religion, we discarded everything—valuable as well as valueless—of the old teachings. In my home we gave a semblance of conforming with the observances and ceremonies of our parents' religion, but outside we joined the young rebels in their defiance of the ruling despotism."[49]

But the views of many of these young people, despite their disclaimers, contained elements that belied their assertions of assimilation. Their negative attitudes were often directed toward the Orthodox and bourgeois leaders of Russian Jewry, not toward Jews as a people. The concept among students and intellectuals of Jews as a parasitic class disappeared over time. They developed new self-awareness when they were rebuffed within the socialist movement and when, after the pogroms, they encountered the stunning indifference of Russian radicals to the violence against Jews.[50]

Abraham Cahan reported that, in the wake of more than two hundred anti-Jewish uprisings that spread across southern Russia and into Poland during 1881 and 1882, young people went to synagogues to demonstrate their solidarity. In Kiev, one speaker confessed to the assembled worshippers: "We are your brethren. We are Jews like you. We regret that we have up to now considered ourselves as Russians and not Jews. Events of the last weeks . . . including the pogroms . . . have shown us how grievously mistaken we have been. Yes, we are Jews."[51] This does not mean that students, intellectuals, and partly assimilated young people generally flocked back to religion; nor does it mean that they gave up on revolution. It does mean that some of them became in varying degrees *Jewish* socialists. The movement was even more infused with Jewish spirit by the participation of the so-called quasi-intelligentsia. This group was recruited mainly in Lithuanian yeshivas, which were centers of religious ferment.[52]

Undoubtedly, conflicts about their own Jewishness existed for many Jews attracted to socialism, and some became hostile or indifferent to Jewish culture. Lev Deutsch, one of the early revolutionaries who stayed active in Russian radical circles even after the pogroms, "wanted the Jews to assimilate as quickly as possible; everything that smelled of Jewishness," Deutsch said "called forth among us a feeling of contempt."[53] But most Jewish radicals were struggling to form new identities out of the mix of the traditional and the modern, and most remained within a broadening Jewish mainstream.[54] The handful who—with Leon Trotsky, Rosa Luxemburg, and Lev Deutsch—were alienated from Jewishness were too few and too far removed in culture and interest from the Jewish masses to directly influence Jewish behavior.

By choosing to be active within the Jewish mainstream, the Jewish intelligentsia influenced—and ultimately played a leadership role for—the Jewish working classes. They helped develop class-conscious socialists among the Jewish artisan and craftsmen, whose numbers grew during the 1890s. In Minsk, Vilna, Kovno, Grodno, Bialystok, and other cities, Jews organized militant trade unions. By 1894 Vilna, with twenty-seven of these unions, was the center of what could be called a Jewish labor movement.

Strikes swept the Pale throughout the 1890s, and by 1897 underground revolutionary groups were in place in Vilna and all the other large towns of Lithuania. In Poland, Jewish labor organizations that were established in Lodz and Warsaw made contact with the Vilna groups. And in Galicia four hundred *tales* (prayer shawl) weavers—"Jews with beards and earlocks"— took an oath on the holy Torah and went on strike.55

The great majority of those who participated in radical labor and political activities, while partly motivated by traditional Jewish values, were significantly younger, more secular, and more acculturated than the *tales* weavers. But it was clear that a Jewish proletariat had developed that was conscious of both its class interest and its cultural identity. This was even more evident in 1897, when many of the local organizations of workers and intelligentsia united to form the first and most important Jewish social democratic party—the Bund.

A revolutionary party with a mass labor base, the Bund (General Jewish Workers' Union), which spread throughout Russia and Poland, moved slowly toward the idea of an autonomous Jewish movement. It combined class war with loyalty to the Jewish people—indeed, to Jewish peoplehood. Few found this synthesis simple. Abraham Liesen, a gifted writer and poet who fled the czarist police and came to the United States in 1897, had given lectures in Lithuania combining socialist propaganda with Jewish history. In the 1890s he wrote:

> When I learned I was a convinced Marxist, I also discovered I was . . . not just a human being (which is merely an abstraction), but a Jew. Marxism intensified my sense of reality, and the reality surrounding me was Jewish. . . . At first I tried to fight off these sinful thoughts . . . just as ten years earlier I had tried to struggle with the religious doubts which tormented me. But I saw that the struggle was lost. I had become a nationalist.56

This personal struggle to fashion a synthesis was evident among the rank and file of the movement as well as its leadership. Bristle workers in Vilna, like the *tales* weavers before them, swore on a Torah scroll not to break a strike. A boycott of Janovsky's cigarette factory in Bialystok was announced to congregations in a number of synagogues, and the term *herem* (excommunication), in its religious context, was persistently employed against exploiters and scabs. In Krynki in 1897 there was a general strike, and some of the worker-organizers were fired. As a result, three hundred Jewish tanners held an outdoor meeting. They stood in the rain for two hours discussing strategy, and all swore on a pair of phylacteries in a solemn religious ceremony that they would support the fired workers. This was immediately followed by everyone singing the "Oath," a Yiddish revolutionary song and the official hymn of the Bund.[57]

Jewish workers, particularly those influenced by Bundists, were using religious imagery and the ethical concepts of their religious tradition to promote secular ideas. Early Zionists (those who looked to Palestine as a potential haven or home), in contrast, held the Jewish Diaspora in disdain. They rejected the Yiddish language and its rich folk culture as well as religious tradition.[58] They strove not to remake a Russia that was more hospitable to Jews and workers but to revolutionize their own Jewish society, to "normalize" the Jewish people, to make it like other peoples. Although Zionism, which came into being after the pogroms of 1881–82, began as a tiny movement, it did produce some thirty to forty thousand Biluim, pioneers influenced by the Russian populist romance with agriculture. The Biluim began organizing in 1882 and settled in Palestine over several decades. But compared to the millions of Jews who came to the United States, and who were vitally in touch with their ethnoreligous traditions, the Biluim formed a relatively insignificant counterflow. Moreover, as Zionism began to grow into a mass movement and to win adherents even among the middle classes and the Orthodox, it, like the Bund, drew on and moved toward a deeper national-religious identity.[59]

A similar dynamic of redefinition took place among the devotees of secular yiddishkayt. Primarily artists and writers, they worked to develop a Yiddish culture as an agent of national identity, while remaining "dedicated to a humanitarian, perhaps even universalist present."[60] For the rising young intelligentsia of Warsaw, Lodz, and Vilna and for the numerous shtetlekh that surrounded these cities, traditional religion remained a powerful source of nourishment and cultural energy; but its excesses of ritual and regulation seemed more and more atavistic. The Yiddishists were well aware of their precarious position. Yiddish poet Abraham Reisen reflected the mood of his confederates with these lines:

> My life I would compare
> To a lamp with a bit of kerosene;
> The lamp continues to flicker,
> But it hasn't the strength to flare.[61]

Nonetheless, Yiddishists worked indefatigably to promote a seeming paradox, a modern culture resting mainly on the Yiddish language.

Many movements in Jewish life, including socialism, came to use Yiddish through expedience, seeing the language as a tool with which to reach the masses; but then they stayed with it out of love. For Yiddishists, however, the love of the language and culture was first and paramount. At the heart of the movement were writers like Sholom Aleichem, Mendele Mokher Sforim, and Isaac Lieb Peretz. These men, and especially Peretz, tried to rediscover Jewish tradition, to reformulate it, and link it to the worldly culture of modern Europe. Yiddishkayt took on an increasingly secular character, but like so many elements in Jewish history it retained strong ties to tradition. We make distinctions, as Irving Howe has said, "between religious and secular ideologies, and we are right to make them; but in the heated actuality of East European Jewish life, the two had a way of becoming intertwined."[62]

The political renewal of the late nineteenth century—particularly socialism and Zionism, and the new cultural emphasis on secular yiddishkayt, stirred the Jews in city and shtetl to a greater awareness of their condition and a new sense of their potential. But without means to fulfill these new aspirations, Jews were simultaneously made aware of how intolerable their life remained. This was made even clearer during the vicious anti-Semitism that at first reinforced the new political and cultural movements, but that, after 1881, threatened to overwhelm the Jews of eastern Europe.

Immediately following the assassination of Alexander II in 1881, the Russian government, in order to deflect peasant discontent and to defend itself against revolutionary criticism and attack, stepped up the accusation that Jews were responsible for the misfortunes of the nation. Government circulars focused on "the harm caused the Christian population by the activity of the Jews with their tribal exclusiveness . . . religious fanaticism and exploitation," and declared that "the people in the Ukraine suffer most of all from the Jews. Who takes the land, the woods, the taverns from out of your hands? The Jews. The Jew curses you, cheats you, drinks your blood."[63]

There followed hundreds of pogroms in southern Russian towns and cities, including Yelizavetgrad and Kiev. There was a massive pogrom in Warsaw in December 1881, with fifteen hundred homes, shops, and synagogues sacked before government troops intervened. An even more bloody and destructive episode took place in the largely Jewish town of Balta in Podolia in late March 1882. In the immediate aftermath of violence in 1881, thirteen thousand Jews, desirous of escaping the physical threat, emigrated from Russia to the United States. This was almost half the number that had gone to America in the entire decade of the 1870s. And Jewish emigrés in 1882 outnumbered those in 1881 by 300 percent. In May 1882, George Price wrote in his diary,

> I am very anxious to leave Russia. Do I not rise daily with the fear lest the hungry mob attack me? . . . Do I not pray that my sisters may escape the clutches of drunkards lest they be raped?. . . Do I not pray that my brothers . . . do not die of hunger? . . . Be thou cursed forever my wicked homeland because you remind me of the Inquisition. . . . In exiling us you deprive yourself of a source of happiness and welfare.[64]

Russian commissions investigating the causes of pogroms concluded that "Jewish exploitation" was at the root of the violence. Based on this finding, the government published the Temporary Laws (the May Laws of 1882), which led to wholesale prohibitions and expulsions. The Jewish collectivity was subject to flagrant discrimination under these laws and, indeed, under Russian law generally. A Russian prince, in 1884, described the Jewish predicament this way: "With regard to all Russian subjects, with the exception of the Jews, the fundamental principle is that everything not prohibited by law is allowed, whereas for the Jews the maxim is that everything which is not positively allowed by law is to be considered prohibit[ed]."[65]

In 1884, though pogroms were temporarily halted, there was serious administrative harassment of Jews, including restrictive educational quotas. In 1886, reacting to the virtual flood of Jews seeking entry to secondary schools and universities, the government limited the number of Jewish students to 10 percent of the student body in the Pale and 3 to 5 percent outside it. In 1887 over twenty-three thousand Russian Jews, many in response to the numerus clausus (quota system) and other restrictions, immigrated to the United States. This was the highest immigration of Russian Jews in a single year up to that point.

By 1891, previously privileged Jews were subject to wholesale expulsion from several Russian cities, and hundreds of thousands of Jews living east of the Pale were forced into the area of confinement. The press continued a campaign of unbridled anti-Semitic propaganda. Konstantin Pobedonostev, the head of the governing body of the Russian Orthodox church and a major instigator of pogroms, clarified the goals of the government when he predicted that "one-third of the Jews will convert, one-third will die, and one-third will flee the country." More than 107,000 Jews left Russia for the United States between 1891 and 1892.

After a short interregnum (1893–98), the strict application of the discriminatory laws continued under Nicholas II (1894–1918). His government subsidized close to three thousand anti-Semitic publications, including the classic forgery *Protocols of the Elders of Zion.* Free reign was given to anti-Jewish agitation, particularly in reaction to the growing revolutionary movement, in which a disproportionate number of Jewish youth took part. An explosion of pogroms filled the years from 1903 to 1906. In contrast to those that took place between 1881 and 1884, these involved much more violence and murder. "At our door four Jews were hanged, and I saw that with my own eyes," said Marsha Farbman, who fled in 1904. "The Gentiles were running and yelling, 'Beat the Jews, Kill them!'" Forty-seven Jews were killed in the Kishinev pogrom of April 1903, and hundreds were severely beaten. In Zhitomer in April 1905, 29 were killed; 100 died in Kiev in July, 60 in Bialystok in August, and 800 in Odessa in October.[66]

In 1906, pogroms became practically uncountable, with many hundreds dead, robbed, raped, and mutilated. Towns not immediately subject to pogroms found out about them, nonetheless. One memoirist remembered the day, in the shtetl of Lentshin (southeast of Lvov), when it was learned from a Hebrew newspaper that a pogrom had taken place in Bialystok:

> No one knew just where Bilestok was. . . . Still, the accounts in the newspaper were terrifying. Yosele translated into Yiddish the report of the atrocities committed against babies, about old men who had been hacked to death with axes, and about pregnant women whose bellies had been slit open. The people in the shul were left pale and shaken. . . . I raged inwardly against a God who would permit such outrages. My parents, who were just as distressed as I, claimed that the massacre had come about as a result of sins committed by Jews. I wouldn't accept such a simplistic explanation.
>
> "It's God's fault!" I cried. "He is evil, evil." My parents clapped hands over their ears to shut out the blasphemous outburst.[67]

The pogroms in the beginning of the twentieth century, like those in the 1880s, were followed not only by increasing erosions of faith but by steep jumps in the Jewish emigration rate from Russia to the United States. In 1900, 37,000 Jews emigrated, in 1904, 77,500. More than 92,400 left in 1905, and 125,200 followed in 1906. A total of 672,000 Jews entered the United States as immigrants between 1904 and 1908, the vast majority from the Russian Empire.[68]

Emigration, of course, was not the only response to anti-Jewish violence; nearly two-thirds of eastern European Jewry chose to remain in the old countries. Some stayed because they had a strong vested interest in tradition and feared the corrosive effects of life in a *treyfa medine* (unkosher land), others because they were too old or too poor to make the voyage.

A small group, mainly Bundists, remained because they thought that Russia could be transformed by revolution into an egalitarian society. In the meantime, they were determined to defend themselves, and in the face of the new wave of pogroms in 1903 the Bundists formed defense societies in every Jewish town. They were joined by Zionists and Socialist-Zionists. Attackers now met with the armed resistance of Jewish youth, who were attempting not only to protect life and property but to "assert the honor of the Jewish nation."[69] Many of these young people would leave after the aborted Russian Revolution of 1905 and the repressive violence that followed. Aspirations raised by cultural renewal would have to be fulfilled elsewhere.

Pogroms alone do not explain the extraordinary movement of the Jewish population between 1881 and 1920, but they were critical. It is true that the highest rate of emigration was experienced in Galicia, where there was economic hardship and some local repression, but virtually no pogroms. Moreover, the Ukraine, the heartland of pogroms in the Russian Empire, produced a relatively low rate of emigration before World War I, and Lithuania, with relatively few pogroms, had a very high emigration rate. Also, concurrent with increasing Jewish emigration was an expanded emigration from the Russian Empire of non-Jewish Poles, Lithuanians, Finns, and even Russians. Jewish emigration in this context can be seen as directly related to the economic strains and dislocations in eastern Europe, particularly in prerevolutionary Russia.[70]

Jews, however, constituting only about 5 percent of the population of the Russian Empire, made up close to 50 percent of the Russian emigrant stream, 60 percent of the emigrants from Galicia, and an astounding 90 percent of the Romanian exodus between 1881 and 1910. These figures, when added to the high correlation between pogroms and Jewish mass exodus, strongly suggest that fear of violent persecution, while not the only cause, was critical in moving an extraordinary 33 percent of eastern European Jews to leave their countries between 1881 and 1920.[71]

Mass Jewish migration had been gathering momentum throughout the 1870s. After 1881, however, Jews had to face anti-Semitism not simply as a permanent inconvenience but as a threat to their very existence. The Russian government was encouraging pogroms as a matter of policy. This was a new and frightening development, distinct from the government's mere indifference to Jewish victimization in the past. By the time of Alexander III, who ruled from 1882 to 1894, and certainly during the succeeding reign of Nicholas II, the desire of the czars was no longer to Russify the Jews but to be rid of them. At a conference of Jewish "notables" in St. Petersburg in 1882, a majority continued to maintain that mass emigration would appear unpatriotic and might undermine the struggle for emancipation. But thoughts about emigration soon became pervasive. Increasing numbers of leaders, including M. L. Lilienblum (1843–1910), a former Maskil and now a Zionist, and Leon Pinsker (1821–91), an Odessa physician, once a fervent assimilationist, and now a Jewish nationalist, perceived anti-Semitism as a deeply rooted disease, incurable in the foreseeable future. And after 1881, more and more believed that emancipation for Jews was not possible within the intolerable conditions of the Russian Empire or, for that matter, anywhere in eastern Europe.[72]

Fear, intensified by new and more violent persecution and deepening poverty, had clearly become a central factor in Jewish life. But even this does not fully account for the stunning uprooting and transplantation of millions of eastern European Jews between 1881 and 1920. As we have seen, there were also the important ingredients of cultural ferment and renewal. In the last third of the nineteenth century, Jews in eastern Europe, in both urban areas and the shtetlekh peripheral to them, struggled to synthesize the forces of modernization with their tradition. A widespread feeling that Jewish culture was experiencing a renaissance emerged in the course of that struggle.

This resurgence reached its height with Bundist socialism, Zionism, and Yiddish secularism. The new ideologies and cultural forms were products of modernity and were "fashioned mostly by men estranged from Judaism's traditional way of life," but all the new belief systems and thought patterns "tapped authentic sources in the Jewish past."[73]

"To become, to achieve," whether in the collective version of messianism or in the individual version of takhles (to accomplish or fulfill), was always central to Jewish culture. Social and economic change redirected that desire; eastern European anti-Semitism frustrated it. For many, uprooting and resettlement appeared to be the only recourse.

Without external assault and increasing poverty, the collective energetic resurgence, rather than producing mass emigration, would likely have promoted a temporary culture of yiddishkayt as the Jews moved toward assimilation. On the other hand, persecution, pogroms, and poverty without cultural revitalization would likely have produced internal upheavals and perhaps new religious enthusiasms rather than a mass exodus. The combination, however, of spiritual hope, physical fear, and poverty provided the requisites for emigration.

Millions of Jews left the shtetlekh and cities in which they had built their lives. Artisans, stewards, and peddlers faced with obsolescence and dislocation, merchants faced with legal disability and discrimination, socialist militants faced with repression from outside their movements and anti-Semitism within them, students and the religiously committed faced with grave uncertainties, and above all innumerable ordinary Jews faced with impoverishment and persecution made the decision to leave eastern Europe in the late nineteenth and early twentieth centuries. They did not merely flee. With a strength born of cultural renewal, they aspired also to accomplish something. The United States as a land of opportunity—and fortunately in a period of industrial expansion and economic growth—provided the context for fulfilling this dream.

✡

CHAPTER TWO

THE IMMIGRATION EXPERIENCE

EMIGRATION is ultimately an individual choice, and most Jews left eastern Europe for personal reasons—to escape the hardships of life under the czar or to fulfill new hopes. The motives of these Jews were similar to those of many other emigrants: a mixture of yearnings for "change, for tranquility, for freedom, and for something not definable in words . . . a readiness to pull up stakes in order to seek a new life."[1] But, unlike the movement of members of other national groups, Jewish migration to America, beginning in earnest in the 1880s, constituted a momentous—and for the most part, irreversible—decision of a whole people.

Greeks, Finns, non-Jewish Russians, and Italians were certainly in motion during these years, and significant numbers of them came to the United States. But none of these groups migrated as a people. Most came from independent nations and represented only a very small percentage of the societies they left behind. Moreover, large numbers of them (approximately 30 percent) returned to their homelands after a sojourn in the United States. Jews, on the other hand, left their old countries at a stunningly high rate; 33 percent of the Jewish population left eastern Europe between 1880 and 1920, and after 1905 only 5 to 8 percent returned. This collective movement of a people was an extraordinary, if not wholly unprecedented, event.[2]

Only a tiny minority of Jews left eastern Europe in organized groups or with ideological intent. The small number of Biluim, who agitated for immigration to Palestine and who themselves departed for the ancient homeland of the Jewish people, constitute one example. The members of the Am Olam movement who also sought new soil on which to replant and re-form Jewish life were another. In their desperation for renewal, Am

Olam visionaries waxed enthusiastic over the possibility of establishing socialist agricultural utopias in America. Abraham Cahan, in flight from the police in 1882, "converted" to this position and committed himself to "journey to that far, far land!" and there "to build a paradise on earth!" where men could "be transformed into angels."[3] Hundreds of others were caught up in this wave of collective excitement, and dozens of Am Olam pioneers marched off to departing trains with the Torah in one hand and a radical tract in the other.

An even more dramatic collective departure began in Romania in 1899. During a severe economic depression, violent denunciations of Jews, who had been pauperized in Romania since the 1880s, were delivered in the legislature. There followed the expulsion of Jews from many districts and a number of pogroms, including a particularly vicious anti-Jewish riot organized by the chief of police in the city of Jassy. In response, young Jewish artisans and workers, acting through spontaneously organized committees, began to leave Romania entirely. They went as *fusgeyer* (walkers), tramping hundreds of miles across the country. On the way they issued broadsides and "newspapers," they sang, gave speeches, and offered amateur theatricals to raise funds. Their commitment, bravado, and exuberance enabled them to reach the port of Hamburg and, finally, America.[4]

More frequent than these organized uprootings were individual and family disruptions. Jewish immigration to America, with its great proportion of females (43 percent) and children under fourteen (25 percent), was much more a movement of families than the immigrations of other European nationalities.[5] Nonetheless, many young men and women eager to escape impoverishment, the draft, and the general circumscription and aspiring to fulfill "hopes unexplainable, but so promising" faced lifelong separation from aging parents.[6] At the moment of his departure, Marcus Ravage saw his mother lose control of her feelings: "As she embraced me . . . her sobs became violent and father had to separate us. There was a despair in her way of clinging to me which I could not then understand. I understand it now. I never saw her again."[7]

Parents tried with difficulty to persuade their sons and daughters to stay home. They stormed and threatened and often warned their children that America was a "corrupt and sinful land."[8] The attraction of the *goldene medine* (golden land), however, was powerful and ultimately overwhelmed parental pleadings. Only "after months of argument and cajolery" was Rose Pessota finally able to "persuade . . . [her] parents to let [her] go to the

United States." And Fannie Shapiro told her father, "If you're not going to let me go to America, I'm going to drown myself."9

The desire for the new life that America promised was intense. The young were always a significant proportion of the immigrants, perhaps because leaving was easier for them than for the old. Moreover, many were stimulated by the Yiddish cultural-political resurgence and would have left even if there had been no worsening of hunger and oppression. Immigrants' autobiographies, memoirs, and interview collections are filled with evidence that Jewish emigrés energetically sought outlets for deeply felt aspirations. Self-actualization was long a central theme of Jewish culture. Modernization redirected and intensified that theme, but increasing Russian, Romanian, and Galician anti-Semitism frustrated it. For large numbers, emigration seemed the only answer.

The unorganized mass of Jews who left, then, resemble in important ways the dedicated members of the much smaller Am Olam and Zionist movements as well as the exuberant *fusgeyers*. For theirs, too, was a collective enterprise filled with hope. And "every emigrating Jew," insisted Abe Cahan, soon "realized he was involved in something more than a personal expedition . . . [that] he was part of an historical event in the life of the Jewish people. . . . Even Jewish workers and small tradesmen . . . joined . . . the move westward to start a new Jewish life. They did so with religious fervor and often with inspiring self-sacrifice."10 That the emigration was more than the sum of individual decisions and more than the consequence of despair is also reflected in the diary of George Price: "We . . . will not be lost upon leaving the land of the Tartars. It is not the first time, and may it be the last, that we fall and rise. Now we are leaving for a land where we will be human beings, and where we will work for ourselves and for others."11

The powerful combination of physical despair and spiritual hope "pushed" the Jews out of eastern Europe. The lure of openness and toleration, economic opportunity and the possibilities for new modes of living "pulled" the Jews to America. As early as 1817 there existed in eastern Europe a Yiddish translation of the *The Discovery of America,* a popular celebration of the United States. And between 1820 and 1870 there had already been a trickle of Jewish immigration (7,500) to America from eastern Europe. Between 1870 and 1890, however, America became more clearly the "distant magnet," a place for potentially enduring renewal for eastern European Jews.12

Mary Antin, who came to the United States in 1891, recalled that in the old country

America had been in everybody's mouth. Businessmen talked of it over their accounts; the market women made up their quarrels that they might discuss it from stall to stall; people who had relatives in the famous land went around reading their letters for the enlightenment of less fortunate folk . . . children played at emigrating; old folks shook sage heads over the evening fire, and prophesied no good for those who braved the terrors of the sea and the foreign goal beyond it; all talked of it, but scarcely anyone knew one true fact about this magic land.[13]

Certainly, fiction and fact blended, creating many myths about America. Letters from relatives (over thirty thousand eastern European Jews had gone to America in the 1870s) sometimes exaggerated the positive dimensions of their experience. They were filled with "glowing accounts of . . . enormous wages, . . . and houses grandly furnished." A correspondent in writer Anzia Yezierska's story, "How I Found America," falsely reported that he ate "meat . . . every day just like the millionaires," but he also told an important truth: "there is no Czar in America."[14]

Steamship agents added to the myths. Transatlantic travel had grown safer, faster, and cheaper, and several companies sent representatives to solicit voyagers. Agents were not above deception, and they often tempted Jews with stories of economic mobility and quick fortunes. Propaganda about the social equality of America had effect, however, only because it resembled the ideas and facts about America that prospective immigrants had already gathered from trusted kin and familiar publications.

Emigrating Jews were responding to visions of their own making but also, as with other immigrant groups, to American realities. The United States in the late nineteenth century was undergoing an economic revolution. Beginning in the 1870s, the increasing rationalization of agricultural production was already significantly changing the nature of the American economy. In 1880, about 50 percent of the United States work force was in agriculture; by 1920, that figure was little more than 25 percent. The completion of a number of transcontinental railroads in the 1880s contributed to the phenomenal growth of the American economy, as did an unprecedented level of industrial mechanization and capital investment between 1870 and 1890. In these years, America experienced a 28 percent growth in the number of its industries and a net increase of 168 percent in the value of production. Between 1880 and 1920, this rapidly expanding industrial economy created tens of millions of jobs for immigrants to fill.[15]

Though some cautious, old-country periodicals warned that "there is no land which devours its lazy inhabitants and those not suited to physical labor like the land of America," few paid heed.[16] Between 1881 and 1910, 1,562,800 eastern European Jewish immigrants, 73 percent of whom were from the Russian Empire, arrived in the United States. The two-million mark was surpassed in 1914, and another quarter of a million Jews arrived before 1924.[17] An immigration commission report in 1909 concluded that "recently arrived immigrants are substantially the agencies which keep the American labor market supplied. . . . [Their] personal appeals . . . promote and regulate the tide of European migration to America."[18]

Letters containing information about job opportunities, wages, and depressions acted as stimuli or brakes. The cost of transportation also affected the numbers who would come. But modest changes in the rate of Jewish immigration pale in the face of the overall numbers for the period 1881–1924. Moreover, and in strikingly higher proportion than for other migrating groups, the *goldene medine* remained the destination of choice for Jews. More than three million Jews crossed borders in Eastern Europe in these years. Seven percent went to western Europe; between 10 and 13 percent went to Canada, Australia, Argentina, South Africa, and Palestine; but more than 80 percent ended up in the United States.[19]

If the agonies of separation made the decision to leave difficult, implementing it was even harder. Numerous obstacles stood in the way, not the least of which was the lengthy and circuitous expedition out of Russia, Romania, and Galicia. Jews from southern Russia usually crossed the Austro-Hungarian border illegally, traveled by train to Berlin or Vienna, and then went on to one of the major European ports—Hamburg, Bremen, Rotterdam, Amsterdam, or Antwerp. There, for thirty-four dollars (in 1903) a steamship ticket could be purchased, if one did not already have one in hand. Jews from western Russia came surreptitiously across the German borders, while the Galicians were able to cross legally. Romanian Jews arrived at the northern ports mainly through Vienna.

Theoretically, there were more direct routes for Russian Jews. For a short time, Libau, in the north, was a popular port of embarkation, but the Russian passport required there was expensive. In addition, Jews, especially men of draft age, risked becoming entangled at Libau with czarist authorities. Despite rapacious peasants and smugglers that Jews confronted along the less-direct, more time-consuming routes, it was judged safer to cross the Russo-German border illegally than to confront Russian officials. This was especially true after 1888, when the czarist government, in its typical perversity, unofficially allowed unhindered departures of millions of Jews at the same time that it made it hard for Jews to obtain passports legally.[20]

The difficulty of getting a passport was the result not only of the intransigence of the central government but also of a mass of conflicting ordinances by regional and local authorities. Each official was interested in securing as much in the way of "fees" as possible for smoothing the way toward obtaining the passport. The average price of the precious document was twenty rubles (about ten dollars), no small amount, and even then applicants had to wait three months for delivery—unless, of course, they paid significantly more to reduce the wait to only one month.

Emigrants often turned to steamship ticket agents for help. Agents were sometimes simply swindlers, who took the money and disappeared, but official agents of the shipping companies could, more or less, be trusted. They frequently relieved the emigrant of the trouble and expense of procuring a passport by "arranging for his delivery" to a port in Germany for an agreed-upon fee, generally amounting to a 50 percent surtax on the cost of a ticket. This would usually include help with route logistics, border crossings, accommodations, and all the necessary bribes.[21]

Somehow, vast numbers of Jews scraped together the money. One young mother said, after listening to a letter from America filled with good news: "Sell my red quilted petticoat." Her children immediately suggested the feather beds and the samovar. "Sure," the mother said, "we can sell everything." Families often did sell everything, which brought them just enough money to get to western Europe and finally to the New World— penniless and bereft of possessions.[22]

In western Europe, the emigrants' difficulties did not quite disappear. Trouble was especially intense in the pogrom-ridden years of 1881–83 and 1903–6, when Jewish migration resembled mass flight. Beginning in 1881, thousands of refugees, fleeing the murderous violence wreaked upon their communities in southern Russia, poured into the Austrian city of Brody. One of the refugees was George Price:

> We arrived in Brody yesterday. God! What Pandemonium! Fifteen
> thousand Jews [more than the entire permanent population of Brody]

are stranded here waiting their turn. For lack of accommodations many are quartered in factories situated on the outskirts. . . . [And] there is a factory in the city which lodges about three thousand emigrants and a stable which accommodates three hundred. In both dwellings the condition of the emigrants is intolerable. They sit on the floor, huddled together, hungry and thirsty. Besides, there are many emigrants in the streets.[23]

The Jewish community of Brody did temporarily shelter some refugees in private homes, but the problem was far too massive for them to handle. Relief soon began to flow into the city through such agencies as the Baron de Hirsch Fund and the Alliance Israélite Universelle. The response, given the scope of the migration from the east, was inadequate; but emigrants were at least enabled to continue their move to port cities in Germany.

Western European Jewish organizations were anxious, on the one hand, to help the victims of the pogroms but, on the other, afraid that the refugees might engulf their countries. These organizations were at first reluctant to encourage, and even ready to oppose, immigration, whenever hope arose that the position of Jews in Russia might be improved. But in the face of growing numbers of refugees who refused to be repatriated and who steadfastly resisted being sent to the United States without their families, western Europeans began to accept the reality of mass Jewish migration from eastern Europe. A group of German Jewish associations organized as the Hilfsverein der Deutschen Juden, in order to help their coreligionists and to avoid being overrun by the mass influx, set up information bureaus. From their offices in Berlin and Bremen, they negotiated special rates with railroad companies and steamship lines and lobbied European governments to ease the emigrants' journey and speed them on their way.

Between 1905 and 1914, seven hundred thousand eastern European Jews passed through Germany; over two hundred thousand were directly aided by the Hilfsverein. Baron Maurice de Hirsch, heir of financiers to the Bavarian Royal Court, who made several fortunes in banking and railway finance, contributed large amounts to improve the conditions of eastern European Jews. In the late 1880s, however, after the pogroms and mass expulsions, the baron encouraged emigration, and in 1891 he set up the Jewish Colonization Association, with vast programs for international resettlement.[24]

These organized efforts at resettlement, while important, played a small part compared to the migration of the vast majority of individuals and families who came to America on their own resources. The journey of these people, as well as those who were directly aided in the emigration process, continued to be filled with tribulation. Even legal travelers had to deal with con men and thieves and with the bewildering confusion of various bureaucracies and the officious manner of German authorities, who—fearful of plague and other diseases—conducted innumerable inspections. There were questions, disinfections, and the constant fear of being sent back or quarantined for "medical reasons."[25]

At the port of embarkation, emigrants were examined by a physician. The increasing strictness of these examinations had less to do with concern for the emigrants' health than with the steamship company's profit. Emigrants with "contagious diseases" who were excluded at American ports were to be taken back to Europe at the company's expense.[26] Sholom Aleichem's short story "Off to the Golden Land," gives us some sense of why the medical examination was so feared by immigrants:

> The time comes to go on board the ship. People tell them they should take a walk to the doctor. So they go to the doctor. The doctor examines them and finds they are all hale and hearty and can go to America, but she, that is Goldele, cannot go, because she has trachomas on her eyes. At first her family did not understand. Only later did they realize . . . that they could all go to America but she, Goldele, would have to remain in Antwerp. So there began a wailing, a weeping, a moaning. Three times her momma fainted. Her papa wanted to stay here, but he couldn't. All the ship tickets would be lost. So they had to go off to America and leave her, Goldele, here until the trachomas would go away from her eyes.[27]

Successfully negotiating all the hurdles of boarding still left the emigrants facing the gruelling transatlantic passage, a thirteen- to twenty-day voyage in steerage. Steerage, which took millions of emigrants from Europe to America, was the brainchild of Albert Ballin, a German Jew and the head of the Hamburg-American line. German ships carried raw materials, particularly timber, from America, but on the return voyage they carried items requiring little space. Realizing the profit potential in the growing emigration traffic, Ballin had the empty holds fitted with rudimentary beds, and the infamous steerage was born.[28]

A steerage berth was an iron bunk with a straw mattress and no pillow. Two water closets were available in steerage, and both were used by both sexes. There was a shortage of receptacles to use in case of seasickness, and as the voyage progressed, conditions became filthy and unbearable. On stormy passages, conditions were far worse, because the decks were filled with vomit, and drinking water was scarce.[29] One immigrant remembered that, upon entering the Atlantic Ocean, "the waves buffeted the ship. Everyone was frightened. Panic-stricken, the passengers huddled together on their cots and spent six days practically without food. . . . It rained continually, inactivity and thirst tormented me, and there was only boiled sea water."[30] Another recollected grimly that "seasickness broke out among us. Hundreds of people had vomiting fits. . . . I wanted to escape from that inferno but no sooner had I thrust my head forward from the lower bunk than someone above me vomited straight upon my head."[31] These tales of suffering were not simply the exaggerations of bewildered and disoriented immigrants. Suffering was real, persistent, and thoroughly documented.

An investigator for the U.S. Immigration Commission reported that a passenger in steerage class would arrive "at the journey's end with a mind unfit for healthy wholesome impressions and with a body weakened and unfit for the hardships that were involved in the beginning of life in a new land."[32] Reforms began as early as 1882 in regard to passenger comfort and cleanliness, but as the Immigration Commission recognized in 1908, "it [was] clear that bad steerage conditions [were] for the most part due to the nonenforcement of the various laws regulating the carriage of steerage passengers rather than to faulty provisions in those laws."[33]

By the early 1900s, there was some improvement. Jewish organizations at various transit points now had more experience and were better able to serve and protect the emigrés. In addition, competition among steamship lines led to innovations: steerage was modified into compartments on newer ships, and the voyage, though still an ordeal, was reduced to between six and ten days. Some immigrants remembered that during this era there was, along with the continued distress, the occasional reprieve of cardplaying and even the music of accordions or fiddles.[34]

The end of the voyage did not mean the end of bewilderment. Still to be negotiated were the admissions procedures at Castle Garden and, after 1891, at Ellis Island. Built as a fort in 1807 near the Battery, at the tip of Manhattan Island, Castle Garden was used by New York State, beginning in 1855, to receive immigrants. By the 1880s, even this massive structure was grossly inadequate; according to one Russian Jew, "The main hall [was] so jammed, that there was simply nowhere to sit . . . or any place to lie down at night—not even on the bare floor. The filth was unbearable, so many . . . pillows, featherbeds, and foul clothing . . . provided great opportunity for vermin."[35]

Between 1881 and 1891, more than five million immigrants were processed at Castle Garden—far too many for its facilities. Employees, harrassed and sometimes overwhelmed, were often cold and oppressive. Abe Cahan felt like a recruit "at a Russian summons for military service," and Emma Goldman—later to become famous as a revolutionary anarchist— though "enraptured by the sight of the . . . Statue of Liberty," found the atmosphere at Castle Garden "charged with antagonism and harshness" and her "first day on American soil . . . a violent shock."[36]

Failure to anticipate the massive wave of immigration accounted for the overcrowding and many of its attendant ills. But in addition, other abuses only indirectly related to overcrowding were turned up by government investigators. Some immigrants were made to pay twice the usual amount for the shipment of baggage, others paid telegraph operators for messages that were never sent, and many were bilked by money changers who hung about the Battery anticipating easy prey. Complaints mounted, and shortly after the federal government dispensed with state control and took over the supervision of incoming aliens, Ellis Island was opened as a modern immigration center in 1892.

As with many reforms, this one was inadequate. New York was the United States' most active port and received approximately 70 percent of newcomers from all nations. An estimated 5,000 immigrants per day were inspected at Ellis Island, and on 17 April 1907, the busiest day in the island's history, 11,745 were processed. Between 1899 and 1910, 86 percent of the Jews heading for America landed in the Northeast, the vast majority in New York City. Overworked and often insensitive immigration employees checked the new arrivals for "defects," tuberculosis (considered "the Jewish disease"), "dull-wittedness," eye and scalp problems, and contagious and "loathsome" diseases.

Squeezed into massive halls in dozens of lines, immigrants underwent incessant pushing, prying, and poking. Immigrants who aroused suspicion were isolated, and their clothes were marked with chalk. Approximately one in six underwent further medical checking. The eye examination was often the most feared. Trachoma was the cause of more than half the medical detentions, and according to one contemporary investigator, "most of those detained by the physicians for trachoma [were] Jews."[37]

Immigrants who passed the medical examination were taken to the registry section to be asked dozens of questions: Your name? How did you pay for your passage? Do you have the promise of a job? Are you an anarchist? Where is your money? Such questions posed dilemmas for Jewish immigrants, especially before 1892, when the Hebrew Sheltering and Immigrant Aid Society was organized to give advice. For example, since stories circulated about persons being deported for violating an 1885 law prohibiting the importation of labor, was it good to have a job waiting or not? The young Fiorello La Guardia, later to become mayor of New York City, worked at Ellis Island as an interpreter, and he bore witness to the fact that these interviews were almost invariably accompanied by "mental anguish . . . disappointment and . . . despair."[38]

Women traveling alone were a special problem, because immigration officials feared they would fall into the hands of the white slave traders who operated around the docks and frequented Ellis Island looking for young prospects. The women were interrogated more intensely and were often detained until relatives came to escort them from the processing center. One woman arriving unaccompanied at Ellis Island failed to recognize her fiance, who had preceded her to America by six months and had come to meet her dressed in American style, with a derby hat. Zealous officials thought they had caught one of the white slavers. The removal of the derby produced recognition on the part of the woman, but Ellis Island officers were not convinced and insisted that the young couple be married then and there.[39]

Some stories did not end so happily. While the average immigrant passed through Ellis Island in a matter of hours, detainees could be at the facility for as long as two weeks. In peak periods, as many as twenty-four hundred persons were put into the detention room, a facility with only eighteen hundred beds. At one point in 1907, the space was so crowded that inspectors were unable to reach persons in the center of the room to discuss with them the reasons for their detention. Overcrowding also meant that it was impossible to keep infection under control. And there were some (between 1 and 2.5 percent) who faced even greater disappointment than delayed entry. For those hapless voyagers diagnosed as having "loathsome and dangerous contagious diseases" or judged so deficient either physically or mentally that they were seen as "likely to become a public charge" there was no admittance, only the ordeal of a return trip to Europe.[40]

The number of those detained or deported varied according to the immigration laws in effect at the time, to the strictness with which they were enforced, and to the existence, commitment, and activities of Jewish immigrant aid societies. The Board of Delegates of American Israelites was active in the field of immigrant relief, and as Jewish immigration began to increase significantly in 1881, the Hebrew Emigrant Aid Society (HEAS) was formed. Although makeshift, short-lived, and led by German Jews ambivalent about, and often resistant to, large-scale immigration from eastern Europe, HEAS and the Hebrew Sheltering Society, organized in 1882, extended aid to some fourteen thousand Russian refugees between 1881 and 1883.[41]

Eastern European Jews themselves got involved in aiding their land-slayt (countrymen) when it appeared to them that German Jews were not doing all they could to prevent the return of paupers or "persons likely to become a public charge." In New York in 1882, twenty-four Polish congregations created the small but effective Hebrew Emigration Auxiliary Society. By the end of 1883, similar relief associations were formed in Philadelphia, New Haven, Indianapolis, and Chicago. Slowly, American Jewry was building an overlapping network of organizations to help immigrants resettle. But after the demise of HEAS in 1884, the aid proferred Jewish arrivals was sporadic and unsystematic until 1892, when the Baron de Hirsch Fund stepped in to bring order to the process. A $400,000 fund was set up to finance the relief efforts, and most of the groups concerned with the welfare of the immigrants were brought together under the umbrella of the American Committee for Ameliorating the Condition of Russian Refugees.

One of the first *major* institutions in America set up and administered by eastern European Jews on their own was the Hebrew Sheltering and Immigrant Aid Society (HIAS). This extraordinary agency originated at an 1892 meeting "called in an East Side store by a *landsmanshaft* anxious to provide burial for Jews who had died on Ellis Island."[42] By 1897 HIAS had grown into an organization that combined under one roof facilities for skills training, interpreters, legal aid, temporary housing, and an employment agency.

On Ellis Island, HIAS agents distributed a Yiddish bulletin containing information about the services available from the society, as well as a great deal of useful general advice. Agents also helped immigrants get past the con men and swindlers who waited on the shore and helped them find their relatives. By 1908 the agency was issuing the *Jewish Immigrant,* a bulletin providing relevant information, including details about what would or would not prevent admission to America. The publication circulated widely in Russia and proved extremely valuable not only in providing practical guidance but for imparting to emigrants a sense that there were supportive people on the other side waiting to help them.

Perhaps most important, HIAS representatives at Ellis Island and at other important points of entry in Boston, Philadelphia, and Baltimore mediated between immigration officials and the newly arriving masses of Jews. The presence, for example, of the sensitive and talented Alexander Harkavy (more famous as the compiler of a Yiddish-English dictionary), who served at Ellis Island from 1904 to 1907, the peak of Jewish immigration to the United States (535,000 newcomers), and of Abraham Alpert, "the man from Kovno," who served at Boston harbor, restrained authorities who might otherwise have been quick to detain or deport.[43] Building on this experience, HIAS by 1914 had grown into a national organization that effectively stemmed bureaucratic and political efforts to restrict immigration. As we have seen, there were agencies predating HIAS that extended relief to Jewish immigrants. At the start, however, none of these German Jewish organizations were so clearly and consistently committed to welcoming and ameliorating the condition of eastern European Jews as HIAS.

Leaders of the German Jewish community admitted in the 1880s that "immigration was not popular among our people" and claimed that the "mode of life" of the Russian Jew "has stamped upon them the ineffaceable marks of permanent pauperism." Nothing but "disgrace and a lowering of the opinion in which American Israelites are held . . . can result from the continued residence among us of these wretches."[44] Even prior to the flight from the first widespread Russian pogroms (1881–83), which appeared to threaten the Germans with a significantly increased burden of impoverished eastern European newcomers, many of the philanthropic agencies cautioned against open immigration. Indeed, in 1880 the United Hebrew Charities of New York and the newspaper *American Hebrew* urged the passage of restrictive immigration laws.

High cost was often cited as the reason for reluctance to welcome masses of immigrants from eastern Europe. The Union of American Hebrew Congregations, suspecting that western European Jewish organizations were "dumping" eastern European immigrants on American Jewry, stated early on that it "no longer assume[d] any charge of . . . material aid for the immigrants arriving in the United States."[45] In Boston the sudden arrival of 415 Russian Jewish refugees in June 1882 so startled local German Jews that they refused to accept them, fearing that the immigrants would become a permanent drain on Boston's hard-pressed charity organizations. The Germans shipped the Russians back to New York.[46]

Resentment and fear over the immigration of eastern European Jewry went beyond economic cost. A representative of the United Charities of Rochester called the Yiddish-speaking Russian Jews "a bane to the country and a curse to all Jews" and warned that the "enviable reputation" German Jews had earned in the United States was being "undermined by the influx of thousands who are not ripe for enjoyment of liberty." All "who mean well for the Jewish name should prevent them as much as possible from coming here."[47] In New York the Russian Emigrant Relief Fund, desperately seeking to limit Jewish immigration to the United States, wrote to the Alliance Israélite Universelle: "Please bear constantly in mind that the position of the Jews is not such that they can afford to run any risk of incurring the ill-feeling of their fellow citizens."[48]

The opposition by German Jews to the unrestricted immigration of eastern European Jews was more directly tied to class and cultural differences and to social insecurity than to the economic burden they might become. From as early as the 1870s, when eastern Europeans were few in number, German Jews, though generous materially, shunned their less assimilated coreligionists. The unofficial slogan of the Harmony Club in New York, perhaps the most prestigious German Jewish social club in the United States, was "More polish and less Polish."[49] Though there were very few visible reminders of their peddler origins, the German Jews in the 1880s were apparently too insecure to feel comfortable with the poverty, the Yiddish, the Orthodoxy, and the socialism of the new arrivals from eastern Europe.

In the last three decades of the nineteenth century, the discomfort of the German Jews was significantly increased by the coincidence of two important changes: immigration from eastern Europe became massive, and anti-Semitism in America intensified. Anti-Jewish feeling in the late nineteenth century was the product of a complex constellation of forces. It was tied to general nativism, rooted mainly in agrarian regions, and was reinforced by elites who perceived their displacment in a rapidly changing society. Anti-Jewish feeling was also promoted by the nouveaux riches. Raised to believe in the ideal of a traditional, stable, nonacquisitive social order, Protestant strivers were troubled by their own materialistic pursuits. The newly wealthy, however, could find in the classic stereotype of the grasping, rootless Jew, rather than in their own behavior, the "reason" for the decline of stability and "community" and for the rise of the new individualistic world of commercial exploitation.

In an era of rapid industrial and demographic change and of increasing mobility and heterogeneity, many people demanded a simple explanation for increasingly complex conditions, which they no longer controlled. Farmers, for example, were confused and angered by the frequent whiplashing they took from market forces and for their precipitous decline in status. In the 1870s and into the 1880s, farmers mostly blamed the railroads and the middlemen, upon whom they had become more and more dependent. By the mid-1880s, farmers, almost always debtors, found themselves caught in a deflationary cycle. Not only was the money they owed worth more than the money they had borrowed, but the prices for their products were seriously declining. Many farmers came to believe in a conspiracy designed to cheat them of the fruits of their labor through the curtailment of the quantity of money and other forms of currency manipulation, and they increasingly turned their wrath upon the banking system and government fiscal policy.[50]

With stereotypes long held and images deeply embedded in Christian tradition, it was but a short jump from banks and government to polemics about "money changers in the temple" and city Jews heading up a worldwide system of money control. Many believed that system was designed to promote deflation by maintaining the gold standard and by defeating any attempts to institute the free coinage of silver. Was not the world of banking pervaded after all by Jewish names like Kuhn, Loeb, and Seligman? And had not powerful Jews like Moses Montefiore and Edmond de Rothschild appeared at the Brussels monetary conference in 1894, at about the same time that Austria-Hungary, Japan, and Russia were deserting bimetalism in favor of the gold standard?[51]

Prejudice against Jews is diffused in the United States because of the absence of a national church and because anti-Semitism has had to compete with other forms of animus, particularly Negrophobia and anti-Catholicism. Also, Jews in newly formed, relatively modern America, did not have to go through any process of emancipation from medieval bonds, as they did in Europe. For these reasons, American anti-Semitism has been milder than European versions. But hatred of Jews was carried to America at the very birth of the nation, and it was nourished by myths that portray Jews as eternally alien to Christendom and as unscrupulous moneylenders.

American history generally was marked by a "traditional linkage of money crazes and anti-Jewish feelings." And from 1870 through the 1890s, "a whole generation of Americans [had been] embroiled . . . in the argument over silver."52 In the late nineteenth century, "the international Jewish conspiracy" became a popular theme in the United States. It was reinforced by the works of patrician intellectuals, writers, and political polemicists like Henry Adams, Ignatius Donnelly, and William Harvey. America's money difficulties and its social and cultural decline were traced to Jews like Hartbeest Schneidekoupon (coupon clipper), in Adams's novel *Democracy* (1880), to the rapacious Jews in total political and financial control in Donnelly's futuristic book *Caesar's Column* (1890), and to the ruthless, anti-American, pro-British Baron Rothe, in Harvey's *A Tale of Two Nations* (1894).53

Although Populist party leader Donnelly was known in some circles as the Prince of Cranks, he was more popularly dubbed the Tribune of the People. In the same year as the publication of his anti-Semitic novel *Caesar's Column,* Donnelly was elected president of the Minnesota Farmers' Alliance as well as state senator. Harvey's work was misleading, gratuitous, and even nonsensical, but he was widely read and praised. His monograph *Coin's Financial School* (1894) sold close to a million copies. Like his novel, it targeted Jews on the silver issue.

Ignatius Donnelly's anti-Semitism raised the larger question of the character and intensity of Populist anti-Semitism, a question that has engendered lively scholarly debate. Defended by some historians as tolerant, democratic idealists and characterized by others as xenophobic and demagogic, the Populists may have been, as Oscar Handlin described them, neither more nor less anti-Semitic than other Americans. Indeed, in their attempt to understand the decline of rural America through analysis of modern capitalist market forces, the Populists distinguished themselves from the mere anti-Semitic conspiracy propagandists of the South, the Midwest, and the Great Plains. But while most Populists were not anti-Semites, several important representative figures like Tom Watson and Ignatius Donnelly clearly disliked foreigners and Jews. Moreover, although anti-Semitic stereotypes portraying Jews as nonproducers, mere manipulators of money, and sinister representatives of international finance had circulated in the United States well before the turn of the century and the rise of the Populist party, in the 1890s they fit Populist political rhetoric very closely.54

Ignatius Donnelly and William Harvey, unlike Henry Adams, did dis-

play a certain discomfort about their prejudice. Blatantly anti-Semitic remarks were occasionally woven together with high praise for Jews. The
same was true for Dan De Quille (the pen name of William Wright), a well-
known journalist in the West. De Quille used anti-Semitic rhetoric in de-
nouncing the gold standard and in demonstrating his Populist sympathies.
At the same time, he wrote a relatively positive account of the Jewish
experience and persistently assured Jews that they were welcome in America. It should be remembered, too, that there were important figures who
tended to balance the anti-Semitism of people like Henry Adams; these
include the renowned minister and reformer Henry Ward Beecher, the
philosopher Josiah Royce, and writers Mark Twain and Lincoln Steffens.
But in the final decades of the nineteenth century, strong feeling both for
and against Jews surfaced and moved to the forefront of American consciousness.

Economic disruptions in the 1890s provided the context for an intensification of negative feelings about Jews. A depression beginning early in
1893 was heightened by a stock market panic in May, and by mid-1894 the
economy appeared exhausted. Farmers reeled at the collapse of wheat and
cotton prices. Banks and businesses failed at astonishing rates. Significant
numbers of "men of substance" were bankrupted, as Henry Adams knew
when he "lamented that his entire generation had had to quit." Joblessness
mounted, reaching as high as 20 percent, and while William Harvey was
readying his work for publication, Coxey's "army of the unemployed" was
marching in protest on Washington. The violent Pullman strike followed
thereafter, soon to be crushed by federal troops sent to Illinois by President
Cleveland. And by the end of 1894, the Populist party, with its monetary
planks and demands for inflation, was making an important challenge to
the strength of the Democratic and Republican parties in the West and
South. People worried about "how far the crisis would carry the country
from its old ways, or how many institutions were still fated to crumble."[55]

Victims of the crisis, and those who perceived themselves as victims,
cried for a quick and simple solution, and the understandable confusion
over the complexity of causes only increased the dogmatism about the cure.
Political rhetoric was filled with images of money conspiracies implicitly
and sometimes explicitly tied to Jews. When William Jennings Bryan, cam-
paigning for the presidency in 1896, peppered his diatribes against the gold
standard with Christian images, he simply, even if inadvertently, added fuel
to the fires of conspiracy theories that had been burning for more than two
decades. The theories, in Richard Hofstadter's words, did not exceed a

kind of "rhetorical vulgarity," since no explicit action was urged against Jews as such; but writing and rhetoric filled with anti-Semitic allusions and phrases like "crucifixion upon a cross of gold" and "put all moneylenders to death" made Jews, particularly the conspicuously successful German Jews, wary.[56]

Moreover, beginning in the late 1870s and on through the 1890s, anti-Semitism went beyond the printed page and the speeches of politicians. There was in these years significant, widespread social discrimination against Jews as well as sporadic anti-Semitic harrassment and violence, particularly in the South. Objective members of the established American Jewish community admitted that the arrival of the new breed of Jews from eastern Europe did not cause the anti-Semitism; nevertheless, many believed the immigrant presence promised only to intensify it.[57] At first German Jews fought open immigration or sought to disperse the immigrants to rural areas. A few, like Rabbi Jacob Voorsanger (1853–1908) of San Francisco, favored shutting off Jewish immigration to the United States altogether and believed that "not a single sensation of sympathy nor any sentiment of affection generated by kinship or religious affiliation should prevent us from appreciating the justice of this ultimate procedure."[58] Voorsanger's view, however, was rare. Julius Goldman, who rendered aid to the new immigrants, admitted finding "much indifference and unwarranted dislike" toward the eastern European Jews, but he had not met a German Jew "who [was] prepared to *close* the ports of the United States to the Russian refugee."[59]

German Jews, at least until the early 1890s, were ambivalent about massive emigration from eastern Europe. This posture was reflected in the behavior of German Jewish organizations and in the pages of the leading German Jewish newspapers, including the *American Hebrew.* In June 1880 the paper advocated restrictive immigration laws and the diversion of immigrants to farms. Only eight months later, the editors demanded uninterrupted immigration: "Hither the tide of immigration should come," they wrote, "these shores . . . have room for all." In November 1881, however, there was a noticeable shift, the paper insisting that America was not the only haven for Russian immigrants. On 30 June 1882, the *American Hebrew* went even further: "Jews of Europe!" the editors warned, referring to the European counterparts of HEAS, "Know that you are inviting a danger to us! You send us hither a multitude of men, women and children whom we cannot sustain."[60]

This last was a somewhat frantic exaggeration; most needy immigrants received aid from previously arrived relatives, landslayt, or their own mutual-aid societies, and no more than 5 percent ever turned to the philanthropic agencies for help. Once again, the worry was not so much over economic cost as over the prejudice that would be generated by masses of eastern European Jews—prejudice "dangerous to the Jews of refinement and culture in this country."[61]

After 1891, however, the desperate straits of Russian Jews under the reign of Nicholas II (see chapter 1) "transcended considerations of comfort among the established [American] Jews or even concern about the rise of anti-Semitism."[62] Indeed, at the same time that Americans in general inclined toward restricted immigration, leaders of the German Jewish community committed themselves to open immigration as well as to aiding the eastern Europeans materially. In 1891 the United Hebrew Charities, for example, began maintaining an agent at the old barge office in New York City, and through March 1893 the Free Employment Bureau run by Boston's German Jews found jobs for 1,158 applicants, thus helping to sustain more than 2,000 persons. The editors of the *American Hebrew* in 1894 not only applauded these and many other philanthropic efforts, they proclaimed their fears for the Jews of Russia. And while occasionally warning against the possibility of millions of eastern European Jews pouring "pell-mell . . . into the country," the staff vehemently resisted all legislative efforts to curtail Jewish immigration.[63]

Any ambivalence on the part of German Jewish leadership regarding the mass influx of Russian Jews disappeared in the face of the horrors of the pogroms in Russia between 1903 and 1906. Not only were these years a period of mass murder and violence against Jews in eastern Europe, they were also the peak period of Jewish immigration to America. The *American Hebrew* and older German Jewish organizations, including the Board of Delegates of American Israelites and B'nai B'rith, responding to the depredations in Russia, dedicated themselves to a full-scale campaign to defeat the efforts of the restrictionists, even though this meant the inevitable numerical dominance of Russian Jews in America. Moreover, in 1906, the new American Jewish Committee joined the fight against restriction, to which it devoted much of its revenues before World War I.

The united effort to beat back the restrictionists was necessary to counteract nativist pressure, which in the last two decades of the nineteenth century moved Congress toward curtailing immigration. From the end of the Civil War until the early 1880s, a relatively optimistic period in U.S.

history, Americans were generally tolerant of immigration; and industrial manufacturers seeking cheap labor were positively encouraging, as were state governments. Beginning in the 1880s, however, a series of challenges to the national confidence brought nativism to the center of American thought and behavior.

The rapidly changing society of the 1880s and 1890s, though often celebrated in terms of "progress," was also feared for its power to destabilize and complicate. During this same period, the number of immigrants entering the United States markedly increased; there were close to three million new arrivals between 1881 and 1884, nearly equaling the total immigration for the entire decade of the 1870s. Another five to six million arrived by 1898, and a stunning fifteen million more by 1920 (table 3).

The shift in the geographic origins of the foreign-born was as important as the increasing numbers. In 1880, 82 percent of foreign-born persons residing in the United States had emigrated from Germany, Ireland, or elsewhere in northwestern Europe. Another 11 percent came from Canada. Only 4 percent were from southern and eastern Europe. By 1920, 46 percent of America's foreign-born came from southern and eastern Europe.[64] The new immigrants, according to historian John Higham, were not only disproportionately Catholic and Jewish, relative to the indigeneous American population, they were perceived to be politically radical, and "they had an exotic look about them for ethnological as well as cultural reasons." The "thought of European immigration [after 1881] suggested strange images of Mediterranean, Slavic and Jewish types."[65]

Advocates of an Anglo-Saxon America argued for the need to radically decrease the number of immigrants and for more selective entry. The Immigration Restriction League, founded in 1894, and racial nativists such as sociologist E. A. Ross and Madison Grant, "the high Priest of racialism in America," warned against the "mongrelization" of the nation and insisted on rigorous restriction on Slavs, Latins, and Asians, the "historically downtrodden, atavistic, stagnant" races.[66]

Although constituting less than 10 percent of the immigrant stream, Jews were nonetheless a special worry for the restrictionists. Goldwin Smith, historian and active anti-immigrationist, wrote in an article in 1891 that the Jewish "character" was inferior. The Jew can not be counted on for loyalty, Smith contended, because he "changes his country more easily than others."[67] And E. A. Ross wrote that "on the physical side the Hebrews are the polar opposite of our pioneer breed. Not only are they undersized and

Table 3. General and Jewish Immigration from Eastern Europe
to the United States, 1871–1920

Year	General	Jewish	% Jewish
1871–80	2,810,000	15,000	0.5
1881–84	2,580,340	74,310	2.9
1885	395,350	19,610	4.9
1886	334,200	29,660	8.8
1887	490,110	27,470	5.6
1888	547,000	31,360	5.7
1889	444,430	24,000	5.4
1890	455,300	34,300	7.5
1891	560,320	69,140	12.3
1892	579,660	60,325	10.4
1893	440,000	33,000	7.5
1894	285,630	22,110	7.7
1895	258,540	32,080	12.4
1896	343,270	28,120	8.2
1897	330,830	20,685	6.25
1898	229,300	27,410	11.9
1899	311,715	37,415	12.0
1900	448,570	60,765	13.5
1901	488,000	58,100	11.9
1902	648,745	57,670	8.9
1903	857,050	76,205	8.9
1904	812,870	106,240	13.1
1905	1,026,500	129,910	12.7
1906	1,100,735	153,750	14.0
1907	1,285,350	149,180	11.6
1908	782,870	103,390	13.2
1909	751,790	57,550	7.7
1910	1,041,570	84,260	8.1
1911	878,590	91,225	10.4
1912	838,170	80,595	9.6
1913	1,197,890	101,330	8.5
1914	1,218,480	138,050	11.3
1915	326,700	26,500	8.1
1916	298,825	15,110	5.1
1917	295,405	17,340	5.9
1918	110,620	3,670	3.3
1919	141,130	3,055	2.2
1920	430,000	14,290	3.3

Sources: Based on data from U.S. Bureau of the Census, *Historical Statistics of the United States to 1957* (Washington, D.C.: Government Printing Office, 1976); Samuel Joseph, *Jewish Immigration to the United States From 1881 to 1910* (New York: Arno, 1969); Simon Kuznets, "Immigration of Russian Jews to the United States: Background and Structure," *Perspectives in American History* 9 (1975): 35–124.

weak-muscled, but they shun bodily activity and are exceedingly sensitive to pain." Furthermore, the Hebrew "immigrants lower standards wherever they enter. . . . The egoistical, conscienceless . . . Jew constitutes a menace."[68]

Restrictionist pressures against the "menace" of open immigration bore fruit. Beginning in 1882, Congress passed a series of acts to regulate and limit immigration to the United States. Up until World War I, most of the bills for radically restricting the number of immigrants were defeated. But several of the bills that did pass caused problems for Jewish immigrants. The first national immigration law called for the exclusion of "undesirables," prostitutes, lunatics, idiots, or "any person unable to take care of himself without becoming a public charge." The vagueness of language, in the last clause particularly, opened the possibility of subjective exclusions and became a major source of contention between immigration authorities and Jewish organizations acting to protect the immigrants.

In 1891 the federal government took over the responsibility of processing immigrants, and an act was passed extending the term *excluded classes* to cover paupers, polygamists, and persons whose tickets were paid for by someone else. Like the "public charge" clause, the ticket question became a major source of dispute between the authorities and antirestrictionist Jewish organizatons. Were persons with tickets bought by a landsmanshaft, a friend, or even a relative to be excluded?

More frustrating and restrictive, another 1891 act called for the exclusion of persons with a "loathsome or dangerous contagious disease." And with the federal takeover, medical inspection became the responsibility of the Public Health Service (PHS). Its officers, inspired by the new germ theory and other medical discoveries of the 1880s, manned depots in the major ports striving to bar germs by barring immigrants who might be carrying them into America.[69] In 1892 the PHS also classified trachoma, which came to be associated with Jews, as a "dangerous, contagious" disease caused by germs.

Even if not intended to be malicious, the new procedures and definitions proved troublesome for Jewish immigrants. Although deportations rarely exceeded 1 percent of arrivals, the proportion of those rejected on medical grounds increased significantly. Between 1895 and 1914, the number of "immigrants denied permission to enter the United States because of ill health grew 1,400 percent."[70] The prominent German Jew and New York attorney Max Kohler testified before the House Committee on Immigration that as many as 35 percent of exclusions at the port of New York were unjustified. In order to "curry favor by making a record for exclusion," he wrote later, "immigration officials are commonly adopting the medical report, no matter how little significance it has."[71]

The new immigrants were no less healthy than the old; increased deportations were mostly the product of prejudice, new biomedical thinking, and bureaucratic zeal.[72] Responding to the dire needs of Russian refugees in 1891 and to the increase in subjective exclusions, four national Jewish bodies joined in protest against restriction and the anti-Semitism inherent in it. B'nai B'rith, the Jewish Alliance of America, the Baron de Hirsch Fund trustees, and the Union of American Hebrew Congregations appointed Simon Wolf (like Kohler, a leading German Jew and New York attorney) to act as spokesman. Wolf immediately wrote to the secretary of the treasury: "To close the avenues of this fine and liberty-loving country, that has always opened its gates to the downtrodden and unjustly persecuted, would be against the underlying genius and theory of our glorious and beloved constitution."[73]

Other agencies also did battle on the immigration front. At the major depots, representatives of HIAS and United Hebrew Charities intervened if they thought PHS officers were certifying Jewish immigrants as mentally deficient when the actual problem was cultural or linguistic. And armed with recent medical evidence, delegates of the American Jewish Committee suggested misdiagnosis in some trachoma cases. In other cases, they cited new findings indicating that a particular disease ought to be classified as noncommunicable or not especially dangerous. In combination with the pressures brought by social reformers like Lawrence Veiller and Ernest Poole, these actions by Jewish organizations kept the PHS from becoming an agent, even if unwitting, of the nativists.[74]

More serious threats to open immigration than the zeal of PHS officers surfaced regularly in Congress. In March 1904 a bill was introduced in the House that would have limited the newcomers from any one country to eighty thousand persons annually. The *American Hebrew* described the proposed legislation as a "silly . . . measure" and vigorously defended the reputation of the immigrant Jew in its columns and editorials. Cyrus Sulzberger, president of the United Hebrew Charities, wrote lengthy pieces about "what the United States owes the immigrant," adding to the pressure that helped defeat this restrictionist measure and other similar proposals.[75]

In 1909 New York Commissioner of Immigration William Williams decreed that each immigrant, in order to be admitted, would have to show possession of twenty-five dollars . The order created a near panic among the detainees at Ellis Island, who, when breaking up their homes in eastern Europe, had had no knowledge of the twenty-five-dollar requirement. The new stipulation also produced mass meetings and angry, nearly riotous protestations on the Lower East Side of New York, by now home to more than a half-million Jews; and it reached even into the shtetlekh of Russia, where as A. Litwin, a correspondent for the *Jewish Daily Forward*, reported: "Thousands of emigrants on the eve of departure don't know what to do." But many "who had a few extra rubles, though not the entire fifty, decided to take a chance and embark." Under pressure from eastern European Jews organized on the Lower East Side and the unrelenting criticism of Abe Cahan's *Forward* and other Jewish bodies, enforcement of the twenty-five-dollar provision was relaxed.[76]

The victory, however, was short-lived. By this time there were already clear signs that the direction in American politics was toward curtailment of immigration. Between 1909 and 1910, congressmen who leaned strongly in the direction of restriction conducted an investigation of immigration. They concluded their work in late 1910 with a forty-volume report recommending a basic shift in government policy from regulation to limitation.

As early as 1897 a bill to exclude persons unable to read or write in their own languages passed the Congress but was vetoed by President Cleveland. Two more chief executives succeeded in beating back literacy proposals through presidential veto—Taft in 1913 and Wilson in 1915. Although Jews were disproportionately literate compared to most other immigrant groups, significant numbers could not read or write, and a literacy law would have been a severe blow.[77] Moreover, there was no guarantee that the ability to read or write exclusively in Yiddish or Hebrew would be acceptable for admission to the United States. When the agitation for a literacy bill began, Jews were adamantly opposed; and when in 1917 Congress finally mustered enough votes to override yet another Wilson veto, Jewish pressure—organized and sustained by German Jews, the supposed enemies of Yiddish—succeeded in getting Yiddish as well as Hebrew recognized as a "literary language."[78] German Jewish lobbyists, including Jacob Schiff and his colleagues in the American Jewish Committee, also managed to have written into the law an exemption for immigrants avoiding religious persecution. The effect on Jews of the literacy test requirement was thereby minimized.[79]

In the immigration struggle, German Jews sharpened their skills in the art of quiet diplomacy. Louis Marshall, a brilliant attorney and for many years the president of the American Jewish Committee, played a crucial role. Along with men like Max Kohler, Simon Wolf, and Cyrus Sulzberger, Marshall took on restrictionists in public debate and in congressional hearings; but he often believed, as he wrote in 1905, that "a public discussion of [the immigration] question at this time by any Jewish organization" would alert Congress "to the fact that we expect a large influx of immigrants from Russia."[80] Not wanting to rouse the deeply rooted anti-Jewish feelings of a Gentile public, Marshall and other German Jewish leaders believed—probably correctly, in this era of increasing nativism—that the best chance of defeating literacy bills and maintaining the free flow of immigration was to make coherent, persuasive, and polite appeals to public officials behind the scenes.

The established Jewish community opposed the restrictionists in print, in legislative battles, and in private meetings with political leaders. In the hope of eroding anti-immigration and anti-Semitic sentiment and of forestalling restrictionist action, they also encouraged and helped organize the dispersal of eastern European Jews from the urban centers of the American Northeast to the interior of the country. To members of non-Jewish circles, German Jews insisted that the immigrant newcomers enriched the northeastern cities where they resided. German Jews publicly challenged the negative stereotypes of the Jewish immigrants head-on, pointing with pride to the eastern Europeans' admirable qualities—virtuous home life, healthy ambition, drive for education, and low level of crime and disease. Paradoxically, at the same time they feverishly made plans to empty the ghettos and direct newcomers to other areas.

German Jews continually coaxed and prodded the immigrants to Americanize as well as to disperse. These established Jews, often mirroring values current in the Progressive era (c. 1900–17), wanted their Old World coreligionists to discard social habits that made them embarrassingly visible and that stood in the way of rational and efficient adaptation. Early on, Yiddish was targeted as an anachronistic jargon, and Orthodoxy as irrational superstition. German Jewish philanthropists also called for an unquestioning compliance with American law and a repudiation of radical political ideologies, like socialism and anarchism.

Dispersal and Americanization were connected in the minds of established Jews and reflected the environmentalist ideology of the Progressive era. Areas of urban Jewish population concentration were viewed by the German Jewish community as ghettos perpetuating a distinctively foreign life-style. Relocated to the interior of the country, the eastern European immi-grant, it was thought, would be unable to depend on a Yiddish-speaking milieu and would be forced to acculturate more rapidly.

Eastern European immigrants were indeed crowded into the great cities of the East and Midwest. Of over one million Jews who arrived in New York between 1881 and 1911, more than 73 percent remained there. Moreover, as many as 60 percent of the Jews in the United States were located in the corridor from Boston to Baltimore, with another 30 percent in Cleveland, Pittsburgh, Chicago, and other large cities of the Midwest. Like other urban newcomers in the period from 1880 to 1920, eastern European Jews massed together in ethnic enclaves, including Chicago's West Side, Boston's North End, South Philadelphia, and New York's Lower East Side.

As early as 1869, Rabbi Bernard Felsenthal of Chicago suggested that Russian and Polish Jews be settled in Kansas, Iowa, and Nebraska. Simon Wolf added the Shenandoah Valley and Washington Territory, which was administered by Edward S. Solomon, a fellow German Jew, and by 1882 more than two thousand immigrants were sent to nearly 170 different locations in the interior of the United States.[81] In order to deal with the hostility of established communities that considered the newcomers a bur-den, the Jewish Alliance of America was created in 1890. By 1900, in re-sponse to growing worry about Jewish congestion in the cities, the dispersal idea began to receive even more serious consideration. B'nai B'rith, now a major national organization, joined those advocating dispersion, and the Baron de Hirsch Fund brought the Jewish Colonization Association, re-named the Jewish Agricultural and Industrial Aid Society, to the United States. Interested mainly in creating a class of American Jewish farmers, the society helped finance more than 160 agricultural settlements.[82]

In 1901, the society also created the Industrial Removal Office (IRO), whose job it was to relocate Jewish immigrants on an individual basis to smaller Jewish communities throughout the United States. Centered in New York, the IRO extended across the entire country and operated as a nonprofit employment agency. Its dozens of local committees, usually orga-nized by B'nai B'rith lodges, kept the main branch informed about the availability of jobs in their cities and towns and committed themselves to accepting a monthly quota of immigrants.

The New York office of the IRO placed ads in Yiddish newspapers; by the end of the first year, over fifteen hundred persons had been relocated. By 1917, after more than a decade and a half of activity, mostly under the able and devoted direction of David Bressler, a young lawyer who became general manager in 1903, the IRO had relocated more than seventy-five thousand persons to 1,670 cities and towns in all forty-eight states and Canada.[83]

Bressler received many appreciative letters: "I thank you for myself and my family from the bottom of our hearts," wrote one immigrant. "You are like physicians bringing people back to life again. . . . I now make a decent living. . . . I wish that you try for everybody as you tried for me . . . for every Jew who is now persecuted in Russia." Another from Denver, Colorado, wrote: I beg "to extend my thanks to you for sending me out of New York. I earn $10 a week, and do not have to work on *shabos* [the Sabbath]!"[84]

But the results of the IRO effort were mixed. Many immigrants faced lost or delayed baggage, or furniture, or tools; trouble over unpaid utilities bills; and misunderstandings about transportation costs (whenever possible, immigrants were expected to pay at least part of this expense). Even more important were complaints from local committees and host towns about being overburdened and about mismatched needs and skills. And there were as many complaints from relocated immigrants about poor conditions and lack of opportunity. "I am sorry to tell you," one unhappy immigrant wrote, "that I caused you a lot of trouble and money to send me to Weatherford [Oklahoma]. . . . It was all a mistake. . . . The party [who employed me] has not got enough for himself. I don't make enough to pay my board."[85]

Most important, it became clear soon after the establishment of the IRO that the vast majority of Jews who came to New York City or Boston or Philadelphia would never leave. The seventy-five thousand who did relocate under IRO auspices between 1901 and 1917 represented only 6 percent of the Jewish newcomers to America. The enthusiasm of the German Jews for social engineering was not generally shared by their potential beneficiaries. The ethnic enclaves or voluntary ghettos of the great cities provided anchors for the newly uprooted. Urban Jewish neighborhoods supplied familiarity, friends, relatives, synagogues, kosher meat, and Hebrew teachers. The ghetto meant yiddishkayt. "If I were [still] in New York," said a recent immigrant earning a decent living in the South, " I could go to the Yiddish theatre in the evenings, hear a lecture, visit people whose conversation I enjoy, join a club or take active part in some movement; in short, after working hours, be a man!"[86]

The absence of a wider Jewish fellowship and the limited cultural opportunities of small towns discouraged immigrants from relocating to the hinterlands. Indeed, even the newest arrivals not yet directly familiar with New York but aware of the promise of the great city were reluctant to choose the American interior. An experiment undertaken by the IRO in 1902 to convince newcomers being processed at Ellis Island to settle in the interior was an abysmal failure and was abandoned after less than two years.[87]

Nevertheless, the flood of immigrants continued. In 1903 and on through 1906, new waves of pogroms broke out in Russia. With Congress in these years coming closer and closer to serious immigration restriction, it appeared to many American Jewish leaders, particularly the noted banker and German-born philanthropist Jacob Schiff, that something more effective had to be devised to distribute the Russian Jewish refugees throughout the United States. He asked Judge Mayer Sulzberger of Philadelphia to think about what could be done "not only to divert the stream of [eastern European] immigrants into the American 'Hinterland,' but even to promote a considerably larger immigration than we now receive."[88] Clearly, Schiff was not only concerned with the deflection and dispersal of immigrants; he wanted to "take every one of our persecuted people out of Russia and bring them to the United States."[89]

German Jewish leaders continued to believe that the most effective way to defuse popular support for restriction legislation was to distribute eastern European immigrants throughout America. By 1904 they reached the conclusion that only by rerouting the immigrant stream to new ports could newcomers be induced to settle in areas other than cities in the Northeast and Midwest. In 1906 a bill establishing an entry station for immigrants in Galveston, Texas, was being debated in Congress. Jacob Schiff and others, including Oscar Straus, secretary of commerce and labor, under whose jurisdiction immigration lay, used their influence to secure passage of the bill.[90]

The Galveston plan, which Schiff called "my project," looked to the Jewish Territorial Organization (ITO) in London and the German Hilfsverein to gather emigrants in Russia, finance their journey to America, and direct them to Galveston. There, the IRO would take over, guiding the immigrants to towns and cities west of the Mississippi. Jacob Schiff pledged half a million dollars to initiate the project, an amount he thought "should suffice to place from 20,000 to 25,000 people" in the American interior.[91] Schiff and other men of wealth and achievement, like Louis Marshall and

Simon Wolf, saw themselves as stewards, obligated along the lines set forth in Andrew Carnegie's famous "Gospel of Wealth" essay, to take on the burdens of the community. Once again, however, the philanthropists took little account of economic realities and immigrant preferences. By 1914, after seven years of operation the Galveston movement had deflected no more than ten thousand immigrants (about 1.2 percent) from the ports of the Northeast.[92]

Another suggested solution to the problem of impending restriction was to create a class of Jewish farmers. The stewards, including the Baron de Hirsch, hoped by this plan both to achieve distribution of immigrants and to "exterminate peddling and petty trading"—the allegedly unproductive pursuits of eastern European Jews. Some among the Russian Jewish immigrants were ready to join hands with their German Jewish benefactors, albeit for different reasons. Members of the Am Olam movement, for example, came to the New World to create agrarian socialist settlements, and in the spring of 1882 thirty-two families established an agricultural colony on Sicily Island, Louisiana. This was soon wiped out by flood. Undaunted, some families regrouped under their leader, poet and publicist Herman Rosenthal, to found Crimea, South Dakota, and nearby, the satellite community of Bethlehem of Judea. Beset by hailstorms, diseased crops, drought, and prairie fires, both colonies were liquidated after three years. New Odessa, near Portland, Oregon, survived a bit longer, but the colony was increasingly overwhelmed by the physical problems of the environment, including distant markets, and unforeseen social stresses, particularly the scarcity of women.[93] "The sex problem" at New Odessa, wrote Abe Cahan in his memoirs, "caused considerable difficulty. . . . Some people confused communism with the concept of eating off the same plate and sleeping in the same bedroom."[94] The Oregon settlement disbanded after five years in 1887.

The Baron de Hirsch Fund colonies, better planned and with some agricultural training for the Jewish settlers, fared better, some enduring for decades. The communities of Alliance, Carmel, Woodbine, and Rosenhayn in southern New Jersey, had "no trouble finding customers for their products" in the large urban markets of New York and Philadelphia. Moreover, these settlements moved away from an exclusively agricultural mode and modified their collectivist orientation in favor of a synthesis of individual enterprise and cooperative organization. Most agricultural ventures, however, were not so flexible or so fortunate, and overall the attempt to make

Jews into farmers failed. The largest number of Jewish farm families in America was about three thousand, reached in 1909, and comprised fifteen thousand people, less than 1 percent of the Jewish population.[95]

Jewish farmers were not the only agriculturalists who failed in this era. The attempt to return Jews to the soil ran counter to the worldwide advance of industrialization as well as prevailing economic trends in the United States. While America rose to be the world's largest agricultural producer, male workers in agriculture dropped from 39.6 to 35.8 percent of all gainfully employed men in the United States between 1900 and 1910.[96]

Jewish farming ventures were, moreover, particularly handicapped. Few Jews had experience with agriculture, and few had internalized the requisite cultural attitudes for farming. They possessed little of the passivity and fatalism necessary to bear the monotonous, backbreaking labor associated with the depressed rural life of Russian serfs and dependent peasants. Some Jews, influenced by the Tolstoyan tradition, had idealized communal agriculture: they believed that as free persons they could fashion vital lives on the soil, only to discover that there was little that was ennobling about farm work, once they actually tried it. When they found themselves caught up in a cycle of disease, fire, and flood, as well as a spiral of downward mobility, they fled. Refugees from New Odessa, for example, returned to New York City in 1887; according to a 1901 report, "one [was] a chemist, one . . . a druggist, and one . . . an engineer, two [were] lawyers, two . . . dentists, one . . . a superintendent of a hospital and one returned to Russia."[97]

It is unlikely that great numbers of others who left agriculture achieved such stunning social mobility as this group. But the economic opportunities, as well as the cultural familiarities of cities were simply unmatched in the hinterlands. The vast majority of eastern European Jews recognized this early on and either refused to leave the cities or soon returned to them. Agricultural colonization as a vehicle for significant dispersion was soon given up. And as early as 1907, the IRO also admitted that "no wholesale solution to our problem is possible." By 1910 it was clear as well that the Galveston experiment, although successful in many individual cases, was, in terms of large-scale deflection and distribution, a failure.

We have seen that the established Jewish community reacted to the influx of eastern Europeans with anxiety over increasing anti-Semitism, and they sought to remove and remold their coreligionists as soon as possible. A number of German Jews, including Jacob Schiff and Louis Marshall, did honestly labor "to weld the two strata into one community," and almost all the leaders of the German Jewish community participated in undertakings and expenditures to ease the hardships of eastern European immigrants.[98] Convinced, however, that removal and Americanization would be in the interest of the immigrant, as well as in the interest of established Jewry, these philanthropists failed to sense their own cultural arrogance.

They saw the eastern European Jew as "inferior . . . ignorant, bigoted, hypocritical," and most particularly, "ungrateful." On the other side, eastern European Jews saw the German Jew as "a cad . . . his philanthropy ostentatious, and insincere."[99] Not surprisingly, neither group had much influence on the other in the short run. In time, however, as we shall see, the increasingly dominant eastern Europeans would help remold the yahudim, as they resentfully called their superiors, and German Jews would become part of the larger ethnically conscious Jewish community. Eastern European Jews, too, would find themselves changed, partly by the institutional frameworks, behavior patterns, and values established earlier by German Jews and partly by the new environment. In the period from 1880 to about 1910, however, the immigrants continued to develop a transitional culture, an amalgam of religious and secular Jewish modes, manners, and forms, neither completely eastern European nor fully American. Nowhere was this dynamic process more evident than on New York's Lower East Side.

CHAPTER THREE

✡

NEW YORK AS THE PROMISED CITY

EASTERN EUROPEAN Jews forged and sustained a unique transitional culture in New York for almost four decades. Fashioned out of both Old World tradition and New World experience, the immigrant culture of the Lower East Side helped ease the pain of accommodation for a people whose recent experience combined at least three kinds of dramatic change: a physical uprooting from the familiar small-town world of eastern Europe to the bewildering vastness of America; a radical shift in class status, mainly from artisan, craftsman, and petty merchant to proletarian; and despite major links of continuity, a separation from the long-standing moral context supportive of Jewish tradition.

It is not surprising, then, that some immigrants in the 1880s and 1890s succumbed to the poverty and confusion of the New World. Some even longed for the old country, with its slower pace and smaller scale, its spiritual and ethical verities, and its more dignified, less lonesome life. Others, disoriented and exhausted, became *farloyrene* menschn, lost souls. More characteristically, however, they were determined to stay afloat. Many immigrants tried to maintain faith and spirituality in the storefront or basement shuln and struggled to weave the social and cultural threads of the old way of life into new patterns in landsmanshaftn and other societies of mutual aid. Many managed to wrest a few moments of pleasure at the Yiddish theater, or a sense of dignity in labor unions and militant strikes. Some even managed, through disciplined effort, to rise. Consciously or not, all were involved in a process of blending secular Jewishness with elements of religion, in a new "interval of equilibrium."[1]

The vast majority of Jewish immigrants were persuaded and relieved that, no matter what else, they had escaped the czars and the pogromchiks.

Although they continued to suffer in America, transplanted Jews could now begin to entertain notions of a better life for their sons and daughters—and even for themselves. These visions, combined with cultural memory and the willingness to adapt, promoted a strategy of survival. Already in the 1880s, immigrants were recreating a Jewish communal existence and culture on the Lower East Side of Manhattan and, about a decade later, in Harlem, the East Bronx, and the Brooklyn neighborhoods of Williamsburg, Boro Park, and Brownsville. In these communities, as well as in the Jewish neighborhoods of Boston, Philadelphia, Chicago, Rochester, Cleveland, and Detroit, Jewish immigrants, with their rewoven culture, gained some measure of control over the process of Americanization. It was a temporary, transitional culture that the immigrants made, but its remnants and echoes continue even in the late twentieth century to nourish important parts of the American Jewish world.

The immigrants ultimately experienced the Lower East Side of New York, as well as the North End of Boston and the West Side of Chicago, as fertile ground for cultural sustenance and renewal. But their initial experience of the ghettos of urban America was one of congested streets, poor housing, and cramped and dangerous work spaces. New York was America's largest city; it was also the most densely populated and the most cosmopolitan, with many of its neighborhoods crowded with immigrants. Ever since the middle of the nineteenth century, the foreign-born and their children had outnumbered Americans of older stock, and by 1900 they constituted more than 75 percent of the city's growing population.[2]

Of the twenty-three million immigrants to the United States between 1880 and 1920, seventeen million came through the port of New York. Although some newcomers dispersed to other places, great numbers collected in immigrant enclaves on the island of Manhattan. No group outdid the Jews in this regard. Practically all eastern European Jewish immigrants arriving after 1870 initially found their way to the Lower East Side, and the vast majority stayed within its nucleus—a twenty-square-block area south of Houston Street and east of the Bowery.

By 1892, 75 percent of the city's Jews lived on the Lower East Side. The percentage declined to 50 percent in 1903 and to 23 percent by 1916; and nearly two-thirds of East Side Jews had left the area by 1905. But the absolute number of Jews, augmented by newcomers crowding into the district, continued to climb until it reached its peak of 542,000 in 1910.[3] The Lower East Side literally bristled with Jews. Jacob Riis, an acerbic and energetic journalist interested in "how the other half lives," observed in the 1890s that "nowhere in the world are so many people crowded together in a square mile" as in the Jewish quarter. The Tenth Ward averaged 730 people per acre by the turn of the century, and some blocks of the Lower East Side in 1895 approached the astounding rate of a thousand per acre. Only Bombay and Calcutta had higher densities. By 1906, of fifty-one blocks in the city with over three thousand inhabitants, thirty-seven were located on the Lower East Side. The neighborhood was bursting at the seams, and its buildings, as Arnold Bennett remarked, "seemed to sweat humanity at every window and door."[4]

The great Jewish influx pushed the district's middle-class Germans and Irish, as well as the remnant of the German Jewish community north of Houston Street, to less crowded quarters. Their places were taken by five major varieties of Jews in an area described by one young immigrant as "a miniature federation of semi-independent allied states."[5] Hungarians were clustered in the northwest section just above Houston Street; the Galicians lived to the south, between Houston and Broome. From Chrystie Street to Allen Street in the west lay the Romanian quarter, within which, after 1907, the Sephardic Jews (mainly from Syria, Greece, Turkey, and Spain) settled. The remainder of the Jewish quarter, from Grand Street south to Monroe Street, was the territory of the Russians—the most numerous and most heterogeneous of the Jewries of eastern Europe.[6]

In every Jewish section there were streets like Suffolk Street, where, as Abe Cahan wrote, one "had to pick and nudge his way through dense swarms of bedraggled half-washed humanity, past garbage barrels rearing their overflowing contents," and "underneath tiers and tiers of fire escapes barricaded and festooned with mattresses, pillows and feather beds not yet gathered in for the night."[7] On Orchard Street, "the crush and stench were enough to suffocate one; dirty children were playing in the street, and perspiring Jews were pushing carts and uttering wild shrieks." It is no wonder that many a newcomer could ask, "Was this the America we had sought? Or was it only after all, a circle that we had traveled with a Jewish ghetto at its beginning and its end."[8]

The streets were crowded but were often preferable to the constriction of the tiny flats. One immigrant, boarding with the family of a cantor, remembered that his two-room apartment on Allen Street contained the two parents, six children, and five other boarders. Two daughters took in dresses to sew at home, and one boarder plied his shoemaking craft in the apartment, as well. The "cantor rehearses, a train passes, the shoemaker bangs, ten brats run around like goats, the wife putters in her 'kosher restaurant.' At night we all try to get some sleep in the stifling roach-infested two rooms."[9]

It was often necessary to take in boarders to help with the rent. Some slept on real folding beds; others were not so fortunate. Charles Zimmerman, who went on to become vice president of the International Ladies' Garment Workers' Union (ILGWU), lived for a while with an uncle in a Ridge Street tenement. He "slept in the kitchen on two chairs with boards laid across," which he "had to dismantle . . . right away in the morning. Otherwise, no other boarder or family member could walk from the front room to the kitchen or to the hall, where the facilities were."[10] A family that could occupy a flat without boarders considered itself lucky.

New York's housing problems had been serious since the 1830s, and mass immigration simply magnified them. The population of Manhattan grew by some two-hundred thousand in the 1890s and another five hundred thousand between 1900 and 1910.[11] On the Lower East Side, dozens of families, amounting to between seventy-five and a hundred people, were often squeezed into a six- or seven-story tenement building. The relatively new dumbbell tenements (so-called because of their shape: a narrow air-shaft separated what were literally two tenements back to back) were the product of an 1879 reform law. They contained four apartments to a floor. Only one room in each apartment received direct light and air from the street. The narrow hallways contained the common water closets, the "special improvement" of the 1879 reform.[12]

Only a few flats had hot running water, and there might be only one hallway water closet for up to ten people. It is no wonder that after working hours every parked wagon in the neighborhood became a lavatory.[13] These conditions persisted despite remedial legislation in 1884 and 1887 regarding water closets, light, air, and fire safety. In 1888 the *American Magazine* described the dumbbell tenements on Ridge, Eldridge, and Allen streets:

> They are great prison-like structures of brick, with narrow doors and windows, cramped passages and steep rickety stairs. They are built through from one street to the other with a somewhat narrower building connecting them. . . . The narrow court-yard in the middle is a

damp foul-smelling place, supposed to do duty as an airshaft; had the
foul fiend designed these great barracks they could not have been more
villainously arranged to avoid any chance of ventilation. . . . In case of
fire they would be perfect death-traps, for it would be impossible for
the occupants of the crowded rooms to escape by the narrow stairways,
and the flimsy fire escapes which the owners of the tenements were
compelled to put up a few years ago are so laden with broken furniture, bales and boxes that they would be worse than useless. In the hot
summer months . . . these fire escape balconies are used as sleeping-
rooms by the poor wretches who are fortunate enough to have windows opening upon them. The drainage is horrible, and even the
Croton, as it flows from the tap in the noisome courtyard, seemed to
be contaminated by its surroundings and have a fetid smell.[14]

In 1901 the New York Tenement Housing Act put an end to the construction of dumbbell tenements and applied some of the new-law regulations to old-law buildings. But the well-intentioned legislation inadvertently caused problems for the poor. Slum clearance and rehabilitation
created a shortage of apartments and caused many poor Jews to crowd in
with relatives or friends or to leave the downtown area altogether. As of 1
July 1903, 43 percent of New York's new tenements were located on the
Lower East Side. But realtors and developers, recognizing the economic
profitability in the new building code, created most of the new tenements as
a middle- to high-rent district within the ghetto.[15]

The poor continued to face congestion and inadequate housing. After
1903, landlords were slow to apply new-law regulations to old-law buildings. As late as 1908 there were still three hundred thousand dark, unventi-
lated, interior rooms south of Houston Street, and between 1902 and 1909,
the Lower East Side, with less than 20 percent of the population, suffered 38
percent of the fire fatalities for all of Manhattan.[16]

Any relatively speedy and enduring solution to the housing problem
would have required an aroused public conscience and a body politic ready
to break with the prevailing notions of laissez-faire in favor of serious urban
planning and public housing. But New York's growth rate exceeded that of
any of the world's great older cities and virtually defied the comprehension
and control of its inhabitants. Such rapid population expansion demanded
unprecedented public expenditures, but legal and political forms were so
inadequate that little was done, and "the city became a veritable frontier in
which near anarchy reigned."[17]

Despite this condition, immigrant Jews continued to pour into the Lower East Side and, to a lesser degree, into Chicago's West End and Jewish ghettos in Philadelphia and Boston; few of the smaller cities and towns of the American interior offered so great a possibility of Jewish communalism and Yiddish-based culture as the great cities. Equally important, the ghettos, particularly the largest one in New York's Lower East Side, offered the possibility of employment for Jews. At the time that masses of eastern European Jews were coming to America, the garment industry was undergoing rapid expansion, and New York City was central to this development. By 1910 the city was producing 70 percent of the nation's women's clothing and 40 percent of its men's clothing, creating jobs for newly arriving Jews. Even if we discount their exaggerations (only 10 percent of eastern European immigrant labor force were actually trained tailors), these Jews brought with them from the old countries significant skills in garment work, one of the few occupations open to Jews in nineteenth-century Europe.[18]

As early as 1890 almost 80 percent of New York's garment industry was located below Fourteenth Street, and more than 90 percent of these factories were owned by German Jews. Lower New York, therefore, was a powerful magnet for the eastern Europeans throughout the period of mass immigration. Immigrants were attracted by jobs and by Jewish employers who could provide a familiar milieu as well as the opportunity to observe the Sabbath. By 1897 approximately 60 percent of the New York Jewish labor force was employed in the apparel field, and 75 percent of the workers in the industry were Jewish.[19]

Within the American needle industry there were three systems and three sites of production. The oldest was the family system, which had been dominant under Irish and German influence in the midnineteenth century. Work was divided among family members and was done at home. In the 1870s, homework, or outside manufacture, declined as factories, the second mode of production, became dominant. But with the coming of eastern European Jews there sprang up a third form of production—the contracting, or sweatshop, system, a variant of the family system.

Contracting utilized section work, which was designed to exploit the economies of a minute division of labor. The contractor, usually an immigrant who had been in America somewhat longer than the newest arrivals (greenhorns) picked up precut, unsewn garments from the manufacturer. He then supervised in his own home, or in a loft or tenement room con-

verted to a shop, a collection of operators: basters, pressers, finishers, zip-
per installers, buttonhole makers, and pocket makers. Some section and
finishing work was given to a subcontractor, who found people willing to
take that work into their own apartments. Exploitation, including exploitation of the self (as the contractors and subcontractors and their family
members often worked alongside the employees), was more intense than in
factories and inside shops. The contractor's profit margin was low and so,
therefore, was pay. The sweatshop, in addition, demanded extremely long
hours in terribly close quarters.

Abe Cahan, in his short story "Sweat-Shop Romance," described the
kitchen in a small Essex Street apartment, filled to overflowing with bun-
dles of cloth, shears, cotton spools, finished garments, people, pots, and
pans. Also present was a "red-hot kitchen stove," which made the work
space a sweatshop in the literal sense.[20]

The worst conditions of the factory and the tenement had come together in one place. Yet to the newly arrived immigrants there were advantages to the sweatshop system. Workers could communicate in their own
language. The work, however arduous, did not prevent the performance of
religious duties, the observance of the Sabbath, or the celebration of religious
festivals. Moreover, working together in small units, immigrants thought
they could preserve the integrity of their families. The "homes of the Hebrew
quarters are its workshop also," reported journalist Jacob Riis.

> You are made fully aware of it before you have travelled the length of a
> single block in any of these East Side streets, by the whir of a thousand
> sewing machines, worked at high pressure from earliest dawn till mind
> and muscle give out together. Every member of the family from the
> youngest to the oldest bears a hand, shut in the qualmy rooms, where
> meals are cooked and clothing washed and dried besides, the livelong
> day. It is not unusual to find a dozen persons—men, women and
> children—at work in a single room.[21]

Skilled and semiskilled Jewish workers, from increasingly industrialized homelands, continued to arrive in the United States at the turn of the
century. Nearly 67 percent of gainfully employed Jewish immigrants who
arrived between 1899 and 1914 possessed industrial skills—a much higher
proportion than any other incoming national group. These men and women
helped to fill the needs of the expanding garment trades in New York. In
1880, 10 percent of the clothing factories in the United States were in New

York City; by 1910 the total had risen to 47 percent, with Jews constituting 80 percent of the hat and cap makers, 75 percent of the furriers, 68 percent of the tailors, and 60 percent of the milliners.²²

Jews were also drawn to innumerable other crafts, including bookbinding, watchmaking, cigar making, and tinsmithing, all of which became part of a growing ethnic economy. It has been estimated that only about a third of the heads of families retained their original eastern European vocations. But almost 24 percent moved out of factory work and into self-employment in small businesses at the earliest opportunity. In the virtually all-Jewish Eighth Assembly District, approximating the Tenth Ward, there were 144 groceries, 131 butcher shops, 62 candy stores, 36 bakeries, and 2,440 peddlers and pushcart vendors.²³

Peddling was enervating, often backbreaking work, with long hours and low profits. But it was a way of avoiding the oppressive discipline of factory labor, and many observant Jews chose to become pushcart vendors in order to have time for study and to avoid breaking the Sabbath prohibition on work. Many women and even some children, mirroring old-country patterns, were involved in the trade as part of the family economy. The Mayor's Pushcart Commission in 1906 reported that male "owners" often had "other occupations [and] regularly . . . let their wives and children attend to the pushcarts."²⁴

In the heart of every pushcart vendor was the hope of becoming the owner of a "real" store. In turn, those who already owned stores dreamed of expansion. The goal of peddlers and vendors then was not simply to remain independent of the restrictive environment of the factory; it was also to take advantage of the market opportunities presented by the ethnic and religious needs of the eastern European Jewish community, particularly dietary. Jewish dietary habits and preferences were determined by a complex amalgam of historical circumstance, religious law, and regional custom. Some foods associated with eastern European Jews—knishes, blintzes, bagels, bialys, herring, whether pickled, baked, fried, chopped, or served in sour cream—had little or nothing to do with Judaism. These were regional dishes that varied only slightly—sometimes just in name—from those enjoyed by Gentile neighbors in the old countries, but these foods had become part of the ethnic diet and were greatly desired. Everywhere Jews came together, they ate; and they preferred the delicacies they had enjoyed before their journey to America. And peddlers, pushcart vendors, and other Jewish entrepreneurs knew how to provide these cultural symbols that East Siders craved.²⁵

Even the enormous quantity of seltzer (artificially carbonated water) consumed on the Lower East Side was the result of cultural preference and only indirectly related to religion. Alcohol is not forbidden to Jews, but drunkenness is (except for two times a year during festival celebrations), and Jews therefore developed a cultural aversion to the regular consumption of intoxicating beverages. They turned instead to seltzer, the worker's champagne, which was cheap and thought to be health enhancing. This stimulated the growth of a large wholesale and retail seltzer enterprise dominated by Jewish bottlers, workers, and teamsters. In 1880 there were only two seltzer companies in New York; by 1907 over a hundred operated in the remarkable ethnic economy Jews had created.[26]

Religious ritual, particularly kashrut (the observance of the dietary laws), was even more important than dietary preference in the growth of the ethnic economy of the Lower East Side. Only the flesh of domestic herbivorous animals that have been humanely slaughtered may be eaten by observant Jews. This produced the need for kosher butchers and shokhetim, or ritual slaughterers, who needed special training and religious piety to perform the sacred ritual.[27]

The mixing of meat and milk products was also prohibited, which required that separate kitchen utensils and dinnerware be used for milk and meat dishes. All of this meant that those who produced food, sold it, or served it in bakeries, restaurants, and cafés had to observe the dairy-meat distinctions. Jews rarely trusted anyone but other Jews in these matters. And every restaurant or food-vending and food-processing establishment intending to serve the Lower East Side Jewish community required the services of a mashgiakh, or supervisor, to ensure compliance with the dietary laws. Many eastern European Jews who had some scholarly background could qualify.

In addition, almost every religious holiday celebrated by Jews involved a special food or beverage: matzo (unleavened bread) and gefilte fish on Passover, hamantash (three-cornered pastry filled with fruit or poppy seeds) at Purim, and challah (egg bread) for the traditional Sabbath meal on Friday evenings. In 1900, seventy bakeries observant of the dietary restrictions and knowledgeable about Jewish holiday needs served the Lower East Side. The number increased to 500 by 1910, and in the Eighth Assembly District alone there were 631 food mongers of every variety. All told, about 20 percent of the Jewish community with their carts and wagons, their retail stores, cafés, and lunchrooms were able to survive, some even to prosper, by catering to the food ways of the remaining 80 percent.[28]

Most Jewish pushcart vendors and peddlers also sold nonfood items. Indeed, they sold just about every conceivable consumer item. They extended credit, promoted their wares, and introduced high-quality goods. Quick to assess the needs of customers and willing to operate on the lowest margins of profit, Jewish street merchants soon turned the peripheral business of itinerant peddling into a vital retail institution. In the process, they sustained themselves and became "self-respecting merchants."[29]

In the late 1890s, Jews in relatively large numbers began moving into the building trades. Earlier, because of the paucity of Jewish building contractors, immigrant workers, fearful of language barriers and of breaking religious taboos by working on the Sabbath or other holy days, avoided this field. But when migration from the Lower East Side stimulated a building boom in Harlem, Brownsville, Williamsburg, and the East Bronx, Jewish entrepreneurs entered the construction industry and made small down payments on lots and buildings. Some Jewish immigrant workers were employed in these new areas, but barriers created by the older unions meant that most would be employed in the alteration and remodeling of old tenements on the Lower East Side—as ironworkers, masons, plumbers, electricians, carpenters, and painters.[30]

The remodeling business, the garment industry, and the general ethnic economy of the Lower East Side provided wide opportunities for Jews seeking employment. But as the descriptions of the tenements and working conditions suggest, most immigrants were poor; indeed, transplantation often resulted, at least in the initial stages, in a worsening of the immigrants' economic plight. This was true not only because wages and profits were meager, but because Jews arrived here with less money and more dependents than non-Jewish newcomers. Moreover, there were other claims on the breadwinner's income. A portion of that income was often earmarked to repay money borrowed for the family's passage or to help other relatives emigrate. In the very early years, virtually all immigrants regularly mailed clothing and food parcels to dependent parents, wives, and children in the old countries. Later, dreams of capitalizing a small business or of putting a son through school led families to sacrifice in order to accumulate the necessary funds. In addition, the religious obligation of tzedakah was so powerfully felt that it too can be seen as a claim on income. Many former East Siders recalled that "almost every family had the pushkas, little boxes. . . . Come Friday . . . you'd throw in a penny for your favorite charity. There were separate boxes for each charity"—Palestine, the yeshiva, poorer people.[31]

Rent was probably the single most expensive item in the working-class family's budget. The average three-room apartment on the Lower East Side was $13.50 a month, which could amount to as much as 30 percent of family income. Paying the rent presented enormous difficulties, especially for garment workers, who had to survive the slack season for three to four months every year.[32] As we have seen, boarders were frequently taken in to help with the rent, but even this did not always prevent eviction. One evicted woman, an observer recalled,

> kept staring at the litter of cheap things in which she must have taken
> no end of pleasure and pride while she had been gathering them one by
> one in the making of her home, now left in pieces in the street, a sym-
> bol of eviction and destitution. Occasionally, she would make the last
> sacrifice—her pride. She brought out a china plate from the folds of her
> dress and placed it on one of the chairs. People would drop pennies
> perhaps even nickels and dimes into that plate—enough to save her
> from being wholly destitute.[33]

Destitution meant that the children often had to be incorporated into the family economy. In future songwriter Irving Berlin's basement apartment on Cherry Street the four youngest girls were daily "bent over bead work," while the middle brothers worked in a sweatshop. Occasionally, young Irving brought home the coins he earned singing songs on corners and in taverns, and at times all the siblings sold newspapers on the street. Pauline Newman, an indefatigable organizer for the ILGWU, went to work at age eleven for the Triangle Shirtwaist Company, later infamous for the fire that killed more than 140 young women and girls. "A section in that factory," Newman remembered, "could have been regarded as a kinder-garten, we were all kids, all youngsters. . . . We worked . . . from 7:30 in the morning to 9 in the evening."[34]

Reliable statistics for the immigrant era are elusive, but most contemporary observations, newspapers, and government reports agree: poverty was pervasive and prolonged for large numbers of Jews from eastern Europe; and it took years of thrift and hard work before they could climb out of it. In the meantime, meager incomes, religious demands, and cultural needs rooted most transplanted Jews in the Lower East Side.

These immigrants knew that, by American standards, their living conditions were abominable, but they also remembered the outrages of the Old World, where many of them had lived in run-down hovels, fearful of drunken peasants, increasing economic dislocation, oppressive czarist decrees, and government sponsored pogroms. They responded to both the American present and the European past, dealing as best they could with their daily burdens. Many Jewish immigrants were determined to climb out of this present situation, and in the meantime they found solace in a fire escape, perhaps, or a lighted hallway, an apartment free of boarders, a private toilet, or windows overlooking the street.

Despite the generally congested and airless living and working conditions, the physical health of the Jews was surprisingly good in comparison to that of both non-Jewish immigrants and native-born Americans.[35] This was partly due to the fact that, despite grim circumstances, traditional Jewish housewives often succeeded in maintaining cleanliness in the home. Contemporary reports suggest that East Side Jewish homes were "hygienic" and that Jewish housekeepers worked hard to clear living quarters of vermin. Dr. Annie Daniel, a pioneer in public health, testified before the Tenement House Committee in 1894:

> The rules of life which orthodox Hebrews so unflinchingly obey as laid down in the Mosaic code . . . are designed to maintain health. These rules are applied to the daily life of the individuals as no other sanitary laws can be. . . . Food must be cooked properly, and hence the avenues through which the germs of disease may enter are destroyed. Meat must be "kosher," and this means it must be perfectly healthy. Personal cleanliness is at times strictly compelled, and at least one day in the week [in preparation for the Sabbath] the habitation must be thoroughly cleaned.[36]

Jews also may have remained comparatively healthier because of their sobriety: Jews rarely drank to excess, preferring seltzer to intoxicants. The comparative death rates from diseases of the liver—diseases linked to consumption of alcohol—are instructive. For eastern European Jews, the rate was five per hundred thousand; for non-Jewish immigrants from Germany, it was thirty-two; and for Irish immigrants, it was seventy-one. Even for the native-born, the rate was thirteen per hundred thousand.[37]

One of the few addictions Jews on the Lower East Side did develop contributed to, rather than threatened, their well-being. "I cannot get along without a 'sweat' (Russian bath) at least once a week, many a Jew [insisted]." The proliferation of privately owned bathhouses in New York (by 1897 over half of the city's sixty-two bathhouses were owned by Jews) was largely attributable to the needs of the Jewish immigrant population.[38]

With the highest average density of tenants per building, the virtually all-Jewish Tenth Ward may nonetheless have been the healthiest in Manhattan. Jewish mortality rates for childbirth, tuberculosis, measles, and scarlet fever were the lowest in New York, as was the overall Jewish mortality rate of 17.4 per thousand. In comparison, the Fourteenth Ward, populated largely by Italian immigrants, had a death rate of 35.2. Jewish immigrants had been perceived by many as particularly unfit physically, but on the Lower East Side, given the trying conditions, they demonstrated resilience and longevity.[39]

While Jews were relatively healthy physically, they were not spared a large share of maladies associated with nervous stress. Hypertension, ulcers, depression, and suicide were more common among Jews in America than in the old countries; and neurasthenia and hysteria were more prevalent among Jews than among their non-Jewish neighbors.[40] The rupture with tradition and the pain of dislocation produced neurosis, mental breakdown, family instability, juvenile delinquency, and criminality. This was reinforced by the fact that in America the immigrant generation was unable to supervise its offspring as closely as had been the custom in the shtetl. Some children worked outside the home, and almost all went to secular schools, where they were taught by strangers intent on Americanizing them. In addition, children fleeing small, crowded apartments spent a great deal of time on congested streets, where they developed behaviors and values at odds with their more traditional parents. One young immigrant recalled that

> the trombeniks [wild ones] represented a sort of underworld in Sheriff
> Street society. They were a loosely associated group ranging from
> would-be tough guys to a few older starkers, strong arm boys. They
> were the disreputable element, the troublemakers, shady characters,
> whom Sheriff Street disowned. Evenings found them hanging out in
> front of Philip's Barber shop. . . . They played cards, threw dice or
> called after any girl that passed. . . . There was something attractive
> about these easy-going, devil-may-care fellows.[41]

Sometimes things got fairly rough. "We had gang fights," Sam Smolowitz remembered, with "rocks, bottles. Against the Irish. It was rough stuff. . . . We loaded up the back of the yard with all kinds of junk, mainly broken bottles . . . for throwing, or . . . stabbing. [Our attackers] had great names [for us]: Jew Boy . . . Fatso, Ginso. . . . We did a job on them. . . . A lot of mussed-up faces. They got the message to pick on some other gang on the block."[42]

Jewish gangs also fought each other. The Ludlow Streeters and the Essex Guerillas in Samuel Ornitz's naturalistic novel of East Side life, *Haunch, Paunch, and Jowl,* were involved in a vicious "civil war" over "differences never quite specified or identified." But participants like Meyer Hirsch, the novel's central figure, found meaning in the gang and its battles. When Meyer joined the Ludlow Streeters, he "swept away the last rag of swaddling clothes and life became real."[43]

Meyer Hirsch, unlike other protagonists in early twentieth-century American Jewish literature, such as David Levinsky in Abe Cahan's monumental novel, or Sara Smolinsky in Anzia Yezierska's *Bread Givers,* had no roots in the shtetl world of eastern Europe. In his relentless pursuit of success at whatever cost, Hirsch failed to integrate the better parts of his cultural heritage into the promise of America. Many youngsters succeeded in making that synthesis, but not without difficulty. The sensitive Gentile journalist Hutchins Hapgood in 1902 described the struggle in the life of the Jewish ghetto boy:

> The struggle is strong because the boy's nature, at once religious and susceptible, is strongly appealed to by both the old and the new. At the same time that he is keenly sensitive to the charm of the American environment, with its practical and national opportunities, he has still a deep love for his race, and the old things. He is aware and rather ashamed of the limitations of his parents. He feels that the trend and weight of things are against them, that they are in a minority; but yet in a real way the old people remain his conscience, the visible representatives of a moral and religious tradition by which the boy may regulate his inner life.[44]

Some ghetto boys, unfortunately, did not have both "old people" around to reinforce the moral tradition. For marital relationships, as well as generational relationships, were marked by the strain and struggle of adjustment to new ways of life, and in the early years of the twentieth century desertion by Jewish husbands became disturbingly evident on the Lower East Side. In 1903 and 1904 the United Hebrew Charities of New York handled more than one thousand applications for relief that came from deserted wives, and by 1905 the organization was using 15 percent of its relief budget to ameliorate problems caused by desertion.[45]

Some of those problems are illustrated in a letter from a young wife and mother to the *Jewish Daily Forward* in 1908: "Max: . . . You lived with me for six years, during which time I bore you four children. And then you left me. Of the four children, only two remain, but you have made them living orphans. Who will bring them up? Who will support us? Have you no pity for your own flesh and blood? Consider what you are doing. My tears choke me and I cannot write any more."[46] The experience of Max's wife was not unique. In 1909 Jewish charities in New York spent $37,000, a significant sum in that era, for desertion relief. And by 1911 the Jewish community admitted the full seriousness of the problem by establishing the National Desertion Bureau, with headquarters in New York City.[47]

Husbands and wives often adjusted to the new environment at different rates. The husband who preceded his wife and family to America sometimes became so Americanized that he felt estranged from the greenhorns when they finally arrived, and desertion beckoned. Others simply "forgot" they were married and took American wives. Perhaps some men, embarrassed by their inability to provide satisfactorily for their families, fled in shame. A boarder could also be a source of trouble. "Scandal is never far off where a boarder works his way in," according to a *Forward* article in 1906.[48]

For some men like Yekl (Jake) in Abe Cahan's novel of the same name, divorce was the way out, and the traditionally close-knit Jewish family on the Lower East Side produced, for a few years at least, one of the highest divorce rates in the city. Various Jewish charities in New York made some effort to deal with this problem. Several organizations sponsored workrooms, which provided job training and day care for unskilled, divorced, widowed, or deserted mothers of young children. But most of these workrooms were short-lived and could, in any case, employ only a small proportion of the needy women.

The problems created by divorce and desertion were acute. In 1913, nearly 20 percent of the Jewish children housed by municipal institutions in New York City were from deserted families, and one of every two inmates of juvenile reformatories was a child from a broken home. Even those children who remained with their mothers and siblings suffered from neglect and the need to help supplement their families' incomes.[49]

Although the great majority of Jewish men remained with their wives and children, the trauma of migration and acculturation clearly took its toll on Jewish family life.[50] Desertion and divorce did great damage, but dissatisfaction and demoralization also battered and destabilized families that remained physically whole. The memoir literature suggests that, among the great majority of fathers who stayed with their families, significant numbers wrestled with the temptation to leave and were made tense and irritable by the struggle. Others, poorly paid and holding jobs lower in status than those they held in the old countries, appear to have suffered bewilderment and loss of hope. The problems were intensified by the difficulties of transplanting to America the forms and traditions of authority and obedience inherent in the Jewish religious culture of eastern Europe.

The resulting family destabilization made it more likely that some children would go astray and that some would become criminals as adults. Some Jews brought criminal histories and patterns of illegal behavior with them from the old countries; other Jewish criminals bore a "made in America" stamp. Historians now recognize that, whether attributable to Americanized second-generation youth or to immigrants already urbanized and felonious in eastern Europe, Jewish criminality in the late nineteenth century became an organic part of the communal life of the Lower East Side and other enclaves where Jews settled in large numbers.[51]

It is true that in 1898 Jews boasted the lowest rate in the nation for crimes of physical violence. But Jewish representation in white-collar crimes, such as fraud, forgery, and embezzlement, was considerably higher. Even here, however, the less serious but widespread violation of Sunday blue laws distorted the Jewish crime rate. More disturbing were charges by several important figures, including Progressive reformers, that Jews were dominant in vice rings. In an article published in 1908, New York City Police Commissioner Theodore A. Bingham claimed that "alien" Jews, amounting to only 25 percent of the population, furnished 50 percent of all the city's criminals. The claim was soon withdrawn as unfounded, but it continued to rankle, especially as it was repeated in other articles and government reports.[52]

Charges that Jews controlled the white slave trade, and stories of Jewish men with sexual prowess who lured girls into prostitution, probably had more to do with fevered imaginations and the fears of repressed patricians than with Jewish ghetto reality. But the heated Jewish reaction to these charges, particularly those in Commissioner Bingham's piece and in George Kibbe Turner's nativist and anti-Semitic article, "The Daughters of the Poor," suggests an element of truth.[53]

For several years before these articles were published, concerned discussion about East Side delinquency and vice had filled many columns in Yiddish newspapers. Moreover, there are enough accounts from Jewish and non-Jewish sources, including the extensive Lexow and Mazet investigations of the 1890s, to indicate that prostitution, gambling, and extortion rackets thrived in the Jewish district, as they did in every poor district in the city. These crimes probably were the perverse result of the American desire to rise as much as they were the result of deprivation. In any case, the names of Jewish gangsters like "Dopey Benny" (Benjamin Fein), "Gyp the Blood" (Harry Horowitz), and "Kid Dropper" (Nathan Kaplan) were well known in the community; and it was hard not to trip over the prostitutes who "sprawled indolently, their legs taking up half the pavement," on Allen Street.54

In public, Jewish leaders and spokesmen denied the connection between the Lower East Side Jewish community and crime and prostitution. But within the community itself, many had to admit the existence of the all-too-visible gangsters, pimps, and whores. The Hertz family, for example, were well-known owners and managers for over thirty years of a string of brothels on the Lower East Side. Mirroring the dynamics of more legitimate Jewish enterprises, "Mother Rosie" Hertz was joined in the business by her husband, Jacob, her brothers, and several cousins. The establishment by brothel owners and procurers of the Independent Benevolent Association, a mutual-aid society with traditional health and death benefits, which stood ready to render "assistance in case of necessity," is further indication of the rootedness of organized vice in the familiar structures of East Side life.55

As the possibilities in American enterprise became clearer, Jews seeking the quickest route to wealth found their way to more sophisticated crime. Isaac Zuker headed a Jewish arson ring, "Mother" Marm Mandelbaum acquired fame as a leading New York fence, and several young men showed a talent for gambling. "Big Tim" Sullivan, a boss of Tammany (the Democratic party machine in New York City) told Arnold Rothstein and his friend Herman Rosenthal, "You're smart Jew boys and you'll make out as gamblers. That business takes brains." Arnold Rothstein "made out"; by 1906 he had become something of a minor folk hero in the Jewish community and had acquired a twelve-million-dollar bankroll.56 In the summer of 1912, Herman Rosenthal was assassinated just after he revealed to authorities the existence of a vice ring operating with police protection on the Lower East Side. With the exception of Police Lieutenant Charles Becker, all of the major figures involved were Jewish.57

In the heated context of charges and disclosures in the period from Police Commissioner Bingham's report in 1908 to gambler Rosenthal's testimony in 1912, both vilifiers and defenders of the Lower East Side Jewish community used and misused data for their own purposes. The statistical picture remains muddy. Crime may very well have been a marginal phenomenon, confined to a relatively small proportion of ghetto dwellers; but that it had roots in the Jewish community and that it befouled the life of the East Side is undeniable.

No one was more disturbed by the revelations of Jewish crime in the downtown ghetto than uptown German Jews. Distressed by the political radicalism and religious Orthodoxy of eastern Europeans and repelled by their "strange ways and speech," German Jews saw their immorality and vice as a great threat to themselves. "If there should grow up in our midst a class of people abnormal and objectionable to our fellow citizens," read the proceedings of the Nineteenth Annual Convention of the Union of American Hebrew Congregations, "all of us will suffer. . . . the question is largely one of self-preservation."[58] Spurred by this insecurity, German Jewish leaders sponsored a series of programs to remake their coreligionists.

These uptowners were very taken with Israel Zangwill's play "The Melting Pot." They saw in it a reinforcement of their own proposed solution for the problems of downtown: the sooner immigrants from eastern Europe gave up their cultural distinctiveness and melted into the homogenized mass, the sooner anti-Semitism would also melt. One program designed in part to achieve this end was the attempt to disperse and deflect immigrants to the interior of the country. But because the Germans grossly underestimated the immigrants' pride in their cultural heritage and their need for the yiddishkayt, which only a concentrated Jewish population allows, experiments in removal were generally unsuccessful. The immigrants would have to be made over in place.

One of the major social and educational vehicles for remaking the eastern Europeans was the Educational Alliance. Leaders of the German Jewish community like Isidor Straus and Jacob Schiff brought about a merger of three agencies, the Hebrew Free School Association, the Young Men's Hebrew Association (YMHA), and the Aguilar Free Library Society. In 1891, the new organization moved into one large center in a five-story building on East Broadway and Jefferson Street. Hailed by its founders as a "center of sweetness and light, an oasis in the desert of degradation and despair," the community house was renamed the Educational Alliance in

1893. It was for several decades an important source of help to eastern European immigrants as well as a major source of friction and hostility between uptown and downtown Jews.[59]

German Jews poured money, time, and energy into the alliance's Americanization programs. But their efforts were accompanied by cultural arrogance. From 9 A.M. to 10 P.M., a wide range of social, cultural, and educational activities were held in classrooms, meeting rooms, the library, and an auditorium, which seated 700. A roof garden and a well-equipped gymnasium, installed to overcome eastern European Jew's "lack of courage and repugnance to physical work," were also in use a good part of the day. While adults were instructed in the "privileges and duties of American citizenship," youngsters were exposed to vocational training, courses in English and English literature, and lectures on American and ancient history. These classes were augmented by training in hygiene, sermons on virtue, and flag-waving exercises on the national holidays.

The German effort to Americanize the eastern Europeans paralleled the efforts of the Irish, who, as leaders of the American Catholic church, devoted vast energies and resources to the Americanization of other Catholic ethnics, particularly Italians and Poles. These efforts had met with resistance and an enduring intergroup hostility and conflict. But the Irish had feared that if the greenhorn Italians and Poles did not acculturate quickly, the Catholic church, which was a target of Protestant nativists, would continue to be regarded as alien, inferior, and un-American. Alliance leaders expressed similar fears over the "medieval Orthodoxy and anarchistic license . . . struggling for mastery [of the eastern Europeans], a people . . . apt to . . . become a moral menace." And likely, no doubt, to tar the uptowner with the brush of the ghetto.[60]

The Educational Alliance probably had an important impact on children, but for at least the first decade of its existence the institution remained literally alien to the adults of the East Side. English, German, and even Russian were spoken in the various citizen education courses, but Yiddish, the actual language of the ghetto, was not. Even at the alliance's People's Synagogue, religious services were conducted in Hebrew and German. Yiddish, the essence of Jewishness in immigrant eyes, remained taboo until shortly after the turn of the century. In the meantime, uptowners insisted that "the new immigrants must be Americanized in spite of themselves, in the mode prescribed by their friends and benefactors."[61]

From its inception, the Educational Alliance came under attack from immigrants of every stripe, who felt they had a culture of their own. In 1900, a group of eastern European Jewish intellectuals set up the short-lived Educational League as a rival institution, and in 1903 one of its founders, Jacob Gordin, wrote a biting parody of the uptowners, called "The Benefactors of the East Side." Immigrant audiences loved it.

Things began to change after the directorship of the alliance was assumed by David Blaustein in 1898. While the formal, stated objective of the alliance remained rapid Americanization, daily programs became more responsive to immigrant needs. Blaustein, himself an acculturated eastern European immigrant who had made his way through Harvard, was sensitive to the immigrants' desire to retain in the New World their cultural supports of language and folkways, religious rites and rituals.[62]

Blaustein and a handful of others eventually came to feel that the more established Jews might even learn something from their "clients." Indeed, by 1905 it was clear that the uptown Americanizers, more than the ghetto dwellers, had been reeducated. Louis Marshall, the prominent German Jewish attorney and philanthropist, admitted in a letter to a friend that the German Jews had "held themselves aloof . . . bringing gifts to people who did not seek [them]. . . . The work was done in such a manner as not only to give offense, but to arouse suspicion of the motives." [63] Marshall taught himself Yiddish to better understand and communicate with the immigrants, and the Educational Alliance lifted its ban on the language in order to help eastern Europeans become Americans in terms of their own Yiddish culture.

Classes held in Yiddish were enormously popular. "Belt-makers, button-hole makers . . . carpenters, cutters, cloak-makers, cigar-makers, [and] embroiderers" came regularly to lectures by the spellbinding Zionist preacher Zevi Hirsh Masliansky, as well as to classes in history, religion, music, and art. (Among the art students were Jacob Epstein, Ben Shahn, and Chaim Gross.) The alliance also increased its popularity by offering a wider variety of vocational training, as well as inexpensive, healthy lunches, free medical examinations, and free vacations in summer camps. As eastern European Jews began to play a more important role in managing and funding the alliance, and as German Jews softened the alliance's Americanizing pressures, the institution and its multidimensional programs became an accepted part of the ghetto world.[64]

Other institutions were created by the Jewish establishment to serve the needs of the ghetto, including Mount Sinai Hospital, which admitted 90 percent of its patients without charge, the Hebrew Orphan Asylum, and the Hebrew Technical Institute for boys and a school to teach domestic arts to girls, both sponsored by the Baron de Hirsch Fund. By 1895, in the heart of the depression that began in 1893, the budget of the United Hebrew Charities in New York, reflecting increased services for the newcomers, had reached the then astronomical sum of $116,000.[65]

The Clara de Hirsch Home, endowed by the baroness in 1897 to provide recreational facilities and vocational training for immigrant girls, soon took on the task of "uprooting the evil" of prostitution by providing young women, Jews and non-Jews, with decent living arrangements, opportunities for employment, and, occasionally, matchmaking. An even more important philanthropic and protective agency was the National Council of Jewish Women, founded in 1893. Female agents of the New York branch of the council were stationed at the New York port armed with pamphlets printed in English, German, and Yiddish warning immigrant girls of dangers and providing them with addresses in sixty cities where they could apply in case of need. The women helped new arrivals find residences in more than 250 towns and cities and made follow-up inquiries. The protection may at times have seemed like smothering, but the "good ladies of the Council and the Hirsch home well understood . . . the social matrix into which the young women landed."[66]

In addition to aid rendered by German Jewish organizations, there were significant efforts by German Jewish individuals to improve conditions in the ghetto. Isaac Seligman, for example, designed and funded the building of a model tenement on Cherry Street, and Felix Adler founded the city's first kindergarten on the Lower East Side. Both projects proved to be positive contributions to beleaguered downtown families. Although German Jews had for a long time been insufferably patronizing and had made little accommodation to the sensitivities of the immigrants, these immigrants ultimately benefited enormously from their philanthropy and even from some of their programs of "uplift."

In creating their philanthropic organizations and agencies, particularly the Educational Alliance, German Jews were very much influenced by the American settlement-house movement of the late 1880s and by such sincere and devoted settlement-house workers as Charles Stover and Jane Addams, who hoped to provide the poor with the social and cultural wherewithal to help themselves.

The very first settlement house in the United States, the Neighborhood

Guild, was founded in tenement rooms on the Lower East Side in 1886. In 1891 under the presidency of Seth Low of Columbia University (later to be mayor of New York City), the Neighborhood Guild became the University Settlement, which acquired a well-equipped five-story building at the corner of Eldridge and Ridge streets in 1898. By then "a picket line of settlements," including the Henry Street Settlement (formerly the Nurses' Settlement), the Educational Alliance, and the Madison Street Settlement House, was a familiar sight to ghetto dwellers.[67] Later, the Neighborhood House was created by the Sisterhood of the Spanish-Portuguese synagogue, Shearith Israel, primarily for Sephardic Jews from Turkey, Greece, Syria, and Arabia, who had immigrated to New York in the tens of thousands beginning in 1890. The Sephardim had all the problems of newcomers and several additional ones, stemming from the fact that they spoke Ladino (Judeo-Spanish) not Yiddish, and that most existing Jewish organizations hardly recognized them as Jews.[68]

Although some settlement workers from patrician and middle-class families were paternalistic and judgmental toward the poor and the immigrants, most were genuinely sympathetic. Moreover, many of these workers were astute Progressives, convinced that the ameliorative work in which they were engaged would be less effective if not accompanied by structural change in the society. As Jane Addams put it, settlement workers had to "arouse and interpret the public opinion of neighborhoods . . . furnish data for legislation and even use their influence to secure it."[69] It was no accident that many political activists in favor of progressive change at state and national levels in the 1920s and 1930s, like Herbert Lehman, Belle and Henry Moskowitz, Eleanor Roosevelt, and Frances Perkins, had earlier been connected to the settlement-house movement.

The impact of settlement work on the Lower East Side was often deeply felt on the local and individual level. Among the first goals of the settlements were the creation of small parks and playgrounds, the building of more schools, and the wider use of school facilities as recreational centers and clubrooms. Some contemporary historians and sociologists complain that these reforms were intended as social control, but relatively few complaints were heard from ghetto youngsters.[70]

Settlement-house workers were role models as well as play supervisors and, undoubtedly, powerful forces for Americanization. But one of the settlement movement's greatest contributions lay "in its insisting that immigrants preserve the customs and traditions of the old country." Workers assured "immigrants that it was not necessary to reject the past to become an American." They also tried to attenuate alienation between parents and their children by reinforcing cultural self-respect through festival pageants and folk art.[71]

One of the most notable settlement-house social workers was Cincinnati-born Lillian Wald (1867–1940). A nurse and the founder of the Henry Street Settlement, Wald grew into "a figure of legend, known and adored on every street" on the Lower East Side. In 1893, Wald, the daughter of a German Jewish bourgeois family, moved with another nurse into a small East Side apartment on Jefferson Street. The two young women made themselves available to anyone asking for aid, whether or not they were able to pay. Needless to say, their tasks were endless. Help in defraying costs came from Jacob Schiff, the German Jewish philanthropist; and a growing number of nurses volunteered their services or worked for nominal pay. Larger quarters were soon necessary, and the Nurses' Settlement was founded in 1895. As her work proved successful, Lillian Wald's reputation grew, and she used it to persuade the city to start a program of public nursing and to put nurses into the public schools. In addition, she actively opposed child labor, supported the playground movement, lined up with the striking cloak makers in 1910, and was a committed pacifist during World War I.

Even as she became a figure of wide renown, Lillian Wald remained dedicated to her East Side neighbors. Within this narrow Jewish world, she was expert at creating links between Germans and eastern Europeans, and she continued to work at gaining the confidence of the former on behalf of the latter.[72] Other attempts to forge links between the two groups were not so successful. Although uptowners and downtowners were often able to put aside some of their mutual hostility and cooperate with one another, a measure of misunderstanding and antagonism continued to mark their relationship and stood in the way of a unified Jewish community in New York.

In response to New York City Police Commissioner Theodore Bingham's accusations in 1908 about the extent of criminality on the Lower East Side, a movement emerged to establish a Jewish communal self-government in New York. Called *kehillah,* to tap into the more successful attempts at communal self-government in sixteenth- through eighteenth-century Russia and Poland, the New York experiment brought hundreds of organizations together in a loosely knit confederation that lasted from 1908 to 1922.

But it never matched its historical namesake in reach or power. While the kehillah did useful work, notably in philanthropy and Jewish education, it failed to fulfill its founders' goal, which, according to the kehillah's foremost historian, Arthur Goren, was to control the unruly ghetto by "molding New York Jewry into a single, integrated community."[73]

Conflicting ideologies—Orthodoxy, Reform Judaism, Zionism, and socialism—contributed to the undoing of the centralized organization. But ultimately, the kehillah did not matter much in the life of immigrant Jews. It was not their own; it was a "Jewish social pacifier" that came from on high, rather than from immigrant experience and vision. The kehillah failed to endure, not because the immigrants were incorrigibly unruly, but because established Jews—Germans and acculturated eastern Europeans—exaggerated the need for order and self-discipline in the ghetto and insisted that the solution to disorder lay in a monolithic hierarchy. The kehillah was more distant, more abstract, and shackled with more organization than the familiar institutions that the immigrants had built for themselves.

Dislocation and poverty, particularly in the early years before a substantial Jewish community had become rooted on the Lower East Side, produced a significant measure of crime, prostitution, desertion, and divorce. But from the start, Jewish immigrants created a web of voluntary organizations and improvised a viable and decentralized pattern for their collective existence. In spite of the disturbing new influences and internal stresses, Jewish immigrants sustained general tranquility and order in the ghetto. The family, the shul, the landsmanshaft, the club, the mutual-aid society, the café, the union, and even many workplaces were arenas of genuine interaction and psychological sustenance. Within these immigrant enclaves, protected from some of the chaos and brutality of the outside world, Jews in association with one another could find support from the Old World and the New. Here they could achieve a sense of order and remake their identities at their own pace.

Informal social networks—neighbors on the block, the rooftop gathering, the group at the candy store—provided some of the same interaction and mutual support. Adolph Held, Yiddish journalist and New York City alderman (1917-19), recognized the importance of both formal and informal association. "Our people are social minded," Held said, noting that they "immediately formed clubs . . . societies, [and] landsmanshaftn."

Jews also congregated on "the sidewalk . . . one of the great islands of Jewish youth" and, like the rooftop, "a terrific agency of communication."[74]

The tenement hallways were also places for communication. More than a few immigrants recalled that

> if you went to the sink to fetch water, you were bound to meet a neighbor or two. . . . Someone . . . would have a cooking pot to fill. And usually a mother would be waiting to fill a tub for her youngsters' baths. Getting the water was important, but just as important was the chance to talk—or listen. Papa called the halls our "talking newspapers." Here was where the gossip was passed around about who was getting married, or expecting a baby, who was ill or dying.[75]

The quintessential association was the family. As we have seen, the family was already challenged in the old country and was seriously beleaguered in the ghetto. But it demonstrated remarkable resilience. Jewish emigration was preeminently a family emigration. Most immigrants made the journey with relatives or came to kin already in the United States; and Jewish families continued to be mutually supportive once they reconstituted themselves here. Pearl Halpern, for example, recalled that, when her husband joined her in America in 1909, "we took in my grandmother, who had already been here. And she took care of my baby when I went out to work."[76]

Families also influenced the nature of the workplace. Garment workers often brought relatives into the factory, instructed them in work routines, and sustained them during slack seasons. Sam Rubin, who came to America in 1908, remembered: "My brother-in-law was an operator and he took me into his shop and he taught me how to be an operator. . . . [He] tried to give me a few dollars more than I was able to earn. . . . My sister gave me food and drink. And when it got slack, she even gave me a few dollars in my pocket."[77]

At the heart of the family were the immigrant parents who, within the cramped apartments, loved, ruled, and tried to protect. The mother, especially in the early years of a family's life in America, appears to have coped best with the strange new world of the tumultuous American city and, through her scrappiness and strength, frequently was able to hold things together. Zalmen Yoffeh tenderly recalled his mother:

> [With] one dollar a day [she] fed and clothed an ever-growing family. She made all our clothes. She walked blocks to reach a place where

meat was a penny cheaper, where bread was a half cent less. She collected boxes and old wood to burn in the stove instead of costly coal. Her hands became hardened and the lines so begrimed that for years she never had perfectly clean hands. One by one she lost her teeth—there was no money for dentists—and her cheeks caved in. Yet we children always had clean and whole clothing. There was always bread and butter in the house, and wonder of wonders, there was usually a penny apiece for us to buy candy.[78]

For the immigrant mother and her family, food remained a central concern. So central was food in fact that Jewish wives and mothers occasionally picketed, boycotted, and even used physical coercion in the face of rising food costs. In early May 1902, for example, when the retail price of kosher meat soared from twelve cents to eighteen cents a pound, while butchers ignored the ensuing protests, immigrant Jewish women organized the Ladies Anti-Beef Trust Association and took to the streets.

"These women were in earnest," observed the *New York Herald*. "For days they had been considering the situation, and when they decided on action, they perfected an organization, elected officers . . . and even went so far as to take coins from their slender purses until there was an expense fund of eighty dollars with which to carry on the fight."[79] The women carried on the fight by staging a successful three-week boycott of kosher meat shops throughout the Lower East Side, parts of upper Manhattan and the Bronx, and Brooklyn. The boycott sometimes led to violent scuffles, the breaking of butcher shop windows, and the dousing of meat with kerosene, but there was no looting. When one of the women was arrested and charged with rioting, she responded, "We don't riot. But if all we did was weep at home, nobody would notice it. We have to do something to help ourselves."[80]

In organizing and participating in the kosher meat protests, immigrant Jewish women were not only acting out of a traditional sensibility that legitimated action in the face of unfair prices for food, nor were they merely following the nineteenth-century eastern European precedent of passive resistance to the *korobke,* or meat tax. These Jewish housewives were also using modern tactics. They addressed themselves to the labor movement and to socialists, as well as to the constituencies of the shuln and landsmanshaftn. And they won enduring sympathy and support from both the *Jewish Daily Forward,* a socialist paper, and the *Yiddishe Tageblatt,* an Orthodox religious daily.[81]

The organizational techniques of these activists and their strategies for mobilization are evidence of a relatively sophisticated political mentality. That mentality was in evidence again during the depression of 1907–8, when in response to rent increases, Lower East Side women staged rent strikes and mobilized hundreds of others to join them. Jewish women in Cleveland organized a kosher meat strike in 1906, and Jewish women in Detroit organized one in 1910.[82]

The boycotting and striking women had begun to grasp their power as consumers and domestic managers and, in the issues of high-priced food and shelter, temporarily found a vehicle for political organization. Many Jewish women, as we shall see presently, also organized and participated in larger social and political movements. But the majority of Jewish wives and mothers, except for occasional forays like the kosher meat protests and rent strikes, stayed close to home, particularly the kitchen.

It was from her kitchen that the Jewish housewife, although later the butt of jokes and the target of anger, inspired generations of sons and daughters. Alfred Kazin in his wonderfully evocative memoir of Brownsville, wrote that "the kitchen gave a special character to our lives, my mother's character. All my memories of that kitchen are dominated by the nearness of my mother sitting all day long at her sewing machine. . . . The kitchen was her life. Year by year, as I began to take in her fantastic capacity for labor and her anxious zeal, I realized it was ourselves she kept stitching together."[83]

Several other Jewish sons, particularly novelist Henry Roth, have given us remarkable portraits of mothers in kitchens, nourishing families with food and love. For daughters, on the other hand, the kitchen was often unremitting drudgery. Whether or not they had paying jobs, girls were expected to help with the housework. Cooking, cleaning, ironing, helping with the younger children, and assisting in the piecework that was the mainstay of so many households meant long hours of toil in the kitchen. Yet it was in the same kitchen that deep psychological and emotional attachments were made between mothers and daughters. As historian Sydney Stahl Weinberg put it: "Mothers could offer little useful advice to daughters on how to behave as young single women, but they set important examples in understanding how to approach life, care for a family's physical and psychological needs, and relate to people." Many daughters "learned to achieve satisfaction from such a life."[84]

Jewish immigrant mothers, as we have seen, usually stayed home. The number of married women working in factories or shops was very small: only 2 percent of eastern European immigrant households reported working wives in 1880, and only 1 percent by 1905. These figures are undoubtedly low, particularly if we include in "working wives" all those women who were partners in small businesses or who took up pushcart operations. Many wives were gainfully employed, but they often did their work at home, where they could continue to nurture their families. Women kept boarders, looked after other women's children, took in laundry, and did piecework in their apartments. Moreover, because many immigrant families lived behind or above their stores, women could shuttle between the store and their domestic duties.[85]

One of those duties was preparing for the Sabbath. It was necessary to have the apartment clean, the best meal of the week prepared, the challah baked, or at least bought, and the wine and candles ready. Although transplantation to America accelerated the fragmentation of Jewish religious culture, a process that had begun in eastern Europe, many Jews tried to hold fast to tradition. Religious sensibility and observance and religious institutions were constantly assaulted by the secular temptations and economic rhythms of American life on the Lower East Side. Yet religious tradition continued to help maintain the equilibrium of many Jews. On Friday nights, with the frenetic workweek finished, decorum reigned again in thousands of immigrant households. In the glow of the Sabbath candles, the whole family could eat together and experience "the pleasure of doing things as everyone knew they should be done."[86]

It is true that in the 1880s and 1890s, the religious community in the ghetto could not provide the organization or the environment for sustaining Orthodox Judaism. The busy city and "the busy season" made it difficult to pray three times a day, to obey the dietary laws with any strictness, or to adhere to numerous other religious regulations. Old World rebbes, who acted as teachers, offered no inspiring model for the children, and religious education was sadly neglected. The question of religious observance became the heart of the generational conflict among the pious, as secular America increasingly beckoned to the young.

By the second decade of the twentieth century, however, many traditional Jews recognized that, in order not to lose their children to secularism entirely, they would have to make accommodations. "We seek," one Jew explained, "to deal effectively and happily with the great task of Americanization . . . in such a way that [it] will not mean the alienation from the principles and practices of traditional Judaism."[87] The Young Israel movement, established on the Lower East Side in 1912, also aimed to develop what would later come to be called Modern Orthodoxy. Within a few years several thousand members were attracted to the movement, where one could feel "thoroughly American and at the same time a true, whole-hearted and loyal . . . Jew."[88]

Although the religious life of observant Jews did not show many signs of vitality on the Lower East Side before 1910, the ghetto's six hundred religious congregations testify to the "authenticity of the Jewish religious imperative to worship," as well as to care for one's own. Many of the shuln on the Lower East Side had developed around landslayt, groups of Jews from the same eastern European towns, and these shuln often operated as mutual-aid societies. Most often, landslayt groups went on to form officially registered landsmanshaftn. Some were independent; most were connected to synagogues, unions, extended family circles, or fraternal orders.[89]

As early as 1892 there were eighty-seven eastern European landsmanshaftn, and by 1910 there were more than two thousand, representing over nine hundred European cities and towns and embracing virtually every Jewish family in New York City. All landsmanshaftn maintained at least a link to the old-country location, particularly in times of crisis, when the shtetlekh from which they sprang were in need of material relief. All maintained a continuation of important communal services, such as burial arrangements and poor relief, as well as a context for a shared expression of nostalgia.[90]

Equally important, the landsmanshaft was a context for reconciling American and eastern European identities. It served as a sanctuary from the strains of acculturation, ambition, and even ideology. And it gave the immigrants a breathing space, a place to be themselves, a place to continue the tradition of tzedakah and self-help, and also a place to play a game of pinochle. At the same time, it resembled an American fraternal order, with its rites and constitutions, its camaraderie, and its opportunity for "doing a little business."[91]

As early as 1901 some landsmanshaftn changed their names. The Independent Young Men of Poniewiez became the Young Men's Association of Manhattan, because they had "no desire to be identified with Russia, or any town in Russia." Most immigrants, however, even after many years in America, still thought of themselves in terms of reference points in the old countries, and their landsmanshaftn kept their original names. They Americanized in other ways. The Kalushiner Society, for example, reported that it had "long given up the idea of being isolated, divided from general Jewish life in America. . . . Its hand is extended to the many other Jewish organizations in America."[92] Other landsmanshaftn Americanized by enlarging their scope *and* changing their names. In 1911 the Ekaterinoslow Ladies Charity Society became the Ladies Charity Society of New York in order "to enlarge the field of its charity . . . to include not only those worthy of charity who originally came from the town of Ekaterinoslow, but to all who may need it in the city of New York."[93]

The world of the landsmanshaft very much reflected the broader themes of American Jewish life and clearly was not a mere nostalgic "brotherhood of memory." The landsmanshaft was a vehicle for mutual aid, philanthropy, health services, insurance, credit, and relaxation; and it was a pit stop of sorts, at which immigrants could refuel and then go on to confront the new society around them.[94]

The strong ethnic and religious ties and the need for mutual aid, which gave birth to the landsmanshaftn, also promoted the creation of other institutions. Eastern Europeans in New York City founded many hospitals, orphanages, and nursing homes that observed Jewish dietary laws and had Yiddish-speaking doctors—including, in 1890, Beth Israel Hospital, which was specifically designed "to meet the peculiar needs of [the] sick poor among the Jewish immigrant population." By 1910 nearly every neighborhood of the city where Jews lived had its own Jewish hospital.[95] In addition there were so many new synagogues, political organizations, labor union locals, philanthropic organizations, loan societies, credit unions, and educational institutions that eastern European Jews, by the second decade of the twentieth century, possessed a more elaborate organizational structure than any other ethnic group in America.

Most of the organizations represented a creative merger of Jewish and American precepts and patterns. Jews were influenced by teachings that gave tzedakah high priority. American-Jewish communities in the early twentieth century were successors of European communities with centuries of experience in helping members through hard times. After the decline of the kehillot in the Old World, charity organizations and mutual-benefit societies were created in European Jewish communities and carried to America by immigrants. The open, less-structured quality of the New World further stimulated the development of these voluntary organizations. Thus, these organizations were not extensions or replications of traditional cultural forms but a reshaping of those forms in a New World context.

Many of the institutions created by eastern European Jews became vital elements in the new transitional culture. Outstanding in this respect was the American Yiddish theater, which also had its origins in the Old World. Performances and skits by Jews were developed in the 1870s as part of a Jewish cultural revival and were centered in the active secular Jewish café life of Jassy, Romania, where Abraham Goldfaden, the father of Yiddish theater, held sway.[96] By the early 1880s many impoverished Yiddish theater companies were performing in wine cellars scattered throughout the larger cities of eastern Europe. But actors suffered harassment from both czarist government officials and Jewish Orthodoxy. Numerous theater people, including Goldfaden's troupe, immigrated to the United States after 1883, when the Yiddish theater was banned by Alexander III in the despotic aftermath of the assassination of Alexander II.

In effect, Yiddish theater arrived in New York City in its infancy and was nurtured there at the turn of the century by its greatest audience—the largest, most heterogeneous aggregation of Jews in the world. In the early years in America, the Yiddish theater overflowed with "corrupt and foolish versions" of the European repertoire as well as "vivid junk and raw talent." It took hold in the public mind only after many trials. But with the emergence of playwrights like Jacob Gordin and actors like Boris and Bessie Thomashevsky and Jacob Adler, larger and larger audiences were attracted. By 1900 there were three major theater troupes in New York City and numerous smaller endeavors in other Jewish population centers. From the late 1890s to World War I, the works of Shakespeare, Ibsen, and Strindberg were adapted to the needs of the immigrant culture, and a flamboyant style of acting was developed. One critic observed that, more than anything else, Yiddish theater, with its overstatement and ritual pageantry, resembled Italian opera without singing.

The theater came to enjoy an unrivaled position on the Lower East Side; it became a major cultural institution, in which all the problems, hopes, and dreams of immigrant Jews were dramatized. The Yiddish theater provided a collective experience for the entire community. It was also a powerful vehicle for fund-raising. Philanthropic, mutual-aid, and labor organizations often sponsored benefit performances. Ticket prices ranged from twenty-five cents to a dollar, not a small outlay for immigrant laborers, but somehow thousands managed to pay it. By 1918 the city boasted twenty Yiddish theaters, which, in a single year—before the inroads of movies—attracted two million patrons to over a thousand performances.[97] Hutchins Hapgood, a keen and sensitive observer and devotee of East Side culture, wrote that Jews of every station and persuasion came to the theater: "The Jews of all the ghetto classes—the sweatshop woman with her baby, the day laborer, the small Hester Street shopkeeper, the Russian Jewish anarchist and socialist, the ghetto Rabbi and scholar, the poet, the journalist. The poor and ignorant are in the great majority, but the learned, the intellectual, and the progressive are also represented."[98]

Although Jewish intellectuals and socialists considered the Yiddishized classics, along with the musical melodramas of Joseph Lateiner and Morris Horowitz, to be *shunde* (trashy), the practice of adaptation led the way to better drama on the Yiddish stage. Jacob Gordin began in 1890 to reform the Yiddish theater according to the best traditions of the Russian theater. He succeeded, to some extent in educating actors and audiences to appreciate sincerity on the stage. But the playwright was also influenced by theatergoers; in his later plays, Gordin inserted comic and musical intrusions as part of the dramatic action.[99]

The involvement of the audience was total and fervent. Crying, always part of an evening at the Yiddish theater, was cathartic for the bone-weary workers who made up most of the house. Laughter at characters with familiar problems was just as prevalent as tears and helped immigrants recognize their own strength and motivation to hold on—even to succeed. Patrons ate and drank, exchanged loud remarks, and unabashedly cheered and hissed. Sometimes they openly jeered actors who lit cigarettes or cigars on stage on Friday night, even while the protestors themselves were obviously not observing the Sabbath, either.[100] Occasionally, patrons yelled out advice, particularly at critical points in the many plays about family conflict. One man was so moved by Jacob Adler's performance in the *The Jewish King Lear,* that he ran down the aisle shouting: "To hell with your stingy daughter, Yankl! She has a stone, not a heart. Spit on her, Yankl, and come home with me. My yidene [Jewish wife] will feed you. Come Yankl, may she choke, that rotten daughter of yours."[101]

Family life and its problems preoccupied Jewish playwrights. Leon Kobrin's comedy *The Next Door Neighbors* dealt with the difficulties faced by a couple who did not immigrate together, and Gordin's *Mirele Efros* (also known as the *Jewish Queen Lear*), a melodrama about a self-sacrificing mother, "instructed" members of the audience to respect their parents. These plays of Gordin and Kobrin, as well as those of David Pinski, Sholom Aleichem, I. L. Peretz, Sholom Asch, and others were performed innumerable times over several decades and were enormously popular with parents and children.[102]

Popularity was largely a result of the fact that stage characters faced problems similar to those of every immigrant: How to be an American *and* a Jew? How to protect the family from destabilization, and religious values from disintegration, in a secular, seemingly normless society? How to enjoy the opportunities for material success in America without giving up the spiritual values of Judaism? These were the questions that befuddled people who were still very much part of two worlds, and the Yiddish theater, like many other transitional East Side Jewish institutions, helped immigrants deal with those questions, in this case by portraying them on stage.

The Yiddish theater also encouraged members of the audience to feel connected to both the American and the Jewish worlds. Patrons felt pride in their Jewishness, as Jewish playwrights and actors expressed Jewish vitality. And Jewish playgoers shared the patriotic enthusiasm of the general American public when they cheered Boris Thomashevsky in *Der Yidisher Yenki Dudl,* or applauded the song "Three Cheers for Yankee Doodle," typical genre pieces.[103] By combining aspects of Old World culture, American culture, and the transitional culture of the ghetto, and by dealing with many of the immigrant dilemmas of that transitional culture, the Yiddish theater held up a mirror to its audiences. It helped them gain a better understanding of their role in the historical process of relocation, and it gave them greater insight into the problems of creating new identities in the New World.

It was possible, as Lincoln Steffens observed, to enjoy the Yiddish theater without knowing Yiddish. But virtually all eastern European immigrants spoke Yiddish. The Yiddish of the Galicians, Poles, and Romanians used different vowels from Lithuanian Yiddish, and Hungarians spoke a variant of Yiddish that was closer to German. But Yiddish was the lingua franca of the East Side, and its growth and development there in the 1880s and 1890s helped Jews of various nationalities feel more like one people.[104]

Lithuanians came to outnumber other Yiddish-speaking groups in the 1880s and inspired the initial attempts to mold a more uniform language. Lithuanian scholar Alexander Harkavy made extraordinary efforts in this regard. He developed a very successful English-Yiddish dictionary, which ran through a dozen editions, and later, "gathering the stray words of the language," Harkavy compiled the first Yiddish-Yiddish dictionary, which eventually replaced the *deitchmerish* versions (dictionaries of Yiddish heavily laden with German vocabulary). Fellow Lithuanian Abraham Cahan and other journalists and writers from the region gave literary currency to the Lithuanian idiom and reinforced its dominance.[105]

Intellectuals and political radicals also had an important role to play in the creation of a reformulated and revitalized Yiddish in New York. Some of this had already been under way in the Old World, where Yiddishists contributed mightily to Jewish cultural revival and Bundists tried to reach the masses in their own language. But as we have seen, there had been little place for Jewish intellectuals, poets, writers, and political activists in the general social and cultural life of eastern European countries. Therefore, unlike the intellectuals and activists of many other nationalities, Jewish intellectuals and activists came to the United States along with the masses and helped enrich the Yiddish culture that ordinary immigrants built here.

As in eastern Europe, many intellectuals and political activists at first viewed Yiddish as merely a useful tool for "enlightening" the masses, but they soon helped develop the language into a compelling means of discourse. Yiddish eventually became a vehicle for Americanization and, ultimately (and ironically), for its own demise. But the continuing mass immigration, the momentum of Yiddish literary activity, and the involvement of Yiddish in the progressive social and political movements of the early twentieth century invigorated the language beyond all expectation.

In New York City, the hub of the Yiddish-American universe, over 150 Yiddish dailies, weeklies, monthlies, quarterlies, festival journals, and yearbooks appeared between 1885 and 1914. Some twenty dailies came into existence during that period, and for a time, at the turn of the century, as many as six competed simultaneously for readers. The *Tageblatt,* founded in 1885, represented the Orthodox religious point of view. The *Morgen Journal* was also Orthodox and was the first (1901) truly successful Yiddish morning paper. The 1890s saw the beginning of the *Forvarts* (*Jewish Daily Forward*), a socialist paper, which, under the guiding hand of Abraham Cahan, became the largest Yiddish newspaper in the world. In the same decade the *Freie Arbeiter Shtime* was born, representing the anarchists. Even the weekly *La America* (1910–25), a Ladino paper for Sephardic readers, printed a Yiddish column to attract advertisers in the greater eastern European community.[106]

Almost all Yiddish periodicals carried literary pieces. Translated tales of adventure and romance, like *The Count of Monte Cristo* and *Don Quixote,* were very popular. Readers even took the time to struggle with translations from Turgenev, Tolstoy, and Zola, and to try to follow the original Yiddish work of I. L. Peretz and Mendele Mokher Sforim. But "all could take instant delight in the homely tales of Sholom Aleichem" and feel the pathos of Morris Rosenfeld's "sweatshop lyrics."[107] Zalman Libin's portraits of life in the tenements and sweatshops and Jacob Gordin's naturalistic sketches were featured in the more radical journals. Buttonhole maker David Edelstadt, who for a short time edited the *Freie Arbeiter Shtime,* and Morris Winchevsky, who published the first socialist pamphlets to appear in Yiddish, also wrote labor poems for the press and won a wide readership.

A group of poets called *Di yunge* (the young ones)—Mani Lieb, Moishe Lieb Halpern, H. Leivick, and others—were linked for a time by their desire to write poetry that was not ideological. The majority of *Di yunge* were still shop workers, but they wanted to develop a freer, more personal poetry that would liberate them from what poet Zisha Landau called "the rhyme department of the labor movement." And they, too, made their first appearances in the Yiddish press.[108]

Whether politically conservative or radical, whether theologically Orthodox or secular, the Yiddish press was often sensationalist and extremist, lashing out at capitalism, socialism, Jewish institutions, or competing papers. Despite this tendency, all soon realized that something remarkable had developed. As Abe Cahan pointed out, "the five million Jews living under the czar had not a single Yiddish daily paper even when the government allowed such publication, while [Russian Jews] in America publish six dailies . . . countless Yiddish weeklies and monthlies, and [enough] books [to make] New York the largest Yiddish book market in the world."[109]

Although it promoted a serious modern Yiddish literature, the press was also a powerfully effective agent of acculturation, nourishing the process of Americanization for the Jewish masses in their own language. Poems and stories dealing with the realities of America and the difficulties of adjustment helped the immigrants understand their new environment and to be less "green." Yiddish newspapers focused on specifically Jewish problems, but editorially they frequently commented on purely American issues. They consistently emphasized the acquisition or development of "desirable" qualities and manners, "taught" American history and geography, and made untiring efforts in correcting civic "deficiencies" in their readers.[110]

Even Abe Cahan's *Forward,* which was dedicated to the propagation of socialism, was equally dedicated to Americanization. As early as 1903, Cahan advised immigrant parents to let Jewish "boys play baseball and become excellent at the game." After all, he admonished, we ought not "raise the children to grow up foreigners in their own birthplace."[111] Cahan was a moderate socialist, whose anticapitalist views were tempered by American conditions. His paper, which excluded theoretical pieces and instead presented the class struggle in the form of stories and news from the marketplace, home, and factory, remained attractive to nonsocialist Jews. At its height, the *Forward* published twelve metropolitan editions from Boston to Los Angeles, with a circulation of a half million (more than a quarter million in New York City alone).[112]

The masses devoured the information and advice that the *Forward* and other papers gave them about life in America. One of the *Forward*'s best-read innovations was the bintl brief (bundle of letters), started in 1906. Letters from readers—often corrected and shortened by editors, and per-haps on slower days entirely concocted by them—were printed daily. It was a marvelous outlet for immigrants troubled by the tensions of a new life and an affirmation that their problems mattered. They wrote about poverty and sickness, love and divorce, unemployment, intermarriage, conflicts of opin-ion, socialism, generational conflicts, declining religious observance, and just about everything else. The responses, written solely by Cahan in the early years and, later by his staff as well, tried to suggest that the immigrants should not make excessive demands on themselves, that they should even enjoy life a little bit. The editors did not advise immigrants to give up their religious or ideological preconceptions entirely, but they did encourage them to make the needs of everyday life primary.[113]

Yiddish papers, as part of the Americanization process, also tried to acquaint their readers with English. Cahan, opening himself to the charge of corrupting the Yiddish language, encouraged his writers to follow the general custom of incorporating English words into their Yiddish articles. The *Tageblatt* went further; it began printing a full English page in 1897. These practices no doubt influenced ghetto conversation. By 1900 the im-migrants were mingling an estimated one hundred English words in their daily speech. *Politzman*, *never mind*, *alle right*, *that'll do*, and other idioms slipped readily from the tongue.[114]

At the same time that the Yiddish press acted as an Americanizing agent, it was, like the Yiddish theater, and the landsmanshaft, and so many other Jewish immigrant institutions, an important part of the transitional, religiously based, ethnic culture of the Lower East Side. This culture, sus-tained by the largest, freest, and most heterogeneous Jewish community in the world, became a Yiddish culture richer and greater than any achieved in eastern Europe.

Producers and disseminators of the vibrant Yiddish culture of the ghetto often met in small restaurants and cafés to eat, talk, and argue. The staff of the *Jewish Daily Forward* were daytime regulars at the Garden Café on East Broadway. In the evenings, writers and poets left their factories and shops to gather in the Café Royale on Second Avenue, in the basement café Zum Essex on Rutgers Square, or in Sachs' Café on Norfolk Street.[115]

"At most hours of the day and night," Hutchins Hapgood reported, "these places are filled with men who have come here to sip Russian tea out of tumblers, meet their friends, and discuss everything under heaven. . . . It is Bohemia."[116] Hapgood also correctly sensed the dominant "socialistic feeling . . . in these cafés," but as writer Harry Roskolenko, who sold papers to the tea-sipping patrons, observed about his customers, they were not ideological purists:

> Ideas about God, the synagogue, the union, intermeshed. It was difficult, then, for me to see how men could be two things—like Zionist-anarchists; or Zionists who were also atheists; or socialists who were Zionists and atheists. It was like a chess game—with no rules. . . .
> Who was not at least two or three separate spiritual and physical entities on the Lower East Side? My father managed socialism, Orthodoxy and Zionism, quite easily, and so did the kibitzers and the serious.[117]

To most immigrants, the cafés probably seemed exotic, perhaps even frivolous, appropriate for free thinkers who "had nothing to do during the day" and who could stay up late into the night, but not for workers who had to rise early to earn a living. What many workers did take seriously were the endless streams of lectures and public meetings sponsored by the Socialists, the Zionists, the unions, the Board of Education, the People's Institute at Cooper Union, and the Educational Alliance. A "certain grandeur of aspiration" was to be found in these people, who toiled long hours in the shops and then somehow mustered the energy to drag themselves to evening lectures in pursuit of learning. On the Lower East Side, learning for its own sake or for the sake of future generations or for the social revolution all merged into one explosion of self-discovery.[118]

Those who mastered at least the rudiments of English often attended the public night school. In 1906 Jews constituted a majority of the hundred thousand students enrolled in New York City evening classes. Almost 40 percent of the students were women. "I admit that I cannot be satisfied to be just a wife and mother," one woman wrote to the *Forward*. "I am still young and I want to learn and enjoy life. My children and my home are not neglected, but I go to evening high school twice a week."[119]

The virtual craze among Jewish adults for secular education appears to have been part of a general release of energy that for generations in the Old World had to be suppressed. The passion for learning that adults displayed was instilled in their children. According to immigrant writer Mary Antin, and repeated in every autobiography, Jewish parents brought their boys and girls to the first day of school "as if it were an act of consecration," and parental encouragement was sustained throughout the child's school career.[120]

The respect and drive for education partly explains Jewish economic and occupational mobility and can help us understand why a dispropor-tionate number of immigrants achieved professional status relatively early. There was no large-scale social ascent to the professions in the immigrant generation or even in the second generation, but by 1907 the number of Jewish doctors making a living on the Lower East Side had doubled to two hundred since the 1880s, and the number of lawyers increased almost as fast. There were also 115 Jewish pharmacists and 175 Jewish dentists serving the ghetto.[121]

Success in small business actually played a more important role than education in the relatively rapid mobility of the Jewish immigrant genera-tion. This was particularly true in Jewish communities of the American interior, where immigrants were less dependent on the garment industry. But it was also the case in New York. As we have seen, thousands of East Siders were involved in the pushcart trade and subcontracting, and hun-dreds more had groceries, butcher shops, candy stores, and bakeries. Al-though many of these businesses remained marginal, some entrepreneurs advanced enough to constitute the beginning of a middle class.[122]

As early as the 1890s the apparel trade and the real estate business also became arenas for immigrant energy and aspiration. By 1905 German Jewish manufacturers and landlords were virtually replaced by eastern European Jews. It was the "Russian-Jewish employer" who hired the "Rus-sian-Jewish laborer," wrote immigrant economist and statistician, I. M. Rubinow in 1905; and it was the "Russian-Jewish landlord" who collected "his exorbitant rent" from the "Russian-Jewish tenement dweller."[123] The vast majority of gainfully employed Jews on the Lower East Side did not be-come manufacturers or property owners; they remained proletarians for at least one generation. But the Jewish middle class was clearly growing. Consumption patterns on the Lower East Side reflected the growing affluence of the immigrant generation as well as the desire of Jews to Americanize. Significant numbers of families, pursuing both the sanctification of the home and the American ideal of social equality, installed gas ovens, turned bedrooms into parlors for daytime use, and bought pianos on the installment plan.[124]

A much smaller number of immigrants grew rich. Harry Fischel, who arrived penniless in New York, became a millionaire in the building industry. Israel Lebowitz, who started as a peddler, graduated to ownership of a men's apparel shop on Orchard Street and, by 1907, was among the largest shirt manufacturers in New York City. This was impressive; but the very thin crust of eastern European wealth remained unimportant in comparison with the wealth of the German Jews or the American elite. Eastern Europeans were not at the center of American economic power. Heavy industry, Wall Street, banking, and insurance remained closed to them. They were primarily confined to real estate, merchandising, and light manufacturing.[125]

Economic mobility often meant residential mobility. For more than thirty years, immigrant Jews from eastern Europe had sustained in the Lower East Side ghetto and in its satellites in Brooklyn, the Bronx, and upper Manhattan a transitional culture laced with elaborate institutional arrangements. But neither the Lower East Side Jewish community nor its spin-offs were destined to be permanent communities, and after 1910 the process of mobility meant lower population density, declining attendance at the Yiddish theater, declining circulation of the Yiddish press, and declining membership in the United Hebrew Trades.

Between 1890 and 1910, however, great numbers of Jewish immigrants still lived on the Lower East Side, and more continued to arrive. A considerable proportion continued to be petty tradesmen, and a large majority remained shop and factory laborers throughout their working lives, about half of them in the garment industry. The real earnings of these workers rose—an annual average rate of 1.3 percent between 1890 and 1914. Life was often hard during these years, especially during the depression of 1893–95, but working and living conditions, general amenities, and incomes improved slowly, enabling immigrants to modestly increase their standard of living and to underwrite education and economic mobility for their children.[126]

Some of the improvements in the physical environment of Jewish ghetto dwellers and laborers were the result of factory and tenement investigations, new legislation, and intensified implementation of older laws. Other material improvements, including better working conditions and increased income, were partly the result of a labor movement that educated and mobilized Jewish workers and became, as we shall see, another vital ingredient in the culture of the Lower East Side.

CHAPTER FOUR

✡

PROPHETS, PROLETARIANS, AND PROGRESSIVES

THE GREAT mass of gainfully employed Jews in eastern Europe had been small businessmen and independent craftsmen for generations. The development of working-class consciousness among them began in earnest only in the late nineteenth century, when large numbers of petit bourgeois Jews suffered economic displacement and were forced to work for wages. The making of the Jewish working class intensified with immigration to large American cities, where most Jewish newcomers confronted a more industrialized environment than they had experienced in eastern Europe. The implications of Jewish proletarianization were articulated and reinforced by the activities of a remarkable group of Jewish radical intellectuals and organizers—young men and women, mostly former students—who provided leadership and a persuasive and attractive socialist critique of capitalism.

The struggle to mobilize and improve the lot of Jewish workers in America, as in eastern Europe, occurred within the ideological framework of socialism. It also occurred almost entirely within the Jewish ethnic economy. Successful Jewish entrepreneurs, German and eastern European, were confronted by mainly Jewish laborers, who were led by an energetic group of radical Jewish organizers. Workers grew increasingly receptive to the radicals, who learned to explain socialism and class struggle in terms of social justice, the prophetic tradition, and the concept of tikkun olam, an injunction to repair or improve the world derived from Judaic religious culture. By invoking a sense of shared Jewish cultural heritage, the radicals demonstrated that they had not strayed so far, after all, from the traditional culture, and they facilitated the temporary conversion of many workers to the new creed.

But most Jewish proletarians were not far removed from their petit bourgeois origins or the religiously based tradition of *takhles* (purposefulness); while sympathetic and responsive to the message of the socialists and the social idealism of the labor movement, Jewish workers retained their own goals of rising *out* of the working class, rather than with it. These workers, in fact, helped teach the organizers and radical intellectuals that immediate incremental improvements were as important as the longer-term goal of restructuring society.

Participation in socialism and trade unionism pulled Jewish workers and labor leaders deeper into the modern world and further into the dynamic processes of American life; but the Jewish labor movement never completely cast off its unique ideological baggage. Although the movement lasted little more than one generation, its accomplishments and progressive echoes continue to reverberate in the contemporary world and to inform American, as well as American Jewish, social and political values.

The Jewish labor movement was one of the principal institutions developed by eastern Europeans in America. But it did not happen overnight. In the early years, there were great difficulties to overcome, some of which stemmed from general economic conditions and the nature of the garment industry, which operated on a low profit margin and whose work was dispersed. Other difficulties included the relative recency of Jewish proletarianization and the fact that the potential organizers of that proletariat were generally inexperienced in labor union mobilization. They were intellectuals who had come to the United States dreaming of revolution. Only a minority of the intellectuals had actual experience in the Russian revolutionary movements. This group included Michael Zametkin, who was a regular at the Odessa police station by the time he was fourteen; Louis Miller, already a seasoned revolutionary in Vilna at thirteen; and Abe Cahan, who arrived in the United States after fleeing the czarist police.

The majority of the intellectuals, whether experienced revolutionaries or not, embraced socialism and anarchism and combinations of the two. Some moved back and forth in their ideologies or cooked up an eclectic stew of European ideas strongly flavored with ethical and moral ingredients. Cahan, after an infatuation with the agrarian communalism of Am Olam, which he ultimately rejected as "utopian," described himself as an anarchist and a socialist. For a short time, he preached the "propaganda of the deed" and advised the poor to "march with iron bars and axes on Fifth Avenue and . . . seize the palaces of the rich."[1] But after the Haymarket affair in 1886, when seven policemen were killed by a bomb at an anarchist meeting in Chicago, Cahan became convinced that the anarchists were "adventurers," and he committed himself more firmly to socialism.

Several other intellectuals among the early immigrants also reaffirmed their commitment to socialism in America, though they still had no developed idea about "going to the people," at least not to the masses of Jewish immigrants who were beginning to arrive in the United States in the 1880s. Loosely organized as the Propaganda Association, many radical Jews did aim to persuade Jewish newcomers not to become strikebreakers. But they continued to speak Russian to immigrants whose language was Yiddish, and they focused most of their attention on the Old World. They believed that "though we find ourselves in a relatively free land, we dare not forget that great struggle for freedom which we experienced in our old home. . . . From far we cannot do much but we can send money."[2]

The attachment to the Russian movements, language, and revolutionary idiom was very strong. Saul Yanofsky, for example, an anarchist editor, attended a meeting of the Russian Progressive Union despite the fact that the subject of the evening was of little concern to him. But "the fact that the meetings were held in Russian . . . interested me very much. [They] took me back, in my fantasies, to the old times, when I was still in Russia, when I had such beautiful and wonderful dreams."[3]

Some of these young people had had the opportunity in Russia to escape shtetl parochialism by attending the gymnasium or university. In the process, they learned formal Russian and came to associate that language with liberation and Yiddish with backwardness. On the East Side of New York or in Philadelphia and Boston, where in the first two decades of the twentieth century Jewish immigrants underwent proletarianization, this elitist attitude toward the folk and its language came to be self-defeating.

Like the radicals who remained in Russia, at least up to the 1890s, these immigrant intellectuals failed to see the possibility of collective working-class resistance emerging from within the Jewish masses. They often withdrew into a self-contained radical community. Morris Hillquit, an important attorney and socialist theoretician, recalled how "unhappy and forlorn" the radicals were in their workshops and factories, "but at night on the roofs they again lived in a congenial atmosphere. Once more they were students among students."4 Without a following, and therefore without even the hope of social power, Hillquit's young men and women friends grew less congenial. Sectarianism generated intense squabbles and made many of them feel even more isolated.

As early as the summer of 1882, Abe Cahan challenged his radical friends to explain how the Jewish workers could understand the Russian language propaganda that the intellectuals were disseminating. It was proposed, almost as a lark, that Cahan lecture in Yiddish. This proved so effective that the so-called folk vernacular quickly became the primary medium of communication. For a time, however, Yiddish was seen strictly as an expedient in the conduct of socialist activity and not of value in itself. Many socialists insisted that, though they were now speaking Yiddish, they were not thereby *Jewish* socialists. In revolt against formal Judaism and very much enamored of progressive universalism, many of these men and women feared being associated with any form of nationalism. As late as 1889, some even imitated the anarchists in an attempt to prove themselves modern, by holding parades and balls on Yom Kippur, the most sacred day in the Jewish calender.

The radicals may have been attempting to exploit the antagonism the masses sometimes felt toward the "pious pillars of the synagogue and community," but the attack on the traditional faith was a grave miscalculation, particularly by the anarchists, who continued to ridicule religion publicly long after most of the socialists had stopped. Even those Jewish immigrants who had given up strict religious adherence were still deeply rooted in traditional religious customs and values. The attacks by the anarchists against religion in New York, Philadelphia, Baltimore, and Boston only put more distance between them and the Jewish masses. "The war against God," one of the organizers of the Yom Kippur balls admitted later, "played a great part in the decrease of anarchist influence in Jewish life."5

Socialists had not come to terms with God, either; they simply recognized that to attack religion publicly was not politic. Just as Yiddish was adopted as an expedient to communicate with the masses, so the "war against God" was dropped to prevent the alienation of those masses. Yet in the United States, and almost simultaneously in Russia, expediency gradually diminished as the radical intellectuals became immersed in the Yiddish-speaking world and worked more closely with the evolving Jewish proletariat.

Exposure to intolerable working conditions increased the sensitivity of the intellectuals to the needs of the Jewish working class. Abe Cahan, Michael Zametkin, Louis Miller, Zalman Libin, Morris Hillquit, and many other intellectuals worked, at least for a time, in the shops. American conditions, which produced the first solid Jewish proletarian bloc and forced the radical intellectuals into the factories, generated the belief in some that there *was* a Jewish working class and that it could be organized.

In 1885 the intellectuals made their first systematic effort to organize the proletariat by creating the Jewish Workingmen's Association, the first union to carry the label *Jewish*. Keeping Jewish workers organized, however, proved to be a difficult task well into the first decade of the twentieth century. The intellectuals, having proceeded directly from messianic politics to labor organizing, continued to place more emphasis on abstract radical principles and less on the specific conditions in individual trades. This gave, and would continue to give, Jewish unions an idealistic character, which distinguished them, as one union executive put it, from the "purely business proposition" of the American Federation of Labor.[6] But in the early years there was repeated failure to keep membership together once strikes ended or during the slack season.

There had been successful strikes by Jewish cap makers, men's coat tailors, and cigar makers in the 1870s in New York and Chicago, but the union locals that emerged in consequence were ephemeral, none lasting more than six years. In 1886 there was a massive cloak makers walkout, which led to the enduring Cloakmakers Benevolent Association, but this was exceptional. In 1888, when the socialists created the United Hebrew Trades, a labor union federation, only typesetters and choristers (choir singers) were firmly organized. John Commons, a prominent labor historian and economist writing at the turn of the century, offered an interpretation of union instability among Jews that focused less on the impractical and abstract orientation of the intellectual leadership and more on the nature of the Jewish worker:

> The Jew occupies a unique position in the clothing trade. His physical strength does not fit him for manual labor. His instincts lead him to speculation and trade. His individualism unsuits him for the life of a wage earner, and especially for the discipline of a labor organization. . . . Jewish workmen . . . are energetic and determined. . . . During a strike large numbers of them are to be found with almost nothing to live upon and their families suffering, still insisting on the streets and in their halls, that their great cause be won.

But once the strike is settled, whether in favor or against the cause, they are contented, and that usually ends the union.[7]

Commons proved to be something less than a seer, but he did identify some truths about Jews and early labor organization. Although between 1888 and 1890 nearly forty unions were established and brought together in the United Hebrew Trades, it continued to be difficult to maintain union solidarity in the off-season or after a strike. This had less to do with the Jew's instincts for trade, however, and more to do with the historical fact that Jews, denied purchase of land and proscribed from participating in a variety of occupations and fields in the Old World, had worked in crafts and small businesses for generations and had come to believe that a "melukhe iz a malkhes" (a trade is a kingdom). The ambitions, therefore, of Jewish immigrant workers often lay elsewhere than in the shop. Bernard Weinstein, who had been converted to socialism by Abe Cahan while the two of them worked in a shop, recognized that "many of the workers . . . wanted to become bosses. It was not very difficult. All one needed was a somewhat larger flat, and one could become a contractor."[8]

Though the contractor often fared no better than his employees, the immigrant's ambition to become an independent entrepreneur was encouraged by the fact that as early as the 1890s the garment industry began to pass from the hands of German Jewish manufacturers to Russian Jewish manufacturers. Israel Barsky, who came to America with the Odessa group of Am Olam, complained that few workers were "class conscious"; each "wants to become a capitalist." Some of the workers would not have put it quite that way. They wanted to escape the torments of the shops; some thought they could do this more quickly as individuals than as members of a class or a union. Labor activist Rose Cohen's father's dream was "some day to lay down his needle and thread and perhaps open a little candy store or a soda water stand." And socialist Louis Glass's father, attempting to convince his son to be a peddler, said: "Louie, if you will keep that job in the shop, you will never be able to crawl out of it. You will be buried in that shop." Louis Glass stayed in the shop; other sons did not.[9]

The horrors of the sweatshop system that led many workers to think about escaping were made possible by the continued arrival of new immigrants in need of immediate income. They were reinforced by former workers who had become competing contractors, offering manufacturers lower bids and speedier deliveries, and by the manufacturers, who naturally encouraged such cutthroat competition. This system and the uneven flow of work caused by the idiosyncracies of the clothing market compelled workers to toil at incredible rates of speed during the busy season only to find themselves unemployed months later. According to some observers, sweatshop work was so enervating that the productive life of an operator was about twenty years.

Factories, or "inside shops," were not much better, and often the routine was worse. Speedups were frequent, and the work was dangerous. Accidents and shop fires were not uncommon. Clocks might be slowed down during working hours, and workers were charged for needles and the cost of electric power to run machines and irons. Until 1907 most workers had to provide their own *katerinka* (sewing machine) and pay a freight charge for transporting it from place to place. There were charges, too, for lockers and chairs, and fines were imposed for damaging garments, breaking needles, and arriving late. Understandably, Jewish workers wanted better jobs than these. Therefore the fluid, fragmented structure of the garment industry, and a relatively steady influx of new immigrants, contributed to an outflow of experienced workers into more tolerable, if not always more profitable, forms of employment. Such fluidity hardly lent itself to stable union membership.

Jews also belonged to other organizations of mutual aid, and union dues were sometimes resented as an additional burden, especially when added to wages missed during strikes. One of the most important organizations of mutual aid was the landsmanshaft; it provided benefits that fledgling socialist unions could not afford. Bernard Weinstein recalled that one worker "would run around carrying an eviction notice, another would complain that he didn't have a scrap of bread in the house. A third had a sick wife, and a fourth's child had died."[10] Union leaders made vague promises of future happiness, but these were no substitute for basic needs, and locals often foundered on their inability to give material assistance.

The ideologically committed labor leaders saw the landsmanshaft, with its regional loyalty and mixed-class membership, as antithetical to unions. But many union members belonged to landsmanshaftn. The rank and file saw no contradiction in belonging to both a hometown society and the labor movement, in singing Old World songs and reading a radical newspaper, in nostalgic reminiscing and aiding striking workers. The labor movement came to accept the concept of mutual-aid associations, and many unions eventually adopted services similar to those offered by the landsmanshaftn. But in the beginning it was difficult for unions to compete with the more pervasive and attractive benevolent societies.

There were other barriers to large-scale mobilization. In 1913 there were still nearly seventeen thousand garment workshops throughout the larger cities of the United States, each employing between five and twenty workers. In addition, ethnic divisions between Jews and Poles and Italians, and even between the trained Jewish tailors from Posen and the more recently arrived, less experienced Russian Jewish needleworkers, often stood in the way of a working-class consciousness.

Another barrier to effective union organization of Jewish newcomers was the lack of encouragement and support from the American labor movement. The reluctance of the more conservative American union leaders, and indeed their discrimination against Jewish workers, was partly a response to the fact that Jewish unions were led by radicals. It was also partly the result of ethnic prejudice. But the basic cause of discrimination within the labor movement was economic interest. The late nineteenth-century American labor movement, represented by the American Federation of Labor, was built around skilled workers organized into craft unions. These unions stressed control over the supply of labor, and when the industrial revolution reduced the role of skill, thereby radically increasing the supply of labor, the unions excluded new workers in order to raise the price of labor.

Most immigrants, then, including Jews, faced the paradoxical situation of an American trade union movement that sought *not* to organize workers. Even the United Cloth Hat and Cap Makers Union, which had a heavy Jewish membership and strong socialist sympathies, considered means to restrict entry into the more skilled jobs during the slow season of 1904. Discrimination within the labor movement lasted for several decades and was overcome only in those instances when a more broadly based independent union was seen either as a threat by the craft union or as a clear addition to an established organization's strength.[11]

Unions were also discouraged by bosses and managers. A variety of techniques—sometimes repressive, sometimes merely manipulative—was used by employers to prevent unionization. Marsha Farbman, who had fled the Kishinev pogrom in 1903, went to work in a New York factory making false braids. She tried almost immediately to organize her women co-workers. "My Yiddish was not so good, but I spoke Russian. A few girls understood . . . so we were able to get together to plan a strike. . . . The forelady spotted right away that I was a socialist. She met with us and raised the wages to avert the strike and unionization. We got the few cents more on the braids and we went back to work. But we didn't get a union."[12]

Despite all this, and despite the depression of 1893, immigrant socialists garnered a mass following in New York and Chicago in the 1890s. Twenty-seven unions and socialist organizations from New York, with a membership close to fourteen thousand, were represented at a United Hebrew Trades conference in 1890, and UHT federations were created in Philadelphia in 1891 and in Chicago in 1896. As late as 1906, the majority of Jewish workers, like the majority of American workers, remained unorganized. But in fits and starts, the combination of unionism and radical propaganda did provide a real connection between the socialists and the masses, even in these early years.[13]

Socialism was a vigorous and vital theme in Jewish immigrant life almost from the beginning, and thousands of Jewish workers made their first entry into American political life in association with the radical movement. The Jewish Workingmen's Association in 1886 formally affiliated with the Socialist Labor party, led by a Sephardic Jew, Daniel DeLeon. In the same year, the association joined a coalition of liberals and socialists to support the New York mayoral candidacy of Henry George. In 1887 two "Jewish" foreign language federations were formed in the Socialist Labor party, section 8 for Yiddish-speakers and section 17 for Russians. Fourteen more Jewish sections were added in the 1890s, and as early as 1889 the party press celebrated the rapid development of socialist influence among Jewish workers.[14]

Later in 1901, Hillquit, Eugene V. Debs, labor lawyer Meyer London, and Milwaukee's Victor Berger, "evolutionary socialists" who demurred from the "intransigent revolutionary determinism" of DeLeon, became founding fathers of the Socialist party of America. One of the factors that sparked the withdrawal from the Socialist Labor party and the creation of the new party was DeLeon's emphasis on dual unionism. This brilliant but unbending class warrior demanded that several UHT unions leave the American Federation of Labor and join the Knights of Labor, an organization DeLeon hoped to control as a revolutionary base. Dissidents from the Socialist Labor party who moved into the Socialist party maintained that socialism was dependent upon the support of existing trade unions. They also believed, in contrast to DeLeon, that working to ameliorate the conditions of the working class through reforms of capitalism was not counter-revolutionary.[15]

Jews came to support the candidates of the new party in increasing and disproportionate numbers. In 1908, Jews, who made up about 39 percent of the Socialist party membership in Manhattan and the Bronx, organized enormous campaign meetings on the East Side for Eugene Victor Debs, the Socialist candidate for president. This is not as impressive as what Jewish votes would do later for the Socialist party, but it was possible for an American journalist to believe in 1909 that "most Jews of the East Side, though not all acknowledged socialists, are strongly inclined toward socialism."[16]

At the same time that the Socialist party was attracting increasing numbers of Jews, the socialist Arbeiter Ring, or Workmen's Circle, was doing the same. A nationwide fraternal order and mutual-aid society, the Workmen's Circle, organized in 1892, had only 872 members in 1901. But in 1905, after the society received a charter from New York State and could offer more reliable and attractive medical and insurance benefits, its membership grew to nearly seven thousand. Members accepted the long-range socialist goals of the radical leaders, as well as the fact that the Workmen's Circle helped finance the socialist movement. In turn, the leadership gave first priority to meeting the immediate needs of workers. By 1908, the Workmen's Circle boasted ten thousand members; most were not members of the socialist party, but the vast majority were sympathetic to the socialist movement.[17]

When, at the turn of the century, John Commons and others declared Jews incapable of sustained collective action, it was less than a decade from the maturation of Jewish socialism as a mass movement and from the enormous and durable growth of union membership in the Jewish trades. Even as late as 1910, the Dillingham Commission reported that southern and eastern Europeans were "unstable" in their industrial relations and tended to "demoralize" labor organizations. Like Commons, these later observers were blinded by ethnic prejudice. Isidore Schoenholtz, who came to America at the age of sixteen in 1906, just prior to the decade of mass labor struggle and victory in the American Jewish world, put it well: "Some did not believe that [Jewish workers] could be organized. . . . Time showed just the opposite. These were false prophets."[18]

The true prophets were those who could talk about the discontent of Jewish shopworkers in terms meaningful to potential recruits for labor activism. Union organizers, intellectuals, journalists, and political activists, in their efforts to mobilize the Jewish proletariat, tried to synthesize the essential values of Jewish culture with the modern goals and values of the socialist movement. They consistently wove biblical references, Talmudic aphorisms, and prophetic injunctions into their socialist appeals. They wrote and spoke particularly about the concepts of tzedakah (righteousness and social justice) and tikkun olam. In all, they emphasized communal responsibility and secular messianism. Even Benjamin Feigenbaum, a writer who had rebelled against Hasidic parents, fiercely attacked the supernatural, and wished for speedy assimilation of the Jews, would frequently make some socialist concept clear and more acceptable by relating it to a Jewish ethical precept. This was no mere expedient on Feigenbaum's part. He himself maintained a deep moral commitment to Jewish commandment.

Abe Cahan was one of the most successful at combining the old and the new values in his work. In the first issue of *Neie Tseit* (New Times) in 1886, he used the theme of Shavuot, the festival of weeks, associated with the receiving of the law, to illustrate socialist principles, and he remained interested throughout most of his career in using Jewish tradition and folk-religious forms in this way. Cahan understood and applauded the fact that the rigid mores of Jewish Orthodoxy had already undergone a loosening in eastern Europe and that in America (the *treyfa medine,* or unkosher land) there was further erosion. But he also knew that Jewish values and traditions were thoroughly embedded in the Jewish imagination, even in that of a professed atheist like himself.

Jewish labor spokesmen were in revolt against formal Judaism, but they were not secular. Indeed, their religious vitality was clearly visible. Religious values and ethnic attachments, in the richest sense of those terms, operated even upon those who thought they had discarded them as backward, and they certainly were meaningful to the average Jewish worker who read the radical Yiddish newspapers. In 1890 Abe Cahan began a weekly column in the *Arbeiter Tseitung* known as the Sedre, the portion of the Pentateuch read each week in Sabbath services. Cahan would begin each essay with a formal element of the liturgy, but after a paragraph or two he connected this to socialist principles and activity.[19] A workman leaving his job on erev shabbos (the eve of the sabbath) and looking forward to a day of rest had this response to one of Abe Cahan's columns:

> One Friday going home from work and considering what paper to buy,
> I noticed a new Yiddish paper. I bought it and began to read it, and

remarkably, this was the thing I wanted. It was a Yiddish, socialist newspaper. Although till then I never heard about socialism, still I understood it without any interpretation. I liked it because its ideas were hidden in my heart and in my soul long ago; only I could not express them clearly. . . . The *Arbeiter Tsietung* preached "Happiness for everyone" and changes for the "betterment of the people." . . . This I could sign with both hands![20]

Abe Cahan's pieces proved so popular that even the anarchists tried to imitate them in the *Freie Arbeiter Shtime* (Free Voice of Labor) with a column called Haftorah—the segment from the prophets used to elucidate the weekly portion of Torah read in the synagogue on Sabbath mornings.

Budding intellectuals as well as proletarians were aided by the radical Yiddish press, which provided a context and sense of direction for dealing with unresolved conflicts and confusions. Morris Raphael Cohen, a philosopher and professor at City College of New York, admitted that "what chiefly helped me in attaining an understanding of my adopted country was the Jewish press, principally the old *Arbeiter Zeitung,* which Abraham Cahan, Feigenbaum and Kranz edited and to which . . . Winchevsky, frequently sent letters from England. . . . The Yiddish press . . . taught me to look at world news from a cosmopolitan instead of a local or provincial point of view."[21]

Even more important to the socialist movement was the *Jewish Daily Forward,* which Abraham Cahan edited at its founding in 1897 and to which he returned permanently in 1903. The *Forward,* along with the United Hebrew Trades and the Workmen's Circle, became a critical component of the Jewish labor movement and Jewish socialism. Cahan quickly changed the somewhat formal language of the paper to the Yiddish of the streets and shops. If "you want the public to read this paper and assimilate Socialism," he told his staff, "you've got to write of things of everyday life, in terms of what they see and feel."[22]

The editor tersely summed up the essentials of the new socialism to be elucidated in the daily paper as "justice, humanity, fraternity—in brief, honest common sense and horse sense." Karl Marx's postulates were tapered to measure. In principle, labor was still the source of all value, and rent was still seen as robbery. But in practice, the *Forward* insisted that so long as capitalism endured, it was better to deal with "honest landlords" and "honest bosses."[23]

Despite their cosmopolitanism and class-war vocabulary, radical leaders and Jewish labor militants did not secede from the ethnic community. They helped Jewish workers in the struggle to create new identities out of traditional materials in a modern context. This struggle was not always conscious or simple. But it was made a good deal easier when, between 1905 and 1910, large numbers of Bundist socialists arrived in New York after the collapse of the 1905 revolution in Russia.

The Bundists, like the radicals who preceded them to America, also celebrated the breakup of religious hegemony, but they strongly resisted further assimilation. They desired to remain Jews—atheists and socialists, but Jews. They brought with them to America sophisticated ideological defenses of this position, and they articulated them with spirit and dedication. They were effective. By 1906 there were three thousand members in Bund branches in America, more even than the enrollment in the Jewish branches of the Socialist party.[24]

The newspapers, the activists, the socialists, and even more so the Bundists furnished the language and the terms of a powerful discourse. They helped immigrant workers on their way to becoming Americans keep their balance between the revitalized values of an ancient past and a nearer past that was falling to pieces.[25] They were effective because, in addition to confronting the objective conditions of American life and avoiding abstraction, the Bundists tapped into and refurbished something that was still alive in Jewish workers—Jewish ethical practice derived from Judaic precepts.

At the same time that Bundists and other socialist labor leaders were invoking the familiar concepts of tzedakah, tikkun olam, and communal responsibility, they were also appealing to the long-standing value of takhles, a commitment to hard work and sacrifice in order to attain an ultimate outcome, a significant individual accomplishment. Immigrant Jews had been raised to believe that there could be neither meaning nor satisfaction in simply living one's life; one had to achieve something. And because socialists were no exception to this belief, they served as role models for the immigrant masses.[26]

Elizabeth Hasanovitz, one of a number of young socialist women who had gone on hunger strikes to persuade their parents to let them go to America, wrote: "I had my hopes, my plans. . . . The hope of doing something worthwhile, hopes unexplainable, but so promising. . . . If I cannot accomplish anything, what is life for then?" Abe Cahan in a letter to a colleague in the 1880s asked: "What can be done to change oneself to rise to the stature of a perfect human being?" And Sidney Hillman was described early in his life by intimates as "believing in his star."[27]

Even as these socialists clung to the militant class feeling and the social idealism of the movement, many shared with the Jewish immigrants, they addressed a desire to rise in the world. Social idealism and personal ambition were not mutually exclusive. The careers of Joseph Barondess, "king of the cloak makers," and David Dubinsky, a Bundist and later president of the ILGWU, are good examples, and their stories were very appealing to immigrant constituencies.

Arriving in New York in 1888, Barondess began as a peddler but soon went to work in a paint factory, followed by a stint in a sugar refinery. When he moved into garment work, the flamboyant and charismatic Barondess quickly climbed the ladder from pants to shirts to cloaks to labor leadership. For years he supplied the East Side with fiery speeches laced with talmudic references, and according to the *New York Journal,* "women and children followed [him] as he went from house to house, kissing his hands and calling him their deliverer." In the late 1890s Barondess, who had become identified with every phase of the immigrant's struggle for justice, retired from labor leadership to enter the insurance business. But he remained loyal to his ideals. His business was virtually a one-man philanthropic society, employment agency, and civic lecture bureau, and through it Barondess continued to serve labor's cause. In 1900 the former cloak maker and agitator was invited to join the National Civic Federation as a labor spokesman for the Lower East Side, and a decade later he was appointed to New York's Board of Education.[28]

David Dubinsky, also an immigrant, came to the United States with experience in radical politics and the desire to become a doctor. Full of energy, he went to work to earn money for his education but soon got caught up in socialism and union affairs. "With double pay for overtime, I was making as much as $50 a week," Dubinsky recalled. "But making money and making soapbox speeches at night for the Socialist Party didn't keep me busy enough. I began to get active in the union." He gave up his job as a cutter and took a full-time union position. "I wanted the job because there was so much to be done." Union leadership proved to be the perfect arena for Dubinsky's energy and ambition. He went on to serve more than fifty years in a labor career, holding many important positions, including the presidency of the ILGWU and a vice presidency in the American Federation of Labor.[29]

Socialist trade unionism appears to have offered to Jews something similar to what the Catholic Church offered Irish Americans: an opportunity to achieve common *and* personal goals. A significant number of Jewish radicals and organizers, almost all of whom had been shopworkers, made careers in the labor movement. Many of them, including David Dubinsky, Max Zaritsky, Fannia Cohn, and Adolph Held, had had opportunities to succeed materially elsewhere but had committed their lives to the union. That involvement went beyond ideology. Jewish unions were not only agents in the class struggle, they were social centers, political forums, and training schools. Ambitious young people could, with practice, learn to hold meetings, to speak publicly, and to develop their ideas and their talents for political leadership. This not only promoted the rise of a professional cadre of Jewish union leaders, it enabled others to rise out of the unions and enter the middle class or to follow intellectual callings.[30]

Men and women who moved along these paths were attractive role models for the Jewish masses. When Jewish workers listened to the speeches of Morris Hillquit, who had risen in less than two decades from indigent cuff maker to socialist theoretician and prosperous lawyer, many in those large audiences, though committed to socialism, must also have been dreaming of repeating Hillquit's meteoric rise for themselves or their children. This desire to rise in station was strong and unrelenting but was also full of shadings and complexities. Just as Jewish socialism was a creative synthesis of older cultural values and the newer requirements of an industrial order, so participation in socialism for some Jews was a merging of individual ambition with collective idealism.

Visions of proletarian solidarity would dim over time to be overshadowed by the remarkable upward mobility of Jewish immigrants and their children. In the meantime, socialists furnished the Jewish labor movement with important vehicles of workers' education and mobilization—the United Hebrew Trades, the Workmen's Circle, and the *Jewish Daily Forward*. With these institutions, eastern European immigrants built the first consciously Jewish power base in America. With that base, the socialist movement set out through strikes and union building to solve some of the more practical problems of the workers.

In response to horrendous working conditions in the garment industry, there were arduous but successful strikes in New York and Philadelphia in

1890, and there was a series of minor victories in several cities in 1899 and the early 1900s. Samuel Gompers, president of the American Federation of Labor (1886–95 and 1896–1924), played an important role as a mediator for Jewish labor at this time. In principle, Gompers was against separate ethnic unions and was a conservative craft unionist and vocal antisocialist. But recognizing the potential power of a mobilized Jewish garment proletariat, Gompers volunteered his assistance to the United Hebrew Trades—between 1894 and 1896, and later as well—in forming Jewish unions.

In 1902 the New York courts affirmed labor's right to strike for the closed shop (only union members to be employed) and reaffirmed that right in 1905. Two years later, after a lockout by New York employers in response to union demands for a closed shop, reefer makers (makers of childrens' cloaks) struck at the height of the busy season. The strike was supported by the *Jewish Daily Forward,* which appealed in its columns for money for the cause and sponsored a theater benefit to raise funds for the strikers. The Workmen's Circle and the United Hebrew Trades did fund-raising of their own and helped raise ten thousand dollars for the reefer makers.

The seven-year old ILGWU brought its resources to bear, and entreaties to the employers' association were even made by the American Federation of Labor and the Orthodox daily *Tageblatt.* After seven long weeks, some of them marked by violence, there was a strike settlement that freed workers from paying for needles and from having to supply their own sewing machines. The closed shop was instituted, and the workweek was reduced from fifty-nine to fifty-five hours. This was an unprecedented victory, but following the strike came the depression of 1907–8. Grievances and tensions increased, but union organizing was inhibited.[31]

Economic recovery reenergized the unions. On 22 November 1909, twenty thousand shirtwaist makers, mostly Jewish women between the ages of sixteen and twenty-five, went on strike. Only a small minority were members of the ILGWU. Yet in the year following this strike, Local 25 alone counted over ten thousand members. The shirtwaist makers' rebellion, the largest strike by women in the United States up to that time, stimulated subsequent strikes and victories. These led to the emergence of the ILGWU as a major force in labor relations and to the formation of stable and enduring socialist unions. It is important, therefore, to examine the conditions that led to the 1909 strike.

Conditions in the shirtwaist factories were somewhat better than in other parts of the garment industry. The shops tended to be newer and

BALTIC SEA

• Riga

• Moscow

GERMANY

KOVNO
Kovno

VITEBSK
Vitebsk

Vilna

VILNA

Minsk

Mogilev

MOGILEV

Bialystock

GRODNO

Warsaw •

Gomel

POLAND

MINSK

VOLYNIA

CHERNIGOV

Zhitomir •

GALICIA

POLTAVA

Poltava •

AUSTRIA-HUNGARY

PODOLIA

KIEV

Ekaterinoslav •

EKATERINOSLAV

Kishinev •

KHERSON

TAURIDA

Odessa

BESSARABIA

**Northwest provinces
(main area of Bund
activity to 1917)**

RUMANIA

Polish provinces

Southwest provinces

Southern provinces

BULGARIA

BLACK SEA

The Jewish Pale of Settlement at the end of the nineteenth century.

On deck, heading for America c. 1893.

Waiting and processing at Ellis Island c. 1910.

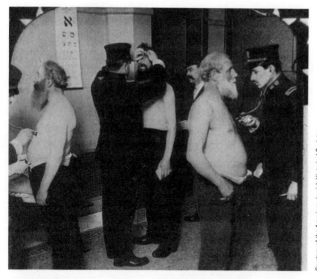

Physical examinations at Ellis Island with Hebrew alphabet eye chart.

```
25  Public School 63
26  Music School Settlement
27  Asch Building
28  Astor Library
29  Cooper Union
30  Hebrew Technical School for Boys
31  Labor Temple
32  Rand School
33  Hebrew Charities Building
34  Metropolitan Life Building
35  Madison Square Garden
36  City College
```

Boundaries of sub-ethnic districts
...... Hungarian
─┼─ Galician
─o─ Rumanian
∿∿ Levantine
── Russian

Shaded blocks indicate Tenth Ward

0   ¼ MILE

THE LOWER EAST SIDE

1 Newspaper Row
2 World Building
3 Chatham Sq. Library
4 Beth Israel Hospital
5 Israel Elchanan Yeshiva
6 Seward Park Library
7 Forward Building on Yiddish Newspaper Row
8 Educational Alliance
9 Henry St. Settlement and Clinton Hall
10 Machzike Talmud Torah
11 Hebrew Sheltering House
12 Hebrew Technical School for Girls
13 Home for Aged
14 Jewish Maternity Hospital
15 Young Men's Benevolent Association
16 Camp Huddleston Hospital Ship School
17 Beth Hamedrash Hagadol
18 Pro-Cathedral Mission
19 University Settlement
20 Grand Theater
21 Yiddish Rialto
22 Thalia Theater
23 Peoples Bath
24 Police Headquarters

Lower East Side of New York.

Hester Street, Lower East Side of New York.

Sweatshop c. 1909.

Family making garters at home c. 1910.

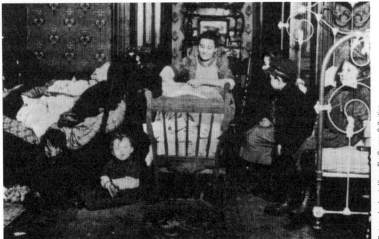

Chairs serve as beds in a New York City tenement.

Making ready for the Sabbath in a coal cellar of a tenement c. 1890.

Shoeshine boys
pitching pennies
on the Lower
East Side of
New York
c. 1915.

Yonah Shimmel's knishe bakery, Lower East Side of New York.

Abraham Cahan.

Educational Alliance library c. 1898.

Clothing and dry goods stands in the Maxwell Street area, Chicago c. 1906.

Russian Jewish quarter near Lombard Street, South Philadelphia.

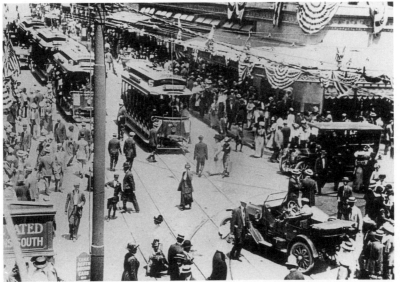

The opening of the Filene's department store at the corner of Washington and Summer Streets, Boston, 1912.

Broadside for Filene's new mark-down store, Boston.

Parading to raise funds for Beth Israel Hospital, Boston.

Abraham and Straus in the 1890s, from peddlers to wagon barons.

Jewish-owned stores on Market Street in San Francisco, 1904.

Jewish-owned stores, Los Angeles c. 1878.

Dora Levine and her daughter in front of their fish store, Portland, Oregon, 1910.

Jewish-owned stores, Omaha, turn of the century.

Neiman-Marcus store, Dallas, Texas.

Lillian Wald, nurse in training,
c. 1890.

Louis Brandeis, Justice of
the Supreme Court of the
United States.

Rabbi Mordecai
Kaplan, founder of
the Reconstructionist
Movement.

Zionist Provisional Committee, 1917–1918, including, *seated left to right,*
Henrietta Szold, Stephen S. Wise, and Jacob De Haas.

cleaner. But hours were long and speedups were common. Moreover, the women were victimized by sex discrimination. Women were paid less than men for the same work, and they were timed when they left to go to the toilet. Bosses took even greater advantage of girls, most of whom they assumed were timid and green. Bosses were not the only exploiters. Male workers did inside contracting by employing girl helpers as "learners" at three or four dollars a week. More than 20 percent of the work force, these women were often kept as learners long after there was little left to learn.

Women were also vulnerable to sexual harrassment. Fannie Shapiro had to leave her job because "the boss pinched" her. She "gave him a crack and he fell. He was very embarrassed; so the whole shop went roaring." The workers laughed, but sexual harassment was a serious problem; it is reported in a significant number of memoirs, and once women were organized and union grievance procedures were established, charges of sexual abuse abounded.[32]

In 1909 the Triangle Shirtwaist Company, one of the largest manufacturers, fired a number of workers suspected of organizing activities. Local 25 of the ILGWU called a strike against the firm in September. The Leiserson shop also went out. Weariness and demoralization set in among the strikers after a month of hunger, beatings by hired thugs, and bullying by police. At a meeting of thousands of workers at Cooper Union on 22 November, Local 25 proposed a general strike. A debate ensued, which dragged on for hours.

One of the strikers from Leiserson's, "a wisp of a girl" who in several weeks of picket line scuffles was arrested seventeen times and had six ribs broken, asked for the floor.[33] Clara Lemlich addressed the audience in Yiddish: "I am a working girl; one of those who suffers from, and is on strike against, the intolerable conditions portrayed here. I am tired of listening to those who speak in general terms. I am impatient. I move a general strike—now!" The enthusiasm of the crowd was tumultuous. The chairman, Benjamin Feigenbaum, who later wrote a book on the labor laws of the Talmud, grabbed the young woman's arm, raised it, and called out in Yiddish, "Do you mean faith? Will you take the old Hebrew oath?" With a sea of right arms raised, the crowd recited, "If I turn traitor to the cause I now pledge, may this hand wither from the arm I now raise." The general strike was on.[34]

Clara Lemlich was no stranger to radicalism and strikes. From the time she was ten years old, in the Ukraine, she had been reading Turgenev,

Gorky, and revolutionary literature. She arrived in America after the Kishinev pogrom of 1903. Within a week, the fifteen-year-old was at work in New York's shirtwaist industry. She was a relatively well-paid draper, saving money for medical school, when in 1906, as she put it, "some of us girls who were more class-conscious . . . organized the first local."[35] Lemlich was one of seven women and six men who founded Local 25 of the ILGWU. She participated thereafter in a number of strikes that led up to the major conflict of 1909, by which time she had become well known in trade union and socialist circles.

Clara Lemlich was part of a growing and important cadre. In many shops, young, unmarried women like her influenced significant numbers of others. They did this through persistent discussion, by invoking a sense of sisterhood, and by example. Most Jewish women workers looked to marriage to save them from the shops. But many, whose aspirations had been raised by changes in the old country and by the promise of the New World, were going to school at night, saving some of their wages, and dreaming of self-sufficiency.[36]

Even though a good part of their wages frequently went to supplement family income, to support the education of brothers, or to help bring relatives across the Atlantic, working women could retain their self-confidence and some hope of eventual independence. Flora Weiss, for example, who came to America at age fourteen, quickly landed a job and almost immediately enrolled in night school. She wanted to learn, and she also "wanted to earn a lot of money." Flora Weiss explained: "I wanted to support myself. I also wanted to organize the workers . . . to do something for mankind. I thought I would see a better world."[37] This combination of high aspiration and social idealism led a disproportionate number of young Jewish women to become active in the labor movement.

Some women, like Pauline Newman, Rose Schneiderman, Theresa Malkiel, Fannia Cohn, and Rose Pesotta, despite the sacrifices and the loneliness, the resistance of union men, and the condescension of the Socialist party, devoted their entire lives to the radical labor movement. Although denied an equitable share of executive positions, these women helped build a number of important union locals. They also pioneered new union programs, which were significant long-term accomplishments, including, for the ILGWU, a successful vacation retreat and an effective worker education department.

The example of activist Jewish women workers energized the entire

Jewish labor movement. The men's great cloak makers' revolt of 1910 was partly the result of the new combativeness and commitment demonstrated by the women in the great uprising of 1909. In July 1910, after careful preparation by the ILGWU, approximately sixty-five thousand workers, mostly male, left their workbenches in the cloak and suit trade to walk the picket lines.[38] Abraham Rosenberg, who had come to America in the 1880s and moved from sweatshop tailor up the ranks of the union hierarchy to become president of the ILGWU (1910–14), described the walkout:

> By half-past two, all the streets in New York from Thirty-eighth Street down and from the East River towards the west, were parked with thousands of workers. In many streets, cars and wagons had to come to [a] halt because of the crowds. Many of our most devoted members cried for joy, at the idea that their long years of labor had at last been crowned with success. I thought to myself such a scene must have taken place when the Jews were led out of Egypt.[39]

The strikers, well organized and financed, made the closed shop an important demand. The manufacturers believed that giving in to this demand would turn control of the industry over to the union, and they opposed it with all their resources. The battle was long and bitter and again, unfortunately, marked by violence. Some leaders of the Jewish community, particularly the uptowners, were distressed by the scandal of downtown Jews warring against each other before the unsympathetic eyes of the public. Invoking Jewish tradition, several among the establishment called for mediation to end the dispute. Jacob Schiff got involved; so did social worker Henry Moskowitz, Boston department store magnate A. L. Filene, attorney Julius H. Cohen, and many other prominent German Jews. Samuel Gompers also intervened for a time, but it took the talents of Louis Brandeis, the Boston "people's attorney," and Louis Marshall to break the deadlock.

The agreement that emerged, the Protocol of Peace, abolished the detested charges and fines, prohibited subcontracting and homework, raised wages, and lowered the workweek to fifty hours. On the issue of the closed shop, Brandeis came up with the preferential shop, a new concept temporarily tolerable to both sides, which called for showing preference in hiring to union members. Of greater consequence were a variety of provisions designed to promote long-term peace in the industry. The union gave up the right to strike in return for the manufacturers' surrender of the lockout. A Board of Arbitration was created to settle major disputes, and a

Board of Grievances was set up for the resolution of minor conflicts and complaints. In addition, a Joint Board of Sanitary Control was established to supervise the maintenance of decent working conditions. Despite evasion and ultimate breakdown, the protocol, which represented an employers' association and unions constituting 60 percent of the industry, pioneered new paths for industrial peace. All subsequent labor conflicts in the apparel field drew upon the protocol experience.[40]

At the end of September 1910, three weeks after the great revolt had been settled, nearly one thousand workers struck in Chicago to protest pay cuts at Hart, Schaffner, and Marx, the city's giant manufacturer of men's clothing. In less than a month there were more than thirty-five thousand strikers on the picket lines, confronting more than fifty firms. The conservative, American-born leadership of the United Garment Workers Union, mainly Irish Catholic and German Jewish, signed an agreement that failed to include the closed shop or even union recognition. The striking workers, consisting mainly of eastern European immigrant Jews and a contingent of eight thousand Italians, angrily rejected the sellout.

The more than seven thousand employees of Hart, Schaffner, and Marx and thousands of other garment workers, through the intervention of an arbitration committee, eventually emerged victorious, and their victory, like the victory of the New York cloak makers, had ramifications beyond their shop and even beyond the garment industry. Permanent arbitration machinery was set up, which eventually grew into the impartial chairman system: agreements, rules, and regulations that recognized the mutual interests of employers and workers, and that were binding upon both. The Chicago tailors, having rebelled against the leadership of the United Garment Workers Union, created one of the most significant experiments in industrial relations—not only in the garment trades but in American industry as a whole. In 1914 these same tailors, joined by others in New York—mostly Jews under the leadership of Sidney Hillman, broke away from the UGW to form the Amalgamated Clothing Workers of America, which became a massive and powerfully effective labor federation.[41]

Although in several cities Jewish labor leaders and workers accepted, and perhaps counted on, mediation by uptown German Jews in settling with downtown Jewish manufacturers, bitter class conflict continued to mark American Jewish life through the period of World War I. Jewish, increasingly Russian Jewish, owners of factories and shops were persistent in their attempts to destroy Jewish union organization. They hired spies, fired activists, and used bribery, threat, and finally brute force against their fellow Jews. In Philadelphia in 1906 one of the largest shirtmakers, Tutelman Brothers and Fagen, determined to rid themselves of unions by any means, including anti-Semitic rabble-rousing, which provoked serious street battles between Gentile and Jewish workers. And in Baltimore in 1913 police reacted so brutally to striking Jewish clothing workers that leaders of the Gentile community were impelled to aid the strikers and walk the picket lines.[42]

The strikes in the period from 1907 to 1913 were marked by violence on both sides. It is clear that the employers were the aggressors, but in order to protect themselves and their picketers, union leaders also sometimes put themselves in league with goons and gangsters. Israel Cohen, for example, a labor leader for the furriers, hired toughs to protect the strikers, who were "bearded and skull-capped Jews or young girls." But these toughs too often turned out to be tar babies—who stuck—and thereafter violence never quite disappeared from labor struggles.[43]

The great labor struggles and victories, starting in 1909 and lasting more than five years, began partly in response to the economic recovery following the depression of 1907–8. Larger factories and the greater concentration of workers also made mobilization easier. In addition, the post-1905 radical immigrants, with experience of "going to the people," began to assume leadership in the unions. At the same time, hopes for revolution in massively repressed Russia waned, moving more radicals to perceive America as home. None of this should slight, however, the accumulation of grievances over more than a decade or the groundwork laid by socialist activists, attorneys, and journalists—the Cahans, Hillquits, Feigenbaums, and Londons—who persisted in recruitment, organization, and the dissemination of propaganda.

Perhaps no single development galvanized Jewish immigrants for militant unionism and socialism more than the Triangle Shirtwaist fire of 1911. The blaze, which killed more than 140 women, broke out in the nonunion shop on the top floors of the Asch Building off Washington Square in downtown Manhattan.[44] The tragedy made a deep impression on laborers and nonlaborers, alike, and touched lives far and wide. Indeed, the news reached into the shtetlekh of Lithuania and deep into the Ukraine, where relatives, friends, and former neighbors of some of the victims lived. Rose Pesotta's sister had worked in the Triangle shop in 1910 and wrote to her parents in Derazhnya in 1911 that two young girls from that provincial town had perished by leaping out a factory window. The Yiddish press repeated the harrowing details of locked doors, inadequate fire escapes, burning bodies. Louis Waldman, a socialist labor lawyer, was an eyewitness. On his way home from Cooper Union, where he was studying, Waldman "looked up at the burning building, saw girl after girl appear at the reddened windows, pause for a terrified moment, and then leap to the pavement below, to land as mangled, bloody pulp."

Louis Waldman and his friends "felt that the workers who had died . . . were not so much the victims of a holocaust of flame as they were the victims of stupid greed and criminal exploitation." Many went to hear Morris Hillquit's address in the aftermath of the fire; they heard "the word 'Socialism' . . . recurring throughout," and their enthusiasm for the movement was aroused or reaffirmed.[45] Even those who had been radicalized in eastern Europe point to the Triangle fire as a critical reinforcement of their commitment. David Dubinsky, a Bundist in the old country, was a member of the Socialist party in America early in 1911 but "just a listener at its rallies until the horrible fire in the Triangle Shirtwaist Company."[46] And Fannia Cohn, who in Russia "imbibed and participated in the revolutionary spirit," said, "it was the triangle fire that decided my life's course."[47] At protest meetings after a stirring mass funeral for the victims of the fire, organizers and activists like Rose Schneiderman, hammered home the message: "I know from . . . experience it is up to working people to save themselves. The only way they can . . . is by a strong working-class movement."[48] Audiences were responsive.

In 1912 another general strike rocked the garment industry. This time some ten thousand furriers walked the picket line. Employer representatives refused to enter the negotiating room with union officials, but Rabbi Judah Magnes's intercession brought a settlement modeled on the protocol agreements. The furriers example was followed in December 1912, when the Brotherhood of Tailors administered a general strike involving nearly fifty thousand workers. And although the United Garment Workers Union only nominally supported the action, the strike brought significant gains and reinforced the principle of arbitration.

Memories of the Triangle disaster still haunted the community in the early months of 1913, and strikes in the shirtwaist, dress, and other industries that employed mostly women attracted wide sympathy from the public. The strikers were supported or encouraged by some of the city's leading preachers, including the Reverend Charles Parkhurst and Rabbi Stephen

Wise, by the middle-class women of the Women's Trade Union League, and by former President Theodore Roosevelt, who called for a state factory investigation. Employers came to terms, and an attempt was made to create a blueprint for future negotiations in the chaotic women's clothing industry.[49]

Still, after years of mutual suspicion and bitter conflict, industrywide peace was hard to achieve. A delicate balance of power and goodwill was required from both sides. But these qualities were strained by the depression of 1913, which reduced union membership and strength and put pressure on employers to cut costs. The Protocol of Peace was unilaterally abrogated by a group of manufacturers in 1915, and in April 1916, there was a massive fourteen-week strike in the garment trades to win back the benefits of the 1909–14 period.

The years from 1909 to 1914 saw increased activity among working-class people throughout America, but the militancy of Jewish workers was particularly intense. In several major cities, as we have seen, tens of thousands of Jewish workers struck for higher wages, better conditions, and union recognition. The United Hebrew Trades experienced a phenomenal growth. In 1910 there were fewer than ninety constituent unions, with approximately 100,000 members; by 1914 there were more than one hundred unions in the federation with 250,000 members. The American labor movement was growing, but Jewish trade unions grew faster. The garment union's 68 percent increase in membership between 1910 and 1913 was a greater rate of growth than that of any other labor union in the country.[50]

In the same period, Jewish socialists broadened their influence in several Jewish communities, especially New York. In addition to actively building and strengthening unions, many Socialists worked for the party, recruiting membership and garnering votes for Socialist candidates. Socialists rarely received more than 3 percent of the votes in New York; but between 1910 and 1914, Jewish assembly districts in the city delivered 10 to 15 percent of their votes to Socialist party office seekers, and after 1914 the figure climbed past 35 percent. Jewish votes in 1917 were responsible for the victories of ten Socialist state assemblymen, seven Socialist aldermen, and a Socialist municipal judge.[51]

Because socialism was also on the rise in America itself and reached a peak of influence between 1912 and 1916, many Jewish Socialists felt that they were part of a movement that in the not too distant future could emerge victorious. This was a miscalculation, but understandable, and based on objective realities as much as on wishful thinking. As early as March 1900, the Socialist party could claim the support of 226 branches in thirty-two states, and in November of that year there were Socialist candidates on the ballot in thirty of those states. Party membership in the United States went from 15,975 in 1903 to 118,045 in 1912, a more than 700 percent increase.

In 1910 the party elected its first congressman, German-born Victor Berger from Wisconsin. It also won control in twelve cities and towns and elected nineteen members to various state legislatures.[52] In 1911 there were seventy-four Socialist mayors and other major municipal officers, and by 1916 twenty-nine Socialist state legislators in eighteen states. This phenomenon was not simply in areas dominated by the foreign-born. Socialists received significant proportions of the vote in several towns dominated by the native-born. In Hagerstown, Maryland, in 1917, where only 1.5 percent of the population was foreign-born, 15 percent of the voters cast ballots for Socialists. In Reading, Pennsylvania, a constituency with 9 percent foreign-born gave a third of its vote to Socialist candidates. And the voters of Hamilton, Ohio, where only 6.7 percent were foreign-born, gave 44 percent to the Socialist party.[53]

Native-born Americans made up an important segment of the Socialist party. In addition, the most militant of revolutionists within the party were generally American-born—William Haywood, Jack London, and Frank Bohn, for example. The leading conservatives in the party—Morris Hillquit, Victor Berger, and John Spargo—were all immigrants. None of this should suggest that we replace the myth of immigrant radicalism with one of native radicalism: neither native-born Americans nor new immigrants were monolithic groups or ideologically homogeneous. But Jewish immigrant socialists received support and encouragement from at least some members of the American host culture. Adolph Held sensed this. "The Americans that came to us," he said, "were always more radical than we were."[54]

There were also some less supportive signals from a culture that was basically antiradical. The death sentence for the Haymarket anarchists in 1886–87 and the popular association of anarchism with foreigners no doubt had a chilling effect on many who contemplated espousing such "dangerous" views. There was a growing anti-immigrant sentiment at the turn of the century, reflected in a series of restrictive laws. In 1903 Congress passed a law that allowed for the deportation of immigrants deemed subversive. Furthermore, the repression of worker militancy in factory and mill towns like Homestead, Pennsylvania, and Lawrence, Massachusetts, was common between 1880 and 1920.[55]

In some metropolitan areas, however—particularly New York, Philadelphia, Boston, and Chicago, where the Jewish working population was significant—there was also innovation and reform. In the years from 1906 to 1915, a period known as the golden age of Yiddish socialism, American urban Progressivism was reaching its peak. Native-born Protestant Progressives, mainly interested in restoring security, morality, and prosperity to American life, pointed to the abuses of modern urbanism and capitalism, and they were often vividly descriptive. Many supported tenement and child labor reform and the regulation of working conditions in factories.[56]

The Progressives, unlike the Socialists, generally opposed a class analysis of society. Many, as noted in chapter 3, were interested in controlling what they considered the pathologies of immigrant life, and often they ministered to the lower classes in condescending fashion. Organized labor, including the ILGWU, recognized and resisted the paternalism inherent in Progressivism and was wary of efforts by social Progressives to eliminate workers' problems by extensive legislation, particularly in the area of hours and wages. But some Progressives went beyond noblesse oblige and legislative reform. Gertrude Barnum, the daughter of a prominent Chicago Democratic family, moved from genteel middle-class reformism to the rough and tumble existence of an organizer for the ILGWU; she represents the less numerous but more militant reformers who actively entered the trade union area.[57]

John Dewey, the Progressive philosopher-educator, and Charles Beard, the activist Progressive historian, also had aims that were much broader than philanthropy or legislative reform. They advocated the right of workers to organize into unions to achieve their own formulated goals.[58] This was true too for the middle-class membership of New York Women's Trade Union League, which contributed to strike funds for women garment workers. Mary Dreier, one of the league's more socially prominent and influential members, was arrested for participating in the shirtwaist strike of 1909 and evoked widespread publicity and sympathy for the picketing garment workers. Jane Addams, founder of the Hull House Settlement in Chicago, who looked forward to the elimination of unemployment and gross inequality, was also an advocate of worker organization. Abraham Cahan spoke kindly of Progressive settlement work and settlement people, and even the fiery anarchist Emma Goldman had positive things to say about Lillian Wald, the Progressive nurse who founded the Henry Street Settlement. Clearly, there were supportive links between American Progressivism, the American-led settlement house movement, and the radical Jewish labor movement.[59]

The Jewish labor movement, by accepting allies in the nonradical world, by incorporating the Progressive tendencies of American life, and by learning to use its power on a day-to-day basis to bring immediate benefits to workers was an important Americanizing agency. But despite their hardheadedness, the radical orientation of the Socialist labor leaders continued to cause unease and cleavage between the Jewish needle trade unions and the American labor movement.

The unease turned to serious concern during World War I, when the leadership of the American Federation of Labor feared that the socialist pacifism of some Jewish unions would call the loyalty of the entire labor movement into question. Some Jewish unions, including the ILGWU, equally concerned about the distance between themselves and the national labor movement, began to support participation in the war effort, and they confirmed their new position with huge purchases of Liberty Bonds. In another accommodation to American sentiment, several Jewish labor leaders continued moving socialist concerns, such as worker control and the restructuring of society, to the periphery of the movement in favor of a Gompers's bread-and-butter unionism. They still believed that socialism would bring the better world, but in the meantime would seek shorter workdays and higher wages.

Idealism and class consciousness continued to mark Jewish unions and were reflected in the fact that Jewish workers often crossed ethnic barriers to forge links with other working-class groups. Italian, German, and Jewish silk workers struck in Paterson, New Jersey, in 1913, and the support they received from New York City came overwhelmingly from Jewish labor. Irish transit workers struck in Harlem in 1916, and crowds of Jews besieged the trollies and tossed out scab conductors. There was a promise that year from other unions, mostly Irish, for a sympathy strike, but only the Jewish unions saw the promise through. The great steel strike of 1919 received approximately $300,000 in support from other unions; $175,000 came from the Jewish-dominated garment unions, $100,000 from the Amalgamated Clothing Workers alone.[60]

Class consciousness remained an important force, but Jewish workers and Jewish labor leaders did not seek to sharpen the class struggle. Instead, as we have seen, they pioneered virtually all the mechanisms for labor-management peace that exist in the field today. As Sidney Hillman put it: "Labor unions cannot function in an atmosphere of abstract theory alone. Men, women, and children cannot wait for the millennium. They want to eat, mate, and have a breath of ease *now*. Certainly I believe in collaborating with employers!"[61]

Jewish unions committed to socialism not only pioneered in labor-management cooperation, they also became laboratories for testing social welfare programs, like the forty-five-hour, five-day week, paid vacations, unemployment and health insurance, pensions, medical care, educational and recreational facilities, credit unions, and low-rent housing cooperatives. Several of these experimental programs were implemented later by the New Deal—in part because union officials, like Hillman and Dubinsky, had a background in the Socialist movement that prepared them for, and moved them toward, participation in the American political process. Here, Jewish union leaders contributed significantly to keeping concepts of human inter-dependence and government responsibility for social welfare in the political dialogue, and they shared responsibility for several decades of reform legislation.

In sum, then, a radical Jewish labor movement combined socialist principles with day-to-day practical experience to build a power base for eastern European Jews in America. The movement, without jettisoning its idealism, used that power to establish an enduring union movement, to institutionalize labor-management cooperation, and to improve the conditions of life and labor under capitalism. In the process, the radical labor movement served immigrant Jews as a powerful agent of acculturation.

✡

CHAPTER FIVE

MOBILITY AND COMMUNITY
BEYOND NEW YORK

MOST discussions of the American Jewish experience have centered on New York City. This focus is justified because the great port and immigrant center, as early as 1880, sheltered 33 percent of American Jewry. Outside of New York, too, the American Jewish experience was essentially urban (see table 4).

By 1920, New York City's share of American Jews was 45 percent—its Jewish population was greater than the total populations of most American cities. Chicago and Philadelphia together accounted for 13 percent of American Jewry, and seven other large or midsize cities in the East and Midwest accounted for an additional 14 percent. More than 72 percent of American Jews resided in major cities, and their experiences were often strikingly similar from place to place.

But Jewish life in every city was not identical. Could Jewish experience in newer, smaller, Midwest Chicago, for example, have been the same as in older, larger, East Coast New York? Or could even a long-established coastal city like Philadelphia, with its quarter-million Jews making up 11 percent of the city's population in 1920, produce the same Jewish history as New York, whose over a million and a half Jews accounted for 26 percent of the general population?

More pointedly, did Jews in mid-sized cities have the same experiences as Jews in major urban centers? Surely Jewish life in even smaller cities had a different quality and texture. There is much to ask about regional differences too. Jews living in the South or the West and in small towns throughout the United States experienced a different America from those in the large northeastern cities.

Table 4. Jewish Population in Selected American Cities, 1878, 1907, 1927

City	1878	1907	1927
New York	60,000	600,000 (33.0)	1,765,000 (44.0)
Chicago	10,000	100,000 (5.6)	325,000 (8.0)
Philadelphia	12,000	100,000 (5.6)	270,000 (6.7)
Boston	7,000	60,000 (3.3)	90,000 (2.3)
Cleveland	3,500	40,000 (2.2)	85,000 (2.1)
Detroit	2,000	10,000	75,000 (1.9)
Newark	3,500	30,000 (1.7)	65,000 (1.6)
Los Angeles	330	7,000	65,000 (1.6)
Pittsburgh	2,000	25,000 (1.4)	53,000 (1.3)
Baltimore	10,000	40,000 (2.2)	48,000 (1.2)
San Francisco	16,000	30,000 (1.7)	35,000
Milwaukee	2,075	10,000	25,000
Cincinnati	8,000	25,000 (1.4)	23,500
New Haven	1,000	8,000	22,500
Rochester (N.Y.)	1,175	10,000	22,500
Minneapolis	172	6,000	22,000
Providence	375	10,000	21,000
Denver	260	5,000	17,000
Louisville	2,500	8,000	12,500
Portland (Or.)	635	5,000	12,000
Atlanta	525	3,000	11,000
Houston	461	2,000	11,000
Indianapolis	400	5,500	10,000
New Orleans	5,000	8,000	9,000
Columbus (Oh.)	420	4,000	8,000
Norfolk (Va.)	500	2,000	7,800
Montgomery	600	1,500	3,000

Source: Adapted from Lee Shai Weissbach, "The Jewish Communities of the United States on the Eve of Mass Migration," *American Jewish History* 78 (September 1988): 79–108.
Note: Figure in parentheses is the percentage of the total population of American Jewry.

The larger the city immigrant Jews settled in, the more likely their community would resemble the Lower East Side of New York: Yiddish-speaking Jews living in large concentrations and working among people very much like themselves. Immigrants in the smaller cities and towns of the interior, on the other hand, were far less dependent on the garment industry and the ethnic economy, generally, and more likely to be self-employed. They were also more dependent on the English language and more likely to have cultural interchange with Gentiles.

It would be wrong, however, to assume that the American interior was a breeding ground for assimilation. Sometimes the opposite was true. The very isolation of the immigrants outside the urban corridors of the North-east or Midwest, in places like Sioux City, Iowa, or Springfield, Massachu-setts, moved them to band together more tightly and to promote Jewish association and consciousness. Certainly the religious congregation, where one could find comfort and guidance, still had a strong hold on the immi-grant who left the East, particularly those in smaller cities and towns. Here Jews were not only inclined to become members of shuln out of their needs for spirituality and continuity but were expected to conform to the Ameri-can practice of attending religious services "like everyone else."

Unfortunately, while we possess a growing number of community studies, efforts to determine and explain the distinctiveness of communities and regions where Jews settled have been rare. There are few systematic and comparative investigations of the religious and ethnic character of host communities or of the size, density, motivation, and background of Jewish settlers. Nor has there been much analysis of the relationships between Jews and non-Jews in different places. A satisfactory synthesis, therefore, is not yet possible; but it is worth drawing here a preliminary sketch of the Jewish experience beyond New York.

After a brief stay in New York City, seventeen-year-old Bernard Hour-wich was told he would find conditions more to his liking in Chicago, the "second America." For Hourwich this proved to be no false promise. The young immigrant arrived in Chicago in 1880, started peddling, and rose over time to become the president of two banks and a prominent figure in Jewish philanthropic circles. Hourwich's odyssey was more like that of mid-nineteenth-century German Jewish immigrants than that of late-nineteenth-century eastern Europeans, whose social mobility was less rapid. But in the early years, most eastern European Jews in Chicago, like Hourwich, did earn their living from peddling, pushcart vending, or small merchandising. Chicago was outstanding among the major American cities in this respect. In each of the four other largest Jewish centers—New York, Philadelphia, Boston, and Baltimore—more individuals worked as sweatshop and factory tailors than as peddlers, merchants, and dealers.[1]

In Chicago, only a minority of gainfully employed Jews were garment workers, and only one in eight were sweatshop workers. Even they dreamed of going into business for themselves in the ethnic economies of their own neighborhoods. They also sensed business opportunity in Chicago's growing Polish and Lithuanian sections, which were far larger than in the North-east, and whose immigrant populations were accustomed to doing business with Jews in the old countries.

When Bernard Hourwich arrived in Chicago in 1880 there were ten thousand Jews in the city, only a fraction of whom were eastern Europeans. In less than two decades, Chicago's Jewish population climbed to almost eighty thousand, and by 1920 had soared to more than a quarter of a million, the vast majority of whom were from eastern Europe. The tens of thousands of Russian and Polish Jews who arrived in Chicago between 1880 and 1920 crowded into an area southwest of downtown. By 1900 they were heavily represented in two sections that stretched from Canal Street west to Damen Avenue and from Polk Street south to the railroad tracks at Six-teenth Street. In the northern section, which contained approximately seventy thousand people, twenty thousand Jews clustered on streets adja-cent to streets dominated by other immigrant groups. But the fourteen thousand Jews in the smaller area to the south totaled 90 percent of the population and constituted a virtual ghetto.[2]

Although Chicago tenements were not as tall as those in New York, housing conditions for the Jewish immigrants in both cities were inade-quate. Indeed, whether in Chicago, Philadelphia, Boston, Baltimore, or a dozen other cities, early eastern European Jewish neighborhoods were most often in older decaying sections. A 1901 housing survey noted that nearly half the dwellings in the heart of the Chicago Jewish neighborhoods were "dangerous." Some were one- or two-story rickety wooden cottages, but most were either ill-ventilated three- and four-story tenements with poor drainage, little light, and no baths, or they were deadly rear tenements with windows facing only foul-smelling back alleys. And "on the narrow pavement . . . in front," one contemporary observer reported, "is found the omni-present garbage-box . . . running over."[3]

The focal point of the Chicago ghetto were the blocks surrounding the intersection of Halsted and Maxwell streets. Here were found the kosher meat markets and chicken stores, matzo bakeries, tailor shops, bathhouses, pushcarts, and peddler stalls. "Every Jew in this quarter," according to an account in the *Chicago Tribune* in 1891, "is engaged in business of some sort. The favorite occupation, probably on account of the small capital required, is fruit and vegetable peddling."[4] There were also rag peddlers, old iron and furniture peddlers, and clothing peddlers.

The preponderance of Jewish peddlers should not obscure the fact that

Chicago also had its garment workers, a disproportionate number of whom were Jews. Side by side with Bohemians, Lithuanians, Poles, and Italians, Jewish workers labored long hours in dark, dirty, and dangerous factories and sweatshops. In 1886, a day after the Haymarket riots in Chicago, more than a thousand Jewish garment workers marched from the southwest districts toward downtown to protest conditions in the shops. At the Van Buren Street bridge, they were beaten and routed by club-wielding police.

In 1894 state investigators visited the Chicago garment "establishments" and described the "shops over sheds or stables, in basements or on upper floors of tenement houses" as "not fit working places for men, women, and children."[5] Conditions in the factories were often no better. There were the same long hours and low wages, and in some shops workers were required to pay the full retail price for damaged materials and were fined heavily for punching the time clock even one minute late.

Although New York was the center for the manufacture of men's clothing, it was Chicago's strike against Jewish employers that laid the foundation for the establishment of the Amalgamated Clothing Workers of America (ACWA). Jews, led by Sidney Hillman and Bessie Abramowitz, were a majority of the more than thirty-five thousand workers who participated in Chicago's prolonged but successful garment strike of 1910; and it was the Chicago and New York Jewish tailors who, on the basis of this success, later broke from the conservative American leadership of the United Garment Workers to form the ACWA.

The established, prosperous German Jews of Chicago's golden ghetto on the South Side, as in many other American cities and towns, were embarrassed by the poverty, radicalism, and Old World ways of the newly arrived eastern European Jews of the West Side, and in the beginning, they resisted their influx. Typically, however, the Germans came to accept the inevitability of mass immigration and ultimately responded with programs of philanthropy and Americanization. Julius Rosenwald (1862–1932), president of Sears, Roebuck, and Company, gave great sums to Jewish charities as well as to education for blacks, housing, the University of Chicago, and the Museum of Science and Industry. Rosenwald also helped found the Chicago Hebrew Institute, later the Jewish People's Institute, which resembled New York's Educational Alliance at its progressive best.[6] German Jews were also crucial in funding the Jewish Training School, one of the first vocational training schools in the United States; the Mandel Clinic, which provided free medical care for poor immigrants; and the Chicago Maternity Center. The Jewish establishment also founded the Maxwell Street

Settlement, the Jewish counterpart to Jane Addams's Hull House on Halsted Street, which was often hailed as the "university of good will, good English, [and] good citizenship."[7]

German Jewish volunteer women were particularly active in organizing and raising funds for social welfare programs. In response to the needs of the new arrivals from eastern Europe, Hannah Solomon worked effectively with American institutions like the Chicago Women's Club and Hull House, but in 1896 she created the Bureau of Personal Service, an institution to be staffed and administered by Jewish women. The bureau investigated the financial needs of immigrants for the Women's Loan Society, studied tenement conditions for industrial reports, directed parents with troubled children to the appropriate agencies, and cooperated regularly with the settlement houses.[8]

The Chicago chapter of the National Council of Jewish Women, which Hannah Solomon helped establish in 1893, created a Sabbath school for girls, as traditional Talmud Torahs did not provide religious education for young women. NCJW members in Chicago, like their sisters in New York, were also largely responsible for the establishment of a separate juvenile court. These women began as inexperienced volunteers but soon became expert in the field of judicial procedures and juvenile delinquency. Several became unpaid probation officers of the court.

Hannah Solomon and other prosperous German Jewish women from Chicago, including Esther Loeb Kohn and Rosa Sonneschein, viewed their participation in Jewish social service as a way to redefine acceptable behavior for women. They were equally committed to their work as a religious duty—an obligation to repair or improve the world. But they also viewed the tasks of uplift and social housekeeping as the privilege and responsibility of their class. And the patronizing attitudes that occasionally surfaced among these more worldly German Jews were often resented by eastern European immigrants.[9] As soon as they could, they created their own self-help agencies. A similar dynamic marked almost every Jewish community in the United States. In Baltimore, for example, German Jews had established the Federation of Jewish Charities, a chapter of the NCJW, and the Federation of Jewish Women, which encompassed some thirty-eight philanthropic societies, involving more than ten thousand volunteers. But eastern Europeans soon created parallel organizations and institutions to provide shelter for immigrants and the aged, as well as burial societies, relief and loan associations, and orphanages.[10]

In Chicago, Orthodox Jewish immigrants established Maimonides

Hospital, later called Mount Sinai, rather than use the unkosher Michael Reese Hospital founded by the Germans; and they created their own orphanage, sheltering society, and old-age home, where traditional eastern European Jews felt more comfortable. Despite the discomfort and suspicion between Germans and eastern Europeans in Chicago, over time there was increasing cooperation, and by 1920 the philanthropic and mutual-aid organizations of the eastern European Jewish community and the German Jewish community merged.

Eastern European Jews also did not feel comfortable, nor were they welcome, in the Reform synagogues of the German Jews. Chicago's Reform movement was led by the nationally prominent Rabbi Emil G. Hirsch (1851–1923), whose Sinai Congregation instituted Sunday services and the reading of prayers in English rather than in Hebrew and eliminated the traditional ark. The ghetto dwellers established more than forty shuln, each built by newcomers from old-country communities. In the synagogues, the immigrants formed auxiliary philanthropic and loan societies, "where 'personal service' is not a fad, but has always been recognized in dealing with the unfortunate."[11] Mutual-aid and philanthropic activity also took place in more than six hundred Chicago landsmanshaftn and in the Jewish Free Loan Society of Chicago, which was established by a handful of "men of small means" who knew that "the loan of a few dollars . . . relieved months of hardship" or furnished start-up capital for a new business.[12]

In addition to mutual-aid societies and synagogues, Chicago Jewish neighborhoods boasted Hebrew schools, Hebrew and Yiddish literary societies, the offices of Yiddish newspapers, including two dailies, and a number of Yiddish theaters. Muni Weisenfreund (Paul Muni) performed in a playhouse on Roosevelt Road near Halsted Street, and New York Yiddish theatrical groups made regular appearances. There was also a branch of the Workmen's Circle, the Jewish socialist mutual-aid organization, which ran secular Yiddish language schools and camps. At its peak, the Workmen's Circle had many thousands of members, most of whom read the New York–based *Jewish Daily Forward,* which at its height printed special editions for twelve cities, including Chicago and Philadelphia.

As in New York, eastern Europeans developed a transitional culture and a viable community on Chicago's West Side. Within that community, there was by 1910 significant amelioration in the economic condition of Jewish immigrants. The benevolence of the German Jews had helped, but trade union activity and the commercial orientation and hard work of eastern Europeans was primarily responsible for the improvements. Combined with the entrepreneurial opportunities of the city and its agrarian surroundings, these improvements promoted Jewish economic mobility.

The immigrant fathers of Benny Goodman and Admiral Hyman G. Rickover had been Chicago tailors. William Paley, founder and president of the Columbia Broadcasting System, was born in the back room of a modest family cigar store near Maxwell Street. And Supreme Court Justice Arthur Goldberg's Russian immigrant father peddled fruit and vegetables on Chicago streets from a wagon pulled by a blind horse, the only horse he could afford at the time.[13]

Not only did the children of the immigrants rise; the parents also made modest gains, mainly through successful small businesses. By 1910 a number of Jews left the Maxwell Street area, but the vast majority of Jews who moved from the area of first settlement relocated three miles to the west, in Greater Lawndale. Dubbed "Deutschland," Greater Lawndale became the largest Jewish community ever to exist in Chicago.

Unlike the Jewish population of Chicago—which grew in great part through the secondary migration of immigrants like Bernard Hourwich who chose to leave the Northeast for better opportunity—the Jewish community of Philadelphia grew mainly from the thousands of immigrants who streamed off boats arriving directly from Europe. The boats docked at the foot of Washington Avenue, and the immigrants settled close by in row house alleys along Fourth and Fifth streets, south of Pine, a small area that resembled New York's Lower East Side. Jewish newcomers also settled north of Market Street, within walking distance from South Philadelphia but separated from the larger Jewish neighborhood by an industrial belt and commercial marketplaces. A third area of original immigrant settlement was Port Richmond, close to the Delaware River. Here William Street became the first exclusively Jewish street in Philadelphia, and the section came to be called Jerusalem. But it was in South Philadelphia that the vast majority of the city's Jews were to settle and remain until after World War II.[14]

Eastern European immigration pushed Philadelphia's Jewish population from about 12,000 in 1880, mostly German Jews, to more than 75,000 in 1900, and nearly 250,000 by 1925. Despite Philadelphia's growing reputation as a "city of homes," a description coined in 1887, there was a severe housing shortage at the turn of the century. The city's emphasis on row house architecture and the absence of New York–style tenements did not prevent a housing shortage nor spare Philadelphia its share of "dark and wretched slums," particularly in immigrant neighborhoods.[15]

In the Jewish sections, Alaska, Gaskell, and Kater streets were especially notorious for their decaying wooden bandboxes, animal excrement in the cobblestone alleyways, and visible evidence of crime and prostitution. These Philadelphia streets were not very different from streets dominated by immigrant Jews in other cities in every region of the United States. Atlanta's Decatur Street, for example, a main commercial thoroughfare and more than 50 percent Jewish, was "lined with two-story attached brick buildings, stores alternating with saloons and poolhalls, which together with the segregated vice district . . . nearby . . . gave the neighborhood an unsavory reputation." Another observer of Decatur Street expressed disdain for "long rows of dingy shops below and dingier dwellings above— markets where everything from eggs, overripe, to women's caresses have their recognized price." Jewish immigrant streets in Boston, Cleveland, Newark, and Minneapolis have been similarly described.[16]

Despite its large Jewish community, its size, its industrial importance, and its status as a port of entry second only to New York, Philadelphia did not become a major center of population for new immigrants, especially non-Jews. Between 1870 and 1920 Philadelphia's foreign-born population averaged only 25 percent, the lowest of all large northern cities and far lower than newer cities like Rochester, Buffalo, Minneapolis, and Chicago. The presence of a significant black population in Philadelphia, as well as a large pool of labor from the old Irish immigration, reduced the need for unskilled immigrants in the city and helps explain the relative dearth of newcomers.[17] Jews, however, rarely sought unskilled work, and they significantly outnumbered the other new immigrants in the city—Italians by two to one and Poles by eight to one. These Jewish immigrants became peddlers and shopkeepers or worked at skilled or semiskilled jobs in the garment industry, which employed 40 percent of them in the 1890s.

Conditions in the apparel trade in Philadelphia, including sweatshops and home contracting, resembled the unwholesome conditions in New York. Yet for almost a quarter of a century, attempts to unionize the Philadelphia garment industries failed. Jewish anarchists in Philadelphia were much too ideological and antireligious for the traditional Jewish workers, the socialist movement was notably weak and divided, and until 1892 there was no Yiddish press to shape or give expression to worker discontent. The *Jewish*

Exponent, the voice of the Jewish establishment, paid little attention to trade unionism, and the Journeymen Tailor's Union and the more recently organized Tailors' National Progressive Union did not seek to recruit Jewish immigrants.[18]

But if they mostly rejected the social and economic philosophy of the anarchists and the socialists, Jewish workers did eventually respond to their trade union programs. At the height of the season in May 1890, the Cloakmakers Union called the first major strike by Jewish workers in the Philadelphia needle trades. A long, bitter struggle, involving the use of scab labor and marked by violence, was ultimately resolved through the mediation of the most prominent Jewish minister in Philadelphia, Rabbi Sabato Morais of the venerable Orthodox congregation Mikveh Israel. In a bold and searing sermon, Morais chastised the wealthy manufacturers and defended his prolabor position by saying, "May the day never dawn, when the disciples of prophets and sages, to whose keeping practical religion has been entrusted . . . may not denounce social inequities."[19]

The strike, mainly by eastern European Jewish workers against German Jewish manufacturers, reflected the deep class division within the Philadelphia Jewish community. Yet the common root of Judaism allowed Rabbi Morais, with the aid of Rabbi Morris Jastrow, to use the prophetic tradition of social justice as the basis for arbitration. The settlement, however, was more significant for being the very first achieved by rabbinical intervention than for making gains for workers. Conditions in Philadelphia's garment industry in 1892, two years after the strike, were still being described as "the worst . . . in the nation."

Before the sweatshop disappeared in the second decade of the twentieth century, many acrimonious labor battles were fought in Philadelphia, Baltimore, and other cities against powerful antiunion employers' associations, which utilized blacklists, lockouts, and strikebreakers. Cloak manufacturers in Philadelphia, particularly Tutelman Brothers and Fagen, seemed willing to use any means to destroy Jewish labor organization, including beatings, the closing of plants, summary firing, and the fomenting of anti-Semitic riots by Gentile workers. In the face of these tactics, the Yiddish press, especially the socialist-oriented dailies, became consistent advocates of the rights of Jewish labor. The Orthodox rabbinate, led by Bernard Levinthal, expressed sympathy with the sweatshop and factory workers, particularly on the issue of work on the Sabbath, and even the staid *Jewish Exponent* slapped the wrists of the manufacturers. Jewish workers also gained allies

from within the newer but burgeoning Italian community of South Philadelphia. Increasing numbers of Italians were entering the clothing trade,
and along with a small number of Lithuanians and blacks, they eventually
joined forces with the Jewish workers.

The garment workers also finally got the attention of New York union
leaders in 1909, when the "great uprising" among the shirtwaist makers of
New York resulted in work being shipped to Philadelphia. The ILGWU
sent representatives, who succeeded in calling a general strike, the first ever
in Philadelphia's apparel trade. Not carefully planned, the walkout was an
abysmal failure. But four years later, in 1913, after a strike of twenty-six
weeks, Philadelphia cloak makers, with the help of the ILGWU, wrung an
agreement from manufacturers modeled on the Protocol of Peace won in
New York in 1910. Time reversed some of the gains. The right to unionize
was still a matter of contention even at the end of World War I. But
machinery for the reconciliation of grievances and the wider use of arbitration were lasting achievements.[20]

German Jews were an old and well-established community in Philadelphia, and they worried now about how Yiddish-speaking eastern European Jews, with their Old World ways and their radicalism, would affect
their own status in the city. The economic rise of Philadelphia's German
Jews, though substantial, was not as sudden as the success of their counterparts in New York, and for several decades Philadelphia's Protestant establishment had been relatively tolerant. But in the status-conscious 1880s, the
Gentile elite quietly built an inviolable caste system, which closed many
resorts, clubs, and neighborhoods to Philadelphia Jews, no matter how
prominent.[21]

Fearful of an even more intensified anti-Semitism, some German Jews
at first attempted to limit or deflect the flow of eastern European Jewish
immigration. As late as 1894, Rabbi Joseph Krauskopf of Kenesseth Israel
opened the National Farm School in Doylestown, north of Philadelphia, to
promote dispersal. But others, like Louis E. Levy, the head of the Association of Jewish Immigrants of Philadelphia, were critical of attempts to slow
the pace of Russian and Polish immigration. Despite feelings of distaste and
even fear, most German Jews in the city expressed an obligation to help
their "poor cousins."

The German Jewish elite in Philadelphia had always been ethnically
cohesive, as well as active and benevolent. But now, recognizing that the
eastern Europeans were destined to be "representative of the race of Israel in

the United States," German Jews entered a particularly creative period of community development and philanthropy. Relief expenditures were increased from twelve thousand dollars in 1880 to forty-two thousand dollars by 1892, and large groups of German Jewish women in Philadelphia, as in most cities, did the sometimes patronizing but always valuable day-to-day work of communal philanthropy. The Jewish elite also established the Hebrew Emigrant Society, a settlement house opened in 1891 at Tenth and Carpenter streets, in the very heart of the immigrant quarter. In addition, German Jewish benefactors doubled the size of the Jewish Foster Home and founded the Federation of Jewish Charities in 1901.[22]

Leading Philadelphia Jews, predominantly intellectuals and scholars like Sabato Morais, Cyrus Adler, Solomon Solis-Cohen, Mayer Sulzberger, and Joseph Krauskopf, were not as wealthy as the businessmen and lawyers who led New York Jewry, but they were committed to Americanizing the newcomers while keeping them attached to Jewish life. Like the New York leadership, they were concerned that unmodified Orthodoxy would alienate the American-born children of immigrants. But they also understood that radical Reform Judaism, so alien to newly arrived traditional Jews, would not be an effective agency in the ghetto. They worked, therefore, to build institutions for a new American Judaism. Recognizing the centrality of New York in the evolving pattern of the Jewish community in America, the Philadelphia group often worked with and through the New Yorkers. But the Philadelphians were important in the building and running of many of the central institutions of American Jewish life, including the Jewish Theological Seminary, the Jewish Publication Society, the American Jewish Historical Society, the American Jewish Committee, and the Baron de Hirsch Fund.[23]

In spite of the difficulties of adjustment, eastern European Jews soon demonstrated equal energy in establishing communal institutions. The 1900 edition of the *American Jewish Year Book* reported some 150 organizations in Jewish Philadelphia, exclusive of branches of established national associations. In the heart of the new Jewish neighborhood, the first Orthodox synagogues of eastern European Jews were consecrated, and by 1893 forty-five places of worship were reported in a half-square-mile area south of Spruce Street. By 1900 six new synagogues had been built within an area of the two city blocks, bordered by Fourth, Fifth, Pine, and South streets.[24]

A rich and vital Yiddish—and to a lesser extent, Hebrew—cultural life flourished. Dozens of newspapers and journals were published, representing almost as many points of view. Of course, New York was irresistible. Journalists and novelists, poets and playwrights, yearned to be on East Broadway, the American haven of the Yiddish word: Abe Cahan arrived in Philadelphia one day and left for New York the next; Leon Kobrin stayed a little longer, but soon he too made New York his permanent home. And the established press of New York—the *Jewish Daily Forward, Der Tog,* and the *Morgen Journal*—printed local supplements for Philadelphia readers, competing with the Philadelphia press. However, in 1914 the Philadelphia paper *Di Yiddishe Velt,* eschewing both ideology and a single religious point of view, won a broad base of Yiddish readers; it continued to publish until 1941.[25]

The Jewish immigrants of South Philadelphia possessed insatiable appetites for learning and for yiddishkayt—the shared experience of Jewish culture and ethnicity. Not only did they support a lively Jewish press, they also attended lectures at the Hebrew Literary Society, which was founded in 1885 at Third and Calhoun streets, and they patronized the Jewish theater on Arch Street, where Jacob Adler and Boris Thomashevsky starred.

The transitional Jewish culture and community of South Philadelphia rooted most Jewish immigrants in the neighborhood. But population density, growing families, unimproved housing, and the slowly rising economic status of some immigrants contributed to a movement away from the area of original settlement. Improved transportation facilities also promoted physical mobility. The last horse-drawn tram in Philadelphia made its final run on Callowhill Street in 1897, and a newly expanded railway system connected the central city with all parts of West Philadelphia.

While many South Philadelphia shopkeepers and professionals remained in the area, keeping it economically diverse, others realized it was no longer necessary to live in the vicinity of their businesses. Taking advantage of Philadelphia's transportation revolution, the turn-of-the-century real estate boom, and the continuing influx of new immigrants eager to rent or buy what others were anxious to leave behind, they secured housing in new neighborhoods. Less-affluent but no less aspiring immigrants combined the financial resources of several families or borrowed money from cooperative loan societies and also moved to the new neighborhoods.[26]

In addition to geographic mobility, there were dramatic instances of social mobility, as some Philadelphia Jews parlayed small businesses into major new enterprises. Sam Paley, for example, built a thirty-million-dollar cigar business from a storefront shop, and Albert M. Greenfield, who started as an office boy, opened a small real estate business and eventually amassed a vast commercial empire, encompassing retail stores, banks, hotels, and transportation companies. Most gainfully employed Jews in Philadelphia remained workers, but even they experienced a slow rise in their standard of living through the first two decades of the twentieth century.[27]

Although the Jewish population of Boston (seven thousand in 1880 and sixty thousand by 1907) grew less rapidly than the Jewish population of Philadelphia, enough Jews settled in the North End at the turn of the century to constitute a ghetto. "I could hardly believe I was in America," wrote Zvi Hirsh Masliansky about his visit to the North End. "The streets of Boston remind me of those of Vilna. Large synagogues, with truly orthodox rabbis. Talmudic study groups . . . Hebrew schools in the old style [and] almost all the stores are closed on Saturdays."[28]

Low rents and the proximity of the waterfront and the business district attracted Jews to the area bounded by Hanover, Endicott, Prince, and Bennett streets. Moreover, neighboring Italian and Irish sections were seen as potential markets by Jewish immigrants at a time when itinerant peddling in the streets of Boston, more so than in New York, offered opportunities to start one's own business.

Most immigrants in the Jewish North End lived in dilapidated, unsanitary tenements, with inadequate light, water, and air. And congestion in the apartments was exacerbated by the need to take in boarders. In the eyes of writer Mary Antin, who lived among them, these Jewish immigrants were "the despair of the boards of health" and "pitiful in the eyes of social missionaries," including those from the Hale House settlement on Garland Street.[29] Conditions in the North End, as in the Jewish sections of other large cities, threatened the stability of Jewish family life, and there was enough desertion and crime to prompt the formation of a special committee of the National Council of Jewish Women and a Jewish Prisoner Aid Society to deal with the problems.

Conditions at work in the Boston garment shops, where the largest number of gainfully employed Jews were found, were no better than in the homes. By the late 1880s, Boston was an important center of clothing manufacture. But as in New York, Philadelphia, Baltimore, and Chicago, it took long years of bitter struggle by Jewish labor unions to stabilize the garment industry and improve working conditions.[30]

In 1889 a small group in the garment industry began organizing Jewish laborers, and by 1900, the Boston Jewish clothing workers participated in the formation of the ILGWU. Sporadic but arduous labor battles followed in Boston in the early twentieth century. These played a role in the "education" of Louis D. Brandeis, a prominent Boston attorney, who helped mediate the struggles. Later, in the great strike of 1910, which was centered in New York, Brandeis introduced the principle of arbitration and helped promulgate the important Protocol of Peace. Like Brandeis, other established German Jews of Boston—including Jacob Hecht, who had risen dramatically from peddler to financier, and Abraham Shuman, the department store magnate—came to the aid of their fellow Jews from eastern Europe. But as in most places where these two groups interacted, acceptance and philanthropy came only after initial repugnance and resistance.

The "Russian invasion," brought fear into the hearts of German Jews in many cities, lest the non-Jewish community associate them with the "uncouth" immigrants. When historian Fredrick Jackson Turner visited the Jewish North End of Boston, the arrogant patrician was filled with revulsion for streets filled with "oriental noise and squalor" and "fairly packed with swarthy sons and daughters of the tribe of Israel . . . some of the latter pretty—as you sometimes see a lily in the green muddy slime."[31] The Germans' fear of being tarred with the brush of the ghetto was understandable in post–Civil War America, and Brahmin Boston was no exception to the era's nativism and anti-Semitism. A bill "to keep Chinese, Negroes, and Jews from neighborhoods where they are not wanted" was hotly debated in the city, and even prominent Jews like Louis Brandeis and Edward Filene met rebuff.[32]

Between 1881 and 1882 only small groups of Russian Jews came to Boston, and these early refugees aroused sympathy among the established German Jews of the city. But when the Mansion House Fund, the London counterpart of the New York Hebrew Emigrant Aid Society, sent 415 refugees to Boston in June 1882, the Boston HEAS refused to accept them and promptly shipped them back to New York. This was not a unique event; other communities also balked as the number of immigrants began to mount. The Baltimore HEAS, for example, demanded in 1882 that New York send no more refugees to their city and went so far as to help finance return trips to Europe for newly arrived immigrants.

The Boston HEAS, in returning refugees to New York, exhausted its funds, and when a small number of Jewish newcomers needed aid in the winter of 1882–83, they were turned away. Some eighteen families asked the Boston Provident Association, a non-Jewish civic philanthropy, to pay their passage back to Russia. When the association agreed, it was besieged by scores of Jews wishing to leave the United States. By making obvious the desperate needs of some immigrants, this incident aroused compassion as well as embarrassment in the Boston German Jewish community, which had failed "to take care of its own." Established Jews resolved never to fail again, and by 1889, they accepted, and even sought out, full responsibility for Jewish immigrants.33

Most eastern European Jews in Boston, as in New York and Philadelphia, found friends and relations to assist them in their first encounters with the New World; some participated in fledgling self-help associations, like the Boston North End Hebrew Benevolent Association, founded by 140 poor Russian and Polish Jews in 1881; but a small number, approximately 5 percent, needed additional help from the established communal Jewish charities. Their poverty was real. According to the *Boston Hebrew Observer,* on any evening in the North End, "you will find little ragged Jewish urchins . . . on corners [where] you are greeted with 'Mister, please buy a paper,' and then, 'Mister, please give me a few cents.'" One boy "turned springs and somersaults at the rate of three for a nickel." Sometimes the behavior of Jewish youngsters in Boston and other cities turned less innocent. In East Baltimore, for example, delinquency was described as "common," and the Federation of Jewish Charities in the city felt compelled to establish a Big Brother League.

German Jews in Boston responded to the problems of the immigrant quarter by forming the Federation of Jewish Charities and a branch of the American Committee for Ameliorating the Condition of the Russian Refugees, which operated as an employment agency and a vocational training school. And from 1880 to 1914, Jewish philanthropy in Boston went from a patriarchal, loosely organized, and relatively inexpensive effort to a well-financed and highly coordinated enterprise.34 Eastern European Jews established several mutual-aid and philanthropic associations themselves, including, in 1891, the Benoth Israel Sheltering Home, which provided newcomers with food and emergency shelter. By 1895 "Russian" and "German" charitable and self-help agencies were able to coordinate efforts, and by 1914, although there remained two clearly distinguishable groups of Jews in Boston, there was movement toward forming common institutions, including hospitals, orphanages, loan societies, and industrial training schools.

Among eastern Europeans themselves, subgroups were also distinguishable. Some immigrants found their place in the Orthodox Baldwin Street shul; the intellectuals gathered at Bersansky's bookstore, where they could read a radical paper or even *Der Yiddisher Odler* and the *Boston Jewish American*. Branches of every Jewish political group, including Socialists, Zionists, and anarchists, had their constituencies, each with their own club room. Several groups, including the Labor Zionists and the Workmen's Circle, established secular Jewish schools to compete with the multiplicity of hederim and the communal Talmud Torah located in the West End.

The cultural, communal, and individual vitality of eastern European Jews was again reflected in their mobility. Immigrant Jews in Boston experienced no large-scale social class ascent in their own generation, but enough carpenters and roofers became builders and enough garment workers and peddlers became contractors or store owners to allow us to talk of a remarkable Jewish occupational and economic mobility. With greater income came geographic mobility, as well. Just as German Jews moved out of the South End of Boston into Brighton, Brookline, and Newton, so eastern European Jews moved out of the North End into the South End and West End, and then into Roxbury, Dorchester, and Mattapan.

Outside of New York in the other great American cities at the turn of the century, immigrant Jews mirrored in microcosm the communal life of the Lower East Side. The North End of Boston, South Philadelphia, East Baltimore, and the West Side of Chicago sheltered dense enclaves of eastern European Jews steeped in a transitional culture built on a combination of new American experiences and the deeply internalized values and habits of yiddishkayt.

It was rare in these cities to find whole blocks inhabited exclusively by Jews, like the Lower East Side of New York, the Brownsville section of Brooklyn, William Street in Philadelphia, and the blocks surrounding Maxwell and Halsted streets in Chicago. Indeed, few streets outside of New York City had as many as 50 percent Jewish residents. But there were large enough pluralities of Jews on significant numbers of adjacent streets, and large enough clusters of Jewish businesses in relatively small areas, for neighborhoods and parts of neighborhoods to beecome known as Jewish—and more importantly, to become public spaces in which Jews interacted with familiarity and into which they transplanted modified versions of Old World cultural forms.

A similar mode and process of transplantation, on a smaller scale, took place outside the larger cities. Jewish immigrant communities in the smaller cities and towns, however, while marked by even greater economic mobility, were less densely settled, and in some cases less culturally and ideologically diverse than those in New York and the larger cities of the eastern seaboard. This stemmed mostly from the fact that these Jewish communities were in good part products of secondary migration—of people uprooting themselves a second time and choosing these destinations, rather than simply disembarking in them.

Cities and towns all over the United States received Jewish newcomers, approximately seventy-nine thousand of whom were assisted in the dispersal and resettlement process by the Industrial Removal Office (IRO) and a vast network of cooperating B'nai B'rith branches, which stretched from Hartford, Connecticut, through Atlanta, Georgia, to El Paso, Texas, and from Providence, Rhode Island, through Kansas City, Missouri, and Denver, Colorado, to Portland, Oregon, and San Francisco, California.[35] After 1907, a much smaller number of immigrants, some ten thousand, were deflected through the port of Galveston, Texas, to interior cities, including Fort Worth, Oklahoma City, Omaha, Minneapolis, and Los Angeles. But the vast majority of eastern European immigrants who ended up outside New York and other major port cities left the crowded ghettos under their own steam, some of them following relatives who had been assisted by the IRO or the Galveston movement.[36]

The immigrant who worked six months in a New York sweatshop to save enough train fare to go to Minneapolis, where his two brothers had settled, was not unusual, nor was the peddler who forsook Boston to join relatives in Cleveland.[37] But several things besides ties of kinship guided the voluntary secondary migration. Immigrants were often drawn to new locations by a landslayt connection. Portland, for example, attracted a disproportionate number of people from Chartoriysk, a town on the ever-changing border between Poland and Russia; Lithuanian Jews, often from the same old-country districts and towns, dominated the Jewish communities in Atlanta and Milwaukee; and Seattle by 1914 was home to six hundred Sephardic Jews, the largest concentration outside of New York City.[38]

Occasionally, the determination to migrate to landslayt or to relatives was reinforced by unforeseen events, as when the Pennsylvania Railroad in 1885 briefly lowered fares from New York to Chicago and St. Louis and when the Baltimore and Ohio Railroad lowered fares on its Baltimore to Chicago route. Many immigrants seized the opportunity to travel these distances for one dollar instead of the usual ten or fifteen.[39]

Clearly, old-country regional ties and the pull of family operated as magnets. Newcomers may also have been drawn to particular cities and towns by immigrant Jewish communities that bore the distinctive ideological stamp of earlier arrivals. It is difficult to explain otherwise why Zionists were disproportionately represented in the immigrant organizations of Chicago and Cleveland; or why Cleveland, with a substantial garment industry and a viable Jewish trade union movement, was never a center of Jewish socialism—while Milwaukee, where Jews were more often involved in commerce, disproportionately sustained the Social Democratic party's rise to power and its control of the municipality for over thirty years.[40]

Immigrant Jews resettled a second time for many reasons. Ultimately, however, most—perhaps a hundred thousand or more—who left large eastern cities without outside assistance, and even a significant proportion of those who left under the auspices of the IRO, saw in places like Detroit, Cincinnati, St. Louis, and Los Angeles better opportunities to enter into or expand small businesses. As much as 35 percent of that small portion of Jews who decided to strike out anew had had entrepreneurial experience; most of the rest were ready to take the risks involved in leaving a known environment to start over, convinced that their skills would enable them to begin careers in trade in new places like Columbus, Ohio; Johnstown, Pennsylvania; Atlanta, Georgia; or Denver, Colorado.[41]

Just as with the German Jews, peddling and other commercial occupations played a much more important role than industrial labor in the working life of eastern European Jews in the smaller cities and towns. Rarely were Jewish immigrants employed in the principle industries of these places: the breweries and iron foundries of Milwaukee, the steel plants of Pittsburgh, the stone quarries and railroads of Columbus, and the textile mills of Malden, Massachusetts, hired few Jews.[42] This was partly the result of discrimination by employers, but it was also the consequence of the petit-bourgeois goals of the Jews themselves. In Providence, for example, Jews were seven times more likely to be peddlers than any other ethnic group, and an extraordinary 65 percent ran small businesses or were self-employed.[43]

Similar proportions of Jewish peddlers, merchants, and self-employed craftsmen were to be found in Springfield, Massachusetts, and Hartford, Connecticut. In such cities as Columbus, Milwaukee, and Minneapolis, too, innovative eastern Europeans followed the paths of the German Jews who preceded them, borrowing capital from friends, relatives, and cooperative loan societies to pursue the risks associated with building small businesses. Many of the businesses were marginal, but Jews were willing to make short-term sacrifices in order to remain linked to the long-term potentialities inherent in the world of commerce.

In Portland, as well, business enterprise prevailed among Jews. Most Jewish immigrants who came to Oregon, including a small number who had first tried cooperative farming at New Odessa or in the agricultural colonies of North Dakota, ended up in Portland, the state's most important commercial city. That Portland was a link in the Pacific overseas economic network and was tied into the transcontinental trade of the United States via the Northern Pacific Railroad was important to relocating Jews, many of whom clustered in the importing and wholesale supply business. Newcomers took advantage of the merchandising network of the Jewish ethnic economy, using extensive trading contacts with relatives and friends in San Francisco and other coastal cities, including Los Angeles, to build innovative retail and wholesale firms.[44]

Los Angeles, with its appealing climate, attracted some Jewish health seekers, but here as well, it was business opportunity that accounted for the remarkable surge in the city's Jewish population from about four hundred in 1880 to seven thousand in 1907 and sixty-five thousand by 1927. With its agricultural potential, warm climate, easy access, and availability of land, the Los Angeles area experienced the celebrated economic boom of the eighties. Peaking in 1886–87, the boom spawned dozens of new West Coast towns and attracted thousands of new settlers, including businessmen and aspiring entrepreneurs anxious to serve the new arrivals.

As they did in so many settlements outside of the Northeast, eastern European Jews who came to the Los Angeles area tended to repeat the economic pattern of the earlier German Jewish generation by struggling to build their own businesses. The usual difficulties were compounded by the fact that Jews were often denied access to established channels of credit. But the venturesomeness of the Jews involved in secondary migrations served them well, as did their networks of relatives, their ethnic cohesiveness, and their cooperative credit associations.[45]

There were dramatic success stories throughout the West, an area which, according to historian Moses Rischin, provided greater social mobility for Jews than the older regions of the country.[46] The story of the Madanic family is a case in point. Hyman Madanic and his son Ben immigrated to the United States in 1889. They took jobs in the sweatshops of St. Louis and saved enough money to bring the rest of the family from Russia in 1893. The Madanics opened their own fairly successful clothing store in Fairfield, Illinois, but in 1908 they moved to the boomtown of Tulsa, Oklahoma, where their business proved so successful that they opened branches in several nearby towns. They changed their name to the May brothers following World War I, and their stores continued to spread across the continent.[47]

Perhaps the most sensational example of the rise from rags to riches in the West is the story of the Hollywood Eight—eight Jewish immigrants who seized the opportunities in a marginal moviemaking business and, by the 1920s, had created eight major companies in complete control of the production, distribution, and exhibition of moving pictures. Dozens of Jews on their way to "inventing Hollywood" began—like Louis B. Mayer, Harry Cohn, and the Warner brothers—in their own East Coast neighborhoods with nickelodeon storefronts and soon graduated to small theater ownership.

As late as 1912, moviemaking was still a fledgling industry. Most American films were produced by approximately a hundred small firms owned mainly by Protestants, some of whom thought they were involved in little more than a passing fad. Jewish theater owners, however, were conditioned to working on the fringes of commercial enterprise; they were seeking new opportunities. They were attuned to the tastes of their audiences and to the developing revolution in manners, morals, and popular culture, and they were determined to make their own films.

Louis B. Mayer, who arrived in Boston at the age of nineteen without enough money for a sandwich, Samuel (Goldfish) Goldwyn, a traveling glove salesman, and several others with great ambition and little capital borrowed money and convinced their families, friends, and landslayt to pool resources. The new moviemakers produced funny, patriotic, egalitarian, sensual, and opulent films, and they built palatial theaters to show them in. The combination attracted large audiences of all classes and made the filmmakers wealthy.

Nicholas Schenck, the head of United Artists, said perceptively, "It is not always greatness that takes a man to the top, it is a gambling spirit." The gambling spirit was significant, along with a strong group cohesion and a desire to Americanize rapidly and to rise. These qualities enabled the Hollywood Eight to build a major new multimillion-dollar industry, which catapulted them into the status of moguls.[48]

Although few eastern European immigrants became moguls, most entrepreneurs—often after at least one failure—gambled again and pulled themselves out of poverty into lives of relative comfort. Indeed, among Jews living in communities beyond the East Coast, there are striking analogies in mobility and occupational patterns. Commerce predominated, whether in the form of peddling and storekeeping in Omaha, Patchogue, Phoenix, Columbus, and Sioux City or in the form of wholesaling and light manufacturing in Portland, junk scavaging in Cleveland, and the slaughter and sale of meat in Kansas City.[49] Even in those cities where the majority of gainfully employed Jews were laborers, as in St. Louis, Louisville, and Rochester, or where significant proportions—40 percent or more—worked in industry, as in Pittsburgh, Cincinnati, Syracuse, Toledo, and Worcester, as many as 25 to 40 percent were peddlers, merchants, or dealers.[50]

In all of these places, the extended Jewish family played a critical role as an economic unit or network. Relatives deployed their collective resources, borrowed from one another, hired, trained, sustained, and encouraged one another. In Cleveland, one young scavenger recalled protesting when the uncle who was "training" him picked unattractive, seemingly worthless junk out of backyards. The older man retorted: "That's business! . . . Everything goes into the wagon. If you're too finicky, you'll never make a living."[51] Relatives and landslayt were also trained and employed by small store owners in such places as Eastport and Setauket, Long Island, and by Jewish wholesalers in San Francisco, among other places, thereby extending family businesses to other towns. And in Hollywood, Louis B. Mayer hired so many of his relatives that Metro-Goldwyn-Mayer (M-G-M) came to be known as Mayer's *gantse mishpokhe* (Mayer's entire extended family).

Like Hollywood, the Catskill Mountains' resort hotels in Sullivan and Ulster counties in New York State were an invention of the immigrant Jews and their networks of relatives and landslayt. Eastern European Jews who tried to do mixed farming in the relatively inhospitable soil of the Catskills found, like their Gentile neighbors, that it was often necessary to take in boarders to make ends meet. For Jewish innkeepers, the early boarders were friends and kin. They came for the clean mountain air, the sun, and to be "in the country." Returning a hundred miles south to New York City, Jewish vacationers told other associates and relatives about the bucolic pleasures to be had in "the mountains."

In response to rising demand, reinforced by the fact that many Gentile-owned Catskill and Adirondack resorts refused accommodations to "Hebrews," Jewish farmhouses were converted to rooming houses, and Jewish farmers, seeing the profitability of taking in boarders, spent less time farming. (As farmers, Jews were as successful as their Gentile counterparts in New York State. Moreover, with the help of the Jewish Agricultural Society, Jews were instrumental in establishing rural credit unions, agrarian sanitation reform, and farmers' cooperatives, which became models for American agriculture.) It was not long before Jewish bungalow colonies, boarding houses, and hotels dotted the Catskills. Between 1900 and 1910, one thousand farms in a ten-mile strip near Ellenville were sold to Jews migrating from New York City. "Nearly every one of the purchased farm houses," according to the *Ellenville Journal* "is used as a summer boarding house." Resentment over the invasion of "Israelites" from the "big city" was modified some when native farmers realized profits from the sale of untillable lands to prospective Jewish innkeepers.

The string of Jewish hostelries eventually became known as the borscht belt, with its impresarios and hotel magnates, whose families, like the Grossinger's and the Brown's, were often engaged in the enterprise season after season and generation after generation. Like the Jewish resorts on the southern New Jersey shore and in Atlantic City, "the mountains" became an important feature of Jewish life and a fixture on the Catskill landscape. Before the general collapse of the Catskill economy in the 1960s, hastened by acculturation, affluence, and jet travel, thousands of hotels, bungalow colonies and rooming houses accommodated more than a million tourists annually, and several resorts rose from shacks to conglomerates with their own post offices, airports, and tinted snow.[52]

In the Catskills, in Hollywood, and in the American interior generally, Jews established family businesses and utilized innovative techniques that promoted a remarkable mobility. A not dissimilar pattern was discernible in the American South, as well. "Jew peddlers" became a fixture of the southern scene, their growing businesses sometimes becoming the nuclei of small towns. Jews were also attracted to the business opportunities of southern cities like Atlanta, the terminus for five railway lines. Whether in small towns or cities, Jewish entrepreneurs broke into commercial networks by filling needs. Like their German Jewish predecessors who established the great southern department stores—Goldsmith's in Memphis, Sakowitz's in Houston, Godstraux's in New Orleans, Rich's in Atlanta, and Cohen Brothers in Jacksonville—eastern European Jews sold on credit and often cultivated a black clientele.[53]

This last could lead to trouble, but more often it simply meant more customers. Jewish businessmen were more interested in customers than in the customs of racial discrimination, and they generally followed the professed philosophy of the owners of Neiman-Marcus, who early on announced: "Anyone alive should be considered a prospect." As one merchant put it: "Selling on credit to the Negro was called 'having a book on the shvartzers.' Do not misunderstand me. *Schvartzers* was not a sign of disrespect. . . . We were probably the first white people in the South who paid the Negro people any respect at all."[54]

Inertia, fear, and the social and cultural comforts of the East Coast ghettos meant that only a small portion of Jewish immigrants left these ghettos for the West and South. Those who did were perhaps more adventurous, more independent, and more acculturated than the millions who remained behind. These traits partly account for the risk taking and rapid economic mobility of the Hollywood moguls, the Catskill hoteliers, the San Francisco wholesalers, the Kansas City meat slaughterers, and the southern department store owners. But did their independence and acculturation mean that these Jewish immigrants assimilated more rapidly?

It is true that in Los Angeles, and in a very small number of other places where Jews settled, a Jewish *"immigrant* milieu hardly came into being."[55] It is also true that Jewish immigrants outside the largest cities were less densely concentrated than Jews in large eastern cities and more likely to share neighborhoods and streets with other ethnic groups—Italians, Irish, Poles, and blacks. Indeed, in places like Columbus, Portland, and Omaha, no single nationality group, including Jews, ever constituted a majority in any area as large as a half-mile square. And even the densely Jewish neighborhoods in Milwaukee, Detroit, and Cleveland were ethnically heterogeneous, with significant numbers of individuals living outside their particular immigrant enclaves.[56]

Thus unlike in East Coast cities, Jews in the interior could not live entirely within the bounds of their own ethnic community. But in these places and in most cities and towns with Jewish residents, there were neighborhoods like the West Colfax section of Denver, the Suffolk Square area of Malden, Massachusetts, Decatur Street in Atlanta, and Water Street in Milwaukee that had a highly visible Jewish immigrant settlement, with a relatively autonomous life, distinct Jewish trades, and familiar street scenes.⁵⁷ The following description by a former Jewish resident of the East Side of Hartford is nearly interchangeable with descriptions of Jewish immigrant neighborhoods in dozens upon dozens of other small American cities and towns: "Rows of two- and three-story tenement houses, packed tightly together, provide homes for the newly arrived. Many used the front of the first floor as a place of business. Windsor Street . . . was alive with people coming and going from these businesses in their homes. The street reverberated, too, with the voices of peddlers hawking their wares from pushcarts and wagons."⁵⁸

Ethnic neighborhoods may have comprised only minor portions of their respective wards in the small cities and towns, but because of the clustering of distinct businesses, trades, and institutions, Jewish immigrant sections were easily identifiable. As Sarah Schwartz of Columbus remembered it: "We lived . . . in our special enclave. . . . It wasn't a ghetto . . . for our neighbors were white Catholic and Protestant—and black. [But] with few exceptions, we lived clustered about our synagogues, the kosher butchers, the Jewish bakeries—yes, and even the mikveh . . . which was in Shapiro's Bath House, on Donaldson, down the street from the Beth Jacob Synagogue. Washington Avenue was our main 'drag,' our own High Street."⁵⁹ Newcomers from eastern Europe, even where they never made up more than half a block's population in any given section, formed their own main drags in the heartland of America—on Ferry Street in Springfield, Massachusetts, or on tree-lined William Street in Buffalo, or on the North Side of Minneapolis, where on Fridays one "could literally smell the Sabbath, the fish and the chicken, and the preparations."⁶⁰

In places even more isolated from the mainstream of American Jewish life, ethnic and religious cohesion was harder to maintain and sometimes disappeared. Jews in such towns as Mora, New Mexico, spoke Spanish, worshipped as Catholics, and ultimately were completely absorbed into the native population.⁶¹ But this was rare. More often, Jews, no matter how few and how distant from the larger centers of Jewish culture, tried, sometimes against great odds, to maintain Jewish identity even as they Americanized. In Phoenix, for example, there were no formal Jewish religious institutions until 1910. High Holy Day services had to be held in homes or rented halls. In 1897 Jewish worshipers had to be sure that their Yom Kippur service at

Elks Hall ended at 8 P.M. so that the lodge members could hold their regularly scheduled meeting.[62]

Even where formal institutions existed, there were problems. Many Jewish communities emerged between Harrisburg and Pittsburgh, each with its own small synagogue but none with a qualified spiritual leader. The same situation prevailed southward from Harrisburg to Baltimore, eastward to Philadelphia, and northward to Rochester. Circuit-riding rabbis like Eliezer Silver, who served in Harrisburg early in his career, traveled often to these communities to provide guidance. Farther west, Benjamin Papermaster of Grand Forks was the only rabbi serving Jews in all of North Dakota and western Minnesota.[63] Many communities, even some of those not far from large cities, imported at least some of their yiddishkayt. On Willard Avenue and Gay Street in Providence, for example, families read aloud from the bintl brief section of the *Forward,* which came in daily from New York, along with the *Tageblatt;* in Sioux City, Iowa, the Chicago edition of the *Forward* was available, as was an occasional Yiddish theater group on tour from New York.

But the resident Jews in such places as Providence, Hartford, Sioux City, Kansas City, Cincinnati, Atlanta, Richmond, and New Orleans also derived their security and identity from Jewish family life, from their landsmanshaftn, from their synagogues, and from their own self-help and cultural institutions.[64]

Although smaller cities and towns were less densely Jewish and less culturally diverse than the larger cities, with the increasing influx of eastern European Jewish immigrants, these places continued to permit and even encourage Jewish ethnic and religious identity. In Springfield, Massachusetts, for example, after 1880 and an influx of new immigrants, a thriving Jewish community emerged, mostly the conscious creation of eastern European Jews. Sioux City witnessed a similar development. German Jews there had practically merged with the Unitarians, but the arrival of eastern European immigrants, with their Zionist as well as socialist elements, their Orthodox Hasidim as well as their free thinkers, breathed new life into the Jewish community.[65] This sometimes happened even in cities of some size. In Cleveland, for example, a Reform rabbi said of the eastern European newcomers: "We look with disfavor upon their quaint customs, particularly . . . their religious observances. [But] if immigration has brought with it a Jewish problem, it has also brought much good, and one is the preservation of Jewish ideals."[66]

Eastern Europeans helped revitalize Judaism in the American interior, but the relationship between the German Jews and eastern Europeans was not a one-way street. Although most newcomers in need of aid were succored by relatives and friends, in the early years a good number of immigrants, particularly refugees from pogroms and those arriving under the auspices of the IRO or the Galveston plan, needed the help of German Jewish institutions.

Established, prosperous German Jews supported their coreligionists by funding relief efforts, providing temporary shelter, and procuring employment. But members of the Jewish elites in the smaller cities and towns, like their large city counterparts, were at first ambivalent about mass immigration and certainly about encouraging large numbers of eastern Europeans to settle in their localities. Sometimes resistance was direct, as when a spokesman for the United Jewish Charities of Rochester claimed that "organized immigration from Russia . . . and other semi-barbarous countries is a mistake."[67]

Sometimes this resistance took the form of directing immigrants elsewhere. In San Francisco several leading German Jews urged the members of Congregation Emanu-El to purchase Baja, California, from the Mexican government in order to settle Yiddish speakers there; in Portland, the International Society for the Colonization of Russian Jews was organized with the goal of settling refugees on land in northern California; and in Cleveland, some new immigrants were assisted to move on to the short-lived Jewish agricultural colony at Painted Woods, North Dakota.[68]

None of these efforts at diversion and dispersal succeeded, and eastern Europeans continued to settle in the cities and towns of the American interior. The Germans initially responded with condescension and social distance. In Milwaukee and Detroit they complained that "the immigrants have been a class that reflects no credit upon their brethren." In Cleveland in 1895, a German Jewish public schoolteacher contended that her immigrant pupils needed to be removed from the influence of their homes and neighborhoods, which were filled with "bigoted followers of the orthodox rabbinical law [and] uneducated paupers . . . whose minds are stunted [and] whose characters are warped." In San Francisco, the leading Reform rabbi and editor of the most influential Jewish periodical in the West described the growing Jewish immigrant neighborhood as a "reeking pesthole." In Columbus, the Germans moved about as far away from the "Russians" as they could get; in Waterbury and Bridgeport, Connecticut, they tried to keep the eastern Europeans out of their synagogues and schools; and in Hartford, as late as 1901, the Touro Club was established for Germans only.[69]

Despite their arrogance and hostility, however, German Jews responded munificently. Rabbi Leo Franklin of Temple Beth-El in Detroit, where feelings seem to have been particularly bitter, reminded his congregation that as Jews their first obligation was to help the unfortunate. "How dare we expect the world to look with unprejudiced eyes upon us so long as Jew stands against Jew."[70] German Jews responded positively to this kind of charge by rabbinical and lay leadership. Settlement houses, federations of Jewish charities, and branches of the National Council of Jewish Women were established in many places, including Kansas City, Portland, San Francisco, Denver, Los Angeles, Indianapolis, Cincinnati, St. Louis, Omaha, Hartford, Pittsburgh, and Atlanta.[71]

Extraordinary amounts of money, time, and energy were spent in philanthropy and Americanization projects. But condescension continued to taint the benevolence. Eastern European immigrants in Rochester saw German aid as "cold charity and colder philanthropy."[72] And charity applicants in such places as Indianapolis, Columbus, Milwaukee, and Atlanta, like charity applicants in New York and Philadelphia, felt demeaned by the impersonal approach of the Germans and by the restrictions and stipulations attached to their benevolence.

The free medical care, the day nurseries, the orphanages and the settlement houses produced important benefits for eastern European Jews, but at least up to the period 1914–20, these failed to assuage entirely the bitterness stemming from German Jewish arrogance. And at the first opportunity (as they had done in New York, Boston, and Baltimore), the eastern Europeans created parallel institutions in almost every city or town they inhabited. In Cleveland, for example, where Germans had established the Russian Refugee Society and the Hebrew Temporary Home, the new immigrants in 1897 built their own Hebrew Shelter Home, which they described as "the only institution in town which asks no questions of its clients." Perhaps the most striking cases of duplication occurred in Denver and Los Angeles: in both cities, both Jewish communities built national institutions dedicated to the treatment of tuberculosis.[73]

The conflict between Germans and eastern Europeans was occasionally bitter, but sometimes it was softened by the sensitivity and commitment of extraordinary Jewish leaders. In Portland, Ben Selling, a businessman and philanthropist, and Ida Loewenberg, who helped found Neighborhood House and a branch of the NCJW, were indefatigable in their relief work and in their efforts to promote cooperation and mutual understanding. Rabbi Stephen Wise, an outspoken social reformer and Zionist who served Portland's Jewish community between 1900 and 1906, also brought his enormous talents to bear on the problem of building bridges between the Germans and the eastern Europeans.[74] In Kansas City, Jacob Billikopf, a young eastern European immigrant trained in America as a professional social worker, worked to bridge the two Jewish communities. Very much reflecting the background, career, and orientation of David Blaustein of New York's Educational Alliance, Billikopf served as secretary of the United Jewish Charities in Kansas City and sponsored the Jewish Educational Institute, one of the most successful settlement houses in the United States.[75]

German Jews of the interior were discomfited by the class and cultural differences of their eastern European coreligionists, and they feared that visible concentrations of new immigrants would generate or intensify hatred of Jews. Their fears were understandable. Anti-Semitism in the form of serious discrimination and physical abuse—as distinct from mental attitude and vulgar rhetoric—may have affected cities more than small towns and may have been more apparent in the East and the older Middle West than in the trans-Mississippi West and the South, but no part of the country escaped entirely the status anxieties, economic discontents, and inner-city ethnic territorial conflicts of the late nineteenth century that promoted anti-Jewish feeling.[76] In most places, the anti-Semitism experienced by eastern Europeans, particularly young children, took the form of verbal abuse. But Jewish adolescents often found themselves engaged in street battles with non-Jewish immigrants or native-born ethnics, and adult immigrant peddlers were beaten and attacked sporadically in such cities as Milwaukee, Detroit, and Rochester, as well as the larger cities.

Occasionally there was a chilling reminder of the Old World, as when Irish workers attacked the funeral procession of Rabbi Jacob Joseph in New York in 1902, or when forty young Irish men in Malden, Massachusetts, armed with iron bars, stones, and broken bottles, converged on the immigrant Jewish neighborhood of Suffolk Square in 1911 with shouts of "death to all the Jews." No one was killed, but the police failed to intervene while two dozen Jewish men and women were bloodied, grocery store and meat market windows were smashed, and an entire community was terrorized.⁷⁷

German Jews were more likely to experience anti-Semitism as social discrimination—exclusion from prestigious clubs and desirable neighborhoods; and they could not help notice that exclusion intensified as Jewish immigration from eastern Europe swelled. But in parts of the West—particularly San Francisco, where German Jews settled early relative to the indigenous population and where they had become relatively prosperous and were influential with non-Jewish elites—they were better able to modify the anti-Semitism directed against themselves as well as against their eastern European cousins. In San Francisco and the West generally, with its Indian, Mexican, and Oriental populations, the drive to maintain white supremacy also helped dilute anti-Semitism. But more important was the fact that the German Jewish arrival and influence in this section predated the crystallization of the status rivalries of the late nineteenth century. In San Francisco Jewish mayors, judges, financiers, and merchants helped construct the basic institutions of the city, and acceptance of Jews extended widely to elite social organizations. This situation remained virtually undisturbed even as the new eastern European immigrants gradually pushed San Francisco's Jewish population to nearly 7 percent of the city.⁷⁸

By contrast, in Minneapolis, where the first German Jewish settlers arrived only in the late 1860s and never acquired a position of any importance in civic affairs, the later Russian and Romanian ghettos faced a much rockier road to integration into city life; and the German Jews, by 1920, were completely shut out of Rotary, Kiwanis, and Lions service clubs, as well as from social clubs and local realty boards.⁷⁹

Anti-Semitism in the South, while sometimes dramatic and explosive, is more difficult to measure and characterize. The region was inhabited by large concentrations of blacks and, like the West, was marked by a strenuous devotion to white supremacy, which undoubtedly deflected some anti-Semitism. Moreover, German Jews arrived in the South relatively early, and their presence as peddlers, merchants, and innovative businessmen was seen as useful and as partly making up for the lack of a native merchant class. In the 1860s and 1870s, before the contentious battles for status, German Jews belonged to fashionable social clubs in several southern cities, and they were admired by many for their inventiveness and commercial energy. There is a thin line, however, separating these perceptions from Shylock images of cunning and avarice. By the 1890s, when the whole country, including the

South, was undergoing rapid economic change, when status concerns became paramount, and when eastern Europeans became more visible below the Mason-Dixon line, a new era appears to have been initiated. It began with the night riders in Georgia, Louisiana, and Mississippi in the early 1890s (see chapter 2) and reached its zenith with the lynching of the German Jewish Atlanta factory manager Leo Frank in 1915.[80]

The second or third largest Jewish community in the Deep South was in Atlanta, which appeared to be hospitable to its enterprising Israelites in the nineteenth century. Between 1874 and 1890, German Jews were deeply involved in Atlanta's civic life and achieved considerable political representation. But the beginnings of status rivalries, the psychological insecurities of Gentile capitalists, and the arrival in Atlanta of several thousand Russian Jews between 1890 and 1910 all came together to create tension and trouble. Between 1890 and 1930, only one person of Jewish descent was elected to office in Atlanta, and he had long since given up any attachment to or identification with Judaism. By the early twentieth century, Jews as a group were excluded from Atlanta's most prestigious clubs. Not long afterward, they were excluded from clubs in Richmond and from elite Mardi Gras festivities in New Orleans.[81] Rabbi David Marx, the spiritual leader of the Reform Hebrew Benevolent Congregation (the Temple) in Atlanta, believed that the presence of unassimilated, lower-class eastern Europeans negatively affected the Gentile community's image of Jews. Significant numbers of German Jews in Atlanta appear to have agreed with Marx; in 1905 they formed the exclusive Standard Club, from which they barred eastern European Jews.[82]

The Germans believed that the "Russians" were the source of the new anti-Semitism; the "Russians" thought the Germans were deceiving themselves about their acceptance in the host society as well as about the gains to be had from rapid assimilation. Tensions within each group as well as between them mounted in 1906, when Atlanta was the scene of a major race riot. Speeches and newspaper articles preceding the riot pointed to Jews as saloonkeepers and brothel owners and fed the popular conviction that Jews encouraged black licentiousness. Jews constituted only a tiny percentage of tavern owners and do not seem to have had any commercial connection to brothels. They did, however, live among blacks, and their small stores were sometimes near or in the same buildings as brothels. This was enough to produce vicious anti-Semitic diatribes and, in the context of antiblack violence, substantial damage to Jewish property.[83] The part of the riot that touched the eastern European community was seen by them as a rather benign American version of a familiar Old World phenomenon. The Germans, on the other hand, were seriously shaken but not as thoroughly shaken as they would be seven years later, when the arrest of Leo Frank encouraged the expression of latent anti-Semitism in Atlanta and in the Deep South, generally.

Leo Frank, brought from New York by his uncle, a respected citizen of long standing in Atlanta, quickly became a member of the Temple community. He married into an established family and was elected president of the local B'nai B'rith lodge. When in 1913, Mary Phagen, a thirteen-year-old employee of his factory, was found brutally murdered, Frank was arrested and, on scanty evidence and contradictory testimony, convicted and sentenced to death. The Reverend Luther Bricker, the murdered girl's pastor, later wrote that "when the police arrested a Jew, and a Yankee Jew at that, all of the inborn prejudice against the Jews rose up in a feeling of satisfaction that here would be a victim worthy of the crime." The courthouse during the course of the trial was surrounded by throngs of people making anti-Semitic speeches and remarks, and Populist Tom Watson's *Jeffersonian* unleashed a series of attacks alleging that Jews were involved in international plots and that they secretly lusted after Christian girls.

Frank's sentence was later commuted to life imprisonment by Georgia's governor. This greatly angered many Georgians, who called for the governor's impeachment. When they were unsuccessful, they took matters into their own hands. In 1915, after one attempt on Frank's life had failed, the prisoner was taken by a mob from the Atlanta penitentiary to Marietta, Georgia, Mary Phagen's hometown, and lynched. While other anti-Semitic incidents and insensitive actions occurred before and after the Frank episode, none equaled it in its impact on the German Jewish community. Unlike in New York, where anti-Semitic violence was mainly confined to Irish workers rioting against Jewish workers, in the South, where Jews were socially mobile, working-class whites had attacked a white middle-class manager. Class antagonism had been added to ethnic and religious anti-Semitism, and the Germans now viewed their acceptance in Atlanta as fragile and tenuous. Some even left the city.[84]

The Frank lynching pales in comparison to the violence in the South to blacks and even to Italians—twenty-two Italian immigrants were lynched by southern mobs between 1891 and 1901. Moreover, although a revived Ku Klux Klan emerged in Atlanta and spread throughout the South, the anti-

Semitism of Klan members appears to have been discharged more often against the imaginary distant Jew—a Rothschild, for example—than it was against Jewish neighbors and merchants.[85]

Recognizing this, Jews made no mass exodus from the South, nor did they retreat behind closed doors. But the events leading up to the Frank lynching ended the most active period of political involvement by Jews in the South prior to World War II. Southern anti-Semitism may have been less consistent and excessive than the anti-Semitism of the Northeast, just as American anti-Semitism in general was less potent and pervasive than that of Europe, but it could have important consequences, nonetheless.[86]

American Jewish life in all regions of the United States was not characterized primarily by struggles against anti-Semitism but was shaped by mobility and the rhythms of the great American balancing act—the need for acculturation on the one side and the desire to retain something of a Jewish world on the other. This dynamic was a central and defining experience for both German and eastern Europeans Jews everywhere in America.

Beyond New York City and other large American metropolitan centers, adventurous eastern European immigrants joined and ultimately vastly outnumbered German Jews. In every place, newcomers created problems for the Jewish establishment, but over time they were accommodated and integrated. Indeed, in many areas the new immigrants, with their penchant for residential and business clustering and their strong Jewish identity, resuscitated the Jewish community. The confluence of Jewish stores, institutions, workplaces, and residences transformed the public character of the neighborhood streets wherever significant numbers of immigrant Jews settled. Less densely populated than the Jewish communities of New York, Boston, Philadelphia, and Baltimore—and perhaps less culturally diverse than the Lower East Side, which could afford the luxury of intramural arguments—Jewish communities in small cities and towns remained manifestly Jewish.

In these places, eastern European Jews like the Germans who preceded them were highly mobile. In the American interior, where Jews were more involved with commerce, business enterprise led more frequently and easily to success than in the Northeast urban corridor, where the majority of immigrant Jews were workers. Even first-generation Jewish immigrants in small cities and towns moved into the middle-class in disproportionate numbers. Those who were successful sometimes changed their neighbor-hoods—but rarely their cities. They repeated their process of clustering in such locations in Cleveland, Atlanta, Chicago, Cincinnati, Columbus, Detroit, Providence, Portland, and Milwaukee. The new settlements were different from one another as well as from the original settlements, but all over the United States immigrant Jews continued to transplant and nourish a recognizable Jewish culture.[87]

CHAPTER SIX

VARIETIES OF RELIGIOUS
BELIEF AND BEHAVIOR

To THE German Jews who settled in the United States in the nineteenth century, the spirit of the times seemed to call for accommodation to the prevailing Protestantism of the new environment. They responded by gradually adapting Jewish religious ideology and form to the Protestant model, ultimately producing an American variety of the Reform Judaism then prevalent in Germany.

Reform emphasized ethical monotheism, rationalism, and the mission of justice as stated in Prophets; and it moved away from the idea of a separate Jewish peoplehood and from the demanding Mosaic code. Leaders of the Reform movement attempted to institute a universal ritual; most congregations, though not without dissent from traditionalists on the inside and from Orthodox believers on the outside, radically abridged the length and content of religious services. They decreased the use of Hebrew in favor of German—and later, English. Many did away with prayer shawls and skullcaps, and some even introduced Sunday services and organ music. These changes were made partly out of concern for Gentile approval but also because it was understood that the pervasive secularism of American culture would make strict adherence to religious law difficult, if not impossible.

As early as 1869 the ideology of radical Reformist David Einhorn was reflected in a platform adopted by fifteen rabbis meeting in Philadelphia. It reinforced the concept of universal mission by proclaiming that the "messianic goal of Israel is not the restoration of the old Jewish state . . . but the union of all men as children of God."[1] The universalism of Reform Judaism appeared to be genuine, transcending tradition even to the point of including women. Most Reform temples permitted women to sit with men in family pews and to sing in the choir. The Reform prayerbook excised the male benediction thanking God, "that I am not a woman," and women were counted as part of the minyan (the ten-person quorum necessary to hold services). Through Reform temple sisterhoods, women administered charitable and other social services and tended to temple maintenance and to the religious education of children.[2]

An attractive blend of egalitarianism, American secularism, and the highest principles of the prophetic tradition, Reform appeared in the 1870s to be at the threshold of making a triumphant sweep through organized Jewish religious life in the United States. Reform leader Isaac Mayer Wise established the Union of American Hebrew Congregations (UAHC) in Cincinnati in 1873 and the Hebrew Union College (HUC) two years later, confident that these institutions would eventually unite and serve all American Jewry. The HUC did not fulfill Wise's initial goal of being the only rabbinical seminary in the nation, but it did flourish and in 1883 graduated a distinguished first class, including David Philipson and Joseph Krauskopf.

Institutional success did not, however, mean the end of religious contentiousness between Reformists and Traditionalists, within the Reform movement or without. In the 1870s in New York City alone, twenty-nine eastern European Orthodox synagogues continued to be an important religious presence. Moreover, in many parts of the United States, congregations that had abandoned Orthodox practices neither joined UAHC nor called themselves Reform. And occasionally the term *Conservative-Orthodox* was employed by those congregations that had instituted moderate changes, such as abridged services. Even those who joined UAHC did not always give up such traditional practices as celebrating the second day of festivals and High Holy Days.[3]

In the context of American secularism and antiauthoritarianism, the organizational rule in most religions was congregationalism. Final authority rested with devotional groups voluntarily associated with a movement or denomination, rather than with the rulings of a central authority. Individual congregants exercised the same freedom to take from the faith what they desired and to ignore the rest. Sometimes the differences generated by voluntarism led to division and sharper denominational definitions. Judaism was no exception. Many Jews, for example, continued to be meticulous in their observance of dietary laws; others accused these traditionalists of practicing an ancient barbaric cult and poked fun at "kitchen Judaism."

The conflict came to an open breach at the *treyfa* (unkosher) banquet in Cincinnati on 11 July 1883, at the celebration of the tenth anniversary of UAHC and the first ordination of HUC graduates. The first course was shellfish, which propelled a number of shocked observant Jews from the room—and eventually from the UAHC. Visible insult had been added to the decades-old verbal attack on traditional Jewish practice. The provocative episode led to an enduring split within American Jewry. Several Jewish leaders and groups, particularly in the East, were outraged by the *treyfa* banquet and even more so by the silence of Isaac M. Wise, president of HUC. The *American Hebrew,* for example, denounced the public flouting of ritual law by a rabbinical school supposedly serving all varieties of Judaism. By 1884 there was mounting pressure on congregations to withdraw from UAHC and to establish a new, more traditional rabbinical seminary in the East.[4] In this context, and in part because of the arrival of new waves of traditional Jews, some Reformists like Kaufman Kohler, the son-in-law of David Einhorn, expressed the need for a declaration of independence from "half-civilized orthodoxy." The goal was to distinguish Reform Judaism not only from the more traditional expressions of the Jewish religion but also from nonsectarian universalism, which was gaining popularity with Jews whose Jewish identity had become marginal.

A major challenge to Reform arose in 1876 with the establishment of Felix Adler's New York Society for Ethical Culture. Adler, a former rabbinical student and the son of the rabbi of the nation's leading Reform synagogue, Temple Emanu-El in New York, saw no need for continued Jewish separation. He aimed to build a more moral theology and, in turn, a more moral world that drew from multiple religious traditions. Throughout the 1880s, Felix Adler, a brilliant and effective orator drew enormous crowds, mostly Jewish, to his weekly Sunday morning lectures.[5]

Threatened from the Left by the universalism of Ethical Culture and from the Right by Orthodoxy, leaders of the Reform movement held a conference in Pittsburgh in 1885. A platform was promulgated emphasizing classical Reform principles that were designed to distinguish people in the Reform movement from the ritualistic traditionalists and the radical universalists. The "Mosaic and Rabbinical laws that regulate diet" were rejected, as was the concept of heaven and hell. But it was maintained that the moral laws of Judaism continued to represent "the highest conception of the God-idea." The Reformers also made it clear that they saw themselves as a modern, progressive religious community and not a people expecting "a return to Palestine."[6]

Isaac M. Wise welcomed the Pittsburgh platform as an American document propounding a Judaism for "American Israelites." He was joined in his enthusiasm for the newly articulated radical Reform principles by rabbis Krauskopf and Philipson, who served as vice president and secretary, respectively, at the Pittsburgh conference. Several other rabbis also accepted the Pittsburgh platform as definitive, including J. Leonard Levy of Pittsburgh, Solomon Schindler and Charles Fleischer of Boston, Henry Berkowitz of Kansas City, Missouri, and Jacob Voorsanger of San Francisco. Fleischer, Krauskopf, and Berkowitz regularly exchanged pulpits with Protestant ministers; and together with Schindler, Voorsanger, and Levy, they encouraged Americanization and a universalism so broad that Gentile and Jew could "join in an adoration of the same God."[7]

For these men the Pittsburgh platform was Reform Judaism; for others it was a declaration no more binding than earlier statements; and in between there was a whole series of intermediate positions.[8] But the radical spirit of the platform in time influenced the entire Reform rabbinate. In 1892, for example, the Central Conference of American Rabbis (CCAR), representing nearly every rabbi serving UAHC congregants, eliminated circumcision and all other initiatory rites and ceremonies as a requirement for conversion to Judaism. It also approved the traditionally prohibited practice of cremation.[9]

Five years later, in 1897, the CCAR eliminated the traditional *gett* (divorce decree) and *ketubah* (marriage contract) and reaffirmed the radical view that all Jewish legal codes were nothing more than "religious literature." In the same year, in response to the emergence of a nascent but energetic Zionist movement, the CCAR rejected once more the goal of establishing a Jewish state. After Kaufman Kohler's assumption of the presidency of HUC in 1903, Zionists and suspected Zionists were dismissed from the faculty.[10]

Even at its peak, radical Reform did not completely dominate Reform Judaism. But Reform Judaism, partly influenced by the radical spirit of the Pittsburgh platform, felt threatening to traditional Jews, and it generated efforts by the Orthodox to put their own house in order and to establish institutional frameworks for recruiting and holding adherents. This competition during the 1880s and 1890s, when a mass influx of eastern European Jews inundated the German Jewish community, led, as we shall see, to the now familiar trifurcation of American Jewry into Reform, Orthodox, and Conservative branches as well as to significant division within each of these loosely organized groups.

Some eighteen to twenty major synagogues in the United States were still Orthodox in 1881 when eastern Europeans began to arrive in large numbers.[11] But for the most part, early newcomers encountered Reform Judaism in America, and they were clearly repelled by it. The apparent rejection by Reformists of Jewish peoplehood, of Halakah, and of time-honored traditions, and their adoptions of such Christian forms as Sunday services and organ music were seen by eastern Europeans as a betrayal. For many recently uprooted Jews, Reform was less acceptable than having no religion at all.

By the nineteenth century, European Judaism had already been partly torn from its moorings. The forces of industrialization and urbanization and the quest among Jews for modernism produced new secular ideologies and movements like the Haskalah, Zionism, and socialism, all of which challenged Orthodoxy (see chapter 1). Adherence to the new ideologies, or even to a generalized secular sentiment, resulted in less rigorous observance of Jewish law. As early as the 1870s, Jewish shops in Odessa were open on the Sabbath. Jews carried money on the day of rest, frequented cafés, and according to some accounts, they "put out their cigarettes on the syn-agogue's outer walls when rushing off to recite the mourner's prayer."[12] Abraham Cahan paints a similar picture for Lemberg, where "Yiddishkayt [was] very weak" in the first decades of the twentieth century.[13]

But a break with Orthodox tradition did not necessarily mean a break with an ethnic culture rooted in the traditions of religious consciousness, which also prevailed in the Jewish community. These were the traditions eastern European immigrants carried as part of their cultural baggage to the New World. It enabled many American Jews to remain Jewish despite their secularism.

An important minority of transplanted Jews continued to live their lives enveloped in Orthodoxy. Others were what some have labeled *orthoprax*, Jews who continued traditional practices without believing the rules were divine revelation. Even larger numbers of immigrant Jews, though less observant, continued to conform to some traditional norms, such as dietary regulations and shul attendance. Participation in synagogue services was especially noticeable during the Jewish High Holy Days of Rosh Hashanah and Yom Kippur. Indeed, in many cities during the Holy Days, congrega-tions could not accommodate all who wished to attend services. On the Lower East Side of New York in 1917, for example, it was necessary prior to Rosh Hashanah to create hundreds of temporary synagogues, with a seat-ing capacity of 164,000.[14] Even many socialists fasted on Yom Kippur and could be seen in shul. Some, like Harry Golden's father, went to shul regularly. When Harry chided his father about the apparent contradiction, the elder Golden replied: "These people are my brethren; they are the people among whom I was raised and I love them. Dudja Silverberg goes to shul to speak with God. I go to shul to speak with Dudja."[15]

Many among the socialists, the less observant Orthodox, and the secularist freethinkers wished to maintain ties with the Jewish community. And indeed, most eastern European immigrants, bound by ethnic commitments and tradition, continued to obey some ritual prescriptions and continued to affiliate with Orthodoxy. In 1881 only a tiny minority of the two hundred major synagogues in America were Orthodox. By 1890, after nearly a decade of mass immigration, the majority of Jewish congregations were Orthodox. And by 1910, 90 percent of more than two thousand synagogues in America called themselves Orthodox. More than half of these synagogues were in the Northeast, where the majority of Jews continued to reside. The Midwest boasted 340 congregations, mostly in the greater Chicago area. More than 130 congregations dotted the South, and even the Far West counted seventy.[16]

The vigor of Jewish religious life in America was reflected in the increasing number of congregations, particularly of the Orthodox branch. Sometimes it appeared that the traditional Jewish religious spirit was being rekindled in America, but this was an illusion. Most congregations— whether in New York or Chicago, Providence, Cleveland, Milwaukee, or Indianapolis, were small landslayt congregations, without permanent rabbis or buildings. They reflected the need for old-country regional ties and social familiarity as well as lingering antagonisms among Ashkenazic and Sephardic Jews. Despite the nominal Orthodoxy of the immigrants, then, the number of synagogues they established may indicate cultural yearning more than religious need. The number of congregations after 1900 actually increased while the percentage of Jews maintaining membership in congregations declined.[17]

The tradition of religious consciousness brought to the New World by eastern European immigrants remained vital, but as we have noted, it had been seriously challenged and diluted even in the old countries. In individualistic America, "a treyfe land where even the stones are impure," Jewish piety never fully dissipated; but it did soften, and many Jews gradually drifted into a secular mode of life.[18]

For some, like Hebrew writer Ephraim Lisitsky, secular America promoted a longing for the old country:

I have never forgotten the impression of my first Saturday in Boston. I compared it to the Sabbath in Slutzk and my heart bled. Actually there was no comparison, for Slutzk, though poverty-stricken, dressed up in glorious raiment in honor of the Sabbath. . . . But in Boston very few Jews observed the Sabbath. . . . Leaving the synagogue after the Sabbath service, the observants were confronted by a tumultuous Jewish quarter; shopkeepers stood in their shop doorways; peddlers on their wagons shouted their wares. . . . As I entered our house it seemed to me that the Sabbath candles were bowed in mourning.[19]

Observant Jews faced great difficulties in America, a place where, as the Slutzker Rav (Rabbi David Willowski) observed, "groups with varying viewpoints came to be settled and no one recognizes any authority."[20] The most poignant figures in the immigrant community were the few eastern European rabbis who came to the United States. Moses Weinberger, who knew first-hand the status of the rabbinate in the old country, drew this picture of its depressed condition in New York in 1887:

In this great city of over 100,000 Jews, and 130 Orthodox congregations, there are no more than three or four . . . rabbis who [can] decide what is prohibited and permitted. Even they . . . came here like everyone else, to find food, and located these positions only after a great deal of trouble and effort. . . . Their regular salaries are so small that it would be shameful to record the amount in print. They thus live penuriously; a small communal stipend, combined with a few isolated gifts, barely cover their basic human needs.[21]

Although the number of eastern European rabbis increased over the next decade, neither their economic situation nor their status improved.[22] Hutchins Hapgood found that as late as 1902 Orthodox rabbis were "mainly poor." They "live in the barest tenement houses" he wrote, "and pursue a calling which no longer involves much honor or standing. . . . The congregations are for the most part small, poor, and unimportant. Few can pay the rabbi more than $3 or $4 a week, and often, instead of having a regular salary he is reduced to an occasional fee for his services at weddings, births and holy festivals generally."[23]

The sad fate of Rabbi Jacob Joseph is an example of the condition of the

Orthodox rabbinate in late-nineteenth-century America. In 1887 an association of downtown New York congregations, in an effort to resolve the chaos and confusion within Orthodoxy, decided to establish the office of chief rabbi. Distinguished rabbis from Europe were invited to apply. It was soon discovered that no truly outstanding rabbinical leader was eager to come to America, where scholarship was little respected and religion ignored. But Vilna Rabbi Jacob Joseph, who was heavily in debt, eventually responded to the invitation to fill the office, which carried a yearly salary of $2,500, plus a stipend for rent, furnishings, and utilities.

The association of congregations chose Joseph primarily to lend unity and prestige to downtown's conglomerate of Jewries and to oversee the chaos of ritual slaughtering in New York. This entailed the imposition of a tax on kosher meat and chicken in order to finance the supervision. Jacob Joseph was well intentioned, and his personality and manner won over even many of his critics; but recollections of the hated *korobke* (Russian meat tax), squabbles between butchers and slaughterers, corruption, and disregard of Jewish law and Board of Health ordinances posed difficulties impossible for the rabbi to overcome. The jealousy and slander from rabbinical rivals, the animosity of radicals, and the resentment of secularized Jews toward even mild authority added to the difficulties and, ultimately, brought disaster. The grandiose title of chief rabbi did little to conceal the powerlessness of the position. Bewildered, suffering from debilitating illness, and beset by general communal indifference, the rabbi was relegated to obscurity. This was relieved only by an extraordinary display of public mourning at the rabbi's death in 1902, when, as if in atonement, downtown Jewry turned out one-hundred-thousand strong at Jacob Joseph's funeral.[24]

The attempt to institute the office of chief rabbi demonstrated a willingness on the part of eastern European Jews to confront their problems and to try to implement solutions. The organization and activity of the Union of American Hebrew Orthodox Congregations in support of the office and objectives of the chief rabbi were indicative of the latent vitality of Orthodoxy. Moreover, the existence of a chief rabbi in New York City moved other communities to institute the same.

Chicago Jewish immigrants invited Jacob David Willowski to be chief rabbi in 1903. On a visit from the old country in 1900, Willowski had characterized America as a *treyfa medine* (unkosher or irreligious land), but he accepted the position nonetheless. Confronted with problems similar to those that engulfed Jacob Joseph in New York, particularly around the issues of kosher food products, Willowski resigned in 1904 and soon left for Palestine, where he spent the rest of his life. Other communities, however, had more success, and several chief rabbis, including Bernard Louis Levinthal of Philadelphia, Eliezer Silver of Cincinnati, Moses Margolies of Boston, Asher Zarchy of Louisville, and Judah Leib Levine of Detroit, supervised ritual preparations, presided over Jewish courts, and generally provided leadership to emerging Orthodox communities.[25]

Eastern European rabbis in the main, however—bearded, Yiddish speaking, dressed in Old World style, and stubbornly resistant to accommodation—were unable to make life bearable for themselves; nor were they able to lead congregants in any meaningful way or to provide appropriate, attractive models for the younger generation. "The average Jewish boy of fifteen," reported the *New York Tribune* in 1905, "lives the life of New York contemporaneous to the minute," while his elders still live in "the existence of Kishinev, Lemberg or Jassy. . . . The laissez-faire spirit of our national life seems in many cases to accomplish what the persecution of ages has failed to bring about—namely, the alienation of the Jewish child from the strict observance of his racial religious rites."[26]

Supportive evidence for the *Tribune* reporter's pessimistic conclusion abounded. A Jewish woman whose daughter had preceded her to the United States wrote to the *Jewish Daily Forward* in dismay: "During the few years she was here without us she became a regular Yankee and forgot how to talk Yiddish. . . . She says it is not nice to talk Yiddish and that I am a greenhorn. . . . She wants to make a Christian woman out of me. She does not like me to light the Sabbath candles. . . . She blows them out."[27] Lincoln Steffens, in the course of his newspaper work "would pass a synagogue where a score or more of boys were sitting hatless in their old clothes, smoking cigarettes on the steps outside, and their fathers, all dressed in black, with their high hats, uncut beards, and side curls, were going in . . . tearing their hair and rending their garments. . . . Two, three thousand years of devotion, courage, and suffering for a cause [were] lost in a generation."[28]

The sympathetic Steffens was premature in his judgment. Jewish spiritual life in America, including Orthodoxy, would undergo redefinition and revitalization in the coming years, particularly after World War I. But Steffens correctly sensed that, in the early years of the twentieth century, there was a drift toward secularization in the Jewish community, as there was in most religious groups.

In these early years, traditional Jews struggled heroically to establish and maintain their own network of institutions, including *kheyderim* (schoolrooms), where an attempt was made to inculcate the ancient faith in the new generation. But the struggle was mostly lost. There were only two Jewish day schools in all of the United States before 1915, and the *kheyderim,* privately run in storefronts or basements, were attended only after a full day of public school. The rebbe, or religious teacher, was often an immigrant Jew who failed in job or business and turned to giving "Hebrew lessons." These lessons were mostly alphabet drills and rote instruction in the mechanics of prayer book reading; rarely was an effort made to bring any of this into a dynamic dialogue with the larger Jewish tradition or the American experience.[29] It is no wonder that the *kheyderim,* staffed by poorly trained, poorly paid, impatient, and frustrated teachers and attended by tired and bored boys, lost more than half their pupils each year. Between 1903 and 1907, only 25 percent of Jewish children between ages six and sixteen were receiving Jewish instruction, and significant numbers of these were taught at home by itinerant rebbes.[30]

There were some schools of quality, particularly the communally run Talmud Torahs in New York. Established for the poor and situated in congested immigrant quarters, the Talmud Torahs on East Broadway and in Harlem, Brooklyn, and the Bronx attracted many pupils. The early policy of educating only the poor was gradually modified, and parents who could afford tuition were charged on a weekly or monthly basis. Ultimately, the Talmud Torah, with afternoon classes from four to seven o'clock, developed a system of grading and school management similar to the public schools. Even in the best circumstances, however, Hebrew schools had to compete for the student's time and interest with the public schools and with such diversions as stickball and other games of the street.[31] Schools were also established by the Labor Zionists, the Workmen's Circle, the anarcho-communists, and the Yiddishists in an effort to link the generations by teaching the Jewish language and religion from a cultural and historical standpoint. These experiments generally remained on the fringe of the immigrant community. They imparted to some a strong attachment to Yiddish and yiddishkayt, but they could not stop the general tide of Americanization and secularization.

If the rabbis mourned the lack of religious observance among Jews, Christian missionaries despaired about the failure to convert Jews. All through the 1890s and early 1900s, Jews were subjected to a campaign of proselytizing by missionaries who established headquarters in many cities. In Cleveland, for example, the Josephine Mission, a branch of the Euclid Avenue Baptist Church, opened its doors in the middle of the Jewish immigrant district and used candy to entice Jewish children to classes.[32]

In some of the settlement houses attended by Jewish children seeking recreation or a hot lunch, the foundations of Judaism were attacked in less blatant but, nonetheless, irritating ways. Walls were adorned with crosses and crucifixes, while Jewish students were taught lessons in Christian ethics, or "universal values." The public schools, too, in their attempts to Americanize the immigrants, presented irksome difficulties for Jews, especially at Christmas time. Explicit attempts at conversion elicited rage and even violence from the immigrants; implicit attempts at Christianization were met with boycotts of public schools and lobbying of school authorities to stop inflicting "repugnant religious convictions on the school children."[33] Despite the uproar, Christian missionaries, official and unofficial, posed little danger for the Jews. As the *New York Herald* put it: "The Jew of the second generation does not become a Christian. He is as far from any such conversion as his father."[34] A more significant threat came from diversions in the Jewish community that competed with religious observance and synagogue attendance, like the theater, night school, the labor union, the fraternal lodge, and the nonreligious Yiddish press.

The greatest danger, however, lay in the secular American environment and the fact that the business life of the nation was adjusted to a Christian calendar. The quest for economic mobility and the need to work on the Sabbath made piety difficult. This "economic factor," Rabbi Mordecai Kaplan complained, "makes even the distinctive religious expression of Jewish life [particularly Sabbath observance] very difficult."[35]

The problem was not unique to New York. In Cleveland, disregard of the traditional Sabbath was already widespread by 1882. In Chicago the Have Emma (lovers of the faith) congregation was jestingly labeled the Halba Emma (half-faith) congregation, because many of its peddler members rode to and from services in horse and wagon. By 1906, an estimated 91 percent of eastern European Jewish immigrants ceased to be strictly Orthodox in their religious practices, and by 1913 almost half the stores and pushcarts on the Lower East Side of New York were open for business on the Sabbath.[36] Nonobservance in America surprised only the most recent arrivals. When Rose Cohen landed here, she found that her father—who had preceded her to the United States by only a few months—had changed.

"I saw a . . . man with a closely cut beard and no sign of earlocks. . . . I could scarcely believe my eyes. Father had been the most pious Jew in our neighborhood." Now he "touched coin on the sabbath. . . . I wondered was it true, as Mindle said, that 'in America one at once became a libertine'?"[37] Over time, as Orthodoxy became less necessary as a cultural and psychological anchor, its ritual aspects and social relations grew increasingly difficult to sustain. The *tsitsis,* the fringed cloth worn by males beneath their outer garments, and the *tefillin,* phylacteries wrapped on the arm and head every morning, were discarded. Wigs, prayer shawls, and skull caps became less obvious. Synagogue attendance and affiliation plummeted.

The consciousness of religious tradition, however, was not lightly abandoned. As we shall see presently, many Jews moved toward a compromise between the need for continuity and the need for change and did not discard their entire heritage. Some observant Jews steadfastly refused to give in to the pressures of altered circumstances and continued to try to recreate the religious milieu they had left behind in eastern Europe. Centered after 1902 in Agudath Harabonim (the Union of Orthodox Rabbis), this constituency, including Jews from New York, New Haven, Providence, Minneapolis, Omaha, and Louisville, sought to reestablish the traditional authority of the European rabbi, and frowned on any attempt at Americanization.[38] The denunciation of the English sermon by the Slutzker Rav was typical. He considered such sermons so dangerous that, if allowed to go unchecked, "there [would be] no hope for the continuance of the Jewish religion."[39]

Others, however, believed that the Jewish religion had no future unless Orthodoxy adapted to an American idiom. This more modern group of traditional Jews, mainly from western Europe, had its nucleus in the Union of Orthodox Jewish Congregations, established in 1898, and was represented by rabbis Henry P. Mendes and Bernard Drachman. Mendes, the spiritual leader of the Spanish and Portuguese (Sephardic) synagogue of New York, also founded the Orthodox Union. The goal of this organization, as distinct from the more traditional Union of Orthodox Rabbis, was to strengthen American Orthodox congregations by attempting to attract eastern European Jews and their offspring. Drachman, an English-speaking minister who very much shared this goal, was one of the first American-born, university-trained, Orthodox rabbis to serve the needs of an American-born population.

In 1902, responding to the need for an Orthodox synagogue to serve modern Jewish young adults in Harlem, Mendes and Drachman joined with local residents in establishing Congregation Shomre Emunah at 121st Street and Madison Avenue. The organizers of this Orthodox Union synagogue pledged to conduct services according to "Orthodox ritual in an impressive decorous manner." They promised their Americanized constituency that the irritating noise, commotion, and unseemly commercialism of the immigrant congregation would find no place in the modern Orthodox synagogue. Another modern Orthodox Union synagogue, Congregation Mount Sinai, was established in Harlem two years later and joined Shomre Emunah in an anti-assimilation crusade. These two congregations were made up of young, mostly New York–born Jews who had recently migrated from the Lower East Side. Their hope was to serve as models for downtown Jews and to attract acculturated English-speaking eastern European Jews who wanted to retain a relatively traditional form of prayer service while eliminating some of the immigrant trappings.[40]

As early as 1900, there was already emerging downtown a new eastern European elite of accomplished men, many of whom readily found common cause with the Orthodox from uptown. Wealthy builders Harry Fischel and Jonas Weil, lawyer Otto Rosalsky, editor Kasriel Sarosohn, and several others had come to America at a young age at the very beginning of eastern European immigration. Each had become Americanized but had retained his religious affinities. Each saw the need for an American Orthodoxy.[41] Rabbis Mendes and Drachman welcomed the participation of these men, who could be role models for younger eastern European Jews. But Orthodox Union congregations, which were neither eastern European nor Reform, were denounced by the Union of Orthodox Rabbis, and they attracted few newcomers. Most eastern European Jews preferred to remain nonobservant (or minimally observant) Orthodox than associate with the new American Orthodox religious life-style.

A minority in the immigrant community, however, was responsive to the anti-assimilation crusade of the modernizers. Eastern European Rabbi Philip Hillel Klein, a leader of the Union of Orthodox Rabbis and head of a large downtown congregation, broke with his organization and joined the Orthodox Union. Klein also opened rooms in his synagogue for late Sabbath afternoon services to accommodate those forced to work in the earlier part of the day. By 1910, Klein was joined in his action by at least two other eastern European rabbis.

A loose coalition of young downtowners—with help from Rabbi Klein and his eastern European colleagues, American Sephardic rabbis H. P.

Mendes and Henry J. Morais, and German American rabbis Bernard Drachman and Henry Schneeberger—established Young People's synagogues, offering "dignified services to recall the indifferent in Jewry back to faith."[42] The English liturgy, the orderly rituals, and the general aesthetic reflected the congregants' growing identity as Americans. And making the late Saturday afternoon service into the major service of the week reflected the realities and rhythms of the American economy. Young People's synagogue leaders did not approve of Sabbath violation, but neither would they condemn Sabbath breakers. They accepted them and served them. At the same time, these leaders tried to make observing the Sabbath easier by lobbying against Sunday closing laws and by fighting for a five-day workweek.[43]

The Young People's synagogues, the Orthodox Union and its unofficial youth division (the Jewish Endeavor Society, established in 1900), and the modern Talmud Torah movement were all part of the anti-assimilation crusade. The goal of this crusade was the adoption of American mores without destroying the essence of Jewish faith and tradition. This was also the goal of the men who founded the Jewish Theological Seminary of America in New York City. Mostly in response to the need for an American Orthodoxy—but also in response to the antinationalistic and antitraditional postures assumed by the Reform movement at Hebrew Union College and in its 1885 Pittsburgh platform—plans were made for a new rabbinical seminary in 1886. Early in the year, Sabato Morais of Philadelphia, Henry Schneeberger, H. P. Mendes and Bernard Drachman of New York, and other Orthodox synagogue spokesmen met with Marcus Jastrow of Philadelphia, Alexander Kohut of New York, and Aaron Bettleheim of San Francisco, all leaders of congregations that had adopted some reforms. These representatives pooled their energies to create a new seminary to revitalize classical Judaism.

Although the seminary developed into the central institution of Conservative Judaism, none of the founders knew at the time that they would be promoting a separate denomination. Indeed, many of those men—who later came to be known as the fathers of Conservatism—were difficult to distinguish from many of their colleagues who stayed in American Orthodoxy. Of the rabbis on the original faculty of the Jewish Theological Seminary, four were considered at the border of Reform, but five—Drachman, Abraham Mendes, H. P. Mendes, Morais, and Henry W. Schneeberger— were Orthodox, and one—Kohut—classified himself as in the "Mosaic-rabbinical tradition." Not only were most of the early JTS associates Orthodox, the seminary's constitution insisted on remaining "faithful to Mosaic Law and ancestral traditions."[44]

The Jewish Theological Seminary, then, was first and foremost a rabbinical seminary dominated by Orthodox Jews committed to combating radical Reform. Many on the faculty and advisory board, however, were dedicated to what Morais called the preservation of "positive historical Judaism," a phrase that suggested discomfort not only with radical Reform but also with rigid Old World Orthodoxy. And it was no accident that the new institution was called the Jewish Theological Seminary, the same name as the spiritual center of the positive-historical school at Breslau.

The positive-historical school, which came into being in central and western Europe in the second half of the nineteenth century, maintained that Judaism was the totality of Jewish experience—a dynamic and, therefore, changing religion. It emphasized the evolving religious experience of the Jewish people in their commitment to God and Torah. And while it spoke for the authority of tradition, it also allowed for *wissenschaft,* freedom of research and expression. This positive-historical perspective was brought to the United States by a group of rabbis, including Benjamin Szold, Marcus Jastrow, and Alexander Kohut. Kohut was the preeminent scholar of the JTS group, and he had the most influence on the program of the seminary. In an address at the exercises opening the seminary in January 1887, Kohut already envisioned an institution where "a different spirit will prevail . . . that of *Conservative Judaism*."[45]

The founders hoped the seminary would produce a rabbinate and, in turn, a Judaism committed to freedom of ideological expression as well as loyalty to traditional observance. In this way, they hoped to unite the vast majority of American Jews. But the seminary, like the movement for an American Orthodoxy, lacked a natural constituency. That constituency—acculturated eastern Europeans and, more so, their grown children—had not yet emerged. In addition, although it unequivocally set forth its purpose, the seminary had no clearly articulated ideology, and it lacked charismatic leadership. By 1900 only seventeen rabbis had been ordained, and six congregations that had been affiliated with the seminary moved into the Reform camp. There were few new students and almost no funds.

It was this depressed set of circumstances that Cyrus Adler was determined to remedy. Adler, an Arkansas-born pupil of Sabato Morais, who went on to earn a doctorate in Semitics at Johns Hopkins, brought the seminary's condition to the attention of Jacob Schiff. An uptown philanthropist known for his devotion to Jewish causes, Schiff had long been committed to the Reform movement. But he saw that a revitalized seminary might succeed, where Reform Judaism had not, in building a bridge to help immigrants cross over to American Judaism and the American mainstream. Jacob Schiff convinced his wealthy friends Daniel and Simon Guggenheim, as well as Mayer Sulzberger and Louis Marshall, to help. In a marvelous demonstration of patrician intelligence and commitment to the preservation of a religious-ethnic heritage, the group raised a half-million dollars to begin to refinance and reorganize JTS.[46]

Solomon Schechter, whose reputation as a brilliant reader of rabbinics at Cambridge had preceded him, was recruited to lead the institution, which was to be housed now in an impressive new building in uptown Manhattan. He arrived in 1902 and brought with him a collection of brilliant scholars, including Louis Ginzberg, Alexander Marx, and Israel Friedlander. All the men were products of traditional eastern European schooling and had continued their studies in the more modern German and American universities. All were sympathetic to the need for a synthesis of the old and the new, the rational and the spiritual. And all were committed to an evolutionary perspective on Jewish law. The outlook of the historical school acquired increased coherence and force with the arrival of this group, which hoped to define "a non-fundamentalist theology . . . that was convincingly traditionalist."[47]

Solomon Schechter harbored a strong dislike of Reform Judaism, which he saw as overly rational, and he continued to be intrigued by Jewish mysticism and the unexplainable in the Scriptures. But in contrast to most Orthodox scholars, Schechter emphasized modern scientific scholarship and believed that it could serve to invigorate Judaism. His *Studies in Judaism,* published in three volumes between 1896 and 1924, established him as a leading exponent of the unique blend of tradition and innovation that was at the heart of Conservatism.

Under Schechter, JTS stressed loyalty to halakah, reverence for the Jewish past, the centrality of the Torah and the synagogue, and perhaps most of all the unity of the Jewish people. Schechter believed that Judaism and Jewish peoplehood had been kept on course in the past by teachers actively shaping tradition as they confronted the contemporary world. These teachers led the Jewish people to define, emphasize, and even reinterpret those dimensions of Judaism relevant to their particular era. Schechter, then, clearly allowed for change when consecrated by general use and the conscience of the Jewish people or, in his words, by "catholic [universal] Israel." Despite his sincere disclaimer about starting a new Jewish denomination, Schechter, almost from the start and throughout his career, described his views by repeatedly using the term *Conservative Judaism* with a capital C.[48]

Israel Friedlander also used the term *Conservative Judaism* with some regularity. And like Schechter and several others, he came to Conservatism through the recognition that some accommodation had to be made to modernization and that American Reform was too radical a departure from tradition. Arguing with the Orthodox, he supported the scientific study of Judaism and the use of history to justify changes in religious practice; arguing with the radical Reformers, he emphasized the "indissoluble historic bond between ethical monotheism, ceremonialism, and Jewish nationality."[49]

Leaders of the Reform movement, especially those associated with Hebrew Union College in Cincinnati, were predictably hostile to the upstart Jewish Theological Seminary, which challenged HUC's hegemony in the field of rabbinic training. Similar sentiments were expressed on the other end of the ideological spectrum: the Union of Orthodox Rabbis in 1904, one year after naming the more traditional Rabbi Isaac Elchonen Theological Seminary (RIETS) in New York as the only legitimate institution for rabbinical training and ordination in America, issued a writ of excommunication against Schechter's seminary. Cut off from the Left and Right in American Jewish religious life, the leaders of JTS began to delineate more self-consciously the contours of Conservative Judaism.[50]

In 1909 work began to establish a union of sympathetic congregations that could promote Conservatism. This effort to create an institutional structure for American Jews outside of Reform or Orthodoxy resulted in the organization of the United Synagogue of America (USA) in February 1913. A union of twenty-two congregations located in various Jewish centers, ranging from Syracuse, New York, through Chicago, to Sioux City, Iowa, and from Newton, Massachusetts, through Norfolk, Virginia, to Birmingham, Alabama, United Synagogue, with its emphasis on "tradition without Orthodoxy," represented perhaps the clearest beginnings of Conservative Judaism in America.[51]

A significant number of delegates to the founding convention of USA were from German American congregations. But the key figures, with whom lay the future of the Conservative movement, were the rabbis of the post-1902 JTS. Graduates Joel Blau, Israel Levinthal, Herman Rubenovitz, and Louis Egelson had become leaders of eastern European congregations in communities outside of immigrant ghettos in Manhattan, Brooklyn, Boston, and Washington, D.C., respectively. By promoting Conservatism, they were attempting to keep mobile, second-generation, acculturated eastern European Jews loyal to the synagogue.[52]

Although the seminary that trained these men did not officially call itself Conservative until 1940, and although a small number of congregations affiliated with United Synagogue of America remained American Orthodox, JTS and USA were by 1913 clearly the linchpins of the Conservative movement. Schechter's seminary taught now with even more confidence and energy that "the Torah is not in heaven. Its interpretation is left to the conscience of catholic Israel." Students and graduates, most of whom went on to lead USA congregations, spoke of "development" and "progress." They reemphasized not only the evolutionary character of Judaism but the responsibility of the Jewish people in each generation to change—albeit carefully and conscientiously—the revered tradition in "accordance with its own spiritual needs."[53]

But what precisely the new movement's theology represented remained unclear. Distinct Conservative practices and rituals were only somewhat more discernible than its ideology. Many aspects of the Conservative service, though everywhere traditional in content and dignified in form, varied from congregation to congregation. A significant number of Conservative synagogues, mirroring Reform synagogues, had organs, mixed choirs, family pews, and English translations of prayers; some, however, had none of these. In other instances, the Conservative service was not distinguishable from what Jews were doing in the Orthodox Young People's synagogues, American Orthodox synagogues, or after 1912, in the Orthodox synagogues associated with the Young Israel movement (see chapter 3).

Conservatives—as distinct from the Orthodox, who believe in a literal, direct verbal revelation from God—felt little pressure to conform to any particular theological doctrine or religious practice. There was instead respect for attempts to harmonize Jewish belief and ritual with modern thought. As a result, a broad spectrum of theological positions, sometimes at odds with each other, were held by the JTS faculty, the Conservative rabbinate, and Conservative congregants. The laity wanted to preserve traditional forms and memories and even the binding nature of Jewish law. But it wanted to choose for itself which specific aspects of traditional Judaism to maintain. Since all acknowledged that halakah was not divinely revealed but a living thing, Conservatism was constantly subject to variation and continues to contain within itself all the quarrels Orthodoxy and Reform have with one another.[54]

The outstanding difference between the Conservative movement and the other Jewish denominations in America developed over the question of Zionism. Although no longer the case, the original classic Reform position emphasized universalism to the point of anti-Zionism.[55] A negative attitude toward establishing a Jewish state also prevailed for several decades in the Orthodox wing. On the other hand, Conservatism, with its emphasis on catholic Israel and Jewish peoplehood, has been the most comfortable home for Jewish nationalism and Zionism in America. Indeed, after Solomon Schechter gave strong support to the kind of redemption Zionism held out for Jews, it came to be seen as a kind of secular equivalent of Conservatism.

No ideology was officially pronounced or sanctioned by the Conservative movement. And when it did attempt to elucidate its theological positions, Conservatism exposed ambivalence toward Jewish rationalism, tension between belief in divine guidance and human endeavor, and ambiguity about the essential, unchanging aspects of Judaism as against the spirit of evolutionary development.[56] This resulted in a series of crises of identity within the movement as it struggled to define itself. It led also to spin-off movements, most notably Reconstructionism. Seeking to deemphasize the purely religious elements in Judaism in favor of its cultural components, Reconstructionism failed to attract many congregations, but it did prove powerfully influential in the realm of ideas, becoming a kind of theological midpoint between Reform and Conservatism.

Conservatism, then, like Orthodoxy and Reform, was not immune to fragmentation and division. Nonetheless, the Conservative movement offered the children of eastern European immigrants a very attractive option—one far more traditional than Reform, yet significantly more American and modern than the Orthodoxy of their parents. Not surprisingly, a number of Conservative congregations appeared even in ghetto areas, and many more, as early as 1916, functioned in areas of second settlement across the United States.[57]

At the turn of the century in America, there existed an Orthodox branch of Judaism, barely coping with the secular environment and already alienating the children of eastern European newcomers; a Reform branch, unable to regenerate itself and clearly unacceptable to the immigrants and their children; and most problematic of all, a distinct trend toward secularization and even antireligion in all sections of American Jewry. The American Jewish religious world needed a new religious modality that would accept the drive toward secularism at the same time that it held onto cherished traditional religious symbols.

Several Orthodox groups attempted to fill the vacuum by establishing aesthetic, decorous religious services with large doses of English and by building modern synagogues with modernized schools and elaborate cultural and recreational programs. One of the greatest efforts in this area was Herbert S. Goldstein's Institutional Synagogue, established in Harlem in 1917. An American Orthodox rabbi ordained at JTS in 1914, Goldstein, like his contemporary, Mordecai Kaplan, the founder and leader of the Jewish Reconstructionist movement, tried to make the synagogue the center of Jewish life. Goldstein's goal, anticipating the Jewish center movement that flourished during the 1920s and 1930s, was to integrate the sanctuary, social halls, and recreational facilities of the synagogue within an Orthodox Jewish atmosphere attractive to an American constituency ready for change.[58]

Even some elements in the Union of Orthodox Rabbis came to accept the idea that a Judaism resistant to change was doomed to extinction in America. Under the lead of rabbis like Philip H. Klein and Moses Z. Margolies, RIETS was gradually transformed from an Old World style yeshiva into an American Orthodox rabbinical seminary. Under pressure from the students themselves, the institution was reorganized in order to provide a more modern course of study. But crucial to the change was the new perception by some in the old Orthodox camp that the future of their children could be left neither to secularists nor to the Conservative teachings of the JTS faculty.

Rabbi Bernard Revel was appointed in 1915 to lead the reorganized RIETS—the nucleus of what would later become Yeshiva University. Revel's goal was to produce Orthodox rabbis knowledgeable about America and able to preach effectively in English. To instruct his students in Talmud, the bedrock of the curriculum, Revel brought in the rabbis of the Union of Orthodox Rabbis. But to teach the ways of America, he chose Orthodox Union leaders like Henry P. Mendes, Herbert S. Goldstein, and Bernard Drachman. By the 1920s, RIETS graduates were on the road to areas of second settlement and suburbia, taking their updated Orthodox messages to second-generation Jews.[59]

Like JTS graduates with whom they were in competition, RIETS men were united in their commitment to the process of reconciling American and Jewish identities. It was the Conservative movement, however, that captured the attention and loyalty of the largest portion of the children of the immigrants as they matured, acculturated, and moved up and out of the old neighborhoods. The attraction of Conservatism was particularly strong for women, who felt stifled within Orthodoxy but who saw the Reform movement as alien—and even Christian.

It is possible to see Conservative Judaism as a dilution of immigrant religious fervor, a middle-class stopover for Jews on the way from Orthodoxy to Reform or to secular assimilation. But from the perspective of the present, Conservatism looks more promising. In the 1970s, religious identity became increasingly attractive again in a culture that was beginning to recognize both the malaise of modernity and the importance of continuity, ritual, and celebration of life. In this context, Conservatism proved particularly durable. The retention of important portions of recognizably Orthodox ritual, a strong attachment to Hebrew, a resonant compatibility with Zionism, and a rabbinate able to adjust to the currents of the twentieth century have kept large numbers of Jews in the Conservative fold. Both the Reform and Orthodox branches, albeit with significant modifications, continue to claim the loyalty of those Jews whose special needs they meet. As long as this continues, the Conservative movement, at the very least, promises to remain a viable, mediating third branch of American Judaism.

✡

CHAPTER SEVEN

PARTICIPATION IN THE AMERICAN POLITICAL SYSTEM

JEWS in the late twentieth century have a well-deserved reputation for active participation in the American electoral process. But before 1914 Jewish immigrants usually viewed party politics with indifference. This was especially noticeable in New York City, which possessed one of the highest concentrations of Jews in the world. The early lack of attention to local politics is traceable to several factors. Like all new arrivals, Jews had to deal with the problems of adjusting to a new culture, earning a living, and improving their lot.[1] Moreover, during the period from 1880 to 1914, the process of naturalization grew more complex, making it harder for immigrants to become citizens and voters.

Even when they did become eligible to cast ballots, eastern European Jews often failed to exercise the privilege. After centuries of forced isolation in the Old World, they had brought with them to America little in the way of political experience. The pious had always thought of secular politics as inherently suspect, and freethinkers and radicals had neither a grounding in routine political processes nor familiarity with the realities of power. "Our exile has created neglect of bureaucratic formalities," Abe Cahan lamented in 1908, "This is why American Jews do not take out citizenship papers; who wants to bother with the technicalities and the paper work?"[2] Inexperienced, wary of bureaucracy, and still haunted by memories of oppressive old-country governments, Jewish immigrants were satisfied to be left alone. And the major political parties accommodated them. Rarely, in the early years of mass immigration, did mainstream politicians address issues vital to the new communities.

Irish domination of urban politics was another factor contributing to the slowness with which eastern European Jews entered American political life. The Irish had several advantages. Early arrival, familiarity with the English language, and an ethnic unity forged within the Catholic church readily translated into Irish political power out of proportion to their number. Moreover, many of the Irish had arrived in the United States fresh from the momentous experience of the Catholic emancipation movement, which served the Irish well in mass politics.[3] At the same time, the Irish carried on here a cultural tradition of viewing formal government as illegitimate. Most were convinced that true sovereignty was reflected only in the informal politics of personal fealty. "All there is in life," said New York City boss Richard Crocker, "is loyalty to family and friends." This mix of cynicism and benevolence made a powerful cement. Through intimate networks built on a combination of graft and services rendered, the Irish came into control of political machines in several large cities.[4]

In New York the Tammany machine interceded with officials to provide jobs, to drop charges and fines, and to help real estate men and contractors gain favors. It also dispensed free coal and food to the needy and helped with medical care, social services, and burial arrangements. Maintaining this system of services took will, talent, and energy, and it brought votes, power, status, and modest affluence to Tammany leaders and operatives. The Irish had no intention of sharing these advantages and losing political control to newcomers, least of all to Jews from eastern Europe.[5]

Jews, moreover, were not exactly breaking down Tammany's doors. The self-help traditions and the elaborate networks of social and charitable agencies in the Jewish community made the "generosity" of Tammany's leaders less necessary. In many ways, Tammany operations anticipated the welfare state and were appreciated in most immigrant communities, but, among Jews, its favors appear to have counted for less.[6]

Eastern European Jews, for all these reasons, saw the politics of American cities—with its quid pro quos and its earthy, rough-and-tumble character—as alien, as something for Gentiles. For some time they maintained their distance. As late as 1912, the predominantly Jewish Eighth Assembly District registered the lowest proportion of voters in New York City. And when Jews did become full participants in the game of American politics, they did not fall into any clearly discernible or predictable voting pattern until the 1920s. Personal issues, class and ideology, group interests, and sometimes even simple ethnic loyalty divided Jews among Democrats, Republicans, Socialists, Fusionists, and Progressives.[7]

Jewish voters, though locating themselves across the political spectrum, viewed politics mainly as a vehicle for achieving justice, and they injected a serious moral dimension into the political dialogue. Their moralism stemmed partly from the influence of socialism in the Jewish world and less directly from the political concepts embedded in the sacred texts. Hebrew Scriptures, particularly Prophets, emphasize social justice and a messianism that looks forward to good government and a just social order. The Book of Joshua explicitly sees politics as a form of moral action and government as a covenant system established by consecrated mutual promise and obligation.[8]

Eventually, these conceptions and inclinations, in combination with the experience of political freedom in America, led Jews to constitutionalism and republicanism. Even radicals among them moved away from the centralized model of revolution imported from the Russian Empire. For the same reasons, Jews also came to support an activist state, one that vigorously pursued the protection of vulnerable individuals and promoted public regulation of individual enterprise on behalf of the common good. Although most clearly manifested in the 1930s, the liberal dimension of the Jewish political profile was already a constant by 1920.

Jewish liberalism, in the sense of support for welfare capitalism, was already perceptible in 1886, when the New York City mayoral candidacy of single-tax theorist and municipal reformer Henry George brought a sizable number of Jews into local political activity for the first time. Impassioned in his speaking style and relatively radical in his views, George was strongly supported by the Jewish Workingmen's Association, which had been established by Socialists Abraham Cahan, Louis Miller, and Morris Hillquit. George placed second in a three-way race, garnering fifteen thousand of his sixty-eight thousand votes in New York's predominantly Jewish Seventh, Tenth, and Thirteenth wards.[9]

In response to George's showing, Tammany grew more careful of Jewish sensibilities, cultivated Jewish voters, and eventually established a dominance in East Side politics. But the Democratic machine never won the loyalty in Jewish neighborhoods that it enjoyed in many other parts of New York City. Significant numbers of Jews were repelled by Tammany's tactics, and many Jews in the 1890s appear to have reverted to political alienation.

But they were ready to reenter the electoral fray on hearing a righteous voice, as in 1897 when an impressive number responded positively to the campaign for mayor waged by James B. Reynolds, the reformist director of an East Side settlement house.

Association with the reform movement was not without its problems for eastern European Jews. Middle-class Progressives often annoyed ghetto dwellers by their attempts to mold immigrants into "acceptable" types. Reformers could also alienate the more radical Jews by emphasizing amelioration rather than basic social change. Nevertheless, the moralistic political consciousness of the downtown Jews drew them to the Progressive reform movement.

Many German Jews, too, found themselves in the Progressive camp. It is certainly true that, after the Civil War, the rapidly rising German Jewish middle class overwhelmingly supported conservative and probusiness party positions and economic policies; it is also true that they never produced a clearly defined proletariat and were rarely associated with labor unions or radical protest movements. But on the national level, even as late as the 1920s, the majority of American Jewish voters, German as well as eastern European, preferred the Republicans—often Progressive Republicans.[10] By the turn of the century, a number of socially conscious German Jews, like Edward A. Filene of Boston and Julius Rosenwald of Chicago, were associated with the Progressive movement, as were the countless German Jewish women who did the day-to-day philanthropic and social welfare work of the National Council of Jewish Women. Moreover, German Jews like Joel Spingarn, Belle and Henry Moskowitz, Lillian Wald, and Louis Brandeis were leading Progressive reformers.[11]

Even a small number of German Jewish Reform rabbis, emphasizing prophetic Judaism and social justice—and following the lead of their Protestant colleagues in the Social Gospel movement—entered the Progressive camp. Henry Berkowitz of Kansas City, Missouri, for example, addressed the problems of poverty in industrial society from a Progressive perspective. He advocated labor and social welfare reform and argued that his proposals were in consonance with the spirit of Mosaic law and the teachings of the prophets of Israel. Beginning in the 1880s, even before there was a significant Jewish proletariat or a pronounced Social Gospel movement in Protestantism, Rabbi Emil G. Hirsch of Chicago was identified with numerous reform causes—the rights of labor, prison reform, women's suffrage, peace, education, and good government. At the conference of rabbis in Pittsburgh in 1885, it was Hirsch who insisted that at least one plank of the projected Reform platform deal with social action. And for the next fifty years, part of the official creed of Reform Judaism read: "We deem it our duty to participate in the great task of modern times, to solve on the basis of justice and righteousness the problems presented by the contrasts and evils of the present organization of society."[12]

In the twentieth century, rabbis Stephen S. Wise and Judah Magnes, bound to the German Jewish community by marriage and position and to the eastern European Jewish community by their democratic social consciousness, continued to promote social reform. Magnes eventually forged intimate ties with the radical wing of the Social Gospel movement. Wise embraced every cause he saw as liberal and just, and his Free Synagogue, established in 1907, pioneered in making social action and social service a central part of its program.[13]

New York's preeminent German Jews, Jacob Schiff and Louis Marshall, were not Progressives, but they shared some Progressive goals, particularly the quest for good government. They had come to support the Republican party as the necessary antidote to Tammany's corruption, but in the 1901 New York City mayoral race, Schiff, Marshall, and other leading German Jews campaigned within the immigrant community for Seth Low and the Fusion ticket. Many downtowners responded positively to the effort to break the stranglehold of Tammany as well as the effort to address the problems of tenement housing and inadequate schools. They were also attracted to the Fusion ticket by the state supreme court candidacy of Samuel Greenbaum, the beloved German Jewish founder of the Aguilar Free Library on the Lower East Side. Eastern European immigrants helped elect Seth Low as mayor, and in the process they reinforced the liberal dimension of the American Jewish political profile and became more attached to the cause of municipal reform.[14]

German Jewish leaders, by their campaign appeals, had indirectly admitted the existence of a Jewish vote. They also appeared to believe that if American Jewry were going to turn political it ought to be under German Jewish direction. It did not always work out that way. In every presidential election between 1900 and 1928, with the possible exception of 1900 and 1916, more Jews voted for Republicans than for Democrats, but this preference seldom extended to local politics. Jewish voters in the cities—when they were not supporting Socialists or reformers like Seth Low and William T. Jerome—tended to vote Democratic. In New York, this meant Tammany.[15]

Ambitious young Jews in New York were beginning to be accepted by Tammany as hangers-on and messengers, and increasingly Jewish recruits found a home in the party clubhouses under the wings of Irish leaders. However, most of the crucial political posts remained in Irish hands for decades; as late as 1907 there was still only one Jewish district leader on the East Side, and by 1923 there were only six, far fewer than Jewish numbers warranted. But some Jews were nevertheless able to fulfill their political aspirations through Tammany. Henry Goldfogle, Tammany's Jewish representative for the Lower East Side, was elected to Congress in 1900; Jacob Cantor became Manhattan borough president in 1901; and in the same year, Aaron Levy was voted Democratic leader of the New York State Assembly.[16]

Tammany appeared to be paying more attention to Jewish interests, as well, especially the crucial question of immigration restriction; unlike the Republicans, Tammany had always supported a liberal immigration policy. Not surprisingly, the Eighth Assembly District, in the heart of the Lower East Side, customarily gave a narrow majority to local Tammany candidates. Elections in the immigrant community were always hard fought, and sizable numbers of Jews continued to vote for Socialists and Progressives as well as for Tammany. Occasionally, they even voted for Republicans, one of whom, with the Teddy Roosevelt landslide in 1904, was nearly carried to Congress, a feat never before approached on the Lower East Side.[17]

Tammany Democrats had gained the edge in the ghetto, and even though they held no monopoly, when a Democratic candidate appealed directly to Jewish interests, he was virtually unbeatable on the Lower East Side. For example, even a reform candidate could not outrun publisher William Randolph Hearst in 1903, when the Hearst newspapers featured accounts of the Kishinev pogrom and appeals for aid to the beleaguered Russian Jews. Hearst's popularity was also a consequence of the fact that his press consistently and passionately made the case for social justice and racial tolerance, sentiments close to the hearts of downtown Jews.[18]

Hearst may have been sincere in expressing these sentiments, but he was also consciously wooing the Jewish voter. This became particularly clear when Hearst went so far as to publish a Yiddish paper (the *Yiddisher Amerikaner*) in 1904. Attempts by one party to entice Jews to the polling booths tended to attract the attention of other parties. In 1906, when Hearst ran as Tammany's gubernatorial candidate in New York, President Roosevelt, partly to divert Jews from a Tammany vote, appointed the first

Jewish cabinet member, Oscar S. Straus, as secretary of commerce. Even earlier, Roosevelt had cultivated good will among Jewish voters: he had invited the Rabbinical Council of America to the White House, several times he publicly praised the new Jewish citizens, and more than once he predicted that a Jew would be president some day.[19]

Clearly the Jews were being drawn into the crucible of ethnic politics—often with positive results. The Lower East Side became an important campaign stop for all political aspirants. That the politicians came increasingly to the immigrants meant that the immigrants could communicate their needs and concerns to City Hall. And on a national level, issues important to Jews, such as immigration policy, relations with Russia, and good government, received a higher priority on the political agenda.

Despite warnings from uptowners about the dangers of behaving like a Jewish voting bloc, the ethnic impulse often seemed a natural one to obey in the polling booth. Jews frequently voted for Jews, and they cheered when Oscar Straus, Henry Morgenthau, Louis Brandeis, and Bernard Baruch were appointed to high office. Since it seemed equally reasonable to Jews, however, to use the ballot to reward their friends and punish their enemies, ethnic politics could also present perplexing problems. When, for example, Oscar Straus was pitted against Tammany's William Sulzer, a Gentile, in the 1912 gubernatorial election, ethnic loyalty dictated a vote for Straus. But Sulzer, the chairman of the House Foreign Affairs Committee, in response to Russian discrimination against Jews, was leading the fight to abrogate the Russian-American Commercial Treaty of 1832. Sulzer won the election, but most Jews had yielded to ethnic ties and voted for Straus.[20]

Voting was easier when there was no controversy about where the Jewish interest lay. Immigration was one such issue. When James M. Curley, a jealous guardian of Irish power but a strong supporter of a liberal immigration policy, ran for mayor of Boston in 1913, he received 85 percent of the Jewish vote. The national campaign in 1912, however, posed a great quandary for Jewish voters, because all four presidential candidates had come out strongly against immigration restriction. The problem was met by ticket splitting, and a sizable proportion of the Jewish vote went to Woodrow Wilson and to Eugene V. Debs, the Socialist party candidate.[21]

Socialism, as noted in chapter 4, never captured the entire community, but with its explicit appeals to moralism and justice, it was an important force on the Lower East Side. Indeed, the rise of the Socialist party vote in the United States from 16,000 in 1903 to more than 118,000 in 1912 was partly the consequence of increasing Jewish support. Socialist candidates were especially attractive to Jews when they represented a combination of ideological and ethnic interests. In this regard, a comparison of the congressional campaigns of Morris Hillquit and Meyer London is instructive. Socialist Morris Hillquit, who was defeated in the 1908 congressional race, though Jewish, had not openly identified with specific Jewish interests. Indeed, at the first rally of his campaign he had said: "If elected to Congress, I will not consider myself the special representative of the . . . special interests of this district, but the representative of the Socialist Party and the interests of the working class of the country."[22]

Hillquit put this forth at a time when the police commissioner's report implied that Jews generated 50 percent of the crime in New York City, when immigration restriction was being hotly debated in Congress, and when the position of the Socialist party on that issue, favoring some restriction, was not attractive to East Side Jews who still had relatives desperate to escape from pogrom-ridden Russia. Like English conservative Edmund Burke, who over a century earlier had run as a representative not of his constituents but of the "realm," the radical Morris Hillquit was roundly defeated.

Meyer London, who replaced Hillquit as the Socialist party's candidate, openly identified himself as a Jew and a Socialist and allied himself with the vital interests of the Lower East Side. Though London lost a bid for a congressional seat in 1910, he outran the rest of the Socialist party ticket two to one. By 1914 London had developed enough support in the district to win. It was rare, even from the Lower East Side, for Socialists to be sent to Congress, yet London was reelected twice, in 1916 and 1920.[23] Combining Socialist ideology and class interest with ethnic interest played a vital role in these victories. London told a crowd of fifteen thousand after his first election: "We shall not rest until every power of capitalism has been destroyed and the workers emancipated from wage slavery." In the same speech, the following words apparently met with the same enthusiasm: "I hope that my presence will represent an entirely different type of Jew from the kind that Congress is accustomed to see."[24]

Ultimately, Morris Hillquit did learn to put ideology and ethnic interest together when appealing to immigrant Jewish voters. When he ran for mayor of New York in 1917, some representatives of the German Jewish community, fearing not only Hillquit's socialism, but his wartime pacifism, advocated voting against him. If Hillquit were "elected by Jewish votes," they thought, "who can doubt that . . . [the] American tradition of tolerance will be imperilled?"[25] Hillquit responded:

This is the old trick of the ruling classes. It is the same old trick Booker T. Washington worked on the Negroes. . . . "Don't assert yourselves or else you will incur the hatred of the ruling classes. . . . Be gentle slaves and you will be all right. And I say to you as a citizen to citizens, as a Jew to Jews, you don't have to be good; you have the right to be as bad as the rest of the world.[26]

Morris Hillquit was not elected mayor. Socialist pacifism during the war had dampened enthusiasm for Socialist candidates generally, and the national party garnered fewer than eighty thousand votes in 1917. But the Socialists in Jewish New York were still strong, electing in that year ten state assemblymen, eleven aldermen, and a municipal judge.[27]

The strength of the Socialist party in the Jewish community should not be overstated. Socialists certainly received disproportionate support from the Jewish electorate, but most Jews were not Socialists. Moreover, in 1914, of eleven Jews elected to the state senate, two were Republicans and nine were Democrats. In the same year, seven Jews sat in the state assembly: only two were Socialists, the rest were Republicans. At the presidential level, in 1912 and again in 1916 Woodrow Wilson's earnest intellectualism and moralism attracted Jews to the national Democratic slate. This included not only former Socialists, but also wealthy Jews with a civic conscience, like Jacob Schiff and Bernard Baruch, both of whom were generous contributors to the campaigns of liberal and moderate candidates.

The gradual shift of Jews from Republican and Socialist to Democratic affiliation on the national level was reinforced by the liberal, progressive role Louis Brandeis played as Wilson's advisor, especially after Brandeis became head of the American Zionist movement in 1914.[28] Later, Wilson's crusade for the League of Nations as well as his initial support for the Balfour Declaration, promising the establishment of a Jewish homeland in Palestine, further strengthened Jewish links to the Democratic party.

It is, however, difficult to determine a clear Jewish voter profile during the postwar years. In New York, substantial secondary settlements of Jewish immigrants and their children had developed in the Bronx and Harlem and in the Brownsville and Williamsburg sections of Brooklyn. These new Jewish American neighborhoods generally reflected the political culture of the original Lower East Side settlement and included centers of Socialist party strength. But in 1920, of the eleven Jewish representatives in Congress, only one, Meyer London, was a Socialist. All the others were Republicans except for Henry Goldfogle, of Tammany, and Adolph Sabbath, a

Chicago Democrat. Moreover, Republican Warren G. Harding's successful bid for the presidency in 1920 was sustained, for reasons still unclear, by a respectable minority of Jewish votes, despite Harding's support of immigration restriction and his opposition in 1916 to the appointment of Louis Brandeis to the Supreme Court. In 1924 Calvin Coolidge, Harding's Republican successor, received a higher percentage of Jewish votes than the Democratic candidate for president, John Davis. But even in that election, it again became clear that a socialist-oriented liberal dimension was to remain a constant of Jewish political culture. In several Jewish districts across the nation, Robert La Follette, the presidential candidate of the newly formed Progressive party, ran well ahead of all other contenders.[29]

If early in their history, immigrant Jews showed little taste for local politics, their interest in foreign affairs was remarkably high. Although intensely preoccupied building lives in their new country, Jews maintained powerful links to k'lal Yisrael, the spiritual community of world Jewry. Traditional nostalgia was reinforced for Jewish immigrants by the fact that many of their relatives and friends remained in the old countries, often in dire need of help. It was interest in the welfare of the landslayt overseas that heightened concern with foreign affairs and stirred Jews to political activism in times of crisis.[30]

It was this interest, too, that helped produce an extraordinary network of Jewish institutions during the first two decades of the twentieth century. In the face of pogroms and the deteriorating condition of Jewish communities in eastern Europe, the American Jewish Committee (AJC) was formed in 1906 by an elite group of German Jews. One of its most important goals was aiding fellow Jews abroad by pressing for diplomatic intercession and by resisting legislation designed to restrict immigration. In turn, another national organization, the American Jewish Congress, was established to confront and transcend the more oligarchic ways of the AJC and to address the interests and minority rights of Jews in postwar Europe.

World War I exacerbated the needs of European Jewry and tested American Jewish will and ability. In order to bring relief to Jewish communities abroad, it was necessary for American Jews to rise above social and religious divisiveness. The challenge was met with the establishment of yet another major organization, the American Jewish Joint Distribution Committee (JDC). The crisis of European Jewry also invigorated Zionism, which itself produced a variety of new organizations and forced American Jews to confront their hyphenated identities. Related to the foregoing events, yet distinct from them in its domestic focus, was the kehillah experiment—New York Jewry's attempt to deal with the cultural and spiritual problems of the New World by adapting an Old World communal structure.

Before we describe these twentieth-century organizations and the intricate politics they generated, it is important to point out that American Jewish political activity in response to needs of Jews abroad had important precedents in the nineteenth century. In 1840 there was an accusation of blood libel against the Jews of Damascus, which led to the arrest there of more than a dozen prominent Jews and sixty children, all of whom were tortured. The American Jewish community responded for the first time in American history with concerted nationwide action. Mass protest rallies were held in New York City, Philadelphia, Charleston, Cincinnati, Savannah, and Richmond. Petitions were sent to the Van Buren administration, although the president had already sent a note of protest. Eventually, through the exertions of Jews worldwide, particularly in Britain by the Board of Deputies of British Israelites, the accused were acquitted and released, but not until four Jews had died and a rash of similar cases had swept Europe.[31]

American Jewry was roused to action again in 1858 with the Mortara incident. The case involved a six-year old Jewish child, Edgar Mortara, who was seized by papal troops and forcibly converted to Catholicism. The boy was alleged to have been secretly baptized as an infant by his nurse. This was enough reason for Pope Pius IX to refuse to return the child to his parents and to insist that he be raised as a Catholic. Meetings were held in many American cities, and requests were made by American Jews for United States intercession. The Buchanan administration, however, rejected the petitions on the ground that "it is the settled policy of the United States" to abstain from all interference in the internal affairs of other countries.[32]

The precedent established by the Van Buren government appeared to be reversed, forcing Jewish leaders to recognize their relative powerlessness and the need for a higher level of unity in the American Jewish community. Consequently, twenty-five congregations, using the British model, came together and established the Board of Delegates of American Israelites. The new organization proved effective. In 1863, Secretary of State William Seward interceded on behalf of the besieged Jews of Morocco, instructing the American consul there "to exert all proper influence to prevent repetition of the barbarous cruelties to which Israelites . . . have been subject."[33]

In the late nineteenth century, the attention of American Jewry was turned increasingly toward the mistreatment of fellow Jews in czarist Russia. The policy of discrimination against Jews in Russia involved the United States in several ways. Most important, Russian anti-Semitism was responsible for the immigration of millions of Jews to American shores. In addition, the czarist regime began in the latter half of the nineteenth century to subject American Jews who returned to Russia on business or visits to the restrictions imposed on Russian Jews.

American Jews called for diplomatic intercession by the United States under the constitutional guarantee of equal protection of the laws. The American government responded, but the Russian government remained adamant in defense of its right to discriminate. Even in the face of Secretary of State James G. Blaine's threat to St. Petersburg in 1881 that the Commercial Treaty of 1832 between Russia and the United States would be abrogated if discrimination against Jews continued, Russia held fast. Jacob Schiff told Adolph S. Ochs, publisher of the *New York Times:* "The moment Russia is compelled to live up to her treaties and admit the foreign Jew . . . on a basis of equality . . . the Russian government will not be able to maintain the Pale of Settlement."[34] But the problem was inherent in the treaty itself, which contained a clause guaranteeing the rights of American citizens in Russia only "on condition of submitting to the laws and ordinances there prevailing."[35]

The Russian government went so far as to suggest that the United States refuse passports to Jews intending to travel to Russia and, thereby, avoid the embarrassment of having its citizens mistreated by a "friendly" foreign power. The State Department acquiesced and actually did reject passport applications from former Russian Jews. This policy ended only in 1892, when the Supreme Court in *Geofrey vs. Riggs* specifically extended the equal treatment clause to treaties.[36]

Although the State Department discontinued its discriminatory practice, the Russians refused to visa the passports of American Jews. There was some increase in Jewish pressure, especially in the context of the anti-Semitic Dreyfus case in France beginning in 1894 (see chapter 8); and the United States government, as it had sporadically since the early 1880s, voiced its displeasure over Russian anti-Semitism. In the 1890s the massive inflow of Jewish immigrants to the United States due to the pogroms and oppression in Russia and Romania became a continuing concern in Washington. President Harrison pointed out that the "banishment . . . of so large a number of men and women is not a local question. A decree to leave one country is in the nature of things an order to enter another."[37] But nothing much was done until the Kishinev pogrom made Russia's anti-Semitic depredations an even more critical matter in the relations between the two countries.

In February 1903 a Christian boy was found murdered near Kishinev, in the Russian province of Bessarabia. For months the Russian government and Orthodox church fomented anti-Semitic agitation, accusing the Jews of having killed the child in order to use his blood for Passover matzo. The campaign was managed so as to culminate in wide-ranging pogroms during Easter. In the riots that took place between 19 and 21 April, thousands of Jewish families were affected. Fifty people were killed; nearly five hundred were injured; rape and pillage was widespread; and Jewish property was destroyed, including seven hundred homes and six hundred businesses, valued at about $1,250,000.

The response of the American Jewish community was immediate. Within a period of little more than two months, nearly eighty protest meetings were held in fifty cities from Boston to San Francisco. The goal everywhere was to raise funds to aid victims and to demand United States government action on behalf of Russian Jews to prevent recurrence. Editorials in leading newspapers in Baltimore, Boston, New York, and dozens of other cities pressed for diplomatic intercession.[38]

It appeared as if President Roosevelt would be sympathetic. He had said publicly that the United States carried a "debt due . . . the Jewish race" and promised that "proper . . . beneficial action" would be taken. Roosevelt, however, had no such action in mind and doubted the usefulness of diplomatic notes "unless we mean to do something further than simply protest." It was not as if the administration was above garnering electoral support through protest notes. But the realpolitik considerations were that Russia might serve as a bulwark to Japanese expansion in the Far East and as a potential market for American goods.[39]

When a B'nai B'rith delegation came to see Roosevelt on 15 June 1903 with a petition to St. Petersburg signed by more than twelve thousand "leading citizens" of the United States, the president and Secretary Hay, with the cooperation of Commerce Secretary Oscar Straus, conceived of a way of deflecting the initiative. The Russian ambassador simply declined to accept the petition, as Hay had predicted, and the issue was not pressed further. Instead, the lengthy document was relegated to the State Department Archives. The administration drafted a diplomatic note in its place, designed not so much for the czar, to whom it would never be presented, but for rabbis to read to their congregations shortly before the upcoming elections.⁴⁰

The leadership of American Jewry did not fail to see that, while it had the ability to arouse public opinion and elicit real sympathy for the plight of Jews overseas, it lacked the organization and power to gain direct government intercession. By 1904 there was some movement away from diplomatic intervention and toward economic retaliation. The new emphasis was reinforced by the desperation American Jews felt as over three hundred pogroms took place in the Russian Empire between 1903 and 1906.

Economic pressure—such as the threat to abrogate the Commercial Treaty of 1832, which governed all commercial relations between the United States and Russia and which gave Russia access to the American market—again became the preferred strategy. In July 1904 an abrogation resolution was introduced in the House of Representatives. St. Petersburg, however, was not moved. On the contrary, Russian authorities, in order to deflect popular anger generated by Russian defeat in the war against Japan (1904–5), initiated a series of new pogroms against the Jews. Jewish bankers also tried to withhold investment capital from Russia, but the efforts of Jacob Schiff, Lord Rothschild, and a small number of others were nullified when French banking houses stepped into the breach.

On 22 June 1906 another congressional resolution was introduced stating that "the people of the United States are horrified by the report of the massacre of the Hebrews in Russia."⁴¹ The ability of Jewish leaders to bring political pressure to bear appeared to be growing. Indeed, at the same time that the resolution was introduced, the newly formed American Jewish Committee succeeded in having a treaty abrogation pledge included in the platforms of the major parties preparing for the presidential election of 1908. Instead of positive action on the part of the government, however, the Jewish leadership watched in dismay and anger as the State Department took yet another step backward. Secretary Elihu Root sent a circular informing all interested parties that the State Department "will not issue passports to former Russian subjects or to Jews who intend going to Russian territory, unless it has the assurance that the Russian government will consent to their admission."⁴²

The AJC charged the State Department with conducting "an uncon-stitutional religious test," and this led to a change in the directive. But it remained clear that threatening Russia and appealing to its self-interest were of little value while the Commercial Treaty remained inviolable. Secretary Root did announce the goal of a complete revision of the treaty, but before any action could be taken, Roosevelt was replaced by Taft and Root by Philander C. Knox.

Taft entered office in 1909 having spoken out forcefully on the treaty issue during the campaign and even at his inauguration. Yet a series of delegations to the White House were unable even to elicit an acknowledge-ment from the new president that American Jews in Russia were entitled to legal protection. Early in 1911, a group representing the AJC, the Union of American Hebrew Congregations, and B'nai B'rith left the Oval Office in anger. Later, Jacob Schiff recalled: "I told the President: . . . 'We had hoped you would see that justice was done us but you have decided otherwise; we shall go to the American people.'"43

Jewish organizations redoubled their agitation on the treaty question and stressed the point that discrimination against American citizens abroad was not a Jewish problem but an American one. Louis Marshall called the behavior of the czarist government insulting to American sovereignty and argued that acquiescence by the United States was "a betrayal of her most sacred principles."44 Newspapers were supplied with relevant data, maga-zines with popular articles, and open meetings were sponsored throughout the country. Finally, after a series of well-publicized congressional hearings and the wooing of key members of both chambers, a resolution calling for the immediate termination of the Commercial Treaty with Russia passed in the House by a vote of 300 to 1 and unanimously in the Senate. Russian wood, pulp, and paper products, which furnished the bulk of Russian trade with the United States, were removed from the most-favored-nation list by the Treasury Department in August 1913.

But 1913 was not a good year to celebrate such victories. A sharp decline in trade brought adverse reaction for American Jews in some quarters of the United States, and in Russia there were anti-American as well as anti-Semitic reprisals. The depth of Russian anti-Jewish animus was evidenced in that year too by the famous Mendel Beilis blood libel case.

It was clear that diplomatic intercession was only partly successful in resolving Jewish problems. But in the process of mobilizing their strength between 1903 and 1913, American Jewish leaders learned that some goals could be achieved by effective organization. Galvanized into action by the pogroms in Russia, especially a second one in Kishinev in August 1905, sixty leading American Jews met in New York City in February 1906 and organized a defense organization called the American Jewish Committee. The AJC was to be a body of the Jewish establishment. Jacob Schiff, Oscar Straus, Cyrus Adler, the Guggenheims, Louis Marshall, and other prominent German Jews would now speak and act in the name of, and for the defense and welfare of, the Jewish community. The concern of Jews of high station with the protection of general Jewish interests was a familiar element of Jewish tradition. The AJC, as a tightly knit prudent group working quietly through government authorities in behalf of fellow Jews, had simply institutionalized the customary function of the *shtadlanim,* court Jews who mediated with the princes and powers of the past.

The single most important figure behind the AJC was the brilliant, fifty-year-old attorney Louis Marshall. He used his talents to plead the causes of American Jews before various administrations in Washington, and he was indefatigable in his struggle for the abrogation of the Commercial Treaty with Russia. Marshall felt little of the disdain for the new Jewish immigrant so often noted among his uptown compatriots, and he was able to serve as a bridge between the preexisting German Jewish community and the new arrivals from eastern Europe. Indeed, Marshall was involved in almost every cause close to the heart of the newcomers, particularly the battle against immigration restriction.[45]

Despite his leadership of what was indeed an ethnic lobby, Marshall continued to be apprehensive about what he saw as the immigrant tendency to think in terms of ethnic politics—that is, to think and act as if Jews had "interests different from those of other American citizens." And despite his relatively tolerant attitude toward eastern Europeans, Marshall continued to be wary of immigrant "radicalism." In order to prevent the newcomers from acting "irresponsibly" or from establishing new radical organizations, and in order to make the AJC more effective, Marshall proposed broadening the base of the committee to include immigrant leaders.

Marshall's proposal met with vehement opposition from Mayer Sulzberger, Oscar Straus, and Adolph Kraus, who asked angrily why it was necessary for the committee to represent "the riffraff."[46] But the idea of democratizing the AJC won the approval of Jacob Schiff, an aristocrat who recognized his obligation to groom the immigrants for a share of the leadership. "A new Jewry had arisen in the United States since 1881," Schiff observed, "and their confidence is necessary for any general representative body."[47] It was decided to proceed with Marshall's plan to make room at the table for representatives of the ghetto. Thirty-five new positions were added to the AJC executive committee, and local advisory councils were created—or adopted, as in the case of the kehillah council in New York.

Most eastern European Jews in America had from the beginning applauded the AJC, whose stated purpose was to help relieve the suffering of their relatives and landslayt in the Old World. The committee's elitism and assimilationism were vigorously attacked by the Socialists and Zionists, but the AJC continued to command general Jewish approval because of its victories in fending off immigration restriction, its successful fight to abrogate the discriminatory Commercial Treaty with Russia, and its role in the passage of the New York State Civil Rights Bill of 1913, which prohibited discriminatory advertising for vacation resorts.[48]

The American Jewish Committee continued to merit support during World War I because of its leadership in organizing both the American Jewish Relief Committee and the Joint Distribution Committee, whose chief beneficiaries were the Jews in war-ravaged eastern Europe. In the war zone, Jews suffered not only incidentally on account of their unfortunate location, they were also targets of deep-seated anti-Semitism, especially in Russia. Indiscriminate rape and murder of Jews accompanied the movement of the czarist armies, and some 300,000 Jews were expelled from their homes as potential spies and traitors.

As reports filtered in, American Jews could no longer doubt that eastern European Jewry had suffered a disaster unparalleled since the Chmielnitsky massacres in the midseventeenth century.[49] Several relief agencies were formed to aid the devastated communities. One of the first was the Central Committee for the Relief of the Jews Suffering through the War, organized in October 1914 mainly by downtowners. It made the point that "no one can tell, today, whether his own relatives are not refugees far from home. . . . You cannot know where your own father or mother, sister or brother is. Your help, through us, may help them."[50] A network of landsmanshaftn and synagogues provided dozens of sites and hundreds of volunteers for the Central Committee's daily solicitations and collections.[51]

Soon the American Jewish Relief Committee joined the effort to raise funds. Mainly the product of the AJC, this organization represented the unprecedented enterprise of a united community; participating national organizations ran the gamut of American Jewish life and included the Orthodox Agudat Harabonim, the Reform Central Conference of American Rabbis, the Conservative United Synagogue of America, and the People's Relief Committee, representing the Jewish labor movement. In the face of crisis abroad, even representatives of the anti-Zionist Workmen's Circle sat with the delegates from the Federation of American Zionists.[52]

Diversity was maintained, but some of the day-to-day contentiousness that marked the life of the American Jewish community was put aside. In November 1914 the different relief committees combined to form the Joint Distribution Committee of American Funds for the Relief of Jewish War Sufferers (JDC, or the "Joint," as it affectionately came to be known). The confederation thought of itself as a purely administrative organization, collecting funds through existing groups and distributing them through established channels of overseas relief work. This posture, which avoided the pitfalls of Jewish community politics, and an efficient executive board with Felix Warburg as its first chairman, helped the Joint raise close to two million dollars in 1915.[53] The following year, Judah Magnes returned from the eastern war zone demanding a goal of ten million dollars for relief. He wrote:

> With my own eyes, I have seen the misery, the slow starvation of thousands. The Jews of America are sharing in prosperity as never before. Will they do their duty by their fellow Jews? Give, I beg of you, to the old men and women, to the young wives whose husbands are at war in the different armies, to the numberless sick who have been brought down by privation, to the children who at times still play and sing despite the cold and the hunger that menace them. Give so that the Jewish people may live.[54]

At a rally in Carnegie Hall, Julius Rosenwald of Chicago made the first of his great pledges, a million dollars. Over a three-year period, he gave more than three million dollars.[55] There were countless small contributions as well, solicited mainly by the Joint's constituent organizations. The Central Committee for the Relief of the Jews, in addition to sponsoring a popular benefit series of cantorial concerts, continued conducting successful appeals in synagogues, and the People's Relief Committee collected large sums in the garment district. All the funds were entrusted to the Joint, which by 1918 had distributed some twenty million dollars.

The efforts of the Joint were concentrated in the Russian Pale and Galicia (Austria-Hungary), where the war proved most devastating to Jewish communities. The organization maintained soup kitchens, distributed clothing and medical supplies, and helped build schools and workshops, some of which managed to survive even under the suspicious eyes of the new Soviet regime established after November 1917. In German-occupied Poland, the Joint channeled its funds through a German Jewish agency operating behind German lines. The Joint was an extraordinary undertaking, and at the peak of its activity 700,000 Jews in eastern Europe were dependent on its largesse.

After the war, nine million homeless Jews tried to put their lives back together in a chaotic, hostile Europe. The difficulties faced by Russian Jewry were intensified by the Revolution and subsequent civil war and by mass pogroms in the Ukraine. In this postwar crisis, the Joint came through once again. With the cooperation of the American government and private national relief agencies, it distributed an additional twenty-seven million dollars for the relief of Russian Jewry. Joint workers organized self-help committees and even small loan societies, and they moved through dangerous war-torn landscapes to distribute food and supplies.[56] Generosity of spirit and efficient use of resources made the Joint synonymous with hope and rescue to the Jews of ravaged Europe. Herbert Hoover, who directed the massive postwar relief effort of the American government, singled out the Joint for praise: "There is," he said in 1923, "no brighter chapter in the whole history of philanthropy than that which could be written of the work of the American Jews in the last nine years."[57]

Several events beginning in 1914 had made it essential that the American Jewish community promptly settle or put aside issues that divided it. Along with the emergencies created in the Jewish communities of eastern Europe, the war brought an unexpected opportunity to realize the Zionist goal of establishing a Jewish homeland in Palestine. But the war also posed a dilemma for the world Zionist movement: Which side should it support? European Jews, after all, were fighting and dying on both sides. Moreover, early in the conflict between the Allies and the Central Powers, the outcome was unclear. European Zionists like Shmaryahu Levin leaned toward the Germans, especially after the Russian Revolution brought to power a regime basically hostile to the Zionist program. Others, best represented by University of Manchester scientist Chaim Weizmann, sided with the British.

Ultimately, the hostility of the Ottoman Turkish Empire, associated with the Central Powers, toward the yishuv—the small Jewish settlement in

Palestine—brought Zionists closer to the British and the Allies. The course of the war itself eventually did the same. This was especially true after the entrance of the United States in mid-1917 dramatically changed the odds in favor of the Allies and after it became clear that the disintegration of Turkey promised to leave the Middle Eastern segments of the Ottoman Empire in British hands.

Since the beginning of the war, Chaim Weizmann had been negotiating with British cabinet members for public endorsement of Zionist territorial aims. Partly out of the desire to woo American and Russian Jewry to the Allied cause, the British seriously considered such a move. They needed assurance, however, that the Wilson administration would back them. Louis Brandeis, Stephen Wise, and Felix Frankfurter, American Zionists who had access to Wilson, used their influence to that end. Despite the anti-Zionism of Secretary of State Robert Lansing and presidential advisor Colonel Edward M. House, Wilson promised his support to British recognition of a Jewish national home in Palestine.

Historians have not been able to agree on the extent of Wilson's commitment to the Zionist cause. But it is at least arguable that, if not for the president, the anti-Zionist posture of the State Department would have triumphed. Reinforced by the influence of Protestant missionaries who were vexed by the unconvertibility of the Jews in the Holy Land and by businessmen interested in Arab oil, the State Department was prepared to quash Zionist plans. But to the evangelical Wilson, the role of facilitating the divine design of Jewish restoration to Zion was appealing. The president was also attracted to Brandeis's vision of a Palestine built on the democratic, progressive ideals Wilson advocated. An endorsement of the Zionist goal also gave concrete proof of the president's concern for national self-determination. And as important, a pro-Zionist position was justified in terms of wartime diplomacy, for the Allies knew that Germany, like Britain, was prepared to use Palestine in a bid for Jewish support.[58]

The final product of the British deliberations, the Balfour Declaration, was announced on 2 November 1917, favoring the establishment of a national home for the Jewish people in Palestine.[59] Marked by ambiguities about sovereignty and about the rights of non-Jewish communities in Palestine, which would haunt the Zionist movement for decades, the Balfour Declaration was nevertheless hailed by Jewish nationalists all over the world. American Zionists called it the Jewish Magna Charta. With a stroke of the pen, the early Zionist vision had been transformed from fantasy to reality.

Hope had also been enhanced by the burst of organizational energy in the United States following Louis Brandeis's emergence as the leader of the American Zionist movement in 1914. This hope, combined with the deteriorated Jewish condition in war-torn eastern Europe and the proposed creation of new nation-states in regions populated with large Jewish minorities, made it critical to have a Jewish delegation at the postwar peace conference. Eastern European Jews in America demanded a part in that enterprise, and American Zionists—buoyed by the international developments described above—took the lead in pressing for the establishment of a new national organization to fulfill this potentially momentous role.

The American Jewish Committee, still relatively elitist in composition and anti-Zionist in ideology, would not do. Instead, a democratically elected representative body, "a Congress for and from all Jews," was urged by publicist and communal activist Bernard Richards, as well as by labor Zionists Nachman Syrkin and Baruch Zuckerman.[60] Many Jewish leaders at first saw the congress idea as a form of Jewish national autonomy and, therefore, as alien to the American political and social structure. At best, Jewish autonomy was considered suitable only to the multinational empires of eastern Europe; in the United States, a Jewish nation embodied in a quasi-parliamentary institution appeared to deny the American concept of equal citizenship and the American dream of one nation.[61]

During the emergency of World War I, however, the concept of the congress was transformed from what looked like a political eccentricity to a pivotal issue in American Jewish life. In 1915 an organizing committee, headed by Louis Brandeis and religious Zionist Gedaliah Bublick, set out to create a democratically elected body to represent the entire American Jewish community. The new organization would be designed to deal with matters affecting the welfare of Jews everywhere. But highest priority was given to securing civil and political rights for Jewish communities in reconstructed postwar Europe.

The Zionists, a small but articulate and dedicated group that played a critical role in the congress movement, hoped it would especially serve their cause: the right and ability of Jews to leave Europe and settle in a new Jewish commonwealth in Palestine. They argued that the congress should fight for "free immigration for all peoples and automatically for Jews." Even if equal rights were guaranteed, many Zionists correctly predicted, "social and economic hostility to the Jews will rise," making "mass emigration . . . the only salvation."[62]

When Louis Brandeis was condemned for furthering the fragmentation of the American Jewish community by lending his name to the American Jewish Congress, as the new organization came to be known, he retorted that only an American Jewry united in a body organized on the principle of Jewish peoplehood and dedicated to mass democratic participation would have the power to obtain equal rights for their brethren in Europe.[63] In March 1916 nearly four hundred representatives of a wide variety of organizations met in Philadelphia to formulate the goals of the American Jewish Congress. These were stated most succinctly by Stephen Wise: "not relief, but redress, not palliatives but prevention, not charity but justice."[64] It was eloquent shorthand not only for the basic grievances of Jews abroad but also for the resentments harbored by eastern European immigrants against the shtadlanim of the AJC.

The AJC recognized in the congress movement a challenge to its hegemony, and Louis Marshall referred to congress supporters as "noisy, blatant demagogues, principally nationalists and socialists."[65] In its confrontation with procongress forces, AJC leaders even went so far as to make an anti-Zionist alliance with the socialist-oriented National Workmen's Committee on Jewish Rights. Still, the AJC was convinced it could do little to prevent the congress from coming into existence, and it finally sought only to limit the new organization's function and duration.[66]

The AJC supported the congress on the condition that the new organization refrain from ideological pronouncements and concern itself only with the postwar problems of Jewry at the peace conferences. At the end of its work, the congress was to disband, and all other existing Jewish organizations were to remain inviolate. Even this compromise proposal was resisted by those in the AJC who saw in the pro-Zionism of the congress movement the implication of dual loyalty and a threat to the foundations of the American Jewish community. But leaders like Schiff and Marshall, though hardly reconciled to the idea of a Jewish political commonwealth, were in sympathy with the idea that a cultural and religious center in Palestine would help revitalize world Jewry.[67] They prevailed, and a compromise was reached in July 1916 covering all the previously cited points, including a dual approach to the Jewish problem in Europe: the congress's delegation to the treaty conferences was to urge the protection of minorities in the various new states to be created; for those Jews who wanted to leave Europe, the delegates were to press for a Jewish national home.[68]

In order to select representatives to the peace conference, a convention of the American Jewish Congress had to be scheduled. This produced a stunningly unique event in American history: on 10 June 1917, one of the nation's many ethnic groups conducted an internal election to choose delegates to the American Jewish Congress, who would, in effect, determine an important part of the future course of American Jewry. Over thirty Jewish organizations and more than eighty cities participated. Some 335,000 votes were cast. Almost four years after the idea had first surfaced, and barely a month before the nations were to meet at Versailles, the American Jewish Congress officially convened in Philadelphia in December 1918. The nearly four hundred delegates elected Judge Julian W. Mack of Chicago as president. A founding member of the American Jewish Committee and president of the Zionist Organization of America, Mack could serve as a symbol of the unity of the committee and the congress in their commitment to their brethren overseas.

The delegation chosen to represent American Jewry at the peace conference also symbolized unity. It was representative of nearly all elements in the American Jewish community. The Zionists included Chairman Mack, Reform Rabbi Stephen S. Wise, and former labor leader Joseph Barondess. Louis Marshall and Harry Cutler spoke for the AJC. Labor-Zionist Nachman Syrkin and the proletarian poet and Socialist Morris Winchevsky represented a segment of the labor movement. Also attending was Orthodox rabbi and religious Zionist Bernard Levinthal of Philadelphia.

German and Russian Jews, Zionists and non-Zionists, Orthodox and Reform, and leaders of labor were united in common purpose; but discordant voices were heard. From the start, the Jewish Socialist Federation and the National Workmen's Committee on Jewish Rights, representing an important body of Socialists, had been unable to decide whether to join or denounce the congress, which included the participation of Zionists and capitalists. From a profound dread of Zionist domination of the Jewish community, Socialist organizations made several ill-timed changes of course, including a temporary alliance with the "bourgeois element" in the congress. By early 1919, the Socialists, infuriated by the pro-Zionist resolutions of the congress and convinced that the system then being implemented in the Soviet Union meant that the solution to the "Jewish question" was already at hand, withdrew from the American Jewish Congress. The American Jewish Committee, not entirely comfortable in the congress delegation, sent its own delegation. In addition, conflicting views as to the order of priorities vis-à-vis Zionist goals and minority rights continued to surface. It took all the energy and skill of Louis Marshall, who replaced Judge Mack as head of the delegation, to maintain unity and discipline.[69]

At home, too, unity was threatened. On 5 March 1919, three days after the American Jewish Congress presented President Wilson with a memorandum urging him to support the Balfour Declaration at the peace conference, an anti-Zionist memorandum appeared in the *New York Times.* Signed by Adolph Ochs, publisher of the *Times,* and by dozens of other members of the anti-Zionist faction of the AJC, the memorandum warned against the "reorganization of the Jews as a national unit to whom territorial sovereignty in Palestine shall be committed."[70] This dissenting voice would not be stilled until the rise of the Nazis in the 1930s made tragically clear the prescience of the Zionist aspiration for territorial sovereignty to serve as a haven for European Jewry.

In addition to the conflicts within the Jewish community, opposition from other quarters posed difficulties for the Zionists. The Arabs, of course, were adamantly opposed to naming Britain, which had issued the Balfour Declaration, the mandatory power in Palestine. France, Britain's traditional rival in the Middle East, joined the dissent, as did the Vatican and Protestant missionary groups. Despite these obstacles, negotiations brought some nominally positive results. Civil rights were guaranteed to Jews and other minority groups within the domain of the newly formed or reshaped nations of Poland, Czechoslovakia, Yugoslavia, Romania, Hungary, and Austria. The guarantees, as several Zionist spokesmen had foreseen, failed in practice to provide protection for the Jews of eastern Europe. But the right of free immigration for all peoples had been asserted. In addition, the mandate over Palestine was granted to Great Britain, and the Balfour Declaration itself would soon be incorporated into the peace treaty with Turkey. Its work completed at Versailles, the congress delegation returned to Philadelphia to make its report. At the end of the session on 30 May 1920, the American Jewish Congress, true to its word, disbanded. But already there were plans afoot to bring it back to life.

The movement for an American Jewish Congress beginning in 1915 had offered an alternative to the elitism of the AJC and the organizational disunity that marked American Jewry. The first effort at order and institutional coherence in the Jewish community, however, had been the kehillah experiment in New York from 1908 to 1922. The New York kehillah warrants our attention as a valiant, perhaps desperate, effort to establish some general form of governance among Jews living in a free society.[71]

Although the immediate move to establish the kehillah was in response to allegations of disproportionate crime rates among Jews in the ghetto (see chapter 3), the kehillah was conceived and developed more generally to meet the need for a single, centralized organization to deal with the social and economic problems faced by the mass of Jews in New York on a daily basis. The guiding spirit was Judah Magnes, the thirty-one-year-old associate rabbi of uptown's Temple Emanu-El. Magnes was no ordinary uptowner. Though he ministered to the needs of the Schiffs, the Seligmans, and the Warburgs in the nation's most prestigious Reform temple, Magnes was equally at home downtown, where he occasionally prayed in the shuln of the Orthodox. He also was an ardent Zionist. Perhaps reflecting his own multifarious personality, Magnes believed that it was possible to create a structure around which the disparate components of New York Jewry might voluntarily coalesce.

In 1909 three hundred delegates, representing more than two hundred organizations—including synagogues, lodges, charitable and educational institutions, mutual benefit societies, and Zionist and religious groups— came together to create the kehillah. There were problems from the start. Conspicuously absent was the socialist-oriented labor movement. More- over, there were furious arguments at the founding convention, particularly between religious spokesmen who thought the kehillah's central purpose ought to be "the protection and care of the . . . interests of the Jewish faith" and those who believed that the organization should be designed primarily to look after the "national, cultural, social [and] economical" interests of the Jewish people. Divisive proposals and counterproposals to amend the neutral declaration of principles were made, and these threatened to wreck the conference. But Magnes, who chaired the session, managed to persuade both sides to withdraw their amendments and to agree on the idea of "union first, dissension after."[72]

Neither the contentiousness of the various delegations nor the absence of the Socialists dampened Magnes's enthusiasm. He was confident that as chairman he could help fulfill the new organization's goals of "democratiz- ing" the community and wiping out the "insidious distinctions between East European and West European, foreigners and natives . . . rich and poor."[73]

The kehillah aimed to teach Jews that they are "one people with a com- mon history and common hopes."[74] This was an ambitious goal but not out of touch with the temper of the times. Affiliations and mergers were occur- ring in the Jewish community on the religious and labor fronts and among landsmanshaftn and philanthropic agencies. Moreover, in the kehillah's desire for efficient community organization and the priority given to bringing order to the ghetto, it is possible to see reflections of the general Progressive spirit abroad in the nation between 1900 and 1920. Magnes even envisioned that other cities would establish similar communal agencies, which would unite in a nationwide federation in association with the American Jewish Committee. Jewish organizational life would be democratized, and yet the influence of the shtadlanim would be retained for the good of the community.[75]

But it was to no avail. Despite the general desire to coordinate Jewish organizational life, there was opposition to the kehillah from the start, and disunity and contentiousness remained a constant in the history of the organization. Immediately, there was tension over the role of the American Jewish Committee. Anxious to expand its popular base while retaining its oligarchic hold, the AJC provided most of the funding for the kehillah. Resentment surfaced over the increasing influence of the AJC in kehillah affairs and intensified when the AJC formally co-opted the twenty-five-member executive board of the kehillah as its New York chapter. The AJC was not the only source of tension. Socialists, in order to have a hand in hammering out the developing agenda of the kehillah, attended the annual conventions in 1911 and 1915; there they formed temporary alliances with the uptowners to check the influence of the Zionists. Indeed, each group, including the Zionists, sought to use the kehillah to further its own objectives.[76]

In the early years, these conflicts did not noticeably interfere with the effectiveness of the kehillah. The organization was divided into bureaus, which focused on special problems: education, philanthropy, morals, religion (particularly dietary laws), labor, and industry. Under the leadership of Dr. Samuel Benderly, the kehillah's Bureau of Education ran an effective consolidated Jewish educational enterprise with two hundred schools, six hundred teachers, and thirty-five thousand students. The Bureau of Education endured beyond the kehillah and is probably the experiment's most conspicuous success. The Bureau of Religious Affairs also brought some order into the chaos surrounding the certification of kosher food, and the Bureau of Labor played an important role in mediating a strike in the fur industry in 1912 and in the men's clothing industry in 1913.

Perhaps most remarkable was the Bureau of Social Morals. A kind of vigilante committee, with its own undercover investigators, this bureau was designed to ferret out prostitution and other wrongdoing in the Jewish community and to gather information to serve as the basis for municipal antivice campaigns. Much depended on the cooperation of the mayor's office and the police. After only a year of investigation, the bureau had a card file of over twenty-five hundred addresses of "undesirable" hangouts and disorderly houses; the kehillah was responsible for closing more than one hundred of these establishments. Upward mobility was more important than the Bureau of Social Morals for the dramatic decline in Jewish crime and prostitution on the Lower East Side, but its efforts between 1912 and 1918 helped curb at least some of the surface manifestations of ghetto vice.[77]

The kehillah and its bureaus continued to seem viable as late as 1918, when 840 delegates attended the annual convention. But all was not well. The cohesiveness of the New York Jewish community, which the kehillah was charged with developing, remained elusive. Even at its peak, the kehillah attracted no more than 15 percent of the Jewish community's organizations. And now it was being challenged by the American Jewish Congress movement and even by experiments in alternative communal structures like the Federation for the Support of Jewish Philanthropic Societies.[78] Moreover, as we have seen, each of the kehillah's member organizations tried to foster its own aims, which exacerbated rather than ameliorated conflict.

In addition, Judah Magnes, perhaps the one figure who could hold the conflicting groups in the kehillah together, stood discredited. As a member of the AJC and of the Provisional Committee of the Zionist Organization of America, as well as chairman of the kehillah, Magnes appeared to be the key person to mediate among Zionists and non-Zionists, uptowners and downtowners—the role he originally hoped for in the rabbinate. But in the struggle between the congress movement and the AJC, Magnes cast his lot with the AJC. He turned upon the Zionists, accusing Brandeis, Wise, and the others of fostering disunity among American Jews. At the same time, he was blind to the shortcomings of the AJC, which did not believe in the ability of the masses to govern themselves, and which failed to negotiate meaningfully. The Zionists no longer trusted Magnes; but his voice carried little weight in the AJC. The kehillah was falling apart, and Magnes's radical pacifism during World War I exacerbated the situation and undermined his supporters.[79]

Contentiousness was also the norm outside the kehillah, where a rich and heterogenous Jewish community remained divided by its differences, all of which were represented in the variety of Jewish communal institutions and in the fact that each organization included subgroups in seemingly perpetual conflict.[80] The Zionist movement alone, between 1898 and 1914, spawned no fewer than 125 different societies in New York City.[81] Such conflict reflected not only the fact that "every shade of religious, social and political thought is represented,"[82] it was also a product of the luxury of Jewish security in America. Despite occasional manifestations of anti-Semitism in the United States, Jews correctly judged that America was different. The sense of insecurity which helped maintain the kehillot in eastern Europe was not duplicated in the United States. Given this condition, and given the rich turbulence of Jewish communal life, the New York kehillah's hope for unity may have been doomed from the outset.[83] Perhaps, as one critic put it, "there was no Kehillah, there was only Dr. Magnes, and there was in his mind the *idea* of the Kehillah."[84]

Judah Magnes believed in an ethnic solidarity among Jews, a solidarity grounded in historical and religious experience, and in the minority group experience of oppression. He assumed that crises would continue to elicit collective Jewish responses.[85] But even Magnes came to understand that, under the relatively free conditions of life in the United States, ethnicity was but one of many attachments—such as class, profession, family, and the greater American culture—shared by groups and individuals. Most Jews would be content with a much more modest vision of ethnic community than the one envisioned by the kehillah. Most would separate themselves from the larger society only to the degree necessary for maintaining Jewish identity, and all would continue to have their own ideas about the content, intensity, and meaning of that identity.

✡

CHAPTER EIGHT

CULTURAL PLURALISM AND ZIONISM

THE VIGOR and variety of Jewish organizational life in America reflected the resilience of the Jewish culture that had its roots in eastern
Europe. Centuries of enforced isolation in the old countries had promoted
a separate Jewish language and literature and a set of distinctive values and
traditions. Indeed, in their predominant presence in the Pale, the Jews—
though hardly sovereign—might even be considered to have had their own
territory as well as their own culture. All of this reinforced a rich and
powerful national-cultural heritage, which was difficult to give up.

The erosion of strict religious observance and belief did not, therefore,
lead to assimilation but to Jewishness expressed in secular form. Even
before the term became fashionable, then, and before the concept became
an ideal toward which America itself groped, the Jews were making their
way to a cultural pluralism within their own community. One form of Jewish identity that grew out of these historical circumstances was Zionism—
the movement to give the separate Jewish national-cultural entity its own
home.

Although Zionism never implied for American Jews a personal imperative to settle in Palestine, the movement provided a vehicle for steering a
course between assimilation and Jewish survival in the United States. More
than the kehillah or the congress movement, Zionism, with its emphasis on
common tradition, history, and fate, offered a spiritual communalism that
buttressed a sense of Jewish peoplehood.

Zionism, or as some would have it, Israelism, is one of the most important elements in American Jewish identity.[1] But at the turn of the century,
Zionism was poorly organized and without a large constituency. Except
among a handful of eastern European Jews in the sweatshops, tenements,

and cafés of New York's Lower East Side, Zionism had little appeal in the unthreatening environment of America.[2] Its strength lay in eastern Europe, where emerging nationalism was everywhere accompanied by strident anti-Semitism.

The bloody pogroms that began in earnest in 1870 in Odessa and other Russian cities and towns helped produce a countervailing nationalism among Jews. Among the first spokesmen to promote a Jewish national-cultural regeneration was the Odessa physician Leon Pinsker. Although an acculturated cosmopolitan, Pinsker in his book *Auto-Emancipation,* published in 1882 while pogroms raged across the Ukraine, rejected the assimilationist solution to the "Jewish question." He focused instead on the possibility of creating a Jewish nation in its own national home, preferably Palestine.

A small number of Lovers of Zion clubs did appear in eastern Europe in the 1880s, but Zionism was neither immediately nor widely popular, even among the victims of pogroms. Orthodox Jews, believing they could not press for redemption through physical means, chose to wait for the Messiah to restore Zion, and they rejected the presumptuousness of the secular nationalists. Believing that anti-Semitism, like all oppressions, was rooted in the rotten soil of capitalism, Socialists worked not to foster Jewish nationalism but to abolish the bourgeois system.[3] For these radicals, a just social order, not the "tribal particularism" of Zionism, would liberate all peoples, including the Jews. A Zionist writer assessed the opposition succinctly: "The very religious consider us heretics who wish to bring the redemption before it is time. The liberals look upon us as fanatics, who obscure the light of civilization with this new fangled idea. The 'Know Nothings' [all other non-Zionists] are against us from sheer inertia."[4]

The difficulty of pulling up stakes and leaving even an inhospitable environment was reinforced by the unattractiveness of Palestine, as either haven or home. Though it had been the site of ancient Jewish territorial sovereignty and continued to shelter a small traditional Jewish population, Palestine did not appear to be the best place to reestablish a Jewish national homeland. Not only was the region ruled by hostile Ottoman Turks, it was poor and disease ridden.

The beleaguered Jews of eastern Europe who sought a haven most often immigrated to America. But a small stream of refugees, encouraged by the Lovers of Zion clubs and various Zionist colonization societies, chose Palestine. Eastern European pioneers in some two dozen agricultural communities faced extreme hardship, and their experience discouraged a major migration. But these eastern Europeans represented at least a beginning for the Zionist movement, which would soon find ideological support in the West.

An upsurge of political and racial anti-Semitism in Austria, Germany, and France throughout the 1880s and 1890s convinced many Jews that emancipation in western Europe had failed. This led to a reawakening of Jewish national consciousness, even among assimilated Jews. Theodore Herzl, an upper-middle-class Hungarian-born journalist, had witnessed the resurgence of anti-Semitism; and in 1894 while serving as the Paris correspondent of the *Neue Freie Presse,* he was profoundly affected by the infamous treason trial and public degradation of Jewish French army officer Alfred Dreyfus. "Death to the Jews!" Herzl had heard the French mob howl, "as the decorations were . . . ripped from the captain's coat." He was convinced that the Dreyfus case, with its travesties of justice and ugly race hatred, embodied "the desire of the vast majority of the French to condemn a Jew, and to condemn all Jews in this one Jew."[5] That France, the very first western European state to emancipate its Jews, could continue to manifest such powerful hatred of Jews reinforced Herzl's growing conviction that anti-Semitism was ineradicable and moved him to publish *Der Judenstaat* in 1896, a proposal for the founding of a modern Jewish state.

Theodore Herzl proved to be a charismatic leader; he gained financial and political support for Zionism in the West and rejuvenated the pioneer Lovers of Zion movement in the East. In 1897 Herzl brought the two groups together at a World Zionist Congress in Basel, Switzerland. Here Jewish leaders dedicated themselves to the promotion of settlement in Palestine, "the organization and binding together of the whole of Jewry" and the strengthening and fostering of "Jewish national sentiment and consciousness."[6]

Jewish nationalist sentiment in the form of the Zionist idea had surfaced in the American Jewish community from as early as the colonial period. Most synagogue-goers, for example, faced east toward Jerusalem during devotions, and their prayer books were peppered with references to the restoration of Zion. In the eighteenth and nineteenth centuries, American Jews were also positively responsive to emissaries from Palestine who collected funds for the *yishuv,* the small Jewish settlement in the Holy Land.

And some American Jews even insisted on being interred with a handful of Palestinian soil. Indeed, Commodore Uriah P. Levy, the first Jew to obtain high rank in the American navy, brought several thousand pounds of such "sacred earth" to the United States aboard his warship.[7]

A number of individuals and groups, Protestant as well as Jewish, promoted actual settlement in Palestine. These included Mordecai Manuel Noah, a minor nineteenth-century politician; Simon Bermann, who, after seventeen years in the United States, moved to Palestine, where he designed plans for an agricultural cooperative; and Warder Cresson, a religious enthusiast who converted to Judaism in 1845 and began an agricultural settlement near Jerusalem, where he waited for the "ingathering of the Jews by divine means." Several Christian groups, though hardly attracted to the idea of conversion to Judaism, were interested in the Jewish ingathering as the prerequisite for the Second Coming of Jesus Christ, and they too attempted settlements in Palestine.[8]

Faced by inhospitable conditions and Arab hostility, the Christian settlements failed in short order. But sometimes it was Christian enthusiasm for Zionism that stirred nationalism among the Jews. The poet Emma Lazarus, for example, who wrote the popular Zionist tract *Epistles to Hebrews* in 1882, was influenced not only by Leon Pinsker's *Auto-Emancipation* but earlier, and as profoundly, by George Eliot's Zionist novel *Daniel Deronda* (1876) and Laurence Oliphant's *Land of Gilead* (1881).

A notable example of Christian enthusiasm for Jewish national redemption was the Blackstone memorandum of 1891. Christian Minister W. F. Blackstone, after a visit to the Holy Land, petitioned President Benjamin Harrison to consider using his office to establish a homeland for "Israelites" in Palestine. The memorandum was signed by more than four hundred prominent Americans, including J. P. Morgan and John D. Rockefeller.

This support for a Jewish home in Palestine developed in the context of Russian depredations against Jews. And in the last two decades of the nineteenth century, the American government, concerned about the flood of impoverished Russian Jewish immigrants, became increasingly open to the possibility of using Palestine as a refuge. As early as 1882, General Lewis Wallace, the American minister to Constantinople, secured the administration's consent for his support of Jewish colonies in Palestine. And Oscar Straus (who served as minister to Constantinople from 1887 to 1889 and from 1898 to 1900), though not a Zionist, on several occasions championed general Jewish immigration and settlement in Palestine.[9]

Although American authorities before World War I paid scant attention to the idea of a Jewish state, they were receptive to any schemes, including Zionism, that promised to deflect the immigrant flow away from the United States. But Zionism was slow to develop among American Jews. The economic difficulties experienced by immigrants in America between 1883 and 1886 and again between 1893 and 1897 drained potential enthusiasm, and the few Lovers of Zion chapters that had been organized by a tiny minority of the newcomers in the early 1880s languished. Zionism, moreover, ran counter to the desire to root oneself in America, which despite occasional economic difficulties seemed to Jews more and more like the true promised land. The Zionist movement therefore won little popularity within any Jewish group, including eastern European immigrants. Chaim Weizmann's description of Zionism in England held equally true for the United States: "A handful of devotees to the cause among the lower middle classes, indifference or hostility among the upper classes."[10]

Hostility was manifest, too, in other Jewish quarters. Reform rabbis, led by Emil Hirsch of Chicago, proud of their universalism and their Americanization and fearing the charge of dual loyalty—ridiculed the Zionists' dream of Palestine. At the same time, Orthodox leaders in America viewed the Zionists as "going against God's will." Like their counterparts in the shtetlekh of eastern Europe, New World traditionalists believed that, if God "wanted us to have Zion again, He would restore it without the help of the so-called Zionists." In addition to opposition from religious groups, Zionism in America faced opposition, just as it had in Russia, from the antinationalist radical labor movement.[11]

In such a context it is not hard to understand why American Jewry was represented by only one official delegate at the first World Zionist Congress in Basel in 1897. This congress itself, however, appears to have served as an energizer for the American movement. Richard Gottheil, a Reform rabbi of German descent who served as an unofficial observer in Basel, organized the Federation of American Zionists (FAZ), the first national Zionist organization. Gottheil served as president from 1898 to 1904, while Stephen S. Wise, a young Hungarian-born Reform rabbi from Oregon and a charismatic orator, became the organization's secretary. More than one hundred local Zionist groups affiliated with FAZ in the first year. By 1900 the combined membership of these groups rose to an unprecedented eight thousand and, five years later, to twenty-five thousand.

American Zionism, however, continued to be plagued by sluggish growth. Twenty-five thousand dues-paying Jews in 1905 represented a very small percentage of the more than one million Jews in the United States, and only a handful were actually active in the movement. Moreover, important American Jewish leaders associated with Reform, like Jacob Schiff and Louis Marshall, continued to express disapproval. Established Reform Jews, mainly of German descent, were particularly distressed when several of "their own," like Gottheil, Wise, and Max Heller, a Cincinnati-trained Reform rabbi, openly identified with Zionism, thereby legitimizing the nationalist dimension of Judaism and making the Reform movement vulnerable to the charge of disloyalty to America.[12] Schiff wrote to Stephen Wise in 1904: "I am an American pure and simple and cannot possibly belong to two nations. I feel that Zionism is a purely theoretical and sentimental proposition and as a practicable one has no future." And Louis Marshall felt compelled to write to Max Heller: "I do not believe that . . . relief for . . . our unfortunate [Russian] brethren . . . will come though Zionism. . . . Eventually Russia will have a free government, and . . . the Jew will receive the same rights and privileges that he possesses in other free countries."[13]

For different reasons, eastern European Jews were also unhappy that Zionist leaders like Richard Gottheil, president of FAZ, were part of the German Jewish establishment. As early as 1898, the Lovers of Zion chapters, the founders of the American Zionist movement, left the federation. In addition, disagreement between FAZ and the World Zionist Organization took its toll; between 1901 and 1903, sixty-three local Zionist societies, constituting over one-third of the membership, withdrew from the federation. A number of religious Zionists led by Rabbi Philip Klein, hoping to form an American branch of Mizrachi, the international religious Zionist movement, also departed.

At the same time, Poale Zion, a socialist labor faction with the aim of synthesizing Zionism and socialism, made its debut. Poale Zionists found themselves at odds with religious and bourgeois Zionists, who resented their socialism, and with anti-Zionist Jewish Socialists, who resented their nationalism. They became an autonomous body in 1909, finally separating from FAZ in 1914. Additional fragmentation came when the Chicago-based Knights of Zion, the largest Zionist group outside of New York, refused to cooperate with FAZ and insisted upon direct relations with the World Zionist Organization.[14]

Even earlier, the territorialists—Jewish nationalists who were concerned more with speedy Jewish resettlement than with any specific locale—engendered a split in the Zionist movement. Under the leadership of Israel Zangwill, who headed the Jewish Territorial Organization (ITO), the territorialists looked for any "suitable" space, and when the British offered Uganda in 1905, the Zangwill group, unlike most of the Zionist movement, favored accepting it. In this way the territorialists alienated the more historically conscious Jews, who sought not only a haven but a regeneration of the Jewish people, and who thus insisted that the Jewish nation be rooted in Palestine, Israel's ancient homeland.[15]

Some of the disunity and loss suffered by FAZ was made up during these years by the administrative ability and energy of attorney Louis Lipsky. He founded and edited the *Maccabean,* which became the official organ of FAZ, and by 1912 Lipsky was the chairman of the federation's executive committee. Zionist momentum was also maintained and aided by the leadership of the Jewish Theological Seminary (JTS). Although several seminary figures, like Judah Magnes and Solomon Schechter, never came to support Jewish political independence, they were men of national stature who brought an important vitality to religious and cultural Zionism. Mordecai Kaplan and Israel Friedlander, too, with their emphasis on Jewish peoplehood, promoted the cause of Jewish cultural nationalism.[16]

Another important element sustaining prewar Zionism was the Jewish women's club movement. Although some women in the movement, like Hannah Solomon, resisted Jewish nationalism, many others saw in Palestine an opportunity to do good works and social housekeeping. Rosa Sonneschein, Mary Fels, and Mrs. Richard Gottheil devoted great energy to the promotion of Palestine as a Jewish refuge and a center for the revitalization of the Jewish religion.[17] And Henrietta Szold, a teacher and educational administrator who ran a night school for Russian immigrants in Baltimore between 1889 and 1893 and who came to be one of Zionism's most prominent and influential figures, made her first pro-Zionist speech in 1896 at a local chapter of the National Council of Jewish Women.

In 1909, at her mother's suggestion, Szold visited Palestine and was shocked by the horrendous quality of health care available to the yishuv. Her Zionist sympathies were reinforced, and by 1912, in addition to having served two years as secretary of the Jewish Agricultural Experimental Station in Palestine, Szold had generated out of a Zionist study circle the American Women's Zionist Organization. Soon renamed Hadassah, the organization emphasized the need for a public health and nursing system for the yishuv and promoted the resettlement of Jewish youth in Palestine. Hadassah grew to become the largest Jewish women's organization in the world and one of the largest women's organizations in the United States.[18]

Substantial Zionist sentiment in prewar America notwithstanding, the movement in 1913 faced major financial and organizational problems. The Federation of American Zionists continued to have difficulties with affiliated societies and with the World Zionist Organization, and it remained wracked by internal jealousies and ideological quarrels. The cultural, religious, and political divisions to which Jewry in general was heir were reproduced in American Zionism, and they were reinforced by the decentralization, pluralism, and voluntary association characteristic of all American Jewish organizations. These forms and modes of operation, however, grew directly out of American political culture and may not have been entirely dysfunctional. They allowed the flexibility required to keep the Zionist movement alive, if not unified, as well as to accommodate its spurts of growth between 1903 and 1905 and again, as we shall see, between 1914 and 1917.

The Zionist movement, despite its apparently unwieldy character, established roots in the Jewish community in the prewar period. In 1913 there were fewer than fifteen thousand members in the organizations associated with FAZ, but that still made the federation the second or third largest among national Zionist federations. In addition, numerous Zionist organizations not associated with FAZ bolstered the Zionist movement. Although the primary loyalty of the Poale Zionists, for example, was still socialism, their abhorrence of anti-Semitism in Europe often outweighed ideology and promoted cooperation.[19]

Even some organizations not Zionist in name were dominated by Jewish nationalists. Indeed, the Jewish Theological Seminary, as mentioned earlier, grew into a veritable bastion of Zionism, especially after 1906, when Solomon Schecter announced his support and published a lengthy vindication of the Zionist movement on both religious and national grounds. In these years, the seminary became increasingly associated with Conservative Judaism, and JTS scholars like Schechter, Friedlander, and Kaplan continued to defend Zionism against Orthodox and Reform opponents. As the number of Conservative Jews in America increased, this group became an important source of Zionist support.

The idea of a sovereign Jewish commonwealth remained anathema for the vast majority of German Jews; but many, including such important figures as Jacob Schiff and Louis Marshall, came to see Palestine as a potential haven for Jews and as a center for the cultural revitalization of Judaism. Schiff and Marshall favored colonization in Palestine and contributed funds for the economic development of the region. Even Julius Rosenwald, the entrepreneur who ran Sears, Roebuck, and Co. and an outspoken anti-Zionist, gave millions of dollars to support specifically Jewish projects in Palestine.[20] Thus, despite attracting only relatively small numbers to official membership, prewar Zionists had not been unsuccessful; without their work, the emergence of the movement in 1914 and 1915 would not have been possible.

Beginning in 1914, certain developments served to strengthen the American Zionist movement in more dramatic ways. First and foremost was the opportunity for the realization of the Zionist dream presented by World War I (see chapter 7). Second was the recruitment of Louis Brandeis to the Zionist cause and his ascendancy to leadership of the movement. Third was the resolution of some of FAZ's long-standing operating difficulties. With Brandeis at the helm, the federation—soon to be renamed the Zionist Organization of America (ZOA)—was restructured in 1915 so that individual members could join it directly. This eliminated some of the problems of coordinating constituent chapters.

But Louis Brandeis brought the Zionist movement more than improved organizational efficiency; he brought a "cloak of respectability" and a way to deal with the charge of dual loyalty. American-born, Harvard educated, a prominent Progressive attorney, and a Woodrow Wilson confidant, Brandeis gave American Zionism a new image.

In his fifties when he began to think about Jewish identity, Louis Brandeis became totally committed to the Zionist cause between 1905 and 1914. A number of reasons have been offered by historians and biographers for Brandeis's conversion. It has been suggested that Brandeis came to Zionism seeking compensation for exclusion from the Wilson cabinet in 1913, or that he openly identified with the Jews only after, and in order to overcome, rebuff by Boston Brahmin society. It has also been suggested that Brandeis, believing his cabinet exclusion to be the result of opposition by influential Jews, determined to cultivate members of that circle. In short, Brandeis is alleged to have come to Zionism in search of a Jewish constituency.[21]

The problem with these postulations is that there is little hard evidence to sustain them. It is difficult to make the case, for example, that Louis Brandeis was a marginal man in mainstream American society. One of the best known and richest lawyers in the United States, Brandeis was called upon regularly to testify before congressional and administrative bodies; he was a valued advisor to Woodrow Wilson and the key architect of the president's domestic policy. Brandeis also counted among his friends and admirers members of the intellectual and political elite of the United States, including Lincoln Steffens, Roscoe Pound, Robert La Follette, and Jane Addams.[22] While Brandeis was shunned by some New England Brahmins, it is important to remember that it was he who rejected them by pursuing a progressivism that threatened to shake the financial basis of their lives and society. It would have been illogical, moreover, for Brandeis to choose Zionism as a way of cultivating elite Jews, most of whom were repelled by the idea of a Jewish state.[23]

More likely, Brandeis's attraction to Zionism grew out of a combination of positive experiences with eastern European immigrants and Jewish nationalists, and disenchantment with Brahmin society. Between 1906 and 1909, it was increasingly apparent to Brandeis that his most valued Progressive ideas, which he associated with Puritan pioneers and Yankees, were rejected by the New England elite. In 1910 however, while serving as chairman of the arbitration board that produced the Protocol of Peace for the garment industry, Brandeis thought he found in the immigrant Jewish community, particularly its labor leaders, new and true carriers of the Progressive tradition. In his speech accepting the chairmanship of the Provisional Committee of the ZOA in 1914, and again in an interview in 1915, Brandeis said that his experience at the negotiating table in 1910 taught him that "the Jewish people had something which should be saved for the world." He had sensed there a deep concern for "true democracy," social justice, and "love of liberty and freedom," concerns that Brandeis shared and that he pursued for most of his adult life.[24]

It was in 1910, too, that Louis Brandeis met Jacob de Haas, who had been Theodore Herzl's secretary. Initial contact led to a series of discussions of Zionism between the two men and a deepening sense of Jewishness for Brandeis. Around the same time, Brandeis was also impressed by the Palestinian agronomist Aaron Aaronson. World famous for his discoveries of wild wheat in Palestine, Aaronson raised funds in the United States for an agricultural experimental station near Haifa. Brandeis, the Progressive, wedded to ideals based on smallness, efficiency, and pragmatic, collective experimentation, as well as to the pioneering spirit of the early Puritans, was much taken with Aaronson's work and was reinforced in his vision of Jewishness as democracy and Zionism as Progressivism.

In 1912 Brandeis formally joined the Federation of American Zionists, and his growing commitment to the movement became publicly known in 1913 when he chaired a Boston meeting to honor Nahum Sokolow, a member of the French Zionist organization, Actions Comité. By the outbreak of World War I in 1914, Brandeis was finally convinced of the urgency of the Jewish situation in Europe and was persuaded by Jacob de Haas to take on the work of American Zionism in a fully committed way.[25]

Brandeis was also profoundly influenced by the ideas of Horace Kallen, a Harvard-educated Progressive who taught philosophy and psychology at the University of Wisconsin before World War I. Between 1913 and 1914, in letters and conversations, Kallen helped his fellow New Englander perceive more clearly the relationship between Americanism, Hebraism, and Zionism.[26] Hebraism, for Kallen, was not mere Judaism or religion but a construct that described the "total biography of the Jewish soul." Its spirit represented the prophetic legacy of social justice, international righteousness, and peace and was inseparable from the American core tradition, with its universalistic and unique democratic mission. Indeed, Kallen believed that the biblical prophets had shaped the Hebraic character traits of the Puritans and, by extension, the American Republic.[27]

The concept of a usable Hebraic past led to Kallen's vision of an America enriched by its distinctive ethnic groups—a rejection of the melting pot and an embrace of what Kallen later called cultural pluralism. Like Jewish nationalist Chaim Zhitlowsky before him, Kallen called upon America to shelter the "commonwealth of national cultures." Not only would the individual be blessed by the life-giving cultural sustenance of ethnic attachment, but the creative unity of a variety of national cultures would lead to mutual enrichment. America would not be a melting pot, but a symphony—a symphony, as Judah Magnes put it earlier, to be "written by the various nationalities which keep their individual and characteristic note and which sound this note in harmony."[28] In this way the individual nationalities would not only deepen and enrich American culture, they would become channels for the most precious gift America could give: a model for a united states of the world.

Louis Brandeis gradually came to accept Zionism and cultural pluralism and, most important, their interdependent relationship. He saw Judaism and Zionism as essential parts of a democratic, ethnically pluralistic society; and he believed that Jews, in pursuing Zionist goals, would revive their great humanistic civilization. Two Jewish centers, America and Palestine, would feed each other, promoting a renaissance vital to American Jewish life as well as to society at large. In his writings and speeches between 1913 and 1915, Brandeis developed the classic syllogism summarizing his position: "To be good Americans, we must be better Jews, and to be better Jews we must be Zionists."[29]

Brandeis not only supplied an epigrammatic refutation of the charge of dual loyalty so often leveled at Zionists; his formulations, emphasizing Zionism's benefit to America and the world, also allowed Jewish nationalists, both religious and secular, to make the case for cultural pluralism and the congruity of Jewish ethics and American ideals. Zionism or Jewish nationalism, like American nationalism, it was argued, gained at least part of its value in its universal mission—its emphasis on democracy and self-determination.[30]

The idea of mission—or the idea that Zionism, like American democracy, could serve as a model and a beacon to the world—had appeared in the words and deeds of Stephen Wise, Judah Magnes, Israel Friedlander, and others. But Brandeis made the idea popular and respectably American, especially after he penetrated the sacred precincts of American political life with his appointment to the Supreme Court of the United States in 1916. Brandeis also recruited notable and talented American Jews to the movement. Felix Frankfurter, Nathan Straus, and Louis Kirstein added stature to American Zionism and credibility to Brandeis's insistence that "there is no inconsistency between loyalty to America and loyalty to Jewry," indeed that "loyalty to America demands . . . that each Jew become a Zionist."[31]

Zionism as it developed in the second decade of the twentieth century not only enabled American Jews to support the ideal of the return of Jews to Palestine without fear of compromising their American patriotism, it also encouraged and helped American Jews to remain Jewish. As early as the 1890s, Richard Gottheil argued that Zionism would keep many Jews in the fold of Judaism who might otherwise depart. Solomon Schechter by 1906 saw Zionism as "the great bulwark against assimilation." The movement "must not be judged," he said, "by what it has accomplished in Zion and Jerusalem but *for* Zion and Jerusalem, by awakening the national Jewish consciousness. Our [American] synagogues and homes show plainly the effect."[32]

Judah Magnes also believed that Zionism would be a tonic for American Jewry. "The entire people must be organized in different forms, in different countries," Magnes wrote to Chaim Weizmann in 1914. "Palestine should be the connecting link, the summit of organized [Jewish life]. The

Jews of the world influence Palestine, Palestine influences the Jews of the world." Israel Friedlander agreed. Indeed, he went so far as to argue that American Jews would disappear unless they retained their vital links to the spiritual center in Palestine and to world Jewry generally.[33]

Cultural pluralists seeking ethnic harmony and a vital civilization promoted the value of Jewishness and the idea that Zionism enriched American life; but Jewish nationalists in their advocacy of Zionism also promoted another complementary goal: the group survival of American Jews. Zionist appeals, however they were pitched, attracted increasing numbers of American Jews in the immediate prewar years. Movement membership climbed from about 13,000 in 1912 to 150,000 in 1914. By 1919, after the reorganization of the FAZ into the more efficient ZOA, and after five years of Louis Brandeis at the helm preaching the need for "Men! Money! Discipline!" the Zionist movement reached a peak of 180,000 members.

Growth promoted optimism, but it hid some important fissures. The Brandeis leadership believed that the political and educational work of the Zionist movement could be ended and that the primary, if not the only, task for Zionists was "the task of reconstruction" in Palestine. Building a potash plant along the Dead Sea appeared to be more important to the Brandeis group than the cultural and ideological programs that emphasized Jewish peoplehood, and this alienated many immigrant Zionists. The narrower focus was reflected at the Pittsburgh convention in 1918, which issued a program concerned primarily with land, natural resources, public utilities, and cooperative organization in Palestine. After a visit to Palestine in 1919, Brandeis was reinforced in his outlook, and he outlined plans for additional projects like reforestation and the eradication of malaria. His plans, in true Progressive fashion, underscored efficiency, scientific management, and the completion of specific, attainable objectives.[34]

To eastern European Jewish immigrants, this American Progressive version of Zionism seemed devoid of yiddishkayt, the stuff of Jewish peoplehood. Brandeis ignored their complaints, further antagonizing the pre-1914 leadership and its immigrant constituency. Brandeis also separated himself from the eastern European rank and file by his refusal to be active in the World Zionist Organization and by his attempt to reach a reconciliation with wealthy German Jews. All of this came to a head at the Cleveland convention of the ZOA in 1921 (covered in detail in the succeeding volume in this series), when the Brandeis leadership was forced to resign. The majority eastern European membership, proud of Brandeis and grateful for his contribution, were nonetheless alienated by his patronizing ways and weak ideological commitment. Practical development and philanthropic Zionism were simply not enough for those who emphasized political action and worldwide Jewish cultural renaissance.

The split contributed to a serious decline in membership—down to twenty-five thousand by 1920 and to less than nineteen thousand by 1921. Zionism, however, even in the face of the "100 percent Americanism" of the 1920s, did not disappear. It stayed alive in movements and organizations like Conservatism and the American Jewish Congress, which was revived after 1921. The growth of these crucial movements in the 1920s and 1930s ensured that Zionist sentiment would remain a foremost component of American Jewish identity. Indeed in 1927, a leading Zionist could declare without fear of contradiction that Conservative Jews viewed Palestine with "an intuitional, unreasoning love" and, like the Torah, "as an ultimate, a thing that is good in itself, whose welfare [they sought] for its own sake."[35]

By the end of the nineteenth century and through the early decades of the twentieth, the nucleus of Jewish communal consciousness in America was not so much Judaism, which no longer commanded a widespread intensity of commitment, but Jewishness, which manifested itself in many forms. Not the least of these forms was Zionism; but as we have seen in earlier chapters, there were other ways of formulating an American Jewish identity.

The Jewish immigrants were in America to stay, and they early sought acculturation. Some, like department store magnate E. A. Filene and journalist Walter Lippman, went further in demanding assimilation. And significant numbers of college students went "so far as to change their names and otherwise attempt to hide their identity."[36] But as one memoirist put it: "The idea that all immigrants should wipe out their past and become simple imitations of the dominant type is neither possible nor desirable. We cannot wipe out the past and we make ourselves ridiculous in the effort to do so."[37]

There were certainly important changes in the immigrants' traditions, tastes, and habits, but as we have seen throughout this volume, these amounted most often to adaptation and acculturation, rather than unreflective imitation or total abandonment of former customs. Some new Jewish identities, for example, were formulated in a separate "American-Jewish-socialist region of heart and mind."[38] From Socialist Abraham Cahan, who had labored mightily to transform Jewish immigrants into a great new American public in terms worthy of their ancient prophetic tradition, through Judah Magnes, who combined radical reform politics and pacifism with Jewish ministry, and Stephen Wise, the energetic rabbi steeped in American social gospel and Jewish messianism, an important segment of American Jews remained "vitally, intensely, and unequivocally Jewish" by its liberal political activism.[39]

There were many other concrete creative amalgamations that went into the reformulation of Jewish identity and that affected even larger numbers of people. For example, immigrant Jews as early as 1904 became American Jews by joining in the celebration of the Fourth of July, Thanksgiving, and Labor Day, while continuing to honor the Jewish High Holy Days and festivals like Passover and Hanukkah. In addition, these holidays were adapted to the new American environment.

Hanukkah, for example, became a much more important festival, one infused with the spirit of shopping that marked Christmas. This was not so much an imitation on the way to assimilation as it was a way of keeping children attached to Jewish tradition by incorporating a pervasive American tradition. The celebration of Passover, perhaps the most popular and conscious manifestation of Jewish identity in America, was also reformulated to reflect the anticipation of ever-higher living standards in the New World as well as remembrance of ancient captivity and liberation. Jews adapted the Old World tradition of festival luxury—that is, the practice of materially distinguishing the sacred from the profane by the use of one's best things on the Sabbath and holidays—to American abundance. The pulse of retail commerce in Jewish neighborhoods rose in anticipation of all the holidays and festivals but, most of all, for Passover, when sometimes households were not only freed of *khomets* (leavened dough) and thoroughly cleaned, but were entirely refurbished.[40]

Marketing, too, like consumption, could serve Jews as a bridge to American culture. Jewish immigrants had more commercial experience than most other newcomers, and the United States, as we have seen in earlier chapters, provided fertile ground for innovation, extension of marketing skills, and mobility. Louis Borgenicht, who started out penniless and established a successful business in children's clothing in New York City in 1890, reflected on the motivation of Jews who moved from poverty to affluence by providing people with goods and services. "There is nothing sinful," Borgenicht argued, "about spreading material goods around to the greatest number." On the contrary, the abolition of scarcity would eliminate war and liberate energies for "human and not jungle-beast activities."[41] Inspired by the prospect of acceptance in the new culture and by the high status of business in America, commercially oriented Jewish newcomers apparently pursued their entrepreneurial calling in the spirit of a democratic crusade. In America, echoes of Jewish messianic redemption could be heard in the radical rhetoric of transplanted socialists, but they could be heard as well in the strivings of merchants and manufacturers.

Jewish immigrants acculturated rapidly but very much on their own terms. They became Americans, and they made important contributions to American life, but in the process they retained and reshaped distinctively Jewish characteristics. In short, they did not "melt." Jews understood—as Louis Levin, Baltimore journalist, social worker, and educator said in a review of Israel Zangwill's play *The Melting Pot* in 1908—that "Mr. Zangwill makes a fatal mistake." The making of a "new type of man does not require that he . . . throw upon the scrap heap all that he has stood for in the past. On the contrary . . . maintaining intact [the best of his past is] the real contribution that he can make to the betterment of the New American."[42] In America, where the temptation to abandon a dual allegiance was great, Jews did not throw the past upon the scrap heap. As a religious community, they attempted to fashion a group identity that would enhance their full integration into American life, while at the same time, as a people, they retained their identification with Jewish civilization.

The religion of the American Jews, as we have seen, was found not only in the realm of synagogue and denominational life but in the activities and ideologies of the wide spectrum of Jewish organizations usually described as secular. Beginning in the era of mass immigration, many American Jews practiced a civil religion, achieving unity, purpose, and identity as a moral community through secular organizations devoted to philanthropy and social work and to the welfare of Jewish people abroad. The early steps in this direction were not always consciously ideological. But the eventual development of a Jewish civil sphere—distinct from, though not necessarily antagonistic to, religious instiutions—was a significant step in the formulation of an American Jewish civil religion.[43]

Civil Judaism articulated and reinforced the attempts of the community to preserve Jewish group life while promoting maximal involvement in American society and polity. It inspired Jewish particularism in the form of support for other Jews; at the same time, it encouraged universalism through the pursuit of social justice. Over several decades of Jewish immigrant life in the United States, Jewish ethnicity and Jewish religion were combined in a number of important new syntheses and placed firmly within the embrace of American liberalism.

Inspired by America's commitment to democracy and pluralism, Jews, albeit through a variety of redefinitions of their original culture, retained their Jewishness. This was a response to individual and communal needs and led to an enrichment of American society, in which Jews found not only a refuge but, increasingly, a home.

EPILOGUE: ALMOST
AT HOME IN AMERICA

W HEN Rose Cohen attended public school in New York City in the early 1900s, she "had a glimpse of the New World," and it produced in her a powerful "desire to get away from the whole old order of things." For a time she "went groping about blindly," but later, having come "to see that the Old World was not all dull and the new not all glittering," Rose stood between them "with a hand in each."[1]

Few Jewish immigrants expressed the ideal of cultural pluralism so succinctly. But most behaved in ways that made the ideal increasingly real. While they demonstrated a profound appreciation of America and loyalty to their newly adopted country, the immigrants retained their Jewishness—through reformulated religious identities and social activism, through mutual aid, communalism, and Zionism. This happy American Jewish combination, however, was not achieved without a struggle. It took an enormous spiritual energy and creativity to forge these new identities. "Never have I felt so strongly that I am a Jew as now," wrote labor activist Baruch Charney Vladeck in 1916, at the height of Zionist agitation in America. He added, "Not a day passes that I do not think about how I should fit my Jewishness into the rest of me without being broken up."[2]

Despite the personal difficulties it engendered, Jews supported the ideal of cultural pluralism. They were ready, even delighted, to accept America's rules, norms, and obligations, while at the same time they wished to keep important elements of their distinctive Jewish culture. The host society, however, often had other ideas and sometimes sent "signals of unwelcome." For many Americans, including some among the nation's intellectual and political elite, cultural pluralism remained suspect, a complex and unwieldy

236

concept. Much more popular was the idea of the melting pot—an idea with clear implications as to who would melt whom.

A leading educator could say without apology in 1909 that southern and eastern European immigrants "tend to settle in groups . . . and to set up here their national manners, customs and observances. Our task is to break up these groups . . . to assimilate and amalgamate these people as part of our American race."3 Even President Woodrow Wilson said, as late as 1915, the same year in which Horace Kallen's classic essay on cultural pluralism and democracy was published, that "America does not consist of groups. A man who thinks of himself as belonging to a particular national group has not yet become an American."4

Withal, Jews continued to perceive of themselves as a people and not merely as Americans of a particular religious persuasion. This increased the possibility that, under certain historical conditions, American Jews would be subject to a variety of exclusions. An especially intense anti-Semitism made itself felt simultaneously in the United States and western Europe in the 1880s and 1890s and again during and immediately after World War I. Both periods of anti-Semitic agitation were marked by such rapid structural change and by economic crises so severe as to suggest the collapse of social systems. And both periods witnessed, as a result, powerful displays of narrowly conceived nationalism and xenophobia—with Jews, the universal and centuries-old scapegoat, prominently targeted.

The last two decades of the nineteenth century saw the rise of racial anti-Semites Adolf Stocker and Karl Lueger in Germany and Austria, the Dreyfus case in France, and in Russia, massive pogroms and the discriminatory May Laws. In the same period, the United States was marked by agrarian and small-town hatred of Jews, widespread social discrimination against Jews, intense patrician anti-Semitism, and rising sentiment against open immigration.5 The second period, from about 1914 to the 1920s, saw the circulation of the notorious forgery, the Protocols of the Elders of Zion in many countries, the resurfacing of violent anti-Semitism in the Ukraine, and the rise of the Nazis in Germany. In the United States, the period began with the lynching of Leo Frank, and by the 1920s, following the artificial, temporary harmony generated by the war, there was a crystallization of anti-Semitic trends in American culture. This was evident (as will become clear in a subsequent volume in this series) in the Jew-baiting crusade of Henry Ford, quotas in colleges and universities, and a virtual locking of America's golden door to southern and eastern Europeans through restrictive immigration legislation.6

In America, the decade after the war was marred by the resumption of conflicts generated by industrialization and urbanization and became known for the extreme nativism that attended these conflicts. There was widespread economic hardship and bitter confrontations between labor and management, including actual pitched battles as in the great steel strike of 1919. In the same year, racial animosities led to riots in twenty-six cities, the worst of which was in Chicago, where blacks and whites terrorized each other for months, leaving many dead and injured and more than one thousand black families homeless.[7]

Also in 1919 a climate of fear, created by the ongoing Bolshevik revolution in Russia, allowed the attorney general of the United States to launch a campaign against radical foreigners. Known as the Red Scare, the crusade led to the deportation of thousands of aliens alleged to be subversives, a sizable number of whom were Jews; it also led to the removal of Socialists and their "alien" ideologies from their elected positions in the New York state legislature. Extreme nativism was reflected too in the growth of the Ku Klux Klan, which expanded its hate list to include Catholics and Jews as well as blacks.[8]

The essential driving force behind these repressive activities was antimodernism, a fear held by many that alien forces were corrupting their country. In the literature of the era, in popular parlance, in the media, and in politcal rhetoric, it is striking to note how frequently Jews, in particular, were blamed for the "ills" brought by modernization.

Anti-Semitism in heterogeneous America was milder than in Europe, because it had to compete with other forms of antipathy, especially anti-Catholicism and racism. It is also true that, in contrast to Germany and Poland, anti-Semitism in the United States has been a distinctly minor feature of historical development, associated with no political party of consequence, no powerful social movement, and no periodic mass violence. But from as early as the 1840s, it is relatively easy to document hostile attitudes and discriminatory acts toward Jews in the United States.[9] And in the xenophobic 1920s, anti-Semitism was plainly and openly expressed by a variety of important people, institutions, and legislative acts.

Henry Ford, a powerful and rustic folk hero, was responsible through his newspaper, the *Dearborn Independent,* for spreading the message that Jews menaced the Unites States. The paper not only published the Protocols of the Elders of Zion, it was filled in the first half of the twenties with pieces on "the international Jew as the world's foremost problem" and "aspects of Jewish power in the United States."

In all of the writings, a deep distrust was expressed of the city, which was identified with Jews. There was also consistent attribution to Jews of traits that Henry Ford refused to recognize in himself. He assigned to Jews extraordinary power to destabilize society, for example, while he was radically enhancing physical mobility and permanently changing the American landscape through the mass production of automobiles. And Ford accused Jews of corruption, while he himself was cheating his stockholders and exploiting his car dealers. Many people were apparently willing to overlook Ford's improprieties and his anti-Semitism. In 1923 more than one-third of 260,000 voters polled supported Henry Ford for president.[10]

As dangerous as Ford's power was, his blatant hatred of Jews probably did less material damage than the more subtle anti-Semitism practiced at American institutions of higher education. Jewish students were admitted to colleges in relatively large numbers, but they experienced social discrimination from the outset, and the practice increased significantly after Russian Jews became more visible on campuses. Unlike their German Jewish predecessors, the newcomers did not seek to adapt themselves to the "genteel tradition," and it was commonly charged that the Russians studied too hard. One resentful Harvard alumnus recalled that "Jews worked far into each night . . . they took obvious pride in their academic success and talked about it."[11] Ambitious Jewish students, who viewed college as a place for serious intellectual endeavor and not merely a place where one achieved social poise, were kept out of the eating clubs at Yale and Princeton. And in 1913 a national fraternity suspended its City College of New York affiliate because the "Hebraic element [was] greatly in excess."[12]

Such insults were usually borne in silence; but when leading educational institutions tried to restrict Jewish entrance in the twenties, Jews felt threatened. Between 1920 and 1922, New York University and Columbia University, whose Jewish enrollments had reached nearly 40 percent, instituted regional quotas. When other universities followed suit—including Harvard, the most prestigious institution of higher learning in the United States—a cry of outrage arose in the Jewish community. It was of little comfort that Harvard, according to President Lowell, had instituted quotas in order better to "absorb" Jews and to decrease the discrimination that allegedly emerged wherever Jews gathered in large numbers. The quotas were repudiated in 1923, but through various subterfuges the number of Jews at Harvard and other elite schools were kept within "reasonable" proportions.[13]

Restriction in the 1920s was not limited to college admissions. An even more significant anti-Semitic discrimination was inherent in the immigration laws of 1921 and 1924. The attempt to limit immigration was almost as old as immigration itself, but in the twenties the restriction movement added a more overt racist dimension with its national origins quota system. The restriction laws passed by Congress in 1921 and 1924 made dangerously invidious distinctions between the old immigration from northern and western Europe, from which rural Americans largely stemmed, and the new immigration from southern and eastern Europe, which included Jews and which flowed mainly to the cities.

Through a complicated legislative formula, Congress ultimately limited immigration to 2 percent of the number of foreign-born residents of each national group who lived in the United States in 1890. Since the vast majority of eastern European immigrants ("filthy, un-American and often dangerous in their habits") came after 1890, the legislation clearly discriminated against them. Jews were not singled out or attacked directly in the new laws. But in fiscal year 1920–21, a record number of 119,000 eastern European Jews entered America, and during hearings on immigration between 1920 and 1924, many proponents of restriction, including Professor Henry Pratt Fairchild and journalist Burton J. Hendrick, cited Jewish criminality, greed, and laziness as reasons why the laws were needed.[14]

General immigration decreased from over 700,000 in 1924 to less than 300,000 in 1925; Jewish immigration declined from 50,000 to 10,000. The concept of northern European supremacy embodied in the law hurt Jews already in America far less, of course, than it hurt those who were stranded abroad by the law and later murdered in the name of the same concept in Nazi-dominated Europe. But the declining faith in the power of Americanization implied in the new restriction laws meant intensifed suspicion and hostility toward "unmeltable" ethnics at home, including Jews.

Still, as Jonathan Sarna has persuasively argued, if America "has not been utter heaven for Jews, it has been as far from hell as Jews in the Diaspora have ever known."[15] Even in the twenties, the picture was mixed. Despite restrictions, the number of Jews on college campuses, in government service, and in the professions increased significantly, as did their affluence. Anti-Semitism was mostly private, never becoming part of the national political agenda, and never strong enough to deny Jews access to the opportunities offered by American society. What the relative mildness of anti-Semitism implied for the group survival of American Jews after 1920 we leave to the subsequent volumes in this history. But between 1880 and

1920, as we have seen here, Jewishness in America displayed great resili-ence. There was disunity, fragmentation, and significant reshaping of tradi-tion—but durability, nonetheless.

Eastern European Jews, settling mainly in the Northeast, challenged the dominance of the German Jewish establishment, which was centered mainly in Cincinnati and Chicago. The less numerous Germans were soon obliged to share their power, but they helped, with some shift in emphasis, to maintain continuity of institutions and patterns of Jewish behavior that they had pioneered.[16] Although the commitment to Judaism diminished for German Jews and eastern Europeans, both groups considered domestic philanthropy and the welfare of Jews abroad their sacred responsibilities. And in Jewish social-philanthropic organizations and federations, in Jewish support for Israel, and in Jewish concern for the Jews in the Soviet Union and Ethiopia, those responsibilities not only continue but remain an essen-tial—perhaps the most essential—part of the civil religion that marks American Jewry in the late twentieth century.[17]

✡

NOTES

Preface and Acknowledgments

1. Jonathan Sarna, "Anti-Semitism in American History," *Commentary* 71 (March 1981): 47.

Prologue: On the Eve of the Great Transformation

1. Samuel Joseph, *Jewish Immigration to the United States from 1881–1910* (New York: Arno, 1969); Liebmann Hersch, "International Migration of the Jews," in *International Migrations,* ed. Imre Ferenczi and Walter F. Willcox (New York: National Bureau of Economic Research, 1931), 2:471–520; Simon Kuznets, "Immigration of Russian Jews to the United States: Background and Structure," *Perspectives in American History* 9 (1975): 35–124; Irving Howe, *World of Our Fathers* (New York: Harcourt, Brace, Jovanovich, 1976), 15–24.

2. On the dynamics of acculturation for immigrants and ethnics generally, see Milton Gordon, *Assimilation in American Life: The Role of Race, Religion and National Origins* (New York: Oxford University Press, 1964); John Bodnar, *The Transplanted: A History of Immigrants in Urban America* (Bloomington: Indiana University Press, 1985). On the reformulation of a new ethnocultural synthesis for the children of Jewish immigrants in particular, see Deborah Dash Moore, *At Home in America: Second Generation Jews in New York* (New York: Columbia University Press, 1981).

3. Henry Feingold, "The Success Story of German Jews in America," in Henry Feingold, *A Midrash on American Jewish History* (Albany: State University of New York Press, 1982), 28.

4. Bernard Martin, "Yiddish Literature in the United States," *American Jewish Archives* 33 (November 1981): 184.

5. Hyman Grinstein, *The Rise of the Jewish Community of New York, 1654–1860* (Philadelphia: Jewish Publication Society of America, 1945), 172; Norton Stern and William Kramer, "The Major Role of Polish Jews in the Pioneer West," *Western States Jewish Historical Quarterly* 8 (1976): 326–44; Naomi Cohen, "The Ethnic Catalyst: The Impact of the East European Immigration on the American Jewish Establishment," in *The Legacy of Jewish Migration,* ed. David Berger (Brooklyn: Brooklyn College Press, 1983), 131–48.

6. Naomi Cohen, *Encounter with Emancipation: German Jews in the United States, 1830–1914* (Philadelphia: Jewish Publication Society of America, 1984), xiii; Hyman Grinstein, "The Efforts of East European Jewry to Organize Its Own Community in the United States," *Publications of the American Jewish Historical Society* 49 (December 1959): 73–89; Feingold, "Success Story," 34–35.

7. Lawrence Bachmann, "Julius Rosenwald," *American Jewish Historical Quarterly* 66 (September 1976): 89–105; Vincent Carosso,"A Financial Elite: New York's German-Jewish Investment Bankers," *American Jewish Historical Quarterly* 66 (September 1976): 67–88; Don Coerver and Linda Hall, "Neiman-Marcus: Innovators in Fashion and Merchandising," *American Jewish Historical Quarterly* 66 (September 1976): 123–36; Saul Engelbourg, "Edward A. Filene: Merchant, Civic Leader, and Jew," *American Jewish Historical Quarterly* 66 (September 1976): 106–22; Robert A. Burlison, "Samuel Fox, Merchant and Civic Leader in San Diego, 1886–1939," *Journal of San Diego History* 26 (Winter 1980): 1–10; Tom Mahoney, *The Great Merchants: The Stories of Twenty Famous Retail Operations and the People Who Made Them Great* (New York: Harper, 1955).

8. Cohen, *Encounter with Emancipation,* 14.

9. Lee Shai Weissbach, "The Jewish Communities of the United States on the Eve of Mass Migration: Some Comments on Geography and Bibliography," *American Jewish History* 78 (September 1988): 79–108.

10. Douglas North, *The Economic Growth of the United States, 1790–1860* (New York: Norton, 1966), 66–74, 177–218.

11. George Rogers Taylor, *The Transportation Revolution, 1815–1860* (New York: Holt, Rinehart, and Winston, 1964), 15–177.

12. Joshua Trachtenberg, *Consider the Years: The Story of the Jewish Community of Easton, 1752–1942* (Easton, Pa.: Centennial Committee of Temple Beth Sholom, 1944), 234.

13. Cohen, *Encounter with Emancipation,* 19–26.

14. Ibid., 27; Bachmann, "Julius Rosenwald"; Coerver and Hall, "Neiman-Marcus"; Engelbourg, "Edward A. Filene."

15. Stephen G. Mostov, "A 'Jerusalem' on the Ohio: The Social and Economic History of Cincinnati's Jewish Community, 1840–1875." Ph.D. diss., Brandeis University, 1981; Marc Lee Raphael, *Profiles in American Judaism: The Reform, Conservative, Orthodox, and Reconstructionist Traditions in Historical Perspective* (San Francisco: Harper and Row, 1984), 12–14.

16. Weissbach, "Jewish Communites"; Rudolf Ganz, "The Spread of Jewish Communities through America before the Civil War," *YIVO Annual* 15 (1974): 7–45.

17. Schwayder Family Oral History Memoir, 26, Oral History Collection, William Weiner Library, New York City.

18. William Kramer and Norton Stern, "Levi Strauss: The Man behind the Myth," *Western States Jewish Historical Quarterly* 19 (April 1987): 257–63; Stephen J. Whitfield, "Commercial Passions: The Southern Jew as Businessman," *American Jewish History* 71 (March 1982): 342–57; Louis Schmeir, "A Jewish Peddler and His Black Customers Look at Each Other," *American Jewish History* 73 (September 1983): 39–55; Bachmann, "Julius Rosenwald"; Coerver and Hall, "Neiman-Marcus"; Engelbourg, "Edward A. Filene."

19. Harriet Rochlin and Fred Rochlin, *Pioneer Jews: A New Life in the Far West* (Boston: Houghton Mifflin, 1984), 69, 86.

20. Calculated from tables in Weissbach, "Jewish Communities," 84–88; and David

Sulzberger, "Growth of the Jewish Population in the United States," *Publications of the American Jewish Historical Society* 6 (1897): 144-45.

21. David Gerber, "Cutting out Shylock: Elite Anti-Semitism and the Quest for Moral Order in the Mid-Nineteenth Century American Market Place," *Journal of American History* 69 (December 1982): 615-37; Stephen G. Mostov, "Dun and Bradstreet Reports as a Source of Jewish Economic History: Cincinnati, 1840-1875," *American Jewish History* 72 (March 1983): 333-53.

22. Abraham Karp, *Haven and Home: A History of the Jews in America* (New York: Schocken, 1985), 191-92.

23. Feingold, "Success Story of the German Jews," 42-45.

24. Steven Hertzberg, *Strangers within the Gate City: The Jews of Atlanta, 1845-1915* (Philadelphia: Jewish Publication Society of America, 1978); Stephen Thernstrom, "Religion and Occupational Mobility in Boston, 1880-1963," in *The Dimensions of Quantitative Research,* ed. W. O. Ayedelotte et al. (Princeton: Princeton University Press, 1972), 124-58; Marc Raphael, *Jews and Judaism in a Midwestern Community: Columbus, Ohio, 1840-1975* (Columbus: Ohio Historical Society, 1979); Howard Chudacoff, *Mobile Americans: Residential and Social Mobility in Omaha, 1880-1920* (New York: Oxford University Press, 1972); Clyde Griffen, "Making It in America: Social Mobility in Nineteenth Century Poughkeepsie," *New York History* 51 (October 1970): 479-99; Mitchell Gelfand, "Progress and Prosperity: Jewish Social Mobility in Los Angeles in the Booming Eighties," *American Jewish History* 68 (June 1979): 408-33; Peter Decker, "Jewish Merchants in San Francisco: Social Mobility on the Urban Frontier," *American Jewish History* 68 (June 1979): 396-407.

25. Jacob Lestschinsky, "Economic and Social Development of American Jewry," *Jewish People: Past and Present* 4 (1955): 78-80; John Higham, "Social Discrimination against Jews, 1830-1930," in John Higham, *Send These to Me: Jews and Other Immigrants in Urban America* (New York: Atheneum, 1975), 144.

26. *Statistics of the Population of the United States at the Tenth Census,* 1 June 1880 (Washington, D.C.: Government Printing Office, 1883), xxix; Weissbach, "Jewish Communities," 87.

27. Weissbach, "Jewish Communities," 79-88.

28. Cohen, *Encounter with Emancipation,* 55-62.

29. Weissbach, "Jewish Communities," 79-88.

30. Cohen, *Encounter with Emancipation,* 39-54.

31. Robert Liberles, "Conflict over Reforms: The Case of the Congregation Beth Elohim, Charleston, South Carolina," in *The American Synagogue: A Sanctuary Transformed,* ed. Jack Wertheimer (Cambridge: Harvard University Press, 1987), 274-96; Leon Jick, "The Reform Synagogue," in Wertheimer, *American Synagogue,* 85-110; Raphael, *Profiles in American Judaism,* 3-19; Cohen, *Encounter with Emancipation,* 159-70; Michael A. Meyer, *Response to Modernity: A History of the Reform Movement in Judaism* (New York: Oxford University Press, 1988), 220-63.

32. J. G. Heller, *Isaac M. Wise: His Life, Work and Thought* (New York: Union of American Hebrew Congregations, 1965); Isaac M. Wise, *Reminiscences,* ed. and trans. David Philipsoin (New York: Central Synagogue of New York, 1945); Isaac M. Wise, *Selected Writings,* ed. David Philipson and Louis Grossman (New York: Arno, 1969).

33. Higham, "Social Discrimination against Jews," 138-73; Cohen, *Encounter with Emancipation,* 249-65.

34. Higham, "Social Discrimination against Jews," 138-73; Cohen, "Encounter

with Emancipation," 249–65; Moses Rischin, *The Promised City: New York's Jews, 1870–1914* (New York: Corinth, 1964).

35. John Higham, *Strangers in the Land: Patterns of American Nativism, 1865–1925* (New York: Atheneum, 1955), 92.

36. David Gerber, "Anti-Semitism and Jewish-Gentile Relations," in *Anti-Semitism in American History,* ed. David Gerber (Urbana: University of Illinois Press, 1986), 3–30.

37. Zosa Szjakowski, "The *Yahudi* and the Immigrant: A Reappraisal," *American Jewish Historical Quarterly* 63 (September 1973): 13–44.

38. *American Hebrew,* 13 May 1881; 2 September 1881; 2 December 1882. Similar sentiments are expressed in numerous other issues.

39. Rischin, *Promised City,* 263.

40. Cohen, *Encounter with Emancipation,* xi.

41. Weissbach, "Jewish Communities," 90–93.

Chapter One. Sources of the Eastern European Migration

1. Simon Kuznets, "Immigration of Russian Jews to the United States: Background and Structure," *Perspectives in American History* 9 (1975): 35–124; Elias Tcherikower, *The Early Jewish Labor Movement in the United States,* trans. A. Antonovsky (New York: YIVO, 1961), 17; Joshua Rothenberg, "Demythologizing the Shtetl," *Midstream* 27 (March 1981): 27–30.

2. Diane K. Roskies and David G. Roskies, eds., *The Shtetl Book* (New York: KTAV, 1975), 286; Rothenberg, "Demythologizing the Shtetl," 26.

3. Maurice Samuel, *The World of Sholom Aleichem* (New York: Knopf, 1962), 26–27.

4. Shalom Muhlstein, "At the Market," in *From a Ruined Garden,* ed. Jack Kugelmass and Jonathan Boyarin (New York: Schocken, 1983), 30–31.

5. Samuel Joseph, *Jewish Immigration to the United States from 1881 to 1910* (New York: Arno, 1969), 42–48.

6. Ruth Gay, "Inventing the Shtetl," *American Scholar* 53 (Summer 1984): 329–49.

7. Bernard Martin, *A History of Judaism* (New York: Basic Books, 1974), 2:113–40.

8. Abraham Cohen, *Everyman's Talmud* (New York: Schocken, 1975), 364–70.

9. Daniel Elazar, "American Political Theory and the Political Notions of American Jews: Convergences and Contradictions," in *The Ghetto and Beyond: Essays on Jewish Life in America,* ed. Peter Rose (New York: Random House, 1969), 203–27; R. J. Zwi Werblowsky, "Messianism in Jewish History," in *Jewish Society through the Ages,* ed. H. H. Ben-Sasson and S. Ettinger (New York: Schocken, 1971) 32–38; Yehezkel Kaufman, "Israel in Canaan," in *Great Ages and Ideas of the Jewish People,* ed. L. W. Schwarz (New York: Modern Library, 1956), 38–53; Will Herberg, "Socialism, Zionism, and Messianic Passion," *Midstream* 2 (Summer 1956): 65–74; Gershom Scholem, *The Messianic Idea in Judaism* (New York: Schocken, 1971), 1.

10. Jacob Katz, *Tradition and Crisis: Jewish Society at the End of the Middle Ages* (New York: Schocken, 1961), 1–5.

11. Babylonian Talmud, Sanhedrin, 99b.

12. Benediction translated from the Talmud by Rabbi William Strongin; Schlomoh

Zalman Havlin, "Hadran," *Encyclopedia Judaica,* 7:1053; Moses Weinberger, *People Walk on Their Heads: Jews and Judaism in New York,* trans. and ed. Jonathan Sarna (New York: Holmes and Meier, 1982), 7.

13. Yekhiel Shtern, "A Kheyder in Tyszowce (Tishevits)," *YIVO Annual* 5 (1950): 156; David Blaustein, quoted in Irving Howe and Kenneth Libo, *How We Lived: A Documentary History of Immigrant Jews in America, 1880–1930* (New York: Marek, 1979), 9.

14. Yoysef Fridman, "A Strike in Kheyder," in Kugelmass and Boyarin, *From a Ruined Garden,* 105–6.

15. Shtern, "Kheyder," 158; Charlotte Baum, Paula Hyman, and Sonya Michel, *The Jewish Woman in America* (New York: Dial, 1976), 58–60.

16. Sydney Stahl Weinberg, *World of Our Mothers* (Chapel Hill: University of North Carolina Press, 1988), 31.

17. Charlotte Baum, "What Made Yetta Work? The Economic Role of Eastern European Jewish Women in the Family," *Response* 18 (Summer 1973): 32–38; Pearl Halpern, 11 November 1965, Amerikaner-Yiddishe Geshichte Bel Pe, YIVO, New York City; Mathew Josephson, *Sidney Hillman: Statesman of American Labor* (Garden City, N.Y.: Doubleday, 1952), 24; Clara Weissman, interview with author, 3 April 1982; Bernard Chasanow, *Tag un Yorn: Funem Leben fun a yidishen arbeiter* (New York: Bernard Chasanow, 1956), 11–12.

18. Weinberg, *World of Our Mothers,* 148; Baum, Hyman, and Michel, *Jewish Woman in America,* 58.

19. Roskies and Roskies, *Shtetl Book,* 186.

20. Moishe Olgin is quoted in Abraham Menes, "The Jewish Socialist Movement in Russia and Poland," *Jewish People: Past and Present* 2 (1948): 356.

21. Roskies and Roskies, *Shtetl Book,* 182–86.

22. Rothenberg, "Demythologizing the Shtetl," 25–31; Ezra Mendelsohn, *Class Struggle in the Pale* (Cambridge: Cambridge University Press, 1970), 25–27.

23. Tcherikower, *Early Jewish Labor Movement,* 8.

24. Michael Stanislawski, *Tsar Nicholas I and the Jews: The Transformation of Jewish Society in Russia, 1825–1855* (Philadelphia: Jewish Publication Society of America, 1983), xii–xiii, 28–48.

25. Roskies and Roskies, *Shtetl Book,* 99–102.

26. Rose Schneiderman, *All for One* (New York: Erikson, 1967), 12.

27. Stanislawski, *Tsar Nicholas I and the Jews,* 67.

28. Roskies and Roskies, *Shtetl Book,* 103; Mendelsohn, *Class Struggle,* 27.

29. Daniel Charny, quoted in Rothenberg, "Demythologizing the Shtetl," 26.

30. Salo Baron, *Modern Nationalism and Religion* (Freeport, N.Y.: Books for Libraries Press, 1971), 15–22.

31. Salo Baron, *Steeled by Adversity* (Philadelphia: Jewish Publication Society of America, 1971), 269–414.

32. Stanislawski, *Tsar Nicholas I and the Jews,* 170–82; Martin Gilbert, *Jewish History Atlas* (New York: Colliers, 1969), 67; Salo Baron, *Russian Jews under Tsars and Soviets* (New York: Macmillan, 1964), 81–84.

33. Sam Davis, interview, 15 November 1980, Oral History of the American Left, Tamiment Library, New York University, New York City.

34. Kuznets, "Immigration of Russian Jews," 35–124.

35. Henry Feingold, *Zion in America: The Jewish Experience from Colonial Times*

to the Present (New York: Hippocrene, 1976), 117–19; Emanuel Litvinoff and Binyimin Eliav, "Russia," in *Encyclopedia Judaica,* 14:451.

36. Ezra Mendelsohn, "The Russian Jewish Labor Movement," *YIVO Annual* 14 (1969): 90.

37. Ibid., 94; Mendelsohn, *Class Struggle,* 8.

38. Tcherikower, *Early Jewish Labor Movement,* 17.

39. Rothenberg, "Demythologizing the Shtetl," 30; Litvinoff and Eliav, "Russia." 451.

40. Stanislawsky, *Tsar Nicholas I and the Jews,* 67; Louis Greenberg, *The Jews in Russia* (New Haven: Yale University Press, 1944), 1:83; Baum, Hyman, and Michel, *Jewish Woman in America,* 71.

41. Pauline Wengeroff, "Memoirs of a Grandmother," in *The Golden Tradition: Jewish Life and Thought in Eastern Europe,* ed. Lucy Dawidowicz (Boston: Beacon, 1967), 164.

42. Leo Shpall, ed., "The Diary of Dr. George M. Price," *American Jewish Historical Quarterly* 40 (December 1950): 174.

43. Stanislawski, *Tsar Nicholas I and the Jews,* 17, 42–67.

44. Mendelsohn, *Class Struggle,* 27–40; Menes, "Jewish Socialist Movement," 365.

45. Morris Winchevsky, "Reminicenses," reprinted in *Jewish Currents* 32 (September 1978): 30–32. See also David Brower, "Student Political Attitudes and Social Origins: The Technological Institute of St. Petersburg," *Journal of Social History* 6 (Winter 1872–73): 202–13.

46. Abraham Cahan, *Bleter fun mein leben* (New York: Forward Association, 1926–31), 1:393, 404.

47. Aaron Lieberman, quoted in Jonathan Frankel, *Prophecy and Politics: Socialism, Nationalism, and the Russian Jews, 1862–1917* (Cambridge: Cambridge University Press, 1981), 33.

48. Allan Wildman, *The Making of a Workers' Revolution: Russian Social Democracy, 1891–1903* (Chicago: University of Chicago Press, 1967), 60; Leonard Shapiro, "The Role of the Jews in the Russian Revolutionary Movement," *Slavonic and East European Review* 40 (December 1961): 148; Robert J. Brym, *The Jewish Intelligentsia and Russian Marxism* (New York: Schocken, 1978), 2–3; Harriet Davis-Kram, "Jewish Women in Russian Revolutionary Movements," (Master's thesis, Hunter College, 1974, 17. In 1897, women constituted nearly one-third of the Bund's membership and apparently held the organization together after the mass arrests of the men in 1898.

49. Gregory Weinstein, *Reminisences of an Interesting Decade* (New York: International, 1928), 8–9.

50. J. Goldhagen, "The Ethnic Consciousness of Early Russian Jewish Socialists," *Judaism* 23 (1974): 479–96.

51. Cahan, *Bleter fun mein leben,* 1:500.

52. Moshe Mishkinski, "Regional Factors in the Formation of the Jewish Labor Movement in Czarist Russia," *YIVO Annual* 14 (1969): 46; Litvinoff and Eliav, "Russia," 452.

53. Deutsch, quoted in Henry J. Tobias, "The Jews in Tsarist Russia: The Political Education of a Minority," in *Minorities and Politics,* ed. Henry J. Tobias and Charles Woodhouse (Albuquerque: University of New Mexico Press, 1969), 26.

54. Gerald Sorin, *The Prophetic Minority: American Jewish Immigrant Radicals* (Bloomington: Indiana University Press, 1985).

55. Mendelsohn, *Class Struggle,* 88–89; Menes, "Jewish Socialist Movement," 366–67; Jacob Bross, "The Beginning of the Jewish Labor Movement in Galicia," *YIVO Annual* 5 (1950): 64–65; C. B. Sherman, "Nationalism, Secularism, and Religion in the Jewish Labor Movement," in *Voices from the Yiddish,* ed. Irving Howe and Elizer Greenberg (New York: Schocken, 1975), 219–33.

56. Abraham Liesen, quoted in Lucy Dawidowicz, ed. *The Golden Tradition: Jewish Life and Thought in Eastern Europe* (Boston: Beacon, 1967), 423; see also Hayim Zhitlowsky, "The Jewish Factor in My Socialism," in Howe and Greenberg, *Voices from the Yiddish,* 126–34.

57. Mendelsohn, *Class Struggle,* 109–10.

58. Dawidowicz, *Golden Tradition,* 54.

59. Arthur Hertzberg, ed., *The Zionist Idea* (New York: Atheneum, 1972), 43–51; the *Encyclopedia Judaica* goes so far as to say: "Within a relatively short period, the revolutionary movement and the Zionist movement brought a tremendous change among Jewish youth. The battei-midrash and yeshivot were abandoned, and dynamism of Jewish society now became concentrated within the new political trends," 14:452.

60. Irving Howe, *World of Our Fathers* (New York: Harcourt, Brace, Jovanovich, 1976), 18.

61. Ibid.

62. Ibid., 16.

63. Simon Dubnow, *The History of Jews in Russia and Poland* (Philadelphia: Jewish Publication Society of America, 1916–20), 2:273; Jonathan Frankel, "The Crisis of 1881–82 as a Turning Point in Modern Jewish History," in *The Legacy of Jewish Migration,* ed. David Berger (Brooklyn: Brooklyn College Press, 1983), 13.

64. Shpall, "Diary of Dr. George M. Price," 173–75.

65. Quoted in Richard Benkin, "Ethnicity and Organization: Jewish Communities in Eastern Europe and the United States," *Sociological Quarterly* 19 (1978): 614.

66. Marsha Farbman, interview, 17 December 1963, Amerikaner-Yiddishe Geshichte Bel Pe, YIVO, New York City; Frankel, *Prophecy and Politics,* 134–71.

67. Roskies and Roskies, *Shtetl Book,* 91–93.

68. Joseph, *Jewish Immigration to the United States;* Kuznets, "Immigration of Russian Jews," 35–124.

69. Litvinoff and Eliav, "Russia," 451.

70. Kuznets, "Immigration of Russian Jews," 86, 88, 89, 121.

71. Joseph, *Jewish Immigration to the United States,* 89–120.

72. Frankel, "Crisis of 1881–1882," 9–22.

73. Dawidowicz, *Golden Tradition,* 50.

Chapter Two. The Immigration Experience

1. Maldwyn Jones, *American Immigration* (Chicago: University of Chicago Press, 1961), 12.

2. Liebmann Hersch, "International Migration of Jews," in *International Migrations,* ed. Imre Ferencezi and Walter F. Willcox (New York: National Bureau of Economic Research, 1931), 2:471–520. Before 1905, Jewish return migration in some years exceeded 20 percent, but the overall Jewish repatriation rate was radically lower than the rate for all other immigrant groups. See Jonathan Sarna, "The Myth of No Return:

Jewish Return Migration to Eastern Europe, 1881–1914," *American Jewish History* 71 (December 1981): 256–67.

3. Abraham Cahan, *Bleter fun mein leben* (New York: Forward Association, 1926–31), 1:506–9.

4. Joseph Kissman, "The Immigration of Rumanian Jews up to 1914," *YIVO Annual* 2–3 (1947–48): 160–79.

5. The averages for other national groups were 30.5 percent females and only 12.3 percent children under fourteen.

6. Elizabeth Hasanovitz, *One of Them* (Boston: Houghton Mifflin, 1918), 33.

7. Marcus Ravage, *An American in the Making: The Life Story of an Immigrant* (New York: Harper, 1917), 55.

8. Irving Howe, *World of Our Fathers* (New York: Harcourt Brace Jovanovich, 1976), 27.

9. Rose Pesotta, *Bread upon the Waters* (New York: Dodd, Mead, 1944), 6, 9; Rose Pesotta, *Days of Our Lives* (Boston: Excelsior, 1958), 219; Sydelle Kramer and Jenny Masur, eds., *Jewish Grandmothers* (Boston: Beacon, 1976), 8.

10. Quoted in Irving Howe, introduction to *The Legacy of Jewish Migration*, ed. David Berger (Brooklyn: Brooklyn College Press, 1983), 4–5.

11. Leo Shpall, ed., "The Diary of Dr. George M. Price," *American Jewish Historical Quarterly* 40 (December 1950): 175.

12. Philip Taylor, *The Distant Magnet: European Emigration to the United States* (New York: Harper and Row, 1971).

13. Mary Antin, *From Plotsk to Boston* (Boston: Clarke, 1899), 12.

14. *Report of the United States Immigration Commission: Emigration Conditions in Europe* (Washington: Government Printing Office, 1911), 4:56–57; Anzia Yezierska, "How I Found America," in Anzia Yezierska, *Hungry Hearts* (Boston: Houghton Mifflin, 1920), 256; Hansen, *Immigration*, 100.

15. *Historical Statistics of the United States* (Washington, D.C.: Government Printing Office, 1976), 164–67.

16. Sanford Ragins, "The Image of America in Two East European Hebrew Periodicals," *American Jewish Archives* 17 (November 1965): 143–61.

17. Simon Kuznets, "Immigration of Russian Jews to the United States: Background and Structure," *Perspectives in American History* 9 (1975): 35–124; Samuel Joseph, *Jewish Immigration to the United States from 1881 to 1910* (New York: Columbia University Press, 1914).

18. Isaac Hourwich, *Immigration and Labor* (New York: Putnam's, 1912), 94.

19. Salo Baron, *Steeled by Adversity* (Philadelphia: Jewish Publication Society of America, 1971), 270–80; Kuznets, "Immigration of Russian Jews," 44–45, 84–85.

20. Howe, *World of Our Fathers*, 28.

21. Zosa Szajkowski, "Sufferings of Jewish Emigrants to America in Transit to America through Germany," *Jewish Social Studies* 39 (Winter-Spring 1977): 105–16; Pamella Nadell, "The Journey to America by Steam: The Jews of Eastern Europe in Transition," *American Jewish History* 71 (December 1981): 269–84.

22. Yezierska, "How I Found America," 259.

23. Shpall, "Diary of Dr. George M. Price," 176–77.

24. Elias Tcherikower, "Jewish Immigrants to the United States, 1881–1900," *YIVO Annual* 6 (1951): 158; Zosa Szajkowski, "Emigration to America or Reconstruction in

Europe," *Publications of the American Jewish Historical Society* 42 (September 1952): 157–88.

25. Deborah Dwork, "Health Conditions of Immigrant Jews on the Lower East Side of New York: 1880–1914," *Medical History* 25 (January 1981): 4.

26. Howe, *World of Our Fathers,* 37.

27. Sholom Aleichem, "Off to the Golden Land," *Jewish Immigration Bulletin* (February 1917): 10.

28. Lamar Cecil, *Business and Politics in Imperial Germany, 1888–1918* (Princeton: Princeton University Press, 1967), 7–14, 39–38.

29. U.S. Immigration Commission, *Report on Steerage Conditions,* S. Doc. 753, serial 5877 (Washington, D.C.: Government Printing Office, 1911), 6–16.

30. Shpall, "Diary of George Price," 180.

31. Quoted in Howe, *World of Our Fathers,* 41.

32. *New York Times,* 13 March 1893.

33. U.S. Immigration Commission, *Report on Steerage Conditions,* 6–16.

34. Nadell, "Journey to America," 282–83.

35. I. Kopeloff, quoted in Milton Meltzer, *Taking Root: Jewish Immigrants in America* (New York: Farrar, Straus, and Giroux, 1976), 43.

36. Abraham Cahan, *The Education of Abraham Cahan,* trans. Leon Stein et al., from Cahan, *Bleter fun mein leben* (Philadelphia: Jewish Publication Society of America, 1969), 2:267; Emma Goldman, *Living My Life* (New York: Knopf, 1931), 11–12.

37. Arthur Henry, "Among the Immigrants," *Scribners' Magazine* 29 (1901): 302.

38. Howe, *World of Our Fathers,* 46.

39. Rhoda Lewin, "Stereotype and Reality in the Jewish Immigration Experience in Minneapolis," *Minnesota History* 46 (Fall 1979): 262–63.

40. August C. Bolino, *The Ellis Island Source Book* (Washington, D.C.: Kensington Historical Press, 1985), 20–21; Alan M. Kraut, "Silent Strangers: Germs, Genes and Nativism in John Higham's *Strangers in the Land,*" *American Jewish History* 76 (December 1986): 142–58.

41. Gilbert Osofsky, "The Hebrew Emigrant Aid Society of the United States (1881–1883)," *Publications of the American Jewish Historical Society* 49 (March 1960): 173–87.

42. Howe, *World of Our Fathers,* 47.

43. Alexander Harkavy, "Diary," American Jewish Historical Society, Waltham, Mass.; Abraham Alpert Papers, American Jewish Historical Society, Waltham, Mass.; Kraut, "Silent Strangers," 152–58; David B. Alpert, "The Man From Kovno," *American Jewish Archives* 29 (1977): 107–15.

44. *American Hebrew,* 1 September 1882; *Jewish Messenger,* 8 September 1882.

45. Irving A. Mandel, "The Attitude of the American Jewish Community towards East European Immigration as Reflected in the Anglo-Jewish Press," *American Jewish Archives* 3 (June 1950): 18–20.

46. Baron, *Steeled by Adversity,* 282–83.

47. Zosa Szajkowski, "The Attitude of American Jews to East European Immigration," *Publications of the American Jewish Historical Society* 40 (March 1951): 232.

48. Ibid., 264–71.

49. Hyman B. Grinstein, "The Efforts of East European Jewry to Organize Its Own Community in the United States," *Publications of the American Jewish Historical Society* 49 (December 1959): 73–89.

50. Walter Rideout, introduction to Igantius Donnelly, *Caeser's Column* (Cambridge: Harvard University Press, 1960); Richard Hofstadter, "*Coin's Financial School* and the Mind of 'Coin' Harvey," in William Harvey, *Coin's Financial School* (Cambridge: Harvard University Press, 1963), 1–80.

51. Henry Feingold, *Zion in America: The Jewish Experience from Colonial Times to the Present* (New York: Hippocrene, 1976), 144–46.

52. Hofstadter, "*Coin's Financial School*," 65, 1.

53. Henry Adams, *Democracy* (New York: Henry Holt, 1880); Rideout, introduction; Hofstadter, "*Coin's Financial School*."

54. Richard Hofstadter wrote in 1955 that "it would be easy to misstate the character of Populist anti-Semitism or to exaggerate its intensity," but he suggested that the "Greenback-Populist tradition activated most of what we have of modern popular anti-Semitism in the United States." *Age of Reform* (New York: Knopf, 1955), 80. These comments stimulated a historiographical debate that lasted more than a decade and that continues to erupt sporadically. Included among the works that "defend" the Populists are Walter Nugent, *The Tolerant Populists* (Chicago: University of Chicago Press, 1963); Norman Pollack, "The Myth of Populist Anti-Semitism," *American Historical Review* 68 (October 1962): 76–80; Norman Pollack, "Fear of Man: Populism, Authoritarianism, and the Historian," *Agricultural History* 39 (April 1965): 59–67; Oscar Handlin, "Reconsidering the Populists," *Agricultural History* 39 (April 1965): 68–74; John Higham, "American Anti-Semitism Historically Reconsidered," in *Jews in the Mind of America*, ed. Charles H. Stember (New York: Basic Books, 1966), 237–58. On the other side, see Irwin Unger, "Critique of Norman Pollack's 'Fear of Man,'" *Agricultural History* 39 (April 1965): 75–80; William F. Holmes, "Whitecapping: Anti-Semitism in the Populist Era," *American Jewish Historical Quarterly* 63 (March 1974): 244–61; Naomi Cohen, "Anti-Semitism in the Gilded Age: A Jewish View," *Jewish Social Studies* 41 (Summer-Fall 1979): 187–210; Leonard Dinnerstein, *Uneasy at Home: Antisemitism and the American Jewish Experience* (New York: Columbia University Press, 1987).

55. Hofstadter, "*Coin's Financial School*," 53.

56. Ibid., 65; W. C. Ford, ed., *Letters of Henry Adams: 1892–1918* (Boston: Houghton Mifflin, 1918), 110–11.

57. Naomi Cohen, "The Ethnic Catalyst: The Impact of the East European Immigration on the American Jewish Establishment," in Berger, *Legacy of Jewish Migration*, 132.

58. *Emanu-El*, 27 January 1905.

59. Julius Goldman to A. Loeb, 2 April 1889, Baron de Hirsch Fund Papers, American Jewish Historical Society, Waltham, Mass.

60. Yehezkel Wyszkowski, "The *American Hebrew*: An Exercise in Ambivalence," *American Jewish History* 70 (March 1987): 344–45; Mandel, "Attitude of the American Jewish Community," 11–36.

61. Wyszkowski, "The *American Hebrew*," 344–45.

62. Naomi Cohen, *Encounter with Emancipation: German Jews in the United States, 1830–1914* (Philadelphia: Jewish Publication Society of America, 1984), 341.

63. *American Hebrew*, 7 September 1894.

64. *Historical Statistics of the United States*, 177.

65. John Higham, *Strangers in the Land: Patterns of American Nativism, 1865–1925* (New York: Atheneum, 1955), 169.

66. Jones, *American Immigration*, 259.

67. Goldwin Smith, "New Light on the Jewish Question," *North American Review* 417 (August 1891): 141–42.

68. Edward Alsworth Ross, *The Old World in the New: The Significance of Past and Present Immigration to the American People* (New York: Century, 1914), 289–90.

69. Kraut, "Silent Strangers," 145.

70. Jenna Weissman Joselit, "The Perceptions and Reality of Immigrant Health Conditions, 1840–1920," appendix A, *Staff Report of the Select Committee on Immigration and Refugee Policy* (Washington, D.C.: Government Printing Office, 1981), 34–36.

71. Max Kohler to David Bressler, 28 March 1910, Galveston Immigration Plan Papers, Box 1, American Jewish Historical Society, Waltham, Mass.

72. Kraut, "Silent Strangers," 152–55; Joselit, "Perceptions and Reality," 34–46.

73. *Official Correspondence Relating to Immigration of Russian Exiles* (Washington, D.C.: Government Printing Office, 1891), 6–7.

74. Kraut, "Silent Strangers," 153.

75. Wyszkowski, "*American Hebrew,*" 346–47.

76. Howe, *World of Our Fathers,* 56.

77. According to the commissioner general of immigration, only 837 of 11,587 Jewish immigrants in 1915–16 were illiterate. Anthony Caminetti, *Annual Report of the Commissioner General of Immigration* (Washington, D.C.: Government Printing Office, 1916), 20. During 1899–1910, however, peak years of Jewish emigration from Russia, 26 percent of Jews fourteen years of age and older were illiterate. Joseph, *Jewish Immigration,* 193–94.

78. Zosa Szjakowski, "The *Yahudi* and the Immigrant: A Reappraisal," *American Jewish Historical Quarterly* 63 (September 1973): 29.

79. Max Kohler to Herbert Friedenwald, 13 October 1911, Kohler Papers, American Jewish Historical Society, Waltham, Mass. Judith Goldstein, "Ethnic Politics: The American Jewish Committee as Lobbyist," *American Jewish Historical Quarterly* 65 (September 1975): 44–45.

80. Charles Reznikoff, ed., *Louis Marshall, Champion of Liberty: Selected Papers and Addresses* (Philadelphia: Jewish Publication Society of America, 1957), 1:111; Louis Marshall to Oscar Straus, 24 March 1908, Marshall Papers, Box 1, American Jewish Historical Society, Waltham, Mass.

81. Baron, *Steeled by Adversity,* 276.

82. Samuel Joseph, *The Baron de Hirsch Fund: The Americanization of the Jewish Immigrant* (Philadelphia: Jewish Publication Society of America, 1935), 104–29.

83. Ibid; Bernard Marinbach, *Galveston: Ellis Island of the West* (New York: State University of New York Press, 1983), 1–3.

84. Chaim Zadick Lubin to IRO, 16 March 1906, IRO Papers, Box 99; Chaim Rachsted to IRO, 7 November 1906, IRO Papers, Box 93, American Jewish Historical Society, Waltham, Mass.

85. Alec Tennant to IRO, 21 September 1906, IRO Papers, Box 116, American Jewish Historical Society, Waltham, Mass.

86. Miriam Blaustein, ed., *Memoirs of David Blaustein* (New York: McBride, Nast, 1913), 208.

87. Marinbach, *Galveston,* 4.

88. Jacob Schiff to Mayer Sulzberger, 27 September 1906, quoted in Gary Dean Best, "Jacob H. Schiff's Galveston Movement: An Experiment in Immigrant Deflection, 1907–1914," *American Jewish Archives* 30 (April 1978): 47–48.

89. *New York Times,* 22 October 1910.
90. Marinbach, *Galveston,* 13.
91. Cyrus Adler, *Jacob H. Schiff: His Life and Letters* (New York: Doubleday, Doran, 1928), 2:98.
92. Minutes, Jewish Information Bureau, 12 January 1914, 9 April 1914, Galveston Immigration Plan Papers, Box 3, American Jewish Historical Society, Waltham, Mass.
93. Uri D. Herscher, *Jewish Agricultural Utopias in America, 1880–1910* (Detroit: Wayne State University Press, 1981).
94. Cahan, *Bleter fun mein leben,* 2:297–303.
95. Joseph Brandes, *Immigrants to Freedom: Jewish Communities in Rural New Jersey since 1882* (Philadelphia: Jewish Publication Society of America, 1971); Gabriel Davidson, *Our Jewish Farmers and the Story of the Jewish Agricultural Society* (New York: Fischer, 1943), 33–34.
96. Baron, *Steeled by Adversity,* 291.
97. Quoted in Thomas Kessner, "The Filter of Ethnicity," in Berger, *Legacy of Jewish Migration,* 170.
98. Cohen, "Ethnic Catalyst," 133.
99. Cohen, *Encounter with Emancipation,* 327.

Chapter Three. New York as the Promised City

1. Irving Howe, *World of Our Fathers* (New York: Harcourt, Brace, Jovanovich, 1976), 169.
2. Moses Rischin, *The Promised City: New York's Jews, 1870–1914* (New York: Corinth, 1964), 9.
3. Leonard Dinnerstein, *Uneasy at Home: Antisemitism and the American Jewish Experience* (New York: Columbia University Press, 1987), 19.
4. E. E. Pratt, *The Industrial Causes of Congestion in New York City* (New York: Longmans, Green, 1911), 19–20; Arnold Bennett, *Your United States: Impressions of a First Visit* (New York: Harper, 1921), 187.
5. Marcus Ravage, *An American in the Making: The Life Story of an Immigrant* (New York: Harper, 1917), 87.
6. Rischin, *Promised City,* 78.
7. Abraham Cahan, *Yekl and the Imported Bridegroom and Other Stories of the New York Ghetto* (New York: Dover, 1970), 13.
8. Quoted in Howe, *World of Our Fathers,* 67.
9. Quoted in Elias Tcherikower, *The Early Jewish Labor Movement in the United States,* trans. A. Antonovsky (New York: YIVO, 1961), 119.
10. Charles Zimmerman, interview with author, 17 May 1982; 11 November 1964, *Amerikaner-Yiddishe Geschichte Bel-Pe,* YIVO, New York City.
11. *Thirteenth Census of the United States, 1910: Population, General Report and Analysis* (Washington: Government Printing Office, 1913), 1023; *Abstract of the Census* (Washington: Government Printing Office, 1913), see supplement for New York containing statistics for the state, counties, and cities.
12. Lawrence Veillert and R. DeForest, eds., *The Tenement House Problem* (New York: Macmillan, 1903), 1:94.

13. New York State Legislature, *Report of the Tenement House Committee of 1894* (Albany: J. B. Lyon, State Printer, 1895), 8, 12, 104.

14. Allen Forman, "Some Adopted Americans," *American Magazine* 9:51–52 (November 1888), quoted in Rischin, *Promised City,* 82–83.

15. *Report of the Tenement House Department of the City of New York* (New York: N.Y. Tenement Department, 1903); Jeffrey S. Gurock, *When Harlem Was Jewish: 1870–1930* (New York: Columbia University Press, 1979), 57, 165.

16. Veillert and DeForest, *Tenement House Problem,* xvii; Jacob Riis, *Children of the Tenement* (New York: Macmillan, 1903), 92–93, 252–53.

17. Rischin, *Promised City,* 10.

18. Thomas Kessner, "Jobs, Ghettoes, and the Urban Economy, 1880–1935," *American Jewish History* 71 (December 1981): 224.

19. *Annual Report of the Factory Inspector's Office of the State of New York, 1897* (Albany: J. B. Lyon, State Printer, 1898), 45.

20. Abraham Cahan, "Sweat-Shop Romance," in Cahan, *Yekl and the Imported Bridegroom,* 191.

21. Jacob Riis, *How the Other Half Lives* (New York: Dover, 1971), 108.

22. Judith Greenfield, "The Role of the Jews in the Development of the Clothing Industry," *YIVO Annual* 2–3 (1947–48): 180–204.

23. Liebmann Hersch, "International Migration of Jews," in *International Migrations,* eds. Imre Ferencezi and Walter F. Willcox (New York: National Bureau of Economic Research, 1931), 2:471–520.

24. Laurence T. Veiller, ed., *Report of the Mayor's Pushcart Commission* (New York: Pushcart Commission, 1906), 39.

25. Alan M. Kraut, "The Butcher, the Baker, the Pushcart Peddler: Jewish Foodways and Entrepreneurial Opportunity in the East European Immigrant Community, 1880–1940," *Journal of American Culture* 6 (Winter 1983): 73.

26. Ibid.

27. Ibid., 77.

28. Tcherikower, *Early Jewish Labor Movement,* 154–55; Kessner, *Golden Door,* 44–70.

29. Andrew Heinze, *Adapting to Abundance: Jewish Immigrants, Mass Consumption, and the Search for American Identity* (New York: Columbia University Press, 1990), 192–202.

30. Rischin, *Promised City,* 59.

31. Quoted in Jeff Kisseloff, *You Must Remember This: An Oral History of Manhattan from the 1890s to World War II* (New York: Harcourt, Brace, Jovanovich, 1989), 41.

32. Alice Kessler-Harris, "The Lower Class as a Factor in Reform: New York, the Jews and the 1890s," Ph.D. diss., Rutgers University, 1968, 179; Louise Boland More, *Wage Earners' Budgets: A Study of Standards and Costs of Living in New York City* (New York: Holt, 1907), 6, 16–21, 33.

33. Marie Ganz, *Rebels Into Anarchy and Out* (New York: Dodd and Mead, 1920), 117.

34. Alexander Woollcott, *The Story of Irving Berlin* (New York: Da Capo, 1983), 13; Pauline Newman, interview, 15 June 1965, Columbia University Oral History Collection, Butler Library, New York City.

35. Deborah Dwork, "Health Conditions of Immigrant Jews on the Lower East Side of New York: 1880–1914," *Medical History* 25 (January 1981): 1; Jacob Jay Lindenthal, "Abi Gezunt: Health and the Eastern European Jewish Immigrant," *American Jewish History* 70 (June 1981): 423.

36. Dwork, "Health Conditions," 30; *Report of the Tenement House Committee of 1894,* 21–22, 47–48.

37. Lindenthal, "Abi Gezunt," 432.

38. Dwork, "Health Conditions," 30.

39. Lindenthal, "Abi Gezunt," 433–35.

40. Dwork, "Health Conditions," 33.

41. Gertrude Ford, *81 Sheriff Street* (New York: Frederick, 1981), 95.

42. Quoted in Neil Cowan and Ruth S. Cowan, *Our Parents' Lives: The Americanization of East European Jews* (New York: Basic Books, 1989), 66.

43. Samuel Ornitz, *Allrightniks Row, "Haunch, Paunch and Jowl," the Making of a Professional Jew* (New York: Weiner, 1986), 35.

44. Hutchins Hapgood, *Spirit of the Ghetto* (New York: Schocken, 1966), 32.

45. Reena Sigman Friedman, "'Send Me My Husband Who Is in New York City': Husband Desertion in the American Jewish Immigrant Community, 1900–1926," *Jewish Social Studies* 44 (Winter 1982): 1.

46. Quoted in Charlotte Baum, Paula Hyman, and Sonya Michel, *The Jewish Woman in America* (New York: Dial, 1976), 117.

47. Ari Lloyd Fridkis, "Desertion in the American Jewish Immigrant Family: The Work of the National Desertion Bureau in Cooperation with the Industrial Removal Office," *American Jewish History* 71 (December 1981): 291.

48. *Jewish Daily Forward,* 12 February 1906; Friedman, "'Send Me My Husband,'" 5.

49. Friedman, "'Send Me My Husband,'" 8.

50. Fewer than eleven thousand Jewish desertions were committed in the United States. See figures in Friedman, "'Send Me My Husband,'" 12; and in Ofri Ben-Yehuda Felder, "Family Desertion among East European Jewish Immigrants: 1900–1930," Master's thesis, Columbia University, 1986, 13–19.

51. Arthur Goren, *New York Jews and the Quest for Community: The Kehillah Experiment, 1908–1922* (New York: Columbia University Press, 1970), 134–58; David Singer, "The Jewish Gangster: Crime as 'Unzer Shtik,'" *Judaism* 23 (Winter 1974): 70–77; Jenna W. Joselit, *Our Gang: Jewish Crime and the New York Jewish Community, 1900–1940* (Bloomington: Indiana University Press, 1983).

52. Abraham Cahan, "The Russian Jew in America," *Atlantic Monthly* 82 (July 1898): 137; Theodore Bingham, "Foreign Criminals in New York," *North American Review* 168 (September 1908): 383–84; Rischin, *Promised City,* 91.

53. Egal Feldman, "Prostitution, the Alien Woman, and the Progressive Imagination, 1910–1915," *American Quarterly* 19 (1967): 196–206; George Kibbe Turner, "Daughters of the Poor," *McClure's* 34 (November 1909):45–61.

54. Daniel Bell, "Crime as an American Way of Life," *Antioch Review* (June 1953): 131–54; Mike Gold, *Jews without Money* (New York: Avon, 1965), 6.

55. Arthur Goren, "Mother Rosie Hertz, the Social Evil, and the New York Kehillah," *Michael: On the History of the Jews in the Diaspora* 3 (1975): 188–210; Goren, *New York Jews,* 137–38; Turner, "Daughters of the Poor," 48.

56. Leo Katcher, *The Big Bankroll: The Life and Times of Arnold Rothstein* (New York: Harper, 1959).

57. Henry Feingold, *Zion in America: The Jewish Experience from Colonial Times to the Present* (New York: Hippocrene, 1976), 141.

58. Tcherikower, *Early Jewish Labor Movement,* 109.

59. Rischin, *Promised City,* 101–3.

60. *Educational Alliance: First Annual Report, 1893; Educational Alliance: Report of the Committee on Moral Culture,* quoted in Howe, *World of Our Fathers,* 231.

61. *Jewish Messenger,* 25 September 1891.

62. Miriam Blaustein, ed., *Memoirs of David Blaustein* (New York: McBride, Nast, 1913), 18–28.

63. Louis Marshall to Samuel Greenbaum, 3 February 1919, quoted in Lucy Dawidowicz, "Louis Marshall's Yiddish Newspaper, *The Jewish World:* A Study in Contrasts," *Jewish Social Studies* 25 (April 1963): 116.

64. *Educational Alliance: Eleventh Annual Report* (New York: Educational Alliance, 1903).

65. S. P. Rudens, "A Half Century of Community Service: The Story of the New York Educational Alliance," *American Jewish Yearbook* 46 (1944–45): 73–87.

66. Naomi Cohen, *Encounter with Emancipation: German Jews in the United States, 1830–1914* (Philadelphia: Jewish Publication Society of America, 1984), 337.

67. Rischin, *Promised City,* 206–7.

68. *American Hebrew,* 27 November 1914; 10 May 1918; Alice Mencken, *On the Side of Mercy* (New York: Covici, Friede, 1933), 17–18; Marc Angel, *La America: The Sephardic Experience in the United States* (Philadelphia: Jewish Publication Society of America, 1982), 6.

69. Allen Freeman Davis, *Spearheads for Reform: Social Settlements and the Progressive Movement* (New York: Oxford University Press, 1967), ix.

70. *Baron De Hirsch Fund Report* (New York: Oppenheimer Printing Co., 1902).

71. Davis, *Spearheads for Reform,* 89.

72. Lillian Wald, *The House on Henry Street* (New York: Holt, 1915); Jacob R. Marcus, *The American Jewish Woman: A Documentary History* (New York: KTAV, 1981), 400; Howe, *World of Our Fathers,* 93.

73. Goren, *New York Jews,* 250–51.

74. Adolph Held, interview, 6 June 1964, Amerikaner-Yiddishe Geshichte Bel-Pe, YIVO, New York City; interview, 1967, Columbia University Oral History Collection, Bulter Library, New York City.

75. Quoted in Milton Meltzer, *Taking Root: Jewish Immigrants in America* (New York: Farrar, Straus, and Giroux, 1976), 70–71.

76. Pearl Halpern, interview, 11 November 1965, *Amerikaner-Yiddishe Geshichte Bel-Pe,* YIVO, New York City.

77. Sam Rubin, interview, 26 June 1965, *Amerikaner-Yiddishe Geshichte Bel-Pe,* YIVO, New York City.

78. Quoted in Irving Howe and Kenneth Libo, *How We Lived: A Documentary History of Immigrant Jews in America, 1880–1930* (New York: Marek, 1979), 43.

79. Quoted in Paula Hyman, "Immigrant Women and Consumer Protest: The New York City Kosher Meat Boycott of 1902," *American Jewish History* 70 (September 1980): 91–105.

80. Susan E. Kennedy, *If All We Did Was to Weep at Home: A History of White Working-Class Women in America* (Bloomington: Indiana University Press, 1979), 65.

81. Hyman, "Immigrant Women and Consumer Protest."

82. Lloyd P. Gartner, *The History of the Jews of Cleveland* (Cleveland: Western Reserve Historical Society, 1987), 247; Robert A. Rockaway, *The Jews of Detroit: From the Beginning, 1762–1914* (Detroit: Wayne State University Press, 1986), 81.

83. Alfred Kazin, *Walker in the City* (New York: Harcourt, Brace, 1951), 66–67.

84. Sydney Stahl Weinberg, *The World of Our Mothers* (Chapel Hill: University of North Carolina Press, 1988), 148.

85. William Z. Ripley, "Race Factors in Labor Unions," *Atlantic Monthly* 93 (1904): 300; Thomas Kessner and Betty Boyd Caroli, "New Immigrant Women at Work: Italians and Jews in New York City, 1880–1905," *Journal of Ethnic Studies* 5 (1978): 25.

86. Howe, *World of Our Fathers*, 171.

87. Quoted in Jenna W. Joselit, "What Happened to New York's 'Jewish Jews'? Moses Rischin's *The Promised City* Revisited," *American Jewish History* 73 (December 1985): 163–72.

88. *Hebrew Standard,* 18 January 1918.

89. Daniel Soyer, "Between Two Worlds: The Jewish *Landsmanshaftn* and Immigrant Identity," *American Jewish History* 76 (September 1986): 5–24; Daniel Soyer, "*Landsmanshaftn* and the Jewish Labor Movement: Cooperation, Conflict and the Building of Community," *Journal of American Ethnic History* 7 (Spring 1988): 22–45; Moses Rischin, "Responsa [to 'A Reexamination of a Classic Work in American Jewish History: Moses Rischin's *The Promised City,* Twenty Years Later']," *American Jewish History* 73 (December 1985): 201.

90. Nathan Kaganoff, "The Jewish *Landsmanshaftn* in New York City in the Period Preceding World War I," *American Jewish History* 76 (September 1986): 61; Hannah Kliger, "Traditions of Grass-Roots Organization and Leadership: The Continuity of *Landsmanshaftn* in New York," *American Jewish History* 76 (September 1986): 25–39.

91. Irving Howe, "Pluralism in the Immigrant World," in Berger, *Legacy of Jewish Migration,* 149–55.

92. Kaganoff, "Jewish *Landsmanshaftn,*" 64; Soyer, "Between Two Worlds," 21.

93. Kaganoff, "Jewish *Landsmanshaftn,*" 64.

94. For a very different view, see: Michael R. Weisser, *A Brotherhood of Memory: Jewish Landsmanshaftn in the New World* (New York: Basic Books, 1984).

95. Abraham J. Karp, *Haven and Home: A History of the Jews in America* (New York: Schocken, 1985), 185.

96. Faina Burko, "The American Yiddish Theatre and Its Audience before World War I," in Berger, *Legacy of Jewish Migration,* 85–96.

97. Henry Feingold, *A Midrash on American Jewish History* (Albany: State University of New York Press, 1982), 83–93; Fred Somkin, "Zion's Harp by the East River: Jewish-American Popular Songs in Columbus's Golden Land, 1890–1914," *Perspectives in American History* 2 (1985): 183–220.

98. Hapgood, *Spirit of the Ghetto,* 113–14.

99. Burko, "American Yiddish Theatre," 85–96.

100. Hapgood, *Spirit of the Ghetto,* 121–22.

101. Feingold, *Midrash,* 91.

102. Burko, "American Yiddish Theatre," 90–94.

103. Somkin, "Zion's Harp," 207–8.

104. Hyman Grinstein, "The Efforts of East European Jewry to Organize Its Own Community in the United States," *Publications of the American Jewish Historical Society* 49 (December 1959): 73–89.

105. Rischin, *Promised City,* 116–17.

106. Mordechai Soltes, *The Yiddish Press: An Americanizing Agency* (New York: Arno, 1969); Milton Doroshkin, *Yiddish in America* (Madison: Farleigh Dickinson University Press, 1969), 97–135; Angel, *La America,* 6.

107. Rischin, *Promised City,* 131.

108. Ruth R. Wisse, "Di Yunge: Immigrants or Exiles?" *Prooftexts: A Journal of Jewish Literary History* 1 (January 1981): 43–61.

109. Cahan, "Russian Jew," 132.

110. Feingold, *Midrash,* 84; Maxine Seller, "Defining Socialist Womanhood: The Woman's Page of the *Jewish Daily Forward* in 1919," *American Jewish History* 76 (June 1987):416–38; Robert Park, "Foreign Language Press and Social Progress," in *Robert E. Park on Social Control and Collective Behavior,* ed. Ralph H. Turner (Chicago: University of Chicago Press, 1967), 133–44.

111. *Jewish Daily Forward,* 6 August 1903.

112. Gerald Sorin, "American Jewish Socialists as Agents of Acculturation," *American Jewish History* 79 (Autumn 1989): 41–44; J. C. Rich, "Sixty Years of the *Jewish Daily Forward,*" *New Leader* 40 (June 1957): 1–38.

113. Isaac Metzker, ed., *A Bintel Brief* (New York: Ballantine, 1971).

114. Rischin, *Promised City,* 117.

115. S. L. Blumenson, "Culture on Rutgers Square: The Fervent Days on East Broadway," *Commentary* 10 (July 1950): 65–74.

116. *New York Tribune,* 30 September 1900.

117. Harry Roskolenko, *The Time That Was Then* (New York: Dial, 1971), 190.

118. Howe, *World of Our Fathers,* 246.

119. Quoted in Baum, Hyman, and Michel, *Jewish Woman in America,* 127.

120. Mary Antin, *The Promised Land* (Boston: Houghton Mifflin, 1912), 198.

121. Goren, *New York Jews,* 18.

122. Thomas Kessner, "The Selective Filter of Ethnicity: A Half Century of Immigrant Mobility," in Berger, *Legacy of Jewish Migration,* 169–85.

123. Isaac M. Rubinow, "Economic and Industrial Condition: New York," in *The Russian Jew in the United States,* ed. Charles S. Bernheimer (Philadelphia: Winston, 1905), 104–21.

124. Heinze, *Adapting to Abundance,* 134–97.

125. Howe, *World of Our Fathers,* 139.

126. Paul Douglas, *Real Wages in the United States, 1890–1926* (New York: Kelley, 1966), 264–65; Albert Rees, *Real Wages in Manufacturing, 1890–1914* (Princeton: Princeton University Press, 1961), 3–6, 126; Heinze, *Adapting to Abundance.*

Chapter Four. Prophets, Proletarians, and Progressives

1. Ronald Sanders, *Downtown Jews: Portraits of an Immigrant Generation* (New York: Harper and Row, 1979), 51; Abraham Cahan, *Bleter fun mein leben* (New York: Forward Association, 1926–31), 2:104–5.

2. Cahan, *Bleter fun mein leben,* 2:105.

3. Quoted in Ezra Mendelsohn, "The Russian Roots of the American Jewish Labor Movement," *YIVO Annual* 16 (1976): 173.

4. Morris Hillquit, *Loose Leaves from a Busy Life* (New York: Da Capo, 1971), 2–6.

5. Elias Tcherikower, *The Early Jewish Labor Movement in the United States,* trans. A. Antonovsky (New York: YIVO, 1961), 257.

6. Morris Feinstone, interview, 4 March 1919. David Saposs Papers, Folder 2, Box 27, State Historical Society of Wisconsin, Madison.

7. *Reports of the United States Industrial Commission* (Washington, D.C.: Government Printing Office, 1901), 15:325, 327.

8. Israel Knox and Irving Howe, *The Jewish Labor Movement in America: Two Views* (New York: Jewish Labor Committee, Workmen's Circle, 1958), 152.

9. Rose Cohen, *Out of the Shadow* (New York: Doran, 1918), 212; Louis Glass, interview, 4 November 1963, *Amerikaner-Yiddishe Geschichte Bel Pe,* YIVO, New York City.

10. Quoted in Daniel Soyer, "Landsmanshaftn and the Jewish Labor Movement: Cooperation, Conflict and the Building of Community," *Journal of American Ethnic History* 7 (Spring 1988): 26–27.

11. Irwin Yellowitz, "Jewish Immigrants and the American Labor Movement, 1900–1920," *American Jewish History* 71 (December 1981): 188–217.

12. Marsha Farbman, interview, 17 December 1963, *Amerikaner-Yiddishe Geschichte Bel-Pe,* YIVO, New York City.

13. Tcherikower, *Early Jewish Labor Movement,* 327; Morris Schappes, "The Political Origins of the United Hebrew Trades, 1888," *Journal of Ethnic Studies,* 5 (Spring 1977): 13–44.

14. Hubert Perrier, "The Socialists and the Working Class in New York: 1890–1896," *Labor History* 22 (Fall 1981): 501.

15. Howard H. Quint, *The Forging of American Socialism* (Indianapolis: Bobbs-Merrill, 1953); David Shannon, *The Socialist Party of America* (Chicago: University of Chicago Press, 1955).

16. Charles Leinenweber, "The Class and Ethnic Bases of New York City Socialism, 1904–1915," *Labor History* 22 (Winter 1981): 43; Ray Stannard Baker, "The Spiritual Unrest: The Disintegration of the Jews," *Leslie's Monthly* 68 (1909): 602.

17. M. Hurwitz, *The Workmen's Circle* (New York: Jewish Labor Committee, Workmen's Circle, 1936).

18. Isidore Schoenholtz, interview, 16 May 1964, *Amerikaner-Yiddishe Geschichte Bel-Pe,* YIVO, New York City.

19. Sanders, *Downtown Jews,* 86–87.

20. "Autobiography," no. 45, YIVO, New York City.

21. Morris R. Cohen, *A Dreamer's Journey* (Boston: Beacon, 1949), 219.

22. Robert Park, "Foreign Language Press and Social Progress," in *Robert E. Park on Social Control and Collective Behavior,* ed. Ralph H. Turner (Chicago: University of Chicago Press, 1967), 133–44.

23. Cahan, *Bleter fun mein leben,* 4:512; Moses Rischin, *The Promised City: New York's Jews, 1870–1914* (New York: Corinth, 1964), 160.

24. Irving Howe, *World of Our Fathers* (New York: Harcourt, Brace, Jovanovich, 1976), 292–94.

25. Moses Rischin, "The Jewish Labor Movement in America: A Social Interpretation," *Labor History* 4 (Fall 1963): 235.

26. Moses Kligsberg, "Jewish Immigrants in Business: A Sociological Study," in *The Jewish Experience in America,* ed. Abraham Karp (New York: KTAV, 1969), 5:249–85.

27. Elizabeth Hasanovitz, *One of Them* (Boston: Houghton Mifflin, 1918), 33; Cahan is quoted in Melech Epstein, *Jewish Labor in the United States of America* (New York: KTAV, 1950), 1:140; Matthew Josephson, *Sidney Hillman: Statesman of American Labor* (Garden City, N.Y.: Doubleday, 1952), 51.

28. Rischin, *Promised City,* 192–93.

29. David Dubinsky and A. H. Raskin, *David Dubinsky: A Life with Labor* (New York: Simon and Schuster, 1977), 48–54.

30. Irving Howe, "Pluralism in the Immigrant World," in *The Legacy of Jewish Migration,* ed. David Berger (Brooklyn: Brooklyn College Press, 1983), 149–55.

31. Rischin, *Promised City,* 178–85.

32. Charlotte Baum, Paula Hyman, and Sonya Michel, *The Jewish Woman in America* (New York: Dial, 1976), 135; Sydelle Kramer and Jenny Masur, eds., *Jewish Grandmothers* (Boston: Beacon, 1976), 11; Alice Kessler-Harris, "The Lower Class as a Factor in Reform: New York, the Jews and the 1890s," Ph. D. diss., Rutgers University, 1968; Marie Ganz, *Rebels Into Anarchy and Out* (New York: Dodd and Mead, 1920), 89.

33. Paula Scheier, "Clara Lemlich Shavelson: 50 Years in Labor's Front Line," in *The American Jewish Woman: A Documentary History,* ed. Jacob R. Marcus, (New York: KTAV, 1981), 574–75.

34. Baum, Hyman, and Michel, *Jewish Woman in America,* 140–44; Mary Jo Buhle, *Women and American Socialism, 1870–1920* (Urbana: University of Illinois Press, 1981), 192.

35. Clara Lemlich Shavelson, "Remembering the Waistmakers General Strike, 1909," *Jewish Currents* 36 (November 1982): 10.

36. Gerald Sorin, *The Prophetic Minority: American Jewish Immigrant Radicals, 1880–1920* (Bloomington: Indiana University Press, 1985), 124–41.

37. Flora Weiss, interview, 15 June 1964, *Amerikaner-Yiddishe Geschichte Bel-Pe,* YIVO, New York City.

38. Louis Levine, *The Women's Garment Workers* (New York: Huebsch, 1924), 146–67; Buhle, *Woman and American Socialism,* 176–226; Baum, Hyman, and Michel, *Jewish Woman in America,* 140–44; Melvyn Dubofsky, *When Workers Organize* (Amherst: University of Massachusetts Press, 1968), 59–60.

39. Abraham Rosenberg, *Di Klokmacher un zeyere yunyons* (New York: Cloak Operators Union, Local 1, 1920), 208.

40. Hyman Berman, "The Era of the Protocol: A Chapter in the History of the ILGWU, 1910–1916," Ph. D. diss., Columbia University, 1956; Hyman Berman, "The Cloakmakers' Strike of 1910," in *Essays on Jewish Life and Thought Presented in Honor of Salo Wittmayer Baron,* ed. J. L. Blau et al. (New York: Columbia University Press, 1959), 63–94.

41. Joel Seidman, *The Needle Trades* (New York: Farrar and Rinehart, 1942), 115–21.

42. Isaac Fein, *The Making of an American Jewish Community: The History of Baltimore Jewry from 1773 to 1920* (Philadelphia: Jewish Publication Society of America, 1971), 168; Maxwell Whiteman, "Out of the Sweatshop," in *Jewish Life in Philadelphia,* ed. Murray Friedman (Philadelphia: Jewish Publication Society of America, 1983), 10.

43. J. B. S. Hardman, interview, 19 July 1966, W. E. Wiener Oral History Library, American Jewish Committee, New York City.

44. Leon Stein, *The Triangle Fire* (Philadelphia: Lippincott, 1962).

45. Louis Waldman, *Labor Lawyer* (New York: Dutton, 1944), 33–39.

46. Dubinsky, *Life with Labor,* 40.

47. Fannia Cohn to E. G. Lindeman, 7 February 1933; Fannia Cohn to Emma [?], 8 May 1953, Fannia Cohn Papers, New York Public Library.

48. Rose Schneiderman, *All for One* (New York: Erikson, 1967), 101.

49. Rischin, *Promised City,* 254–55.

50. Louis Ruchames, "Jewish Radicalism in the United States," in *The Ghetto and Beyond,* ed. Peter Rose (New York: Random House, 1969), 237.

51. Melvyn Dubofsky, "Success and Failure of Socialism in New York City, 1900–1918: A Case Study," *Labor History* 9 (Fall 1968): 370–71.

52. James Weinstein, "The Socialist Party: Its Roots and Strengths, 1912–1919," *Studies on the Left* 1 (Winter 1960): 5–27; Ira Kipnis, *The American Socialist Movement, 1897–1912* (New York: Monthly Review Press, 1952), 345.

53. Richard W. Fox, "The Paradox of Progressive Socialism: The Case of Morris Hillquit, 1901–1914," *American Quarterly* 26 (March 1974): 127–40.

54. Adolph Held, interview, 1967, Columbia University Oral History Collection, 4, Butler Library, New York City.

55. John Higham, *Strangers in the Land: Patterns of American Nativism, 1865–1925* (New York: Atheneum, 1955), 35–106, 158–94; Robert Wiebe, *The Search for Order, 1877–1920* (New York: Hill and Wang, 1967), 38–106.

56. Wiebe, *Search for Order,* 11–195; John D. Buenker, *Urban Liberalism and Progressive Reform* (New York: Scribner's, 1973), 1–117, 198–239.

57. Irwin Yellowitz, *Labor and the Progressive Movement in New York State, 1897–1916* (Ithaca: Cornell University Press, 1965), 49–99; Dubofsky, *When Workers Organize,* 24; Kessler-Harris, "Lower Class as a Factor in Reform," 231–34.

58. Yellowitz, *Labor and the Progressive Movement,* 49–99; Dubofsky, *When Workers Organize,* 24; Kessler-Harris, "Lower Class as a Factor in Reform," 231–34.

59. Kessler-Harris, "Lower Class as a Factor in Reform".

60. Dubofsky, *When Workers Organize,* 126–51.

61. Quoted in Matthew Josephson, *Sidney Hillman: Statesman of American Labor* (Garden City, N.Y.: Doubleday, 1952), 439. Also see Steven Fraser, *Labor Will Rule: Sidney Hillman and the Rise of American Labor* (New York: Free Press, 1991).

Chapter Five. Mobility and Community beyond New York

1. Joel Perlmann, "Beyond New York: The Occupations of Russian Jewish Immigrants in Providence, Rhode Island, and in Other Small Jewish Communities, 1900–1915," *American Jewish History* 72 (March 1983): 391.

2. Irving Cutler, "The Jews of Chicago from Shtetl to Suburb," in *Ethnic Chicago,* ed. Melvin Holli and Peter d'A. Jones (Grand Rapids: Eardmans, 1981), 49; Edward Mazur, "Jewish Chicago: From Diversity to Community," in *The Ethnic Frontier: Essays in the History of Group Survival in Chicago and the Midwest,* ed. Melvin G. Holli and Peter d'A. Jones (Grand Rapids: Eardmans, 1977), 272–74.

3. Charles Zeublin, quoted in Milton Meltzer, *Taking Root: Jewish Immigrants in America* (New York: Farrar, Straus, and Giroux, 1976), 76.

4. *Chicago Tribune,* 19 July 1891, in Cutler, "Jews of Chicago," 55.

5. Florence Kelley, quoted in Meltzer, *Taking Root,* 101.

6. Lawrence P. Bachmann, "Julius Rosenwald," *American Jewish Historical Quarterly* 66 (September 1976): 89–105.

7. Philip Davis, quoted in Meltzer, *Taking Root,* 176.

8. June Sochen, "Some Observations on the Role of American Jewish Women as Communal Workers," *American Jewish History* 70 (September 1980): 23–34; Deborah Golomb, "The 1893 Congress of Jewish Women: Evolution or Revolution in American Jewish Women's History?" *American Jewish History* 70 (September 1980): 52–67.

9. Sochen, "Some Observations," 55; Golomb, "1893 Congress," 66.

10. Sochen, "Some Observations," 51.

11. Cited in Cutler, "Jews of Chicago," 51–52.

12. Richard Benkin, "Ethnicity and Organization: Jewish Communities in Eastern Europe and the United States," *Sociological Quarterly* 19 (Autumn 1978): 614–25.

13. Cutler, "Jews of Chicago," 58.

14. Murray Friedman, ed., *Jewish Life in Philadelphia, 1830–1940* (Philadelphia: Jewish Publication Society of America, 1983), 3–11; Maxwell Whiteman, "Philadelphia's Jewish Neighborhoods," in *The Peoples of Philadelphia,* ed. Allen F. Davis and Mark Haller (Philadelphia: Temple University Press, 1973), 231–54.

15. Whiteman, "Philadelphia's Jewish Neighborhoods," 238–44.

16. Steven Hertzberg, *Strangers within the Gate City: The Jews of Atlanta, 1845–1915* (Philadelphia: Jewish Publication Society of America, 1978), 112.

17. Caroline Golab, "The Immigrant and the City: Poles, Italians and Jews in Philadelphia, 1870–1920," in Davis and Haller, *Peoples of Philadelphia,* 203–30.

18. Maxwell Whiteman, "Out of the Sweatshop," in Friedman, *Jewish Life in Philadelphia,* 64–79; Isaac Fein, *The Making of an American Jewish Community: The History of Baltimore Jewry from 1773 to 1920* (Philadelphia: Jewish Publication Society of America, 1971), 164–65.

19. Maxwell Whiteman, "Western Impact on East European Jews: A Philadelphia Fragment," in *Immigrants and Religion in Urban America,* ed. Randall Miller and Thomas Marzik (Philadelphia: Temple University Press, 1977), 117–37.

20. Whiteman, "Out of the Sweatshop."

21. E. Digby Baltzell, Allen Glickman, and Jacquelyn Litt, "The Jewish Communities of Philadelphia and Boston: A Tale of Two Cities," in Friedman, *Jewish Life in Philadelphia,* 290–313.

22. Edwin Wolf, "The German-Jewish Influence in Philadelphia's Jewish Charities," in Friedman, *Jewish Life in Philadelphia,* 125–42; Evelyn Bodek, "'Making Do': Jewish Women and Philanthropy," in Friedman, *Jewish Life in Philadelphia,* 143–62; Philip Rosen, "German Jews vs. Russian Jews in Philadelphia Philanthropy," in Friedman, *Jewish Life in Philadelphia,* 198–212.

23. Maxwell Whiteman, "'The Philadelphia Group,'" in Friedman, *Jewish Life in Philadelphia,* 163–78.

24. Robert Tabak, "Orthodox Judaism in Transition," in Friedman, *Jewish Life in Philadelphia,* 48–63.

25. Maxwell Whiteman, "The Fiddlers Rejected: Jewish Immigrant Expression in Philadelphia," in Friedman, *Jewish Life in Philadelphia,* 80–98.

26. Whiteman, "Philadelphia's Jewish Neighborhoods," 250–54.

27. Dan Rottenberg, "The Rise of Albert M. Greenfield," in Friedman, *Jewish Life*

in Philadelphia, 213–34; Joseph Eckhardt and Linda Kowall, "The Movies' First Mogul," in Friedman, *Jewish Life in Philadelphia,* 99–124.

28. Quoted in Isaac M. Fein, *Boston—Where It All Began: An Historical Perspective of the Boston Jewish Community* (Boston: Boston Jewish Bicentennial Commission, 1976), 42.

29. Arnold Wieder, *The Early Jewish Community of Boston's North End* (Waltham: Brandeis University Press, 1962), 65–66; Mary Antin, *The Promised Land* (Boston: Houghton Mifflin, 1912), 183.

30. Fein, *Boston,* 48–49.

31. Quoted in Stephen Whitfield, "A Critique of Leonard Dinnerstein's 'The Origins of Black Anti-Semitism in America,'" *American Jewish Archives* 39 (November 1987): 194.

32. Baltzell, Glickman, and Litt, "Jewish Communities of Philadelphia and Boston."

33. Jacob Neusner, "The Impact of Immigration and Philanthropy upon the Boston Jewish Community, 1880–1914," *Publications of the American Jewish Historical Society* 42 (December 1956): 71–85.

34. Ibid.

35. John Livingston, "The Industrial Removal Office, the Galveston Project, and the Denver Jewish Community," *American Jewish History* 68 (June 1979): 434–58.

36. Bernard Marinbach, *Galveston: Ellis Island of the West* (New York: State University of New York Press, 1983).

37. Rhoda Lewin, "Stereotype and Reality in the Jewish Immigrant Experience in Minneapolis," *Minnesota History* 46 (Fall 1979): 263.

38. Steven Lowenstein, *The Jews of Oregon, 1850–1950* (Portland: Jewish Historical Society of Oregon, 1987), 76; Hertzberg, *Strangers in the Gate City,* 78–80; Lloyd Gartner and Louis Swichkow, *The History of the Jews of Milwaukee* (Philadelphia: Jewish Publication Society of America, 1963), 86; Marc Angel, "The Sephardim of the United States: An Exploratory Study," *American Jewish Year Book* (1973): 77–138.

39. Lloyd Gartner, *History of the Jews of Cleveland* (Cleveland: Western Reserve Historical Society, 1987), 2d ed., 106–7.

40. Rivka Lissak, "Myth and Reality: The Pattern of Relationships between the Hull House Circle and the 'New Immigrants' in Chicago's West Side, 1890–1919," *Journal of American Ethnic History* 2 (Spring 1983): 25–30; Gartner, *History of the Jews of Cleveland,* 248; Gartner and Swichkow, *History of the Jews of Milwaukee,* 65, 166.

41. Max Vorspan and Lloyd Gartner, *History of the Jews of Los Angeles* (San Marino, Calif.: Huntington Library, 1970), 35; William Toll, "Fraternalism and Community Structure on the Urban Frontier: The Jews of Portland, Oregon—A Case Study," *Pacific Historical Review* 47 (August 1978): 388; Marc Lee Raphael, *Jews and Judaism in a Midwestern Community: Columbus, Ohio, 1840–1975* (Columbus: Ohio University Press, 1979); Ewa Morawska, "A Replica of the 'Old Country' Relationship in the Ethnic Niche: East European Jews and Gentiles in Small Town Western Pennsylvania, 1880s–1930s," *American Jewish History* 77 (September 1987): 27–86.

42. Raphael, *Jews and Judaism,* 135–37; Richard Klayman, *The First Jew: Prejudice and Politics in an American Community* (Malden, Mass.: Old Suffolk Square, 1985), 21–29; Gartner, *History of the Jews of Cleveland,* 160–66; Ida Cohen Selovan, "Jewish Wage Earners in Pittsburgh, 1890–1930," *American Jewish Historical Quarterly* 65 (March 1976): 272–85.

43. Eleanor Horvitz, "Old Bottles, Rags, Junk! The Story of the Jews of South Providence," *Rhode Island Jewish History Notes* 7:2 (1976): 189; Perlmann, "Beyond New York," 379.

44. William Toll, "The Female Life Cycle and the Measure of Social Change: Portland, Oregon, 1880–1930," *American Jewish History* 72 (March 1983): 309–32; Lowenstein, *Jews of Oregon,* 74.

45. Mitchell Gelfand, "Progress and Prosperity: Jewish Social Mobility in Los Angeles in the Booming Eighties," *American Jewish History* 68 (June 1979): 420; Vorspan and Gartner, *History of the Jews of Los Angeles,* 93.

46. Moses Rischin, "Introduction: The Jews of the West," *American Jewish History* 68 (June 1979): 389–95.

47. Gary Watters, "The Russian Jew in Oklahoma: The May Brothers," *Chronicles of Oklahoma* 53:4 (1975–76): 479–91.

48. Lary May and Elaine Tyler May, "Why Jewish Movie Moguls: An Exploration in American Culture," *American Jewish History* 72 (September 1982): 6–25; Neal Gabler, *An Empire of Their Own: How the Jews Invented Hollywood* (New York: Crown, 1988).

49. Bernard Shuman, *A History of the Sioux City Jewish Community, 1869 to 1969* (Sioux City: Bostein Creative Printing, 1969), 162; Helene Gerard, "Yankees in Yarmulkes: Small-Town Jewish Life in Eastern Long Island," *American Jewish Archives* 38 (April 1986): 28; Gartner, *History of Jews of Cleveland,* 125; Lowenstein, *Jews of Oregon,* 129; Marc Lee Raphael, "The Utilization of Public Local and Federal Sources for Reconstructing American Jewish Local History: The Jews of Columbus, Ohio," *American Jewish Historical Quarterly* 65 (September 1975): 10–35.

50. Perlmann, "Beyond New York," 388–89.

51. Gartner, *History of the Jews of Cleveland,* 126.

52. David Gold, "Jewish Agriculture in the Catskills, 1900–1920," *Agricultural History* 55 (January 1981): 31–49; Stefan Kanfer, *A Summer World* (New York: Farrar, Straus, and Giroux, 1989); Betsy Blackman, "Going to the Mountains: A Social History," in *Resorts of the Catskills,* ed. Alf Evers et al. (New York: St. Martin's, 1979), 79.

53. Stephen J. Whitfield, "Commercial Passions: The Southern Jew as Businessman," *American Jewish History* 71 (March 1982): 342–57; Louis Schmeir, "A Jewish Peddler and His Black Customers Look at Each Other," *American Jewish History* 73 (September 1983): 39–55.

54. Stanley Marcus, *Minding the Store: A Memoir* (Boston: Little, Brown, 1974), 186; Irving Howe and Kenneth Libo, *We Lived There Too* (New York: St. Martin's/Marek, 1984), 327–28.

55. Vorspan and Gartner, *History of the Jews of Los Angeles,* 114. Emphasis mine.

56. Howard Chudacoff, *Mobile Americans: Residential and Social Mobility in Omaha, 1880–1920* (New York: Oxford University Press, 1972), 60–85; Gartner, *History of the Jews of Cleveland,* 123; Raphael, *Jews and Judaism,* 91; William Toll, "Mobility, Fraternalism, and Jewish Cultural Change: Portland, 1910–1930," *American Jewish History* 68 (March 1979): 459–91.

57. Gartner and Swichkow, *History of the Jews of Milwaukee,* 87; Gartner, *History of the Jews of Cleveland,* 155.

58. Quoted in Sandra Hartwell Becker and Ralph L. Pearson, "The Jewish Community of Hartford, Connecticut, 1880–1929," *American Jewish Archives* 31 (November 1979): 184–214.

59. Howe and Libo, *We Lived There Too,* 318.

60. James A. Gelin, *Starting Over: The Formation of the Jewish Community of Springfield, Massachusetts, 1840–1905* (New York: University Presses of America, 1984), 6–7; Selig Adler and Thomas E. Connolly, *From Ararat to Suburbia: The History of the Jewish Community of Buffalo* (Philadelphia: Jewish Publication Society of America, 1960), 185–87; Lewin, "Stereotype and Reality," 264.

61. Floyd S. Fierman, *Guts and Ruts: The Jewish Pioneer on the Trail in the American Southwest* (New York: KTAV, 1985), 172.

62. Blaine Lamb, "Jews in Early Phoenix, 1870–1920," *Journal of Arizona History* 18 (Autumn 1977): 299–318.

63. Aaron Rothkoff, *The Silver Era in American Jewish Orthodoxy: Rabbi Eliezer Silver and His Generation* (New York: Yeshiva University Press, 1981), 50; Isadore Papermaster, "A History of North Dakota Jewry and Their Pioneer Rabbi," *Western States Jewish Historical Quarterly* 10: 2 (1978): 170–84.

64. Horvitz, "Old Bottles," 230; Shuman, *A History of the Sioux City Jewish Community,* 162–63; Deborah Dash Moore, "The Construction of Community: Jewish Migration and Ethnicity in the United States," in *The Jews of North America,* ed. Moses Rischin (Detroit: Wayne State University Press, 1987), 105–20.

65. Gelin, *Starting Over,* 5; Shuman, *History of the Sioux City Jewish Community,* 162–63; Bernard Marinbach, *Galveston: Ellis Island of the West* (New York: State University of New York Press, 1983), 187.

66. Gartner, *History of the Jews of Cleveland,* 179.

67. Stuart Rosenberg, *The Jews of Rochester, 1843–1925* (New York: Columbia University Press, 1954), 66.

68. Fred Rosenbaum, "San Francisco–Oakland: The Native Son," in *Like All the Nations? The Life and Legacy of Judah Magnes,* ed. William M. Brinner and Moses Rischin (New York: State University of New York Press, 1987), 24; "Portland Jewry Collects for Russian Refugees," *Western States Jewish Historical Quarterly* 10 (1978): 343–56; Gartner, *History of the Jews of Cleveland,* 105–6.

69. Robert A. Rockaway, "Anti-Semitism in an American City: Detroit, 1850–1914," *American Jewish Historical Quarterly* 64 (September 1974): 51; Gartner, *History of the Jews of Cleveland,* 110; Rosenbaum, "San Francisco–Oakland," 23; Raphael, *Jews and Judaism,* 122; Becker and Pearson, "Jewish Community of Hartford," 204.

70. Quoted in Robert A. Rockaway, *The Jews of Detroit: From the Beginning, 1762–1914* (Detroit: Wayne State University Press, 1986), 135.

71. Steven A. Leibo, "Out the Road: The San Bruno Avenue Jewish Community of San Francisco, 1901–1968," *Western States Jewish Historical Quarterly* 11:2 (1979): 99–110; Allen duPont Breck, *The Centennial History of the Jews of Colorado, 1859–1959* (Denver: Hirschfield, 1961), 107–9; Beth Wenger, "Jewish Women of the Club: The Changing Role of Atlanta's Jewish Women (1870–1930)," *American Jewish History* 76 (March 1987): 311.

72. Judith Endelman, *The Jewish Community of Indianapolis, 1849 to the Present* (Bloomington: Indiana University Press, 1984), 96–101; Rosenberg, *Jews of Rochester,* 66–69.

73. Gartner, *History of the Jews of Cleveland,* 108; Livingston, "Industrial Removal Office," 455–58.

74. Lowenstein, *Jews of Oregon,* 79–81.

75. Joseph D. Schultz, ed., *Mid-America's Promise: A Profile of Kansas City Jewry* (Kansas City, Mo.: Jewish Community Foundation of Greater Kansas City, 1982), 1–54; Marinbach, *Galveston,* 191.

76. John Higham, "Social Discrimination against Jews, 1830–1930," in John Higham, *Send These to Me* (New York: Atheneum, 1975), 138–73; David Gerber, ed. *Anti-Semitism in American History* (Urbana: University of Illinois Press, 1986), 3–56.

77. Klayman, *First Jew,* 102–3.

78. Irena Narell, *Our City: The Jews of San Francisco* (San Diego: Howell-North, 1981); Earl Raab, "'There's No City Like San Francisco,'" *Commentary* 10 (October 1950): 369–71.

79. Charles I. Cooper, "The Jews of Minneapolis and Their Christian Neighbors," *Jewish Social Studies* 8 (1946): 32–33.

80. Louise A. Mayo, *The Ambivalent Image: Nineteenth Century America's Perception of the Jew* (Madison: Fairleigh Dickinson University Press, 1988), 42–46, 177–82.

81. Steven Hertzberg, "The Jewish Community of Atlanta from the End of the Civil War until the Eve of the Leo Frank Case," *American Jewish Historical Quarterly* 62 (March 1973): 250–85; Higham, "Social Discrimination."

82. Mark Bauman, "Role Theory and History: The Illustration of Ethnic Brokerage in the Atlanta Jewish Community in an Era of Transition and Conflict," *American Jewish History* 73 (September 1983): 71–95.

83. Hertzberg, "Jewish Community of Atlanta," 282–85.

84. Leonard Dinnerstein, *The Leo Frank Case* (New York: Columbia University Press, 1968); Arnold Shankman, "Atlanta Jewry—1900–1930," *American Jewish Archives* 25 (November 1973): 131–55.

85. Stephen J. Whitfield, "Jews and Other Southerners: Counterpoint and Paradox," in *Turn to the South: Essays on Southern Jewry,* ed. Nathan M. Kaganoff and Melvin I. Urofsky (Charlottesville: University Press of Virginia, 1979), 76–104.

86. Raymond Arsenault, "Charles Jacobson of Arkansas: A Jewish Politician in the Land of the Razorbacks, 1891–1915," in Kaganoff and Urofsky, *Turn to the South,* 55–77.

87. As late as 1960, 75 percent of American Jewry was concentrated in five states. Peter L. Halvorsen and William M. Newman, *Atlas of Religious Change in America, 1952–1971* (Washington, D.C.: Glenmore Research Center, 1978), 12.

Chapter Six. Varieties of Religious Belief and Behavior

1. W. Gunther Plaut, *The Growth of Reform Judaism* (New York: World Union for Progressive Judaism, 1965), 30.

2. Michael A. Meyer, *Response to Modernity: A History of the Reform Movement in Judaism* (New York: Oxford University Press, 1988), 230–60; Norma Fain Pratt, "Transitions in Judaism: The Jewish American Woman through the 1930s," *American Quarterly* 30 (Winter 1978): 682.

3. Jeffrey S. Gurock, "A Generation Unaccounted for in *American Judaism*," *American Jewish History* 77 (December 1987): 247–59.

4. Yehezkel Wyszkowski, "*The American Hebrew:* An Exercise in Ambivalence," *American Jewish History* 76 (March 1987): 349–53.

5. Meyer, *Response to Modernity,* 264–65.

6. Quoted in Plaut, *Growth of Reform Judaism*, 33–34.

7. Marc Lee Raphael, *Profiles in American Judaism: The Reform, Conservative, Orthodox, and Reconstructionist Traditions in Historical Perspective* (San Francisco: Harper and Row, 1984), 36; Marc Lee Raphael, "Rabbi Jacob Voorsanger of San Francisco on the Jews and Judaism: The Implication of the Pittsburgh Platform," *American Jewish Historical Quarterly* 63 (December 1973): 189–91; Nathan Glazer, "Four Rabbis in Search of American Judaism: Commentary on a History of Boston's Temple Israel," *Commentary* 19 (February 1955): 151–54; Joseph Schultz, ed., *Mid-America's Promise: A Profile of Kansas City Jewry* (Kansas City, Mo.: Jewish Community Foundation of Greater Kansas City, 1982), 5.

8. Jonathan Sarna, "New Light on the Pittsburgh Platform of 1885," *American Jewish History* 76 (March 1987): 358–68; Meyer, *Response to Modernity*, 265.

9. Raphael, *Profiles in American Judaism*, 37.

10. Herbert Parzen, "The Purge of the Dissidents: Hebrew Union College and Zionism, 1903–1907," *Jewish Social Studies* 37 (Spring-Fall 1975): 291–322.

11. Jenna W. Joselit, "What Ever Happened to New York's 'Jewish Jews'? Moses Rischin's *The Promised City* Revisited," *American Jewish History* 73 (December 1985): 163–72.

12. Steve Zipperstein, *The Jews of Odessa: A Cultural History, 1794–1881* (Stanford: Stanford University Press, 1985), 131.

13. Abraham Cahan, *Bleter fun mein leben* (New York: Forward Association, 1931), 5:144–46.

14. Arthur Goren, *New York Jews and the Quest for Community: The Kehillah Experiment, 1908–1922* (New York: Columbia University Press, 1970), 195.

15. Isaac Metzker, ed., *A Bintel Brief* (New York: Ballantine, 1977), 70.

16. Uriah Z. Engelman, "Jewish Statistics in the United States: Census of Religious Bodies (1850–1936)," *Jewish Social Studies* 9 (April 1947): 127–39.

17. William Toll, "Fraternalism and Community Structure on the Urban Frontier: The Jews of Portland, Oregon—A Case Study," *Pacific Historical Review* 47 (August 1978): 379; Eleanor Horvitz, "Old Bottles, Rags, Junk! The Story of Jews in South Providence," *Rhode Island Jewish Historical Notes* 7: 2 (1976): 219–21; Lloyd Gartner and Louis Swichkow, *The History of the Jews of Milwaukee* (Philadelphia: Jewish Publication Society of America, 1963), 170; Gartner, *History of the Jews of Cleveland* (Cleveland: Case Western Reserve Historical Society, 1987), 142, 165; Judith Endelman, *The Jewish Community of Indianapolis, 1849 to the Present* (Bloomington: Indiana University Press, 1984), 64; Charles Liebman, "Orthodoxy in American Jewish Life," *American Jewish Year Book* (1965): 21–97.

18. Aaron Rothkoff, "The American Sojourns of Ridbaz: Religious Problems within the Immigrant Community," *American Jewish Historical Quarterly* 57 (June 1968): 557–72.

19. Quoted in Irving Howe and Kenneth Libo, *How We Lived: A Documentary History of the Immigrant Jews in America, 1880–1930* (New York: Marek, 1979), 96.

20. Aaron Rothkoff, *The Silver Era in American Jewish Orthodoxy: Rabbi Eliezer Silver and His Generation* (New York: Yeshiva University Press, 1981), 18.

21. Moses Weinberger, *People Walk on Their Heads: Jews and Judaism in New York*, trans. and ed. Jonathan Sarna (New York: Holmes and Meier, 1982), 42.

22. One unpublished study has traced 350 rabbis who arrived between 1881 and

1914. Arthur Goren, however, estimates that in all likelihood twice that number immigrated. Arthur Goren, "Preaching American History: A Review Essay," *American Jewish History* 79 (Summer 1990): 544–45.

23. Hutchins Hapgood, *The Spirit of the Ghetto* (New York: Schocken, 1966), 61.

24. Abraham J. Karp, "New York Chooses a Chief Rabbi," *Publications of the American Jewish Historical Society* 44 (March 1955): 129–98.

25. Raphael, *Profiles in American Judaism,* 133–34.

26. *New York Tribune,* 15 October 1905.

27. *Jewish Daily Forward,* 9 July 1917.

28. Lincoln Steffens, *The Autobiography* (New York: Harcourt, Brace, 1931), 243–45.

29. Liebman, "Orthodoxy in American Life," 21–97.

30. Irving Howe, *World of Our Fathers* (New York: Harcourt, Brace, Jovanovich, 1976), 202.

31. Aaron Rothkoff, *Bernard Revel: Builder of American Jewish Orthodoxy* (Philadelphia: Jewish Publication Society of America, 1972), 10–13.

32. Lewis Fried, "Jacob Riis and the Jews: The Ambivalent Quest for Community," *American Studies* 20:1 (1979): 5–24; Jeffrey S. Gurock, "Jacob A. Riis: Christian Friend or Missionary Foe? Two Jewish Views," *American Jewish History* 71 (September 1981): 29–47; Gartner, *History of the Jews of Cleveland,* 177.

33. Leonard Bloom, "A Successful Jewish Boycott of the New York City Public Schools," *American Jewish History* 70 (December 1980): 184; *American Hebrew,* 15 December 1906; *American Israelite,* 22 December 1904.

34. *New York Tribune,* 15 October 1905.

35. Quoted in Geoffrey Wigoder, ed., *American Jewish Memoirs* (Jerusalem: Institute of Contemporary Jewry, 1980), 12.

36. Gartner, *History of the Jews of Cleveland,* 143; Edward Steiner, *The Immigrant Tide* (New York: Revell, 1909), 176.

37. Rose Cohen, *Out of the Shadow* (New York: Doran, 1918), 69, 78.

38. Bernard Drachman, *The Unfailing Light* (New York: Rabbinical Council of America, 1948), 280; Joselit, "What Ever Happened?" 168; Rothkoff, *Bernard Revel,* 14–15.

39. Rothkoff, "American Sojourns of Ridbaz," 561–62.

40. Jeffrey S. Gurock, *When Harlem Was Jewish, 1870–1930* (New York: Columbia University Press, 1979), 116–17.

41. Gurock, "A Generation Unaccounted For," 252–55.

42. *Hebrew Standard,* 21 March 1902; 28 April 1905.

43. Benjamin Kline Hunnicut, "The Jewish Sabbath Movement in the Early Twentieth Century," *American Jewish History* 69 (December 1979): 196–225.

44. Raphael, *Profiles in American Judaism,* 84–85.

45. *American Hebrew,* 7 January 1887.

46. Cyrus Adler, *I Have Considered the Days* (Philadelphia: Jewish Publication Society of America, 1945), 243–44; Cyrus Adler, *Jacob Schiff: His Life and Letters* (Garden City, N.Y.: Doubleday, Doran, 1928), 2:52–59; Louis Marshall to Aaron Neustadt, 10 April 1922, in Charles Reznikoff, ed., *Louis Marshall: Champion of Liberty, Selected Papers and Addresses* (Philadelphia: Jewish Publication Society of America, 1957), 2:1165.

47. Baila Shargel, *Practical Dreamer: Israel Friedlander and the Shaping of American Judaism* (New York: Jewish Theological Seminary, 1985), 103–8; Abraham Karp, "The Conservative Rabbi—'Dissatisfied But Not Unhappy,'" in *The American Rabbinate: A Century of Continuity and Change, 1883–1983,* ed. Jacob Marcus and Abraham Peck (Hoboken, N.J.: KTAV, 1985), 98–172.

48. Raphael, *Profiles in American Judaism,* 84–96.

49. Shargel, *Practical Dreamer,* 119.

50. Raphael, *Profiles in American Judaism,* 89.

51. Ibid., 90.

52. Jeffrey S. Gurock, "From Exception to Role Model: Bernard Drachman and the Evolution of Jewish Religious Life in America, 1880–1920," *American Jewish History* 76 (June 1987): 481.

53. Raphael, *Profiles in American Judaism,* 91–93; Shargel, *Practical Dreamer,* 112–17.

54. Howard Singer, "The Judaism Born in America," *Commentary* 82 (December 1986): 41–47.

55. Right from the start, however, some Reform rabbis were Zionists, including Bernard Felsenthal and Maximillian Heller. Meyer, *Response to Modernity,* 290–95.

56. Sidney Schwarz, "Conservative Judaism's 'Ideology' Problem," *American Jewish History* 74 (December 1984): 143–57; Shargel, *Practical Dreamer,* 116–19.

57. Jack Wertheimer, *The American Synagogue* (Cambridge: Cambridge University Press, 1987), 111–49; Stuart E. Rosenberg, *The Jewish Community of Rochester* (New York: Columbia University Press, 1954), 172–80; Henry Schnitzer, *Thy Goodly Tent: The First Fifty Years of Temple Emanu-El* (Bayonne, N.J.: Temple Emanu-El, 1961), 3–8; Max Vorspan and Lloyd Gartner, *History of the Jews of Los Angeles* (Philadelphia: Jewish Publication Society of America, 1970), 162–63; Deborah Dash Moore, *At Home in America: Second Generation Jews in New York* (New York: Columbia University Press, 1981), 128; Schultz, *Mid-America's Promise,* 18–19; Carole Kruckoff, *Rodfei Zedek: The First Hundred Years* (Chicago: Rodfei Zedek, 1976), 17–31; Alan DuPont Breck, *The Centennial History of the Jews of Colorado, 1859–1959* (Denver: Hirschfield, 1961), 218; W. Gunther Plaut, *The Jews of Minnesota* (New York: American Jewish Historical Society, 1959), 192–201.

58. Gurock, *When Harlem Was Jewish,* 116–17.

59. Aaron Rothkoff, "The Attempt to Merge the Jewish Theological Seminary and Yeshiva College, 1926–1927," *Michael: On the History of the Jews in the Diaspora* 3 (1975): 254–80; Gurock, "From Exception to Role Model," 485.

Chapter Seven. Participation in the American Political System

1. Moses Rischin, *The Promised City: New York Jews, 1870–1914* (New York: Corinth, 1964), 221–30; Melvyn Dubofsky, "The Political Wilderness," *American Jewish History* 73 (December 1985): 157–61; Melvyn Dubofsky, *When Workers Organize* (Amherst: University of Massachusetts Press, 1968), 13–19.

2. *Jewish Daily Forward,* 9 November 1908.

3. Rudolf Glanz, *Jew and Irish: Historical Group Relations and Immigration* (New

York: Rudolf Glanz, 1966), 83–83; William V. Shannon, *The American Irish* (New York: Macmillan, 1966), 134–35.

4. Andrew Greeley, *That Most Distressful Nation: The Taming of the American Irish* (Chicago: Quadrangle, 1972), 46–48; Morris R. Werner, *Tammany Hall* (Garden City, N.Y.: Doubleday, Doran, 1928), 144; Shannon, *American Irish,* 78; Arthur Mann, "When Tammany Was Supreme," in *Plunkitt of Tammany Hall: A Series of Plain Talks on Very Practical Politics,* ed. William Riordan (New York: Dutton, 1963), vii–xxii.

5. Edward Levine, *The Irish and Irish Politicians* (Notre Dame: University of Notre Dame Press, 1966), 109–31; Riordan, *Plunkitt of Tammany Hall,* 3–6, 37–40; Werner, *Tammany Hall,* 444–52.

6. Charles S. Bernheimer, *The Russian Jew in the United States* (Philadelphia: Winston, 1905), 263–64.

7. Rischin, *Promised City,* 228–235.

8. Gerald Sorin, *The Prophetic Minority: American Jewish Immigrant Radicals, 1880–1920* (Bloomington: Indiana University Press, 1985); Daniel Elazar, "American Political Theory and the Political Notions of American Jews: Convergence and Contradiction," in *The Ghetto and Beyond,* ed. Peter I. Rose (New York: Random House, 1969), 203–27.

9. Jacob Oser, *Henry George* (New York: Twayne, 1974), 114–21; Edward Rose, *Henry George* (New York: Twayne, 1968), 119–22; Dubofsky, *When Workers Organize,* 2, 19.

10. Naomi Cohen, *Encounter with Emancipation: German Jews in the United States, 1830–1914* (Philadelphia: Jewish Publication Society of America, 1984), 195, 324–44; Nathan Glazer, "The Jews," in *Ethnic Leadership in America,* ed. John Higham (Baltimore: Johns Hopkins University Press, 1979), 19–35; Lawrence Fuchs, "American Jews and the Presidential Vote," in *American Ethnic Politics,* ed. Lawrence Fuchs (New York: Harper and Row, 1968), 32–53.

11. Lawrence Bachmann, "Julius Rosenwald," *American Jewish Historical Quarterly* 66 (September 1976): 89–105; June Sochen, "Some Observations on the Role of American Jewish Women as Communal Workers," *American Jewish History* 70 (September 1980): 23–34.

12. Joseph Schultz, *Mid-America's Promise: A Profile of Kansas City Jewry* (Kansas City, Mo.: Jewish Community Foundation, 1982), 12–13; Cohen, *Encounter With Emancipation,* 197–202.

13. Melvin Urofsky, "Two Paths to Zion: Judah Magnes and Stephen S. Wise," in *Like All the Nations? The Life and Legacy of Judah Magnes,* ed. William Brinner and Moses Rischin (New York: State University of New York Press, 1987), 85–98.

14. Naomi Cohen, "The Ethnic Catalyst: The Impact of the East European Immigration on the American Jewish Establishment," in *The Legacy of Jewish Migration,* ed. David Berger (Brooklyn: Brooklyn College Press, 1983), 144–45.

15. Fuchs, "American Jews and the Presidential Vote," 32–53.

16. Bernheimer, *Russian Jew in the United States,* 259; Samuel Ornitz, *Allrightniks Row: "Haunch, Paunch, and Jowl," the Making of a Professional Jew* (New York: Wiener, 1986), 175–79; Werner, *Tammany Hall,* 444–52.

17. Rischin, *Promised City,* 228–32.

18. W. A. Swanberg, *Citizen Hearst: A Biography of William Randolph Hearst* (New York: Scribner's, 1961), 195–207.

19. Lawrence Fuchs, *The Political Behavior of American Jews* (Glencoe, Ill.: Free Press, 1956), 51–53.

20. Rischin, *Promised City,* 232–33.

21. Fuchs, "American Jews and the Presidential Vote," 32–53.

22. *New York Call,* 12 September 1908.

23. Arthur Gorenstein, "A Portrait of Ethnic Politcs: The Socialists and the 1908 and 1910 Congressional Election on the East Side," *Publications of the American Jewish Historical Society* 50 (March 1961): 202–28.

24. *New York Call,* 9 November 1914.

25. *New York Times,* 2 November 1917.

26. *New York Times,* 4 November 1917.

27. Melvyn Dubofsky, "Success and Failure of Socialism in New York City, 1900–1918: A Case Study," *Labor History* 9 (Fall 1968): 361–75.

28. Fuchs, "American Jews and the Presidential Vote," 32–53; Charles Reznikoff, ed., *Louis Marshall, Champion of Liberty: Selected Papers and Addresses* (Philadelphia: Jewish Publication Society of America, 1957), 1:vi, xxi, xxx; Marshall to Jacob Schiff, 14 November 1917; Marshall to Adolph S. Ochs, 5 March 1919, in Reznikoff, *Louis Marshall,* 2:710–11.

29. Deborah Dash Moore, *At Home in America: Second Generation Jews in New York* (New York: Columbia University Press, 1981); Jeffrey Gurock, *When Harlem Was Jewish, 1870–1930* (New York: Columbia University Press, 1979); Gerald Sorin, *The Nurturing Neighborhood: The Brownsville Boys Club and Jewish Community in Urban America, 1940–1990* (New York: New York University Press, 1990); Henry Feingold, *Zion in America* (New York: Hippocrene, 1976), 235–37.

30. Daniel Soyer, "Between Two Worlds: The Jewish Landsmanshaftn and Immigrant Identity," *American Jewish History* 76 (September 1986): 5–24.

31. Cyrus Adler and Aaron Margalith, *With Firmness in the Right: American Diplomatic Action Affecting Jews, 1840–1945* (New York: Arno, 1977), 3–11; Abraham Karp, *Haven and Home* (New York: Schocken, 1985), 41–44.

32. Adler and Margalith, *With Firmness in the Right,* xxvii.

33. Ibid., 20; Allen Tarshish, "The Board of Delegates of American Israelites (1859–1878)," *Publications of the American Jewish Historical Society* 49 (September 1959): 16–32.

34. Cyrus Adler, *Jacob Schiff: His Life and Letters* (Garden City, N.Y.: Doubleday, Doran, 1928), 2:151–52.

35. Adler and Margalith, *With Firmness in the Right,* 234.

36. Feingold, *Zion in America,* 240.

37. Quoted in Samuel Joseph, *Jewish Immigration to the United States from 1881 to 1910* (New York: Arno, 1969), 199.

38. *Baltimore American,* 9 May 1903; *Boston Globe,* 28 May 1903; Philip E. Schoenberg, "The American Reaction to the Kishinev Pogrom of 1903," *American Jewish Historical Quarterly* 63 (March 1974): 262–83.

39. Cyrus Adler, *The Voice of America on Kishineff* (Philadelphia: Jewish Publication Society of America, 1904), 472; Oscar S. Straus, *Under Four Administrations: From Cleveland to Taft* (Boston: Houghton Mifflin, 1922), 216; Stuart E. Knee, "The Diplomacy of Neutrality: Theodore Roosevelt and the Russian Pogroms of 1903–1906," *Presidential Studies Quarterly* 19 (Winter 1989): 71–78.

40. Kenton J. Clymer, "Anti-Semitism in the Late Nineteenth Century: The Case of John Hay," *American Jewish Historical Quarterly* 60 (June 1971): 344-54.

41. Adler and Margalith, *With Firmness in the Right,* 276.

42. "The Passport Question," *American Jewish Year Book* 12 (1911): 79.

43. Quoted in Naomi Cohen, *Not Free to Desist: The American Jewish Committee, 1906-1966* (Philadelphia: Jewish Publication Society of America, 1972), 69.

44. Louis Marshall, "A Defense of American Rights: An Address," *Commentary* 23 (May 1957): 463-65.

45. Louis Marshall to Arthur Brisbane, 4 November 1915, in Reznikoff, *Louis Marshall,* 2:1155-60.

46. Melvin Urofsky, *American Zionism from Herzl to the Holocaust* (Garden City, N.Y.: Anchor, 1975), 75.

47. Quoted in Moses Rischin, "The Early Attitude of the American Jewish Committee to Zionism (1906-1922)," *Publications of the American Jewish Historical Society* 49 (March 1960): 190.

48. Judith Goldstein, "Ethnic Politics: The American Jewish Committee as Lobbyist, 1915-1917," *American Jewish Historical Quarterly* 65 (September 1975): 36-58; Jeffrey Gurock, "The 1913 New York State Civil Rights Act," *Association for Jewish Studies Review* 1 (1976): 93-120.

49. *Jewish Daily Forward,* 5 April 1915; 10 April 1915.

50. Morris Engelman, *Four Years of Relief and War Work by the Jews of America, 1914-1918* (New York: Shoen, 1918), 2-10.

51. Soyer, "Between Two Worlds," 9; Zosa Szajkowski, "Private and Organized American Jewish Overseas Relief and Immigration (1914-1938)," *American Jewish Historical Quarterly* 57 (December 1967): 191-253.

52. Cohen, *Not Free to Desist,* 53.

53. Joseph C. Hyman, "Twenty-five Years of American Aid to Jews Overseas: A Record of the Joint Distribution Committee," *American Jewish Year Book* 41 (1939-40): 141-79.

54. Judah Magnes to M. H. Rosenberg, 21 December 1915, Magnes Collection, Klau Library, Hebrew Union College–Jewish Institute of Religion, New York City.

55. Bachmann, "Julius Rosenwald," 89-105.

56. Hyman, "Twenty-five Years of American Aid."

57. Quoted in ibid., 179.

58. Naomi Cohen, *American Jews and the Zionist Idea* (New York: KTAV, 1975), xi-xvi, 18-24.

59. *Universal Jewish Encyclopedia* (New York: Universal Jewish Encyclopedia, 1939-43), 2:47.

60. *Jewish Daily News,* 14 May 1914, cited in Karp, *Haven and Home,* 228.

61. Jonathan Frankel, "The Jewish Socialists and the American Jewish Congress Movement," *YIVO Annual* 16 (1976): 202-7.

62. Nachman Syrkin, *Yidisher kongres in Amerike* (New York: Jewish National Workers Alliance of America, 1915), 3.

63. Cyrus Adler to Louis Marshall, 2 February 1915, in Louis Marshall Papers, Box 2, American Jewish Historical Society, Waltham, Mass.; Reznikoff, *Louis Marshall,* 2:xxxiv-xxxvii; A. Leon Kubowitzki, *Unity in Dispersion: A History of the World Jewish Congress* (New York: World Jewish Congress, 1948), 19.

64. Stephen S. Wise, *Challenging Years* (London: East and West Library, 1951), 203.

65. Louis Marshall to Adolf Kraus, 12 June 1915, in Reznikoff, *Louis Marshall,* 1:509–10.

66. Frankel, "Jewish Socialists and the American Jewish Congress Movement," 202–342.

67. Evyatar Friesel, "Jacob H. Schiff Becomes a Zionist: A Chapter in American-Jewish Self-Definition, 1907–1917," *Studies in Zionism* 5 (April 1982): 55–92; Louis Marshall to Adoph S. Ochs, 5 March 1919, in Reznikoff, *Louis Marshall,* 2:724–25.

68. Kubowitzki, *Unity in Dispersion.*

69. Frankel, "Jewish Socialists and the American Jewish Congress Movement," 202–342; Reznikoff, *Louis Marshall,* 1:xxx–xxxviii.

70. *New York Times,* 5 March 1919.

71. The discussion of the New York kehillah draws heavily on Arthur Goren, *New York Jews and the Quest for Community: The Kehillah Experiment, 1908–1922* (New York: Columbia University Press, 1970), an extraordinarily thorough book.

72. Ibid., 44–55.

73. Judah Magnes, quoted in Norman Bentwich, "The Kehillah of New York, 1908–1922," in *Mordecai Kaplan Jubilee Volume,* ed. Moshe Davis (New York: Jewish Theological Seminary, 1953), 74.

74. Ibid.

75. Urofsky, "Two Paths to Zion," 94.

76. Goren, *New York Jews and the Quest for Community,* 38–58, 223–38.

77. Arthur A. Goren, "Mother Rosie Hertz, the Social Evil and the New York Kehillah," *Michael: On the History of the Jews in the Diaspora* 3 (1975): 188–210.

78. Deborah Dash Moore, "From Kehillah to Federation: The Communal Functions of Federated Philanthropy in New York City, 1917–1933," *American Jewish History* 68 (December 1978): 131–46.

79. Urofsky, "Two Paths to Zion," 94–96.

80. Daniel Elazar, *Community and Polity: The Organizational Dynamics of American Jewry* (Philadelphia: Jewish Publication Society of America, 1976).

81. Geoffrey Wigoder, *American Jewish Memoirs* (Jerusalem: Hebrew University Press, 1980), 9–19.

82. Louis Marshall to *American Israelite,* 4 May 1912.

83. Wigoder, *American Jewish Memoirs,* 12.

84. I. A. Berkson, transcript of interview with Arthur Goren, 28 October 1965, in Oral History Collection, William Wiener Library, American Jewish Committee, New York City.

85. Evyatar Friesel, "Magnes: Zionism in Judaism," in Brinner and Rischin, *Like All the Nations?* 69–81.

Chapter Eight. Cultural Pluralism and Zionism

1. Charles Liebman and Steven Cohen, *Two Worlds of Judaism: The Israeli and American Experience* (New Haven: Yale University Press, 1989).

2. Melvin Urofsky, *American Zionism from Herzl to the Holocaust* (Garden City, N.Y.: Anchor, 1975), 33.

3. Arthur Hertzberg, *The Zionist Idea* (New York: Atheneum, 1972), 40–51.

4. *Shulamit,* 21 June 1889, quoted in Henry Feingold, *Zion in America* (New York: Hippocrene, 1976), 196.

5. Quoted in Alex Bein, *Theodore Herzl: A Biography* (Cleveland: World, 1962), 115–16.

6. "Basel Program," *Universal Jewish Encyclopedia* (New York: Universal Jewish Encyclopedia, 1939–43), 2:103.

7. Manin Feinstein, *American Zionism, 1884–1904* (New York: Herzl, 1965), 13.

8. Naomi Cohen, *American Jews and the Zionist Idea* (New York: KTAV, 1975), 1.

9. Ibid., 2.

10. Quoted in Urofsky, *American Zionism from Herzl to the Holocaust,* 33.

11. Feinstein, *American Zionism, 1884–1904,* 57; Urofsky, *American Zionism from Herzl to the Holocaust,* 23, 43, 101.

12. Gary P. Zola, "Reform Judaism's Pioneer Zionist: Maximillian Heller," *American Jewish History* 73 (June 1984): 375–97.

13. Jacob Schiff to Stephen Wise, 20 April 1904, quoted in Stephen S. Wise, *The Challenging Years* (London: East and West Library, 1951), 10; Louis Marshall to Maximillian Heller, 20 December 1905, in Charles Reznikoff, ed., *Louis Marshall: Champion of Liberty* (Philadelphia: Jewish Publication Society of America, 1957), 1:112.

14. Urofsky, *American Zionism from Herzl to the Holocaust,* 102–4.

15. Ibid., 105.

16. Henry Feingold, "Assessing an Assessment: The Case for American Zionism," *American Jewish History* 75 (December 1985): 165–74.

17. June Sochen, "Some Observations on the Role of American Jewish Women as Communal Workers," *American Jewish History* 70 (September 1980): 23–34; June Sochen, *Consecrate Every Day: The Public Lives of Jewish American Women, 1880–1980* (Albany: State University of New York Press, 1981), 56.

18. Joan Dash, *Summoned to Jerusalem: The Life of Henrietta Szold* (New York: Harper and Row, 1979), 106–7.

19. Urofsky, *American Zionism from Herzl to the Holocaust,* 95, 149.

20. Evayatar Friesel, "Jacob H. Schiff Becomes a Zionist: A chapter in American-Jewish Self-Definition, 1907–1917," *Studies in Zionism* 5 (Spring 1982): 55–92; Louis Marshall to Adolph S. Ochs, 5 March 1919, in Reznikoff, *Louis Marshall,* 2:724–25; Lawrence Bachmann, "Julius Rosenwald," *American Jewish Historical Quarterly* 66 (September 1976): 89–105.

21. Yonathan Shapiro, *Leadership of the American Zionist Organization, 1897–1930* (Urbana: ersity of Illinois Press, 1971), 30, 61–70, 264–68; Yonathan Shapiro, "American Jews in Politics: The Case of Louis D. Brandeis," *American Jewish Historical Quarterly* 55 (December 1965): 199–211; Allon Gal, "In Search of a New Zion: New Light on Brandeis' Road to Zionism," *American Jewish History* 68 (September 1978): 19–31.

22. Phillipa Strum, *Louis D. Brandeis: Justice for the People* (Cambridge: Harvard University Press, 1984), 229–34.

23. Melvin Urofsky, *A Mind of One Piece: Brandeis and American Reform* (New York: Scribner's, 1971).

24. Michael M. Hammer and Samuel Stickles, "An Interview with Louis Dembitz Brandeis," *Invincible Ideal* 1 (June 1915): 17.

25. Jacob de Haas, *Louis D. Brandeis: A Biographical Sketch* (New York: Bloch, 1929).

26. Sarah Schmidt, "The Zionist Conversion of Louis D. Brandeis," *Jewish Social Studies* 37 (January 1975): 18–34.

27. Moses Rischin, "The Jews and Pluralism: Toward an American Freedom Symphony," in *Jewish Life in America,* ed. Gladys Rosen (New York: KTAV, 1978), 70.

28. Horace Kallen, "Democracy vs. the Melting Pot," *Nation* 18 and 25 February 1915; Horace Kallen, *Culture and Democracy* (New York: Arno, 1970), 124–25; Magnes, quoted in Arthur Goren, *New York Jews and the Quest for Community: The Kehillah Experiment, 1908–1922* (New York: Columbia University Press, 1970), 4.

29. Louis Brandeis, *Brandeis on Zionism* (Washington, D.C.: Zionist Organization of America, 1942), 49–50.

30. Edward M. Burns, *The American Idea of Mission* (New Brunswick: Rutgers University Press, 1957), 3; Allon Gal, "The Mission Motif in American Zionism, 1898–1948," *American Jewish History* 75 (June 1986): 363–85; Shapiro, *Leadership of the American Zionist Organization,* 248–61.

31. Jacob de Haas, *Louis D. Brandeis: A Biographical Sketch* (New York: Bloch, 1929), 181.

32. Solomon Schechter, *Seminary Addresses and Other Papers* (New York: Arno, 1969), 93–100.

33. Deborah Dash Moore, "A New American Judaism," in *Like All the Nations? The Life and Legacy of Judah Magnes,* ed. William Brinner and Moses Rischin (New York: State University of New York Press, 1987), 41–56.

34. Evyatar Friesel, "Brandeis' Role in American Zionism Historically Reconsidered," *American Jewish History* 69 (September 1979): 34–65.

35. *Proceedings,* Rabbinical Assembly of America, 2 (1927): 32, 51, quoted in Samuel Halperin, *The Political World of American Zionism* (Detroit: Wayne State University Press, 1961), 103.

36. Saul Engelbourg, "Edward A. Filene: Merchant, Civic Leader, and Jew," *American Jewish Historical Quarterly* 66 (September 1976): 106–22; Stephen J. Whitfield, "From Publik Occurrences to Pseudo-Events: Journalists and Their Critics," *American Jewish History* 72 (September 1982): 52–81; "Religious Work in the University," *Central Conference of American Rabbis Year Book* 19 (1909): 40.

37. Morris Raphael Cohen, *A Dreamer's Journey* (Boston: Beacon, 1949), 220.

38. Moses Rischin, "Abraham Cahan: Guide across the American Chasm," in *The Legacy of Jewish Migration,* ed. David Berger (Brooklyn: Brooklyn College Press, 1983), 73–84.

39. Arthur Goren, "Between Prophet and Priest," in Brinner and Rischin, *Like All the Nations?* 62–63; Melvin Urofsky, "Two Paths to Zion," in Brinner and Rischin, *Like All the Nations?* 86–88; Wise, *Challenging Years,* 32.

40. Andrew Heinze, *Adapting to Abundance: Jewish Immigrants, Mass Consumption and the Search for American Identity* (New York: Columbia University Press, 1990), 51–69, 89–104.

41. Louis Borgenicht, *The Happiest Man: The Life of Louis Borgenicht* (New York: Putnam, 1942), 370.

42. J. Vincenza Scarpaci, "Louis H. Levin of Baltimore: A Pioneer in Cultural Pluralism," *Maryland Historical Magazine* 77 (June 1982): 183–84.

43. Jonathan Woocher, *Sacred Survival: The Civil Religion of American Jews* (Bloomington: Indiana University Press, 1986), 13–21; see also Robert Bellah and Phillip

Hammond, *Varieties of Civil Religion* (San Francisco: Harper and Row, 1980), 121–37, 138–63.

Epilogue: Almost at Home in America

1. Rose Cohen, *Out of the Shadow* (New York: Doran, 1918), 246.

2. Quoted in Melech Epstein, *Profiles of Eleven* (Detroit: Wayne State University Press, 1963), 346.

3. Ellwood P. Cubberly, *Changing Conceptions of Education* (Boston: Houghton Mifflin, 1909), 15–16.

4. Woodrow Wilson, *President Wilson's Addresses,* ed. G. M. Harper (New York: Holt, 1918), 150.

5. John Higham, *Strangers in the Land: Patterns of American Nativism, 1865–1925* (New York: Atheneum, 1955), 68–105; John Higham, "Social Discrimination against Jews, 1830–1930," in John Higham, *Send These to Me: Jews and Other Immigrants in Urban America* (New York: Atheneum, 1975), 138–73.

6. David Gerber, ed., *Antisemitism in American History* (Urbana: University of Illinois Press, 1986), 3–36.

7. Howard Chudacoff, *The Evolution of American Urban Society* (Englewood Cliffs, N.J.: Prentice-Hall, 1975), 179–208.

8. William Preston, *Aliens and Dissenters: Federal Suppression of Radicals, 1903–1933* (Cambridge: Harvard University Press, 1963); Robert K. Murray, *Red Scare: A Study in National Hysteria, 1919–1920* (Minneapolis: University of Minneapolis Press, 1955).

9. Louise A. Mayo, *The Ambivalent Image* (Rutherford: Fairleigh Dickinson University, 1988).

10. Leo P. Ribuffo, "Henry Ford and *The International Jew,*" *American Jewish History* 69 (June 1980): 437–77.

11. Quoted in Henry Feingold, "Anti-Semitism and the Anti-Semitic Imagination in America: A Case Study—The Twenties," in Henry Feingold, *A Midrash on American Jewish History* (Albany: State University of New York Press, 1982), 185.

12. S. Willis Rudy, *The City College of New York: A History, 1847–1947* (New York: City College Press, 1949), 249.

13. Bruce Kuklick, *The Rise of American Philosophy: Cambridge, Massachusetts, 1860–1930* (New Haven: Yale University Press, 1977), 407.

14. Feingold, "Anti-Semitism and the Anti-Semitic Imagination," 177–92.

15. Jonathan Sarna, "Anti-Semitism in American History," *Commentary* 71 (March 1981): 47.

16. Naomi Cohen, "The Ethnic Catalyst: The Impact of the East European Immigration on the American Jewish Establishment," in Berger, *Legacy of Jewish Migration,* 131–48.

17. Jonathan Woocher, *Sacred Survival: The Civil Religion of American Jews* (Bloomington: Indiana University Press, 1986).

✡

BIBLIOGRAPHICAL ESSAY

The endnotes give the sources upon which this volume is based. The references that follow are a selective guide to the most accessible materials for those who wish to explore the subject further.

Bibliographies

A good recent annotated guide to articles in the scholarly journals is *The Jewish Experience in America: A Historical Bibliography* (Santa Barbara: ABC-Clio, 1983). Sharad Karkhanis, ed., *Jewish Heritage in America: An Annotated Bibliography* (New York: Garland, 1988) contains references to books as well as articles but is somewhat idiosyncratic in its selections. The best work of this kind is Jeffrey Gurock, *American Jewish History: A Bibliographical Guide* (New York: Anti-Defamation League, 1983). All, however, need to be supplemented by consulting the recent indexes of journals in the field, including *American Jewish History, American Jewish Archives, Jewish Social Studies, YIVO Annual, Modern Judaism, Studies in Contemporary Jewry,* and the *Journal of American Ethnic History.*

Primary Sources

The most important repository of primary materials for this study is the American Jewish Historical Society Library on the campus of Brandeis University in Waltham, Massachusetts. The papers of leading figures and witnesses such as Louis Marshall, Stephen Wise, Philip Cowen, and Alexander Harkavy were particularly useful. In addition, the Baron De Hirsch Fund papers and the letters and documents in the Galveston Immigration Plan collection proved to be a rich mine of both institutional and social history.

The archives at YIVO (the Max Weinreich Center for the Study of Judaism) in New York City were indispensable. The collections of letters, clippings, and autobiographical essays, and an invaluable set of interviews with labor activists in the 1960s, most in Yiddish, were very useful. The Tamiment Institute Library at New York University has an outstanding labor collection, including the papers, letters, notebooks, and typescripts of several important figures in the trade union and socialist movements. Here also is the Oral History of the American Left, interviews with radicals, some in Yiddish, conducted from the 1960s through the 1980s.

The New York Public Library, Jewish Division, the Columbia University Oral History Collection, and the William E. Weiner Oral History Library at the American Jewish Committee also hold important letters, notes, diaries, and interviews, including materials for Lillian Wald, Adolph Held, Isaac Berkson, and Samuel Gompers. The libraries of the Hebrew Union College–Jewish Institute of Religion were likewise useful, particularly for papers and letters of Judah Magnes and a small number for Henrietta Szold.

The most important newspaper for the eastern European immigrant experience and its expression is Abraham Cahan's the *Forverts,* or *Jewish Daily Forward,* an incomparable reservoir of contemporary opinion, reportage, and social history. The *Tageblatt* and the *Morgen Journal* are also useful, especially for the more traditional religious perspective. English language papers containing important material and editorial commentary—particularly for the turn of the century, and particularly for the more established Jewish community—are the *American Hebrew* and the *American Israelite.*

Government documents that were most useful and that are most accessible to readers include the *Report of the Industrial Commission,* done between 1900 and 1902, and the *Report of the Immigration Commission, 1907-11.* United States censuses, especially the eleventh through thirteenth (1890, 1900, 1910), also proved valuable.

Memoir Literature

Among the best written and most useful memoirs for students of the American Jewish experience in the years from 1880 to 1920 are Mary Antin, *From Plotsk to Boston* (Boston: Clarke, 1899), and Mary Antin, *The Promised Land* (Boston: Houghton Mifflin, 1912), proud expressions of Americanization combined with moments of lucid sensitivity in regard to Jewish immigrants; Miriam Blaustein, ed., *Memoirs of David Blaustein* (New York: McBride, Nast, 1913), is especially good for the reform impulse of the 1890s and for the Educational Alliance; Louis Borgenicht, *The Happiest Man* (New York: Putnam, 1942), is insightful on economic mobility and the entrepreneurial mentality and is valuable for information on garment manufacturers; Abraham Cahan, *Bleter fun mein leben,* 5 vols. (New York: Forward Association, 1926–31), like the *Forverts,* is a gold mine of social and political detail; and for readers without facility in Yiddish, Abraham Cahan *The Education of Abraham Cahan,* trans. Leon Stein et al. from Cahan, *Bleter fun mein leben,* vols. 1 and 2 (Philadelphia: Jewish Publication Society of America, 1969), is at least a beginning. One of the most evocative memoirs of East Side life is Samuel Chotzinoff, *A Lost Paradise: Early Reminiscences* (New York: Knopf, 1955). But many others ought to be read as well; these include Morris R. Cohen, *A Dreamer's Journey* (Boston: Beacon, 1949), for the 1890s as well as for life at the City College of New York; Rose Cohen, *Out of the Shadow* (New York: Doran, 1918), and Theresa Malkiel, *Diary of a Shirtwaist Striker* (New York: Cooperative Press, 1910), for women and for trade union militancy; Morris Hillquit, *Loose Leaves from a Busy Life* (New York: De Capo, 1971), for the socialist milieu; Marcus Ravage, *An American in the Making: The Life Story of an Immigrant* (New York: Harper, 1917), and Alfred Kazin *A Walker in the City* (New York: Harcourt, Brace, 1951), for serious, often moving reflections on the struggles of acculturation; Harry Roskolenko, *The Time That Was Then* (New York: Dial, 1971), is both informative and entertaining; Lillian Wald, *The House on Henry Street* (New York: Holt, 1915), is useful for Progressivism and relations between German Jews and eastern European Jews; Moses Weinberger, *People Walk on Their Heads: Jews and Judaism in New York,* ed. and trans. Jonathan Sarna (New York: Holmes and Meier, 1982), was written in the 1880s and remains a valuable source for early Orthodox reaction to religious life in secular New York; Anzia Yezierska, *Red Ribbon on a White Horse* (New York: Persea, 1978), is a poignant portrait of an immigrant woman's search for identity and artistic expression.

Among the astute Gentile observers of the immigrant scene is Hutchins Hapgood, whose sensitive writings for the *New York Tribune* about the Jewish East Side are anthologized in *The Spirit of the Ghetto* (New York: Schocken, 1966); portions of Lincoln Steffens, *The Autobiography* (New York: Harcourt, Brace, 1931), are insightful about Jewish life, and the same is true for Jacob Riis, *How the Other Half Lives* (New York: Macmillan, 1971), though Riis is less sympathetic.

Novels that can be read for literary pleasure as well as for their historical and sociological value include Abraham Cahan, *The Rise of David Levinsky* (New York: Harper, 1960), and *Yekl and the Imported Bridegroom and Other Stories of the New York Ghetto* (New York: Dover, 1970); Mike Gold, *Jews without Money* (New York: Avon, 1965); Samuel Ornitz, *Allrightniks Row "Haunch, Paunch, and Jowl," The Making of a Professional Jew* (New York: Weiner, 1986); and Anzia Yezierska's *Bread Givers* (New York: Persea, 1975), and *Hungry Hearts* (New York: Arno, 1975).

Bibliographical Essay

General Secondary Sources

For an overview of this period of American history, see Nell Irvin Painter, *Standing at Armageddon: The United States, 1877–1919* (New York: Norton, 1987), and the older but still useful Robert Wiebe, *The Search for Order, 1877–1920* (New York: Hill and Wang, 1967). For the Progressive context, Robert M. Crunden, *Ministers of Reform: The Progressive's Achievement in American Civilization, 1889–1920* (New York: Basic Books, 1982), is best but should be supplemented with Allen F. Davis, *Spearheads for Reform: Social Settlements and the Progressive Movement* (New York: Oxford University Press, 1967).

Eastern Europe

There are several well-edited anthologies of contemporary writings on Jewish life in nineteenth-century eastern Europe, including Lucy Davidowicz, ed., *The Golden Tradition: Jewish Life and Thought in Eastern Europe* (Boston: Beacon, 1967); Jack Kugelmass and Jonathan Boyarin, eds., *From a Ruined Garden* (New York: Schocken, 1983); and Diane K. Roskies and David G. Roskies, eds., *The Shtetl Book* (New York: KTAV, 1975). Works of history especially relevant to the period in which the future emigrés to the United States were growing up include Simon Dubnow, *History of the Jews in Russia and Poland,* trans. I. Friedlander, vol. 2 (Philadelphia: Jewish Publication Society of America, 1916–20); Jonathan Frankel, *Prophecy and Politics: Socialism, Nationalism, and the Russian Jew, 1862–1917* (Cambridge: Cambridge University Press, 1981); Ezra Mendelsohn, *Class Struggle in the Pale* (Cambridge: Cambridge University Press, 1970); Joshua Rothenberg, "Demythologizing the Shtetl," *Midstream* 27 (March 1981): 25–31; and Michael Stanislawski, *Tsar Nicholas I and the Jews: The Transformation of Jewish Society in Russia, 1825–1855* (Philadelphia: Jewish Publication Society of America, 1983).

Immigration

For an overview of general immigration, Philip Taylor, *The Distant Magnet: European Emigration to the United States* (New York: Harper and Row, 1971), and Maldwyn Jones, *American Immigration* (Chicago: University of Chicago Press, 1960), are best; Oscar Handlin's classic, *The Uprooted* (Boston: Little, Brown, 1951), is still worth reading for immigrant motivation and the social and psychological consequences of dislocation; but John Bodnar's more recent *The Transplanted* (Bloomington: Indiana University Press, 1985) is more persuasive, particularly on who comes to America and why and on the resilience of family, tradition, and culture. On these themes, also see Milton Gordon, *Assimilation in American Life* (New York: Oxford University Press, 1964), and Victor R. Greene, *American Immigrant Leaders, 1800–1910: Marginality and Identity* (Baltimore: Johns Hopkins University Press, 1987).

For detailed analysis and interpretation of Jewish immigration, the following are indispensable: Liebmann Hersch, "International Migration of the Jews," in *International Migrations,* eds. Imre Ferencezi and Walter F. Willcox (New York: National Bureau of Economic Research, 1931), 2:471–520; Samuel Joseph, *Jewish Immigration to the United States from 1881 to 1910* (New York: Arno, 1969); and Simon Kuznets, "Immigration of Russian Jews to the United States: Background and Structure," *Perspectives in American History* 9 (1975): 35–124. Particular dimensions of the Jewish immigration experience are intelligently explored in Pamela Nadell, "The Journey to America by Steam: The Jews of Eastern Europe in Transition," *American Jewish History* 71 (December 1981): 269–84; Alan Kraut, "Silent Strangers: Germs, Genes, and Nativism," *American Jewish History* 76 (December 1986): 142–58; and Jonathan Sarna, "The Myth of No Return: Jewish Return Migration to Eastern Europe, 1881–1914," *American Jewish History* 71 (December 1981): 256–67.

The dynamics of adjustment, acculturation, and mobility in the immigrant generation are dealt with in Thomas Kessner, *The Golden Door: Italian and Jewish Immigrant Mobility in New York City, 1880–1915* (New York: Oxford University Press, 1977); Jenna W. Joselit, *Our Gang: Jewish Crime and the New York Jewish Community, 1900–1940* (Bloomington: Indiana University Press, 1983); Moses Kligsberg, "Jewish Immigrants in Business: A Sociological Study," in *Jewish Experience in America,* ed. Abraham Karp (New York: KTAV, 1969), 5:249–84; Hannah Kliger, "Traditions of Grass-Roots Organization and Leadership: The Continuity of Landsmanshaftn in New York," *American Jewish History* 76 (September 1986): 25–39; Daniel Soyer, "Between Two Worlds: The Jewish Landsmanshaftn and Immigrant Identity," *American Jewish History* 76 (September 1986): 5–24; Deborah Dwork, "Health Conditions of Immigrant Jews on the Lower East Side of New York, 1880–1914," *Medical History* 25 (January 1981): 1–40.

Valuable studies on the effects of dislocation and transplantation focusing primarily on women include Charlotte Baum, Paula Hyman, and Sonya Michel, *The Jewish Woman in America* (New York: Dial, 1976); Sydney Stahl Weinberg, *World of Our Mothers* (Chapel Hill: University of North Carolina Press, 1988); Ari Lloyd Fridkis, "Desertion in the American Jewish Immigrant Family," *American Jewish History* 71 (December 1981): 285–99; and Reena Sigman Friedman, "'Send Me My Husband Who Is in New York City': Husband Desertion in the American Jewish Immigrant Community, 1900–1926," *Jewish Social Studies* 44 (Winter 1982): 1–18.

Bibliographical Essay

German Jews and Eastern European Jews

The most comprehensive work on German Jews, including their interaction with their "Russian" cousins, is Naomi Cohen, *Encounter with Emancipation: German Jews in the United States, 1830–1914* (Philadelphia: Jewish Publication Society of America, 1984). For a concise and balanced view of the relationship, see Zosa Szajkowski, "The *Yahudi* and the Immigrant: A Reappraisal," *American Jewish Historical Quarterly* 63 (September 1973): 13–44. Also useful here are Gary Dean Best, *To Free a People: American Jewish Leaders and the Jewish Problem in Eastern Europe, 1880–1914* (Westport, Conn.: Greenwood, 1982); Bernard Marinbach, *Galveston: Ellis Island of the West* (Albany: State University of New York Press, 1983); and June Sochen, *Consecrate Every Day: The Public Lives of Jewish American Women, 1880–1980* (Albany: State University of New York Press, 1981).

Anti-Semitism

A recent and insightful monograph on anti-Semitism is Louise A. Mayo, *The Ambivalent Image* (Rutherford: Fairleigh Dickinson University Press, 1988). Leonard Dinnerstein's collection of essays *Uneasy at Home: Anti-semitism and the American Jewish Experience* (New York: Columbia University Press, 1987), is reflective and provocative, and David Gerber's anthology of articles by scholars from several disciplines, *Anti-Semitism in American History* (Urbana: University of Illinois Press, 1986), is valuable generally and also valuable particularly for Gerber's introductory historiographical essay. Other important essays include John Higham, "Social Discrimination against Jews, 1830–1930," in John Higham, *Send These to Me: Jews and Other Immigrants in Urban America* (New York: Atheneum, 1975), 138–73; Naomi W. Cohen, "Anti-semitism in the Gilded Age: The Jewish View," *Jewish Social Studies* 41 (Summer-Fall 1979): 187–210; and Jonathan Sarna, "Anti-Semitism and American History," *Commentary* 71 (March 1981): 42–47. For the general xenophobic context of America in the era of mass immigration, see John Higham's classic *Strangers in the Land: Patterns of American Nativism, 1865–1925* (New York: Atheneum, 1955) and a series of recent reappraisals of Higham's work in *American Jewish History* 76 (December 1986).

New York

Moses Rischin, *The Promised City: New York's Jews, 1870–1914* (New York: Corinth, 1964), is a comprehensive, detailed work of meticulous scholarship. His book remains the place to begin for a background on Jews in New

York. For a recent reappraisal by scholars, see *American Jewish History* 73 (December 1983). Irving Howe's *World of Our Fathers* (New York: Harcourt, Brace, Jovanovich, 1976) is a beautifully written, evocative portrayal, particularly good on socialism and Yiddishism. Other work important for understanding the New York Jewish experience includes Arthur Goren, *New York Jews and the Quest for Community: The Kehillah Experiment, 1908-1922* (New York: Columbia University Press, 1970); Jeffrey Gurock, *When Harlem Was Jewish, 1870-1930* (New York: Columbia University Press, 1979); and Deborah Dash Moore, *At Home in America: Second Generation Jews in New York* (New York: Columbia University Press, 1981).

Labor and Socialism

Elias Tcherikower, *The Early Jewish Labor Movement in the United States,* trans. A. Antonovsky (New York: YIVO, 1961), is essential on the subject of labor and socialism. Several articles in *YIVO Annual* 16 (1976) are also useful, as are Irwin Yellowitz, *Labor and the Progressive Movement in New York State, 1897-1916* (Ithaca: Cornell University Press, 1965), and Gerald Sorin, *The Prophetic Minority: American Jewish Immigrant Radicals, 1880-1920* (Bloomington: Indiana University Press, 1985). The best concise essay remains Will Herberg, "The American Jewish Labor Movement," *American Jewish Year Book* (1952): 3-74.

Beyond New York

Two important articles that forecast new research directions on Jews outside of New York are Lee Shai Weissbach, "The Jewish Communities of the United States on the Eve of Mass Migration: Some Comments on Geography and Bibliography," *American Jewish History* 78 (September 1988): 79-108, and Joel Perlmann, "Beyond New York: The Occupations of Russian Jewish Immigrants in Providence, Rhode Island and in Other Small Jewish Communities, 1900-1915," *American Jewish History* 72 (March 1983): 369-94.

Useful community and regional studies include: William Toll, *The Making of an Ethnic Middle-Class: Portland Jewry over Four Generations* (Albany: State University of New York, 1982); Marc Raphael, *Jews and Judaism in a Midwestern Community: Columbus, Ohio, 1840-1975* (Columbus: Ohio Historical Society, 1979); Steven Hertzberg, *Strangers within the Gate City: The Jews of Atlanta, 1845-1915* (Philadelphia: Jewish Publication Society of America, 1978); Stuart Rosenberg, *The Jews of Rochester, 1843-1925* (New York: Columbia University Press, 1954); Selig Adler and Thomas E. Connolly, *From Ararat to Suburbia: The History of the Jewish Community of Buffalo* (Philadelphia: Jewish Publication Society of America, 1960); Robert Rockaway, *The Jews of Detroit: From the Beginning, 1762–1914* (Detroit: Wayne State University Press, 1986); Murray Friedman, ed., *Jewish Life in Philadelphia, 1830–1940* (Philadelphia: Jewish Publication Society of America, 1983); Judith Endelman, *The Jewish Community of Indianapolis, 1849 to the Present* (Bloomington: Indiana University Press, 1984); Isaac Fein, *The Making of an American Jewish Community: The History of Baltimore Jewry from 1773 to 1920* (Philadelphia: Jewish Publication Society of America, 1971); Nathan Kaganoff and Melvin Urofsky, eds. *Turn to the South: Essays on Southern Jewry* (Charlottesville: University Press of Virginia, 1979); Lloyd Gartner, *History of the Jews of Cleveland* (Cleveland: Western Reserve Historical Society, 1987); Lloyd Gartner and Louis Swichkow, *History of the Jews of Milwaukee* (Philadelphia: Jewish Publication Society of America, 1963); Max Vorspan and Lloyd Gartner, *History of the Jews of Los Angeles* (San Marino, Calif.: Huntington Library, 1970); Uri Herscher, *Jewish Agricultural Utopias in America 1880–1910* (Detroit: Wayne State University Press, 1981).

Religion

The best introduction to Jewish religion is Marc Lee Raphael, *Profiles in American Judaism: The Reform, Conservative, Orthodox, and Reconstructionist Traditions in Historical Perspective* (San Francisco: Harper and Row, 1984). Useful collections of essays include Jacob Marcus and Abraham Peck, eds., *The American Rabbinate: A Century of Continuity and Change, 1883–1983* (Hoboken, N.J.: KTAV, 1985); Jack Wertheimer, ed., *The American Synagogue: A Sanctuary Transformed* (Cambridge: Cambridge University Press, 1987). A recent masterful survey of the Reform movement is Michael A. Meyer, *Response to Modernity: A History of the Reform Movement in Judaism* (New York: Oxford University Press, 1988). For Orthodoxy, see Charles S. Liebman, "Orthodoxy in American Jewish Life," *American Jewish Year Book* (1965): 21–97, and Aaron Rothkoff, *Bernard Revel: Builder of American Jewish Orthodoxy* (Philadelphia: Jewish Publication Society of America, 1972). A useful source book on Conservative Judaism is Pamela S. Nadell, ed., *Conservative Judaism in America* (Westport, Conn.: Greenwood, 1988). For Reconstructionism, see Charles Liebman, "Reconstructionism in American Jewish Life," *American Jewish Year Book* (1970): 189–285.

Zionism

A valuable general overview of Zionism is the introductory essay in Arthur Hertzberg's anthology *The Zionist Idea* (New York: Atheneum, 1972). For the

American Zionist movement, see Melvin Urofsky's readable and comprehensive *American Zionism from Herzl to the Holocaust* (Garden City, N.Y.: Anchor, 1975) and Naomi Cohen's concise analysis, *American Jews and the Zionist Idea* (New York: KTAV, 1975). Also worth consulting are Samuel Halperin, *The Political World of American Zionism* (Detroit: Wayne State University Press, 1961); Yonathan Shapiro, *The Leadership of the American Zionist Organization, 1897–1930* (Urbana: University of Illinois Press, 1971); and Allon Gal, *Brandeis of Boston* (Cambridge: Harvard University Press, 1980).

✡

INDEX

neighborhoods, 63, 70, 149, 152; Jewish working class, 133, 138, 149–50
Boston Hebrew Observer, 151
Boston Jewish American, 152
Boston North End Hebrew Benevolent Association, 151
Boston Provident Association, 151
Brandeis, Louis D., 197; and labor movement, 127, 150, 228; progressivism, 194, 199, 210, 228, 231; as Supreme Court justice, 200, 230; as Wilson advisor, 199, 210, 227, 228; in Zionist movement, 199, 210, 211–12, 217, 227–30, 231–32
Bread Givers (Yezierska), 82
Bressler, David, 64
Bricker, Rev. Luther, 167
Bridgeport, Conn., 162–63
Brody, Austria, 43–44
Brooklyn, N.Y., 199
Brotherhood of Tailors, 130
Bryan, William Jennings, 54
Bublick, Gedaliah, 211
Buchanan, James, 201
Bund (General Jewish Workers' Union), 30, 31, 35, 36, 102, 121
Burke, Edmund, 198
Businessmen, 4, 5–6, 106, 154–55, 159

C

Caesar's Column (Donnelly), 53
Cahan, Abraham, 27–28, 82; and Americanization, 103, 104, 232–33; on European Jewry, 29, 174; on immigrant communities, 66, 71, 75, 83; immigration to America, 40, 47, 110, 148; as *Jewish Daily Forward* editor, 61, 102, 103–4, 120; and Judaism, 119; in labor movement, 112, 113, 114; on political participation, 191; and Progressivism, 133–34; socialism, 28, 39, 103–4, 110–11, 114, 119–20, 121–22, 193; and Yiddish, 101, 104, 112, 120
California, 2, 4
Canada, 42, 57, 64
Cantor, Jacob, 196
Capitalism, 135, 193; populists and, 53;

progressives and, 133; socialists and, 109, 117–18, 120, 220
Carnegie, Andrew, 65–66
Castle Garden, 46–47
Catskill Mountains, 157–58
Central Committee for the Relief of the Jews Suffering through the War, 207, 208
Central Conference of American Rabbis (CCAR), 173, 207–8
Chicago, Ill.: Haymarket riots, 111, 140; Jewish immigration to, 138, 139, 140, 143, 241; Jewish institutions, 7, 49, 140–42, 154; Jewish neighborhoods, 63, 70, 74, 139, 142–43, 152; Jewish population, 136, 139; Jewish working class, 133, 138–40, 143; labor movement in, 113, 117, 128, 140; racial violence, 238; synagogues, 142, 175, 177
Chicago Hebrew Institute, 140
Chicago Maternity Center, 140
Chicago Tribune, 139
Chicago Women's Club, 141
Children, 95; Americanization, 81, 87, 96, 103, 233; of broken homes, 83, 84; education, 87, 106, 180; employment, 76, 79, 81; immigration, 39–40; religious education, 15, 16, 96, 179
Christianity, 24, 52, 174, 179–80, 222
Cincinnati, Ohio, 4, 7, 171, 172, 241
Circumcision, 173
Cities: anti-Semitism in, 164, 239; eastern European, 23, 24, 25, 26, 29, 33; employment in, 116, 133, 137, 154–55, 157; Jewish neighborhoods, 63, 64, 70, 74, 139, 152–53, 159–60, 169, 199; Jewish populations, 4, 136–37, 153, 155; Jewish settlement in, 3–4, 6, 63, 67, 109, 154, 161, 169, 240
City College of New York, 239
Clara de Hirsch Home (New York), 89
Class conflict, 30, 128, 167
Class consciousness, 109, 114, 116, 134–35
Class struggle, 24–25, 104, 109, 123, 133, 134–35
Cleveland, Grover, 54, 61
Cleveland, Ohio, 154, 180; Jewish immi-

Index

Union of American Hebrew Orthodox Congregations, 177
Union League Club, 9
Union of Orthodox Jewish Congregations, 181, 182, 183, 189
Union of Orthodox Rabbis (Agudath Harabonim), 181, 182, 186, 189, 207–8
United Cloth Hat and Cap Makers Union, 116
United Garment Workers Union (UGWU), 128, 130, 140
United Hebrew Charities, 50, 56, 60, 82, 89
United Hebrew Trades (UHT), 113, 114, 117, 120, 123, 124, 131
United States, 3, 37; anti-Semitic violence in, 9, 55, 129, 145, 164–65, 167; anti-Semitism in, 9, 51–55, 168, 218, 237, 238–40; immigration restrictions, 56, 59, 60, 61, 237, 240; Jewish population, 1–2, 7, 12, 42, 224; Russian Commercial Treaty (1832), 197, 202, 204, 205, 206, 207; and Russian repression, 202, 203, 204; in World War I, 210, 237; and Zionist movement, 210, 211, 223
U.S. Congress, 62; immigration restrictions, 56, 59, 60, 61, 65, 132–33, 198, 240; Jewish representatives, 196, 198, 199–200; and Russian repression, 204, 205
U.S. Department of State, 202, 204–5, 210
U.S. Department of Treasury, 205
U.S. Immigration Commission, 46
U.S. Supreme Court, 200, 202, 230
United Synagogue of America (USA), 186, 187, 207–8
Universities, 239
University Settlement (New York), 90

V

Valley National Bank of Arizona, 5
Van Buren, Martin, 201
Veiller, Lawrence, 60
Vilna, Lithuania, 27–28, 29, 30
Vladeck, Baruch Charney, 236
Voluntarism, 141
Voorsanger, Rabbi Jacob, 55, 173

W

Wald, Lillian, 91, 133–34, 194
Waldman, Louis, 130
Wallace, Lewis, 222
Warburg, Felix, 208
Warsaw, Poland, 23, 30, 32
Washington, Booker T., 199
Waterbury, Conn., 162–63
Watson, Thomas E., 53, 167
Weil, Jonas, 182
Weinberg, Sydney Stahl, 95
Weinberger, Moses, 176
Weinstein, Bernard, 114, 115
Weinstein, Gregory, 28
Weiss, Flora, 126
Weissman, Clara, 17
Weizmann, Chaim, 209, 210, 223, 230
Wengeroff, Pauline, 26
Western states, 4, 156, 165
White supremacy, 165
Williams, William, 60–61
Willowski, Rabbi Jacob David (Slutzker Rav), 176, 177–78, 181
Wilson, Woodrow, 61, 197, 199, 210, 213–14, 227, 228, 237
Winchevsky, Morris, 27, 103, 213
Wise, Rabbi Isaac Mayer, 4, 8, 171, 172, 173
Wise, Rabbi Stephen S., 164, 195, 233; and American Jewish Congress, 212, 213, 217; and labor movement, 130–31; and Zionism, 210, 217, 223, 224, 230
Wolf, Simon, 60, 62, 63, 65–66
Women, 19, 66, 93–94; education, 17, 18, 105–6, 141; employment, 17–18, 76, 95–96, 126; in garment industry, 124–25, 126–27, 129; housewives, 95; immigration, 39, 48, 89; and Judaism, 170–71, 190; kosher meat boycotts, 94, 95; in labor movement, 124, 125, 126–27, 133; prostitution, 89; voluntarism, 141, 147, 194; and Zionism, 225–26
Women's Loan Society, 141
Women's Trade Union League, 130–31
Working class, 79, 109–10, 111–13, 116, 117–18, 134, 198

Index

Workmen's Circle (Arbeiter Ring), 118, 120, 123, 124, 142, 152, 179, 208
World War I, 134, 199, 200, 207, 208-10, 211, 227, 237
World Zionist Congress (1897), 221, 223
World Zionist Organization, 224, 226, 231
Wright, William, 54

Y

Yale University, 239
Yanofsky, Saul, 111
Yekl (Cahan), 83
Yelizavetgrad, Ukraine, 32
Yeshivas, 15, 16-17, 29
Yeshiva University, 189
Yezierska, Anzia, 41, 82
Yiddish, 36, 111, 137, 178; culture, 31-32, 40, 104-5, 147-48; dictionaries, 101; in eastern Europe, 13, 14, 32, 101, 102; education, 17; Educational Alliance and, 87, 88; German Jews and, 61, 62, 63; literature, 14, 25, 61, 102-3; newspapers, 102, 103, 104, 148; socialists and, 112; theater, 99-101; Zionists and, 31
Yiddisher Amerikaner, 196
Yiddishe Tageblatt, 94, 102, 104, 124, 161
Yoffeh, Zalmen, 93-94
Yom Kippur, 112, 160-61, 174, 175
Young Israel movement, 97, 187
Young Men's Association of Manhattan, 97
Young Men's Hebrew Association (YMHA), 7, 86
Young People's synagogues, 182-83, 187

Yugoslavia, 214

Z

Zametkin, Michael, 110, 113
Zangwill, Israel, 86, 225, 234
Zarchy, Rabbi Asher, 178
Zaritsky, Max, 123
Zhitlowsky, Chaim, 229
Zhitomer, Ukraine, 34
Zimmerman, Charles, 72
Zionism: American Jewish Committee and, 207, 211, 212, 214, 217; American Jewish Congress, 211-14, 217, 232; American Jews and, 154, 218, 219-20, 221-22, 223-32; anti-Semitism and, 221, 226; Balfour Declaration (1917), 199, 210, 213-14; Conservative Judaism and, 188, 190, 226, 232; in Europe, 27, 31, 32, 36, 40, 174, 211, 220-21; and Jewish identity, 219, 227, 232; Nazism and, 214; Orthodox Judaism and, 31, 188, 220, 223; Reform Judaism and, 173, 188, 223, 224; Russian pogroms and, 31, 35, 220, 222; socialists and, 213, 216, 220, 224, 226; Uganda proposal, 225; U.S. and, 210-11, 222-23; women and, 225-26; World War I and, 200-201, 209-10, 211, 227; World Zionist Congress (1897), 221, 223
Zionist Organization of America (ZOA), 227, 228, 231. *See also* Federation of American Zionists
Zuckerman, Baruch, 211
Zuker, Isaac, 85

✡

ABOUT THE AMERICAN
JEWISH HISTORICAL SOCIETY

THE TWENTIETH CENTURY has been a period of change for the American Jewish community, bringing growth in numbers and in status and, most important, a new perception of itself as part of the history of the United States. The American Jewish Historical Society has also grown over the century, emerging as a professional historical association with a depth of scholarship that enables it to redefine what is *American* and what is *Jewish* in the American saga. To record and examine this saga and to honor its own centennial, the society has published this five-volume series, *The Jewish People in America.*

The society was founded on 7 June 1892 in New York City, where it was housed in two crowded rooms in the Jewish Theological Seminary. At the first meeting, its president Cyrus Adler declared that it was the patriotic duty of every ethnic group in America to record its contributions to the country. Another founding father emphasized the need to popularize such studies "in order to stem the growing anti-Semitism in this country." As late as the 1950s, the society was encouraging young doctoral students in history to research and publish material of Jewish interest, even though such research, according to Rabbi Isidore Meyer, then the society's librarian, would impede the writers' advancement in academia. In this climate, the early writings in the society's journal, *Publications of the American Jewish Historical Society,* were primarily the work of amateurs; they were narrowly focused, often simply a recounting of the deeds of the writers' ancestors. However, these studies did bring to light original data of great importance to subsequent historians and constitute an invaluable corpus of American Jewish historiography.

The situation has changed materially. One hundred years later, the society has its own building on the campus of Brandeis University; the building houses the society's office space, exhibit area, and library. The Academic Council of the society includes sixty-three professors of American history whose primary interest is American Jewish history. Articles in the society's publication, now called *American Jewish History,* meet the highest professional standards and are often presented at the annual meeting of the American Historical Association. The society has also published an extensive series of monographs, which culminates in the publication of these volumes. The purpose of *The Jewish People in America* series is to provide a comprehensive historical study of the American Jewish experience from the age of discovery to the present time that both satisfies the standards of the historical profession and holds the interest of the intelligent lay reader.

Dr. Abraham Kanof
Past President
American Jewish Historical Society
and Chairman
The Jewish People in America Project